映像作家100人

Japanese Motion Graphic Creators

Published by	BNN, Inc. 11F Shinjuku Square Tower Building 6-22-1 Nishishinjuku Shinjuku-ku Tokyo 163-1111 Mail: info@bnn.co.jp
Edited by	Kurando Furuya Yusuke Shouno Natsumi Fujita Masanori Hattori
Cover Design	Tsuyoshi Hirooka
Illustration	Hiroshi Iguchi
Translated by	Ryutaro Uchiyama
Assistant Staff	Azusa Iwasaki, Emiko Suzuki, Pino, Kanako Takeuchi, Akihiro Takeda Sou Ootsuki, shoe
Thanks To	David D'Heilly, Takamori Kadoi Unnon, Jiro Ohashi

ISBN 4-86100-362-8

Printed in Japan by Shinano, Ltd.

本書は、日本の映像クリエイター精鋭 100 人の作品を収録した作家ファイルです。また、付録の DVD では、半数以上の映像作家の実際の映像作品を観ることができます。この本は、映像ジャンルにおいて優れた作家を探しているクライアントの方々、また、映像表現を手掛けているクリエイターたち、そして今後この発展途上のジャンルに参入してみたいと思っている意欲的な若者、そんな人々に向けて作られています。

まず、断っておかなければならないのは、100 人とはいえここに掲載されたクリエイターたちが、優れた仕事をしている映像作家のほんの一部であるということです。彼ら、彼女たちの 100 人のリストは、この本を作る過程での、偶然の出会い、あるいはクリエイターたちの友情のネットワーク、そしてこの領域の先輩方々のアドバイスを通じて形作られました。その中の何かひとつでも欠けることがあれば、この本がこのような形になることはなかったと思います。

今回、作家の選択をする際に、できるだけ若く、新鮮な作品を作り出している作家に焦点を当てることにしました。また、映像というジャンルにおいて今、生まれつつある新しい表現領域の全体像を描けるよう心掛けました。すでにいくぶんかの歴史を持つに至った映像クリエイティブの世界において、現在進行しつつある新しい映像表現の形は何なのか。その可能性のアウトラインを描くこと、それが本書のもうひとつの狙いです。

今、映像表現の世界では、個をベースにした作家性、オリジナリティを持つ表現が開花しつつあります。無数の作家が新たな映像の技を繰り出し、しのぎを削り合う、まさにスタイルの戦争、スタイルウォーズが始まったのです。機材の低価格化、そしてアプリケーションの革新は、とどまる所を知りません。映画というジャンルが今もそうであるように、かつて映像という表現は、集団による力、つまり強力な組織力と、資金力を必要としていました。それが今日では、安価な機材が手に入るようになり、誰でも購入可能なコンピューターの上で編集が行われています。映像表現はまさしく個人のものとなったのです。

今、映像の領域は未来を担う作家たちが押し寄せる、巨大な実験場となりつつあるようです。映像はその歴史において、第二の創世記を迎えた、といってもよいでしょう。プロモーションビデオの世界で、CM の世界で、またインターネットや、ギャラリー、クラブミュージックなどのシーンにおいて、さまざまな場所、場面で、個人作家、つまりあなたがたの才能が求められているのです。また、そのような多様で生まれたばかりの領域にこそ、まだ見ぬ新しいクリエィティブ、無数のスタイル、表現の前衛が花開くことができるのです。願わくば本書が、ほんの少しでもその一端をのぞき見る助力となれば、と考えています。

最後に、この本の制作に協力してくれた、たくさんの映像クリエイター、アドバイスをくれた先輩方々、そしてこの本の制作に関わってくれた友人たちへ、最大限の感謝を贈りたいと思います。

This book is a documentation of the works of 100 noteworthy Japanese motion graphic artists. The attached DVD contains clips of the actual works of most of these artists. We hope that this book becomes an object of interest for people such as project directors searching for a talented creator, artists involved in the scene, and young people who are considering diving into this rapidly developing realm.

We must first make it clear that the 100 creators listed in this book are only a portion of the motion graphic artists leading distinguished practices in Japan. The list has been shaped through coincidental acquaintances, the advice of numerous people, and the artists networks of friendship. In choosing the artists to include into this book, we focused mainly on young artists who are creating works with a fresh quality. We aimed to depict a holistic image of the new modes of expression that are currently emerging within the field of motion graphics, and draw an outline of the possibilities they bear.

Currently, authorship based on the individual, and an accompanying form of expression that emphasizes originality are prospering in the field of motion graphics. You can find countless artists, armed with diverse production techniques, engaging in their style wars. A while ago, the production of a motion graphic work required the capacities and financial power of an organization, but today, with affordable equipment becoming available, and the rapid proliferation of the personal computer, this medium is opening up to individuals. New talent has been pouring into the realm of motion graphics, and it is developing into an immense field of experimentation. The demand for individual creators is rising in various scenes such as music videos, TV commercials, the Internet, art galleries, and the club music scene. It is in this kind of fresh environment that innovative imagery, manifold styles, and unprecedented forms of expression are able to blossom. We hope that this book allows you to catch a glance of this whirlwind of creativity.

Finally, we would like to send massive thanks to the motion graphic artists, the seniors of the industry who provided us with advice, and our friends who assisted us in creating this book.

INDEX

※本文中の各連絡先・URLアドレスは、2006年1月時点のものであり、予告なしに変更される可能性がございます。弊社ではサポート致しかねることをご了承下さい。
※本文中の作品名、プロジェクト名、クライアント名、ブランド名、商品名、その他の固有名詞、発表年度に関しては、作家各自より提示された情報をもとに掲載しています。

CREATORS INDEX

CREATORS INDEX

DVD INDEX

※付録 DVD に収録した映像は、オリジナル作品を短くカットするなど再編集がなされており、いずれも各作家1分程度となっております。
※再生には、DVD ビデオ対応の再生機を用いてください。各再生機の操作に関しては、ご使用になる機器の取扱説明書をご参照ください。尚、DVD 専用再生機で再生すると、よりきれいな画質でご覧になれます。
※一部の作品に、明滅を繰り返す光を画面演出に用いた映像表現があります。明るい部屋で少し離れた位置からご鑑賞されるよう、ご注意ください。
※有償・無償に拘らず、無断で貸与・複製・公衆送信・上映等を行うことを禁止致します。

01
ARTIST テンケイ / アウターリミッツ
10K / OUTERLIMITS Inc.
CONTENT ALTZ, *BOOGIE ALTZ*
CREDIT Staring: BAKI3, YOSSY, Camera: kO-Op man
(時空 / LASTRUM CORPORATION, 2005)

02
ARTIST 馬場 淳
ACCI BABA
CONTENT ORANGER, *GOING UNDER*
CREDIT (GH9 Co.,Ltd. / Jackpine Social Club., 2003-2005)

03
ARTIST アダプター
ADAPTER
CONTENT 三上ちさこ Sachiko Mikami,「相対形」*Soutaikei*
CREDIT (YAMAHA Corpolation, 2005)

04
ARTIST エイジズ・ファイブ・アンド・アップ
AGES5&UP
CONTENTS &CREDIT
1. *DOTS_Expansion/Shringkage* (Mori Art Musium+TOHO Chinemas 2004)
2. *Japanese* (Private, 2004)
3. *PoPoRon* (DIGITALOGUE, 1997)
4. *h/m/s* (Tachibana Hajime Design, 2001)
5. *union_v* (Tachibana Hajime Design, 2001)
6. *cell* (Mori Art Musium+TOHO Chinemas, 2004)
7. *1999* (GASBOOK, 1999)

05
ARTIST 亜妃子
AKIKO
CONTENT *flower*
CREDIT (2004)

06
ARTIST キャッチパルス
CATCHPULSE
CONTENT *school oi (MUZIKHIZOMISSION VERSION)*
CREDIT By catchpulse, Tatuki Saito, cavilll (Zuinosin)
Artwork: 土 babilll (ggow) (de-fragment, 2005)

07
ARTIST 松本 力
CHIKARA MATSUMOTO
CONTENT 「48 のネオン」*48 no neon*
CREDIT Music: "cormworm", organ-o-rounge
(electronica, 2002)

08
ARTIST 橋本大佑
DAISUKE HASHIMOTO
CONTENTS *Show reel digest*
CREDIT Director + Animation + Music:
橋本大佑 Daisuke Hashimoto
(©daisuke hashimoto)

09
ARTIST 島田大介 / 四つ葉加工房
DAISUKE SHIMADA / YOTSUBA KAKOUBOU
CONTENTS Great Adventure, *GREAT&FUNKY*
CREDIT (RESERVOIR RECORDS, 2004)

10
ARTIST デラウエア
DELAWARE
CONTENTS *cry_dog_cry*
CREDIT (2004)

11
ARTIST デバイスガールズ
DEVICEGIRLS
CONTENTS *RYUKYUDISKO, ZAN - in waves -*
CREDIT (MUSIC ON! TV Inc.®+©compactsounds, 2004)

12
ARTIST ドラびでお
DORAVIDEO
CONTENT *DORADORA*
CREDIT (2004)

13
ARTIST エレクロトニック
ELECROTNIK
CONTENT *WWW.HIFANA.COM*
CREDIT Director: ELECROTNIK, Sound: HIFANA
Producer: +CRUZ, KENJI TANAKA, ELECROTNIK
Screenwriter: ELECROTNIK, W+K TOKYO LAB
Production Company: ELECROTNIK
(©Wieden+Kennedy Tokyo Lab / Polystar Co., Ltd., 2005)

14
ARTIST エンライトメント
ENLIGHTENMENT
CONTENT *BIRDS*
CREDIT (2005)

15
ARTIST 本木秀明
HIDEAKI MOTOKI
CONTENT Rays, *MOONFLOWERS*
CREDIT (HORIZON / liquid recordings, 2004)

16
ARTIST 光J
HIKARU J
CONTENT 「お客様が神様です」
Okyakusama ga Kamisamadesu
CREDIT Music: DJ KOHNO & DJ TATSUTA
(©Dreamusic, 2005)

17
ARTIST 井口弘史
HIROSHI IGUCHI
CONTENTS *HELL*
CREDIT (2002)

18
ARTIST 中尾浩之
HIROYUKI NAKAO
CONTENT *trainsurfer*
CREDIT Director: 中尾浩之 Hiroyuki Nakao, Producer: 松居秀之 Hideyuki Matsui, CG: JINNI'S Animation Studios, 山本倫裕 Norihiro Yamamoto,
Music: 戸田色音 Irone Toda,
Production by P.I.C.S. (©MTV JAPAN / P.I.C.S. Hiroyuki Nakao, 2003-2004)

19
ARTIST 西郡 勲
ISAO NISHIGORI
CONTENTS ACIDMAN shortfilm
「彩 -SAI-(前篇)/ 廻る、巡る、その核へ」
-SAI- / Revolving...to the core
CREDIT Director + CG: 西郡勲 Isao Nishigori
CG: 米澤拓也 Takuya Yonezawa, 伊藤まゆみ Mayumi Ito, Produce: 松居秀之 Hideyuki Matusi
Production by P.I.C.S. (© 東芝 EMI, 2004)

20
ARTIST 堀切 潤 / ポータブルコミュニティ
JUN HORIKIRI / PORTABLE[K]OMMUNITY
CONTENT *s3ga markIII*
CREDIT (ICC, 2004)

21
ARTIST ジュウリョク
JURYOKU
CONTENTS
1. *BOTANICA* (2005)
2. *The poetry of suburbs* (2004)

22
ARTIST タナカカツキ
KATSUKI TANAKA
CONTENT 「タナカカツキ映像作品集 DVD『赤ちゃん』ジングル映像」*Akachan Jingle*
CREDIT Sound Composer: 長野孝豊 Nagano Takatoyo
(icca/DDD 製作委員会, 2005)

23
ARTIST 若野 桂 / ガール・スタジオ
KATSURA MOSHINO / GIRL STUDIO
CONTENT nobodyknows+,「ココロオドル」*Kokoro Odoru*
CREDIT Director + Animation: Katsura Moshino
Editing Studio: Digital Tank, Music: nobodyknows+
Shooting Studio + Lighting Staff: Naoya Hatta from HEAT
Director of Photography: Hideo Fujiwara
Video Engineer: Shin Hasegawa from GRAN
Shooting Coordination: Digital Tank
Model Corporation: Central Japan
Dance: Rose Hips, Styling: CHISA
Break Dance: top up production
Software Coorporation: Adobe Systems Incorporated
(Sony Music Entertainment Inc., 2004)

24
ARTIST カワイオカムラ
KAWAI+OKAMURA
CONTENT 「ヘコヒョン 7」*Ficfion7*
CREDIT Voice: Shirou Gou, Co-Writer: Toshiro Kimura
Costume Production: Yoko Nishikawa
(Kawai+Okamura, 2004)

25
ARTIST 横井 謙
KEN YOKOI
CONTENTS &CREDIT
1. *Landscape Laundry* (2001)
Co.Produce: 竹中直樹 Naoki Takenaka
2.「2Fスナッカー」*2F Snacker*
デジスタ・アウォード 2002
オープニングタイトル (NHK, 2002)
3.「M市とC市とG町の戯画」
Modern Chouju Giga (NHK, 2003)
4.「ミュージックビデオのための試作」
Making for Trial purposes for Music Video (2003)
5.「デジタルアートフェスティバル東京 2003・オープニング」*Digital Art Festival tokyo 2003*
(NHK Enterprizes, 2003)
6.「送ってみよう!・ケータイ俳句・タイトル」
(NHK, 2004)
7.「デジタル・スタジアム・2005 年 BGV」
Digital Studium 2005 (NHK, 2005)
8.「デジスタ・アウォード 2005・オープニングタイトル」*Digital Studium Awards 2005* (NHK, 2005)

26
ARTIST 西田幸司
KOJI NISHIDA
CONTENT *RAKU-GAKI* -http://raku-gaki.com/-
CREDIT Producer + Graphic + Design + Flash:
Koji NISHIDA (2002~)

27
ARTIST 山村浩二
KOJI YAMAMURA
CONTENT 「頭山」*Mt. Head*
CREDIT (©Yamamura Animation, 2002)

28
ARTIST 空気モーショングラフィックス
KOO-KI MOTION GRAPHICS
CONTENTS &CREDIT
1.「Mr. デニロー」*Mr. Deniroo* (2005)
Director: 木綿達史 Tatsushi Momen
Animation: 髙村剛 Tsuyoshi Takamura
2. *NINJA GROOVY*
Director: 竹清仁 Hitoshi Takekiyo
Animation: 村上ヒロシナンテ
Hiroshinante Murakami
カートゥーン ネットワーク ジャパン
Cartoon Network Japan, 2005
3.「替え玉」*Stand-in* (2004)
Director: 江口カン Kan Eguchi

BNN | DVD VIDEO | ALL | 片面一層 MPEG2 | 字幕無し 複製不能 | JASRAC V-056576 | NTSC | 4:3

JAPANESE MOTION GRAPHIC CREATORS' **DVD** / 2006 / COLOR / 60 min. / STEREO & MONO / ©4D

29
ARTIST **小野浩太**
KOTA ONO
CONTENTS *hypnos*
CREDIT Drawing + Sound: Andrew Deutsch & niji (360° RECORDS), Photography: Andrew Deutsch
Sound Design: niji (360° RECORDS)
Director: Kota Ono, Produce: 360° RECORDS
(360° RECORDS, 2005)

※この作品には、明滅を繰り返す光を画面演出に用いた映像表現があります。明るい部屋で少し離れた位置からご鑑賞されるよう、ご注意ください。

30
ARTIST **加藤久仁生**
KUNIO KATO
CONTENTS 「或る旅人の日記」*Aru Tabibito no Nikki*
CREDIT Director + Animation: 加藤久仁生 Kunio Kato, Music: 近藤研二 Kenji Kondo, Producer: 日下部雅謹 Masaaki Kasukabe, 松本絵美 Emi Matsumoto, SE: 日高貴代美 Yoshimi Hidaka (ONPa), Production by ROBOT

31
ARTIST **ランリュウ**
LANRYU
CONTENT *lifepack* (2004)
CREDIT Director: lanryu Music: KINKA, Kontrajaz, Uhyo, 江戸からかみ砂子 Edo karakami sunago by Genki
Ticket Illustration: Sato Yoshiro

32
ARTIST **ルドビック・グザスデラ**
LUDOVIC XASDERA
CONTENT 「たけやぶやけた」*Takeyabu yaketa*

33
ARTIST **石浦 克 / ティ・ジー・ビー・デザイン**
MASARU ISHIURA / TGB design.
CONTENT COM.A, *Lights, Camera, Hallvcination: COM.A*
CREDIT (©ROMZ record & TGB design., 2005)

34
ARTIST **michi / 石多 未知行**
michi a.k.a. MICHIYUKI ISHITA
CONTENTS 1. *Sound+Dance+Visual vol4*
2. *video works [hikari]*
CREDIT Collaborate with ISANOID (music)

35
ARTIST **ミズヒロ・サビーニ**
MIZUHIRO SAVINI
CONTENT *pulse to pulse*
CREDIT Director + Animation + Music: Mizuhiro Savini
(2001)

36
ARTIST **生意気**
NAMAIKI
CONTENTS *Whiter hair, softer teeth*
CREDIT Released by Gas As Interface Co., Ltd
Distributed by Nowonmedia, inc. (GAS DVD, 2002)

37
ARTIST **宇川直宏**
NAOHIRO UKAWA
CONTENT *No Future without Meeting*
CREDIT (2005)

38
ARTIST **喜田夏記**
NATSUKI KIDA
CONTENT *cage* (MTV Station-ID)
CREDIT Director + Art + Animation: 喜田夏記 Natuki Kida
CD: 小池美奈子 Minako Koike, Animation: 喜田直哉 Naoya Kida, 奥田寛 Hiroshi Okuda, 池亀沙織 Saori Ikekame, Camera: 小宮山みつる MitsuruKomiyama, Light: 保坂温 On Hosaka, Music: 益田泰地 TaichiMasuda (2002)
映像提供：MTV JAPAN

39
ARTIST **タナカノリユキ**
NORIYUKI TANAKA
CONTENTS *VISUAL ADDICT*
CREDIT (2004)

40
ARTIST **パワーグラフィックス**
POWER GRAPHIXX
CONTENTS *Roundscape*
CREDIT (Power Graphixx, 2005)

41
ARTIST **黒川良一**
RYOICHI KUROKAWA
CONTENTS *read #5*
CREDIT Under licensed by daisyworld discs* medium,inc.
Contact: medium@daisyworld.co.jp / info@tches.org
(©daisyworld discs and RYOICHI KUROKAWA, 2004)

42
ARTIST **サッカク**
SAKKAKU
CONTENT *spiral*
CREDIT By SAKKAKU OHJI
(2005)

43
ARTIST **ヨシマルシン**
SHIN YOSHIMARU
CONTENTS 「いろいろ MIX」*iroiroMIX*
CREDIT (朝日美穂 Asahi Miho, 戸田誠司 Seiji Toda, ザ・ワークス THE WORKS, 2003-2005)
By Shin Yoshimaru, Ai Tsuchikawa

44
ARTIST **シンポ**
SIMPO
CONTENT *EXP ENSEMBLE/LIVE (2005.10.22)*
CREDIT VJ: SIMPO

45
ARTIST **菅原そうた**
SOTA
CONTENT 「悟り」*Satori*
CREDIT (Sota Sugawara, 2004)

46
ARTIST **大月 壮**
SOU OOTSUKI
CONTENT *NANA SONG*
CREDIT (nos Inc., 2005)

47
ARTIST **山本信一**
SYNICHI YAMAMOTO
CONTENT *Pine Wheel*
CREDIT Music: パードン木村 Pardon Kimura
(Go-Pha, 1997)

48
ARTIST **山口崇司**
TAKASHI YAMAGUCHI
CONTENT *Wave*
MACHINE=EROS PROJECT
CREDIT (2004)

49
ARTIST **タケイグッドマン / ウィズ エンターテインメント**
TAKEI GOODMAN / WIZ ENTERTAINMENT
CONTENT 小沢健二 Ozawa Kenji,
「夢が夢なら」*Yume Ga Yume Nara*
CREDIT (Licensed by TOSHIBA-EMI LTD., 1996)

50
ARTIST **井上 卓**
TAKU INOUE
CONTENT *pilot*
CREDIT Director + Script + Character Design + Edit: 井上卓 Taku Inoue Producer: 上里滋 Shigeru Agari Animation: 井上卓 Taku Inoue(2D) / JINNI'S animation studios (3D)
Music+Sound: 益田泰地 Taichi Masuda
(2004)

51
ARTIST **村田朋泰**
TOMOYASU MURATA
CONTENTS 1.「さかだちくん、ひたすら走る!」*Sakadachi-kun Hitasura Hashiru!*
2.「白の路」*Shiro no Michi*
3.「睡蓮の人」*Suiren no Hito*
4.「冬の虹」*Fuyu no Niji*
5.「とおりゃんせ」*Toryanse*
CREDIT (©Tomoyasu Murata Company., 2000-2005)

52
ARTIST **梅川良満**
UMEKAWA YOSHIMITSU
CONTENT 「デミサン」*Demisan*
CREDIT Staring: Demisan a.k.a. NIPPS
(2004)

53
ARTIST **ウオヌマ**
UONUMA
CONTENT *4F*
CREDIT By Shingo Abe, Sayaka Maruyama

54
ARTIST **栗田やすお**
YASUO KURITA
CONTENT 「緑玉紳士」*Monsieur Greenpeas*
CREDIT (©Yasuo Kurita+Monsieur Greenpeas Production Committee, 2004)

55
ARTISTS **河村勇樹**
YUKI KAWAMURA
CONTENT *JOUR DE REVE*
CREDIT Music: Yoshihiro HANNO
(2005)

56
ARTIST **宅野祐介**
YUSUKE TAKUNO
CONTENT 「ファクトリー」*Factory* (MTV Station-ID)
CREDIT Director: 宅野祐介 Yusuke Takuno
Producer: 清水忠 Tadashi Shimizu
Camera: 吉田好伸 Yoshinobu Yoshida
Music: 益田泰地 Taichi Masuda
Production by P.I.C.S.
(2003)
映像提供：MTV JAPAN

57
ARTIST **ゼログラヴィティ・オプティカルアート**
ZEROGRAVITY OPTICAL ART
CONTENTS NAN, *ERECTION*
CREDIT (2004)

各ジャンル
映像作家
インタビュー

SIX INTERVIEWS OF
SIX EXPERTS
IN DIFFERENT GENRES

VJ

ダンスフロアにおけるVJの存在はもはや、当たり前のものになってきた。どんなクラブにも大小のなにかしらプロジェクターとスクリーンが用意され、VJたちが場に思い思いのビジュアルを添える。そんな光景を日本中のクラブでみることができる。数多くの映像表現があるが、VJほど現場と密接な映像表現者はいないだろう。宇川直宏はVJとして今年で16年間、日本のクラブカルチャー史とともにフロアを渡り歩いてきたことになる。フロアのバイブスを先陣を切って受け止め、スウィッチャーを介してフロアに彩りを添え続けてきた。なお、2005年のVJ年間本数は52本!!! 共演したDJ陣は以下。DANIEL WANG、Francois K.、DJ MARK FARINA、DERRICK CARTER、GOLDIE、FLYING RHYTHMS、PANSONIC、YOUTH、BOY GEORGE、SLY MONGOOSE、CARL CRAIG、KEN ISHII、MAURICE FULTON、MU、DJ TASAKA、MILK10周年でのFORCE OF NATURE、京都WORLD4周年でのF.P.MとEMMA、名古屋MARGO 9周年でのMOODMAN、高橋透、FLASH TOURでのTOWA TEIとの全国巡礼!!!『WIRE』『FUJIROCK』『RAWLIFE』『渚』『METAMORPHOSE』。そしてEYヨとの7HOURS、石野卓球との7HOURS、WIREでのSECRET CINEMA、FUMIYA TANAKA、FRANK MULLER、JORIS VOORN、REINHARD VOIGT、RENATO COHEN、ABE DUQUE、RAWLIFEでのCRYSTALとPEECHBOY!!!!!!!!!!!! などなど、多数の強者と共演を果たしている!!!!!!!!!!

Today, the presence of the VJ on a dance floor is a matter of course. In just about any club, you can find a projector and a screen, and a VJ throwing inventive images into the space. This kind of scene appears in clubs all over Japan. There are many modes of motion graphic expression, but none is as tightly connected to the actual site of presentation as the VJ. Now in his 16th year of VJing, Naohiro Ukawa has hopped through countless dance floors hand in hand with the history of the Japanese club scene, transmitting visual sensations onto crowds and absorbing their vibes. For your info, he did 52 VJ performs in 2005!!! With DJs such as: DANIEL WANG Francois K.,DJ MARK FARINA, DERRICK CARTER, GOLDIE, FLYING RHYTHMS, PANSONIC, YOUTH, BOY GEORGE, SLY MONGOOSE, CARL CRAIG, KEN ISHII, MAURICE FULTON, MU, DJ TASAKA, FORCE OF NATURE at Milk's 10th anniversary, F.P.M and EMMA at World's fourth anniversary in Kyoto, MOODMAN at Margo's 9th anniversary, pilgrimage of TOWA TEI's Flash tour!! "WIRE" "FUJIROCK" "RAWLIFE" "Nagisa" "METAMORPHOSE". And at EYE's 7 HOURS, Takkyu Ishino's 7 HOURS. With SECRET CINEMA, FUMIYA TANAKA, FRANK MULLER, JORIS VOORN, REINHARD VOIGT, RENATO COHEN, ABE DUQUE at "Wire", CRYSTAL and PEECHBOY!!!!!!!!!!!!! He has co-performed with numerous plucky fellows such as above!!!!!!!!!!!

宇川直宏 UKAWA NAOHIRO

宇 UK NA

祝！
VJ16周年!!

——宇川さんのVJが特に注目され始めたのは、ボアダムスでのライブVJ以降だと思うのですが、そのころはどういったスタイルでプレイしてたのですか？
VHSとHi-8（笑）。そのころはまだテープメディアしかなかったからね。89年にオープンしたばかりの芝浦のクラブ、「GOLD」5FのLOVE&SEXや川崎クラブチッタで、森田君という友人と組んでいた今でいうところのAUDIO VISUALユニット"GRAVESTYLE"としてプレイしたのが最初で、その頃にEYヨちゃんと友達になって、90年に2000Vのボアダムスのライブでしたのが最初かな。

——今はVJデビュー16周年なわけですね。その時、宇川さんいくつですか？
VJやり始めたのは、19歳から20歳くらい。クラブ歴は長いよ。実はワケあって独り暮らしを始めた高校時代に、すでにもう東京に友人がいたから、ほぼ毎週新幹線をキセルして四国から東京のクラブへ来てた。当時『イントロ』っていうフリーペーパーがあって、そこに藤原ヒロシ、高木完、ダブマスターX、ラファエロ、大貫憲章、ランキンタクシーとかのDJスケジュールが載っかってて、そこからずうーっとパーリーピーポ。卒業後、すぐ東京に越してきて、ツバキハウス、ピカソ、クラブD、第三倉庫、モンクベリーズ、バブリン・ダブ、下北ナイトクラブ、バンク、ヒップフェロー、六本木サーカス、芝浦インクとか……、とにかく夜な夜な激踊りできるフロアを求め毎夜クラブハシゴしてました。そこでヘイタさんや、高橋透にハウスの洗礼を受けて……。

——当時のVJの様子はどうでしたか？
89年に俺ら世代がプロジェクターを使ってクラブという空間に映像を持ち込んだのが、今のVJシーンの黎明期だと思うよ。確実に91年にはVJと自称してたし、ね。でも"VISUAL JOCKEY"ではなく"VIDEO JOCKEY"を略していたんだけど。今と違ってソフトがVHSとHi-8しかなかったから。そういう意味では今だに"VIDEO JOCKEY"だけど（笑）。その時期ってGOLDも、CAVEもできたばっかりだったし、まだまだ東京全体にバブリーな空気がモクモクと漂ってて、桑原茂一さんがプロデュースしたピテカン以降、本格的に東京にクラブシーンといえるものが根付く勢いがあったね。（そうした場があったから）みんな音楽以外に現場に何かを持ってこようとしていた時期だった。ちょうど坂本龍一と原田大三郎のやってたラジカルTVと、立花ハジメがコモドール64やAMIGAを使って、ライブにビデオパフォーマンスを導入しているのをリアルタイムで観てきた世代だから。そういう表現に関してはショックを受けたと思うんだけど、当時は家電のテクノロジーが全くそこまで達してなかったから、特権階級にしか解放されてなくて、取り組みようがなかった時代。だからやり始めたのはAMIGA、Mac以降だよね。

——それにしてもまだ一般的な値段ではなかったわけですね。
デスクトップの領域ではやっとDTPって言葉が出てき始めた時代で、MacintoshもIIfxが一番速かったころだよね。当時俺30回ローンでIIci買ったんだけど、実はVideo Toasterの威力にすごいショックを受けてて、友だちのAMIGA使ってるやつと合体させていろいろやってた。田中秀幸とピエール滝のプリンストンガはいまだにVideo Toasterも使ってるでしょ。本当にリスペクトだよ。Director 1.0とSwivel 3Dの1.0と、PhotoshopもIllustratorも1.0だった。そこで何ができるかということで、当時RasterOpsの364っていうビデオがキャプチャリングできるボードがあって、それ

16th year as a VJ!

——You began to attract lots of attention as a VJ after doing the visuals for Boredoms concerts. What kind of style were you using around that time?
VHS and Hi-8 (laughs). It's because only tape media was available at the time. I began VJing at places like Club Citta in Kawasaki and Love & Sex, which was on the fifth floor of Gold, a disco that opened in 1989 in Shibaura. It was for a unit called Gravestyle, which I formed with a friend called Morita. I guess in today's terms it would be referred to as an audio-visual unit. Around that time, I became friends with EYヨ, the leader of the Boredoms, and the first time I VJed for them was in 1990 for a concert at 2000V.

——And so it's been 16 years since then. How old were you at the time?
I began VJing when I was 19 or 20. My clubbing history is long. I was living by myself during high school, and just about every week, I would sneak a free ride on the Shinkansen [bullet train] from Shikoku to Tokyo, to go clubbing with friends I had there. In the train, I would sleep in either the dining car or the lavatory. There used to be a free magazine called "Intro," which listed the schedules of DJs like Hiroshi Fujiwara, Kan Takagi, Dubmaster X, Raphaelo, Kansyo Ohnuki, and Rankin Taxi, so I would always check that and find a great party. At the time, I was what you would call a hardcore clubber. Once I moved to Tokyo right after graduating from high school, I was always searching for a place where I could dance my ass off, mainly at clubs like Tsubaki House, Picasso, Club D, Daisan Souko, Monkberry's, Bubblin Dub, Night Club in Shimokitazawa, Bank, Hip Fellow, Circus in Roppongi, and Shibaura Ink.

——What was the scene like when you first began VJing?
My generation was the first to bring motion graphics into the club space in 1989, by utilizing projectors. I think this was the dawn of today's VJ scene. By 1991, I was definitely calling myself as a VJ, even though I was abbreviating "video jockey" and not "visual jockey." I'm not kidding when I say that I only had VHS and Hi-8. It was an era in which Tokyo still had that bubble-economy-atmosphere. Ever since the popularity of the club Pithecan Thropus Erectus, produced by Moichi Kuwahara, an authentic club scene was rooting in Tokyo. Gold was the foremost club, and Cave had also just opened. Everyone was trying to bring things other than music into this new field. My generation witnessed Ryuichi Sakamoto and Daizaburo Harada's "Radical TV," and Hajime Tachibana introducing video performance into his live acts, using a

と VideoExpander っていうのを IIci に導入して試行錯誤を繰り返していた時期だったね。ボアダムスには当時ゴッドママっていうダンサーがいて、彼女をモデリングしてガキガキの 3DCG を動かしたりしてたよ。レイトレーシングがなかった時代。あと、それにトッドラングレンが作った「フローフェザー」っていうアブストラクトなスクリーンセーバーと MIX したりしてた。mini DV もファイアーワイアーももちろんないし、Hi-8 をモニター上で制御するのに驚いてたような子供騙しなテクノロジーが幅を利かせてた時代だったから（笑）。VJ の歴史は家電としての液晶ビデオプロジェクターの進化なくしては語れないよね。ちょうどそのころシャープが 30 万円台の一眼でけっこう明るいプロジェクターを出して、それまでにも一眼のプロジェクターはあったけど全然光源がパワー不足で灯籠みたいだったの（笑）。まともなプロジェクターは RGB 三眼の当時 200 万円くらいするものしかなかった。それこそ、中古のベンツが買える金額でしょ。そういう意味では黎明期はビデオプロジェクターの進化とともに歩んだ時代だよね。それで当時、GOLD にシャープのそのプロジェクターが入ってたんだよ。DEEP には三眼のでっかい 200 万くらいのが入っていた。CAVE にはビデオプロジェクターがなかった代わりに小さいレーザーが入ってた。ちょうどアンビエントとブリープが盛り上がったころ。毎週通ってたね。それでシャープのプロジェクターを自分で購入したのね。当時って、VJ の内容以前に“プロジェクターを持っていること =VJ”っていう、せこい特権があったように思う（笑）。この頃が日本の、というか世界の VJ カルチャー黎明期と言っても過言ではないかも……。プロジェクターは日本製なんだから。そのころは、自分と、松木靖明と、田中秀幸、あと後にアナーキック・ア・ジャストメントに参加する西海岸のユニットのハイパーデリックビデオあたりが、クラブ VJ って意味では始祖的な立ち位置なんだと思うんだ。あとはやっぱり M.M.delight の森田さん。彼も 90 年から GEOIDO で VJ を始めてるし、久保憲司が主催してた黎明期のリキッドルームのクラブビーナスっていう重要なパーティーでも VJ していた。誰に影響受けるワケでもなくそれぞれが手探りで始めた時代だったから。あの頃、俺とかまだ全然ショボかったと思うよ（笑）。

――今のようなスイッチング（複数の映像を切り替えること）は当時からやっていたんですか？

VJ やる前は DJ やってたから、リアルタイムでミックスしないと意味ないと思ってて、もちろん最初っからロングミックスやってたよ。最初に使ってたスイッチャーが当時リリースされたばかりの SONY XV-Z10000 っていう定価で 75 万もするマシンで、半業務用の重い重いそのマシンを毎回クラブに運んでた。以降そのブッといフェーダーが馴染みすぎて、ほかのスイッチャーは使えなくなった。大きくて太くて固いフェーダーがお好みです！（爆笑）そんなイツモツで初体験しちゃったワケだから、EDIROL の V4 も KORG の krossfour も平行で使ってるんだけど、いまだにメインはずぅーっと SONY XV-Z10000。17 年前のマシンだからもちろん店頭に並んでるワケもなく、レストアしてくれるワケもなく、ヤフオクでもマメにチェックしてて、今使ってるマシンで 13 台目、今年は 6 台壊したよ（笑）。主にはシャンパンこぼしてコントローラー破損って感じなんだけど、最もヤバかったのは、FUJI ROCK で（石野）卓球さんの VJ やっている最中にいきなり壊れたから、OHP の書画カメラに切り替えて、ピンクのポスカで「スイッチャー！急遽破損!! 今から山くだって V-4 取りに行って来ます！」って手書きで書いて、1 万人以上いる会場に黒飴一袋バラまいたらオーディエンスが逆に興奮して（笑）。俺以上にハードコアにフェーダー動かす VJ は多分いないと思うよ。1 分に 30 回として 1

Commodore 64 and an Amiga. We were blown away by these forms of expression, but the technology of home electronics wasn't what it is today, so these options were available only for a privileged class. I was able to begin this kind of activity only after I got my hands on an Amiga and Macintosh.

If we're going to discuss about the VJ culture, it's inevitable that we come to the topic of the evolution of the liquid crystal video projector. Not many people discuss about this, but it was a significant topic for the people on the site. Around that time, Sharp released a fairly bright single-lens projector for around 300,000 yen. There were other single-lens units before this, but their light sources were so weak, they were more like lanterns than projectors (laughs). The only alternative was to buy a three-lens RGB projector, which cost something like 2,000,000 yen at the time. You could buy a used Mercedes of decent

quality for that price (laughs). So the onset of the VJ culture advanced hand in hand with the evolution of the video projector. At the time, club Gold had that Sharp projector. Deep had a 2,000,000 yen three-lens unit. Cave was still a new venue, but they had a small laser instead of a projector. Mr. Kudo's party was using that laser, with the whole lower floor in a pitch black state. All you could see in the darkness was this thin green outline, so it was really weird. Nobody could see what you were doing on the dance floor, so there were guys who were groping girls' bodies (laughs). But if you think about it now, that place was the most progressive techno venue in Japan. It was around the time when ambient and bleep were on the rise. I was there every week. I've strayed off of the topic a little, but anyway, I bought my own projector. I think that at the time, it was a strange situation in which whether you owned a projector or not was more important for the reputation of a VJ than

マンス！この中に今までアーカイブした映像をすべて入れ込んだらもうVHSすべていらないからさ。

——てっきり、VHSの劣化具合を楽しんでるのかなと思ったんですけど。
んなアホな(笑)。NumarkのVMO3のモニターと、ラックマウントのDVDプレイヤーDVD01があれば完璧に現場でピッチ合わせられるよ。Numarkさん、僕もモニターになりたいです。

——DVDのほかに最近ではローランドのビジュアル・シンセサイザーを使ってるようですね。
そうそう。EDIROLのCG8を今年のWIREから導入したんだけど、さすがシンセの老舗メーカー。その発想がスゴすぎ！ だってJPGから3D動画をつくって、その映像をパッドエアシンセみたいなD-ビーム使って、XYZ軸にリアルタイムでコントロールできる。言ってみれば映像で演奏する感覚。60年代にナムジュン・パイクやステファン・ベックがVIDEOシンセサイザーって実際に使ってたけど、感覚的にはあれを進化させたモノだと思う。70年代のSCANIMATEとかEMSのSPECTREみたいにさ。本当にこれは発明でしょう。

時間に1800回で平均一晩10時間プレイしたとして18000回！ それを毎週やってたら壊れて当たり前だよね。あとはパイオニアからモニターとして頂いたPioneer DVJ X-1が今やフル稼動。もうDVJなしでは生きていけない体だよ。だから最近の自分のVJはDVJ X-1でピッチも追いかけて合わせてるし、ブレイクでスクラッチもしてる。あとはDVD 3台とシャープのVC-LXっていう6年前にリリースされたモニター付きVIDEOデッキが5台と、KORGのKAOSS PAD entrancerと、秘密兵器のELMOの書画カメラでリアルタイム手書きVJ。みんなマネすんなよなー手書きVJ（笑）。

——特にVHSにこだわっているわけじゃないんですね？
VHSでやる意味なんて実は全然ないよね。カサバるし、時間軸がリニアだから現場でループ組めないし。落としたら割れるし、お客さんにワインこぼされて、今まで300本位ベタベタになって捨ててるし。だけど逆にこだわってる。今となっては（笑）。VJブースのうしろに大量にビデオ積んでると見た目がヤバいからね。すんごい威圧感ない？ もちろん、今、素材はDVDに焼いてるから、新しいネタはVHSで作らないよ。Motion DiveとかのVJソフトもいろいろなモノを試したんだけど、初期のころだったから、短い尺をハーフサイズでループさせても、まだまだVHSの方がクオリティ高かったの。でももちろん今はフルサイズだし、コンソールパッケージで購入しなきゃ。だからmotion dive .TokyoコンソールでMIDIリンクはライブ表現において必須でしょ。あと、やっぱりKORGのKaptivator。サンプラーとして、エフェクターとして、ミキサーとして使えるあり得ないパフォー

virgin experience was with a prick like this, so even though I now use an Edirol V4 and a Korg Krossfour in parallel, my main switcher is still the Sony XVZ-10000. The machine was released 17 years ago, so it's impossible to find it in any stores, nobody will repair it for you, and there aren't any spare parts that you can buy to fix it. So I constantly alert people at Yahoo! Auctions that I'm looking for this switcher. The one I'm using now is my 13th one!! This year alone, I've broken 6 units (laughs)! Most of the time, the controller malfunctions because of spilt champagne or something, but the craziest time was when it broke down in the middle of my VJ set for Takkyu Ishino at Fuji Rock Festival. I immediately switched to an OHP, and wrote "The switcher broke!! I'm climbing down the mountain to get a V4!" with a marker, and gave away lots of candy to the crowd of over 10,000 people before I left. For some reason, this got them really

the content of his visuals (laughs). That really was the dawn of the VJ culture in Japan. It may even be possible to say "the world," since the projectors are made in Japan.

——Were you doing the kind of switching (alternating between different visual feeds) that you do today?
I was DJing even before I began VJing, so my philosophy was that there was no meaning unless you mixed in realtime. I was doing longmixes from the very beginning. The first switcher I bought was the Sony XVZ-10000, which was just freshly released, with a retail price of 750,000 yen. Since there weren't many VJs around at the time, I had to carry the semi-industrial equipment to the club every time. It was very heavy. I got so used to the unusually thick crossfader on that switcher, I now feel uncomfortable pinching anything else. Yes, I like my faders big, thick, and hard (laughs)!! My

音と映像の蜜月史
100年

——VJのフロアでの役割っていうものをどう考えていますか？　宇川さんのVJを見て思うのは、象徴的なハットをかぶってやってるっていうのが先陣切ってもらってる感じになってるというか。

クラブってすごくトライバルな儀式空間だと思うのね。いってみればDJは司祭で、全身全霊をかけてフロアのヴァイブを自らに憑依させ、ダイアモンドの針を通じて音をフロアに投げかけるワケでしょ。DJにしてもVJにしても、フロアのオーディエンスを忘我的な恍惚に誘える人たちがやるべき表現ですよね。そんな司祭によって導かれたフロアでの連帯意識は何ごとにも代えがたき大きな糧として、退屈な日常に華を添えるんだと思う。だからまずVJは、DJにとっての良きトランスレイターでなくてはならないと思うのね。DJが投げかけた音を映像としてトランスレートするのがVJの一つの役割だから。違う言語に置き換えるという意味では同時通訳と同じだよね。それは直訳であってもダメだし、意訳も混在してくるのが醍醐味であって……。さらにそこからオーディエンスとのインタラクティブな関係性が重要になってくるよね。一貫して言えることはVJの方が視覚だからDJに比べてダイレクトな情報量を持ってるじゃない。だからイメージを限定しちゃう恐れがあるでしょ。だけど音楽ってイメージを限定せずに、送り手のもとから離れた段階で、あとは受け手に委ねられる。もちろん送り手が頭の中でビジュアルを想定したものを音の中に擦り込んでいくこともあるけれど、限定はされないと思うんだよね。オーディエンスがフロアで踊っていて、その場のヴァイブレーションを感じてDJがまた音を送り返す。そうした双方向のコミニュケーションがフロアで形成されていると思うのね。すべては波動です。そこに映像が入ったとき、より限定したイメージに持っていっちゃう可能性がすごく強い。だから3者の相乗効果が得られてフロアのヴァイブを高められる関係じゃないと。

今、オーディオビジュアルいう言葉があるけど、MTVが始まったときからすでに音と映像の蜜月は始まっていたワケだし、例えばミュージッククリップにおいてオーディオとビジュアルがシンクロしてるのはすでに当たり前でしょ。要するにあらかじめシンクロさせることの方が、DJとVJの関係性でもってフロアに連帯をもたらすことより、むしろ表現としては容易いワケで。それをハードディスクやDVDからプレイしたら当然100%のシンクロ率なんだよ。オーディオとビジュアルの予定調和なんてまったく双方向の自由度がない。ライブの背景を埋める映像なら、クラフトワークやコーネリアスのようにその方法がもちろん有効なんだけど。

——今は、音と映像がシンクロするってことをオーディオビジュアルって呼ぶ傾向がありますよね。

そんな言葉はエレクトロニカやトリップホップと一緒。ドリルンベースもインテリジェントテクノも、もう誰もこっぱずかしくって、使わないでしょ(笑)。消費されてすぐ死ぬ言葉だよね。最近「VJは終わった。これからはオーディオビジュアルだ」って言ってる人たちがいて唖然としたんだよ。VJとオーディオビジュアルは全く別ものだよ。映画がサイレントからトーキーへと変わった状況を振り返ってみようよ。フィルムがサウンドトラックを持っていなかった当時、サイレント映画の上映時には弁士がいて、隣にチェロなんかを演奏している人がいた。映像を見ながら演奏していたわけだよね。自分が譜面を用意してきて演奏しているわけではなく、映像を見てその場で譜面を起こしているようなもの。逆だけどこれがVJとDJとMCの関係性というか……。そして映画がトーキーへと移り変わることによって、ぴったり口の動きと

hyped up, and I was able to keep them entertained until I came back (laughs). But Masahiro Hidaka, the director of the event organization company, coincidentally happened to be there during the occurrence, and he was like “It's broken huh (laughs).” So these days, I'm even using malfunctions as part of my performance. They're inevitable, because I don't think there's any VJ who uses the crossfader more fiercely than I do. I flick it maybe 30 times per minute, so that's 1800 times per hour, and on an average of 10 hours per night, that's 18,000 flicks! Since I do that every week, that's close to 100,000 flicks every month, so it's not so strange that it breaks down so often. I'm also constantly using the Pioneer DVJ X-1 now, which Pioneer has provided me with for assessment. I can't live without this machine anymore. So in my recent VJ sets, I use the DVJ X-1 to adjust the speed of my visuals to the DJ's beat, and I even scratch during breaks. I also use three DVD players, five Sharp VC-LXs, which are VCRs with monitors attached to them, a Korg Kaoss Pad Entrancer, and my weapon of choice: an Elmo OHP, which I use to VJ with hand drawings! Hey all you guys, stop it with the hand-drawn VJing, it was my idea first (laughs). I've done VJ sets with nothing but drawings at shows for EYƎ, Pardon Kimura, and Flying Rhythms. Right now, I'm exploring the deep realm of real-time hand drawing.

——Oh, I thought you had a special thing going for VHS.

There's actually no incentive in using VHS. The equipment is bulky, and the time axis is linear, so you can't create loops on the site. It breaks easily when you drop it, and I've had to throw away at least 300 sticky tapes so far, because people spill wine and stuff on them. The reason I started using it in the first place was because VHS, along with Beta and Hi-8, were the only media available for consumer use back then. I was VJing with VHS as the media for something like twelve years. So even when I created new material on my computer, I would often be recording it onto VHS tapes from my hard drive. But actually, I do have a thing going for VHS. I didn't before, but I do now (laughs). Because, it looks wicked when there's a huge mass of videotapes stacked behind the VJ booth. Isn't it daunting as hell (laughter)? It kind of makes me look like one of those homeless guys that sell stacks of thrown-away magazines at the train station.

——I hear that besides DVD, you re also using a Roland visual synthesizer.

Yes, The Edirol CG8! I began using it at this year's Wire. I've got to give it to them, they're experience as a long-time synthesizer manufacturer has led

リップシンクしたサウンドトラックを持つに至った。当たり前でしょ、今となっては(笑)。これってオーディオビジュアルだよね。あと、MTVの歴史を掘り下げることは制作現場としては有効だと思うよ。とにかく音と映像は同時に進化してきたと思うのね。そしてお互い寄り添いながら存在しているものだと思う。あとナムジュン・パイクとかフルクサスとかビル・ビオラのビデオアートに話をそこから飛躍させられるし。それから現場の話なら、最初のサマー・オブ・ラブの時代に西海岸で実験してたゼラチンライトやスライドショー、OHPなんかを使ったサイケデリックパフォーマンスと、ライトショー。当時は赤坂のMUGENでもやってたから。アングラ、サイケ、ハレンチの時代に米軍の黒人が福生からやって来て。その後に、ピンクフロイドらがレーザーを導入した後に、初めてローリー・アンダーソンのビデオパフォーマンスの話ができると思うんだ。80年代のユーミンのライブも(笑)。

——注目しているVJはいますか？

まずKROMAでしょ。彼らはメタフォルフォーゼのVJ周辺を仕切っていて、毎年誘ってくれるんだけど、ここ何年間も最も注目してる。自分も5年前リリースした『Scanning of Modulation』みたいにオプやフリッカー、モアレ的なアブストラクトな方向性だけで探求している世界観を持っているんだけど、KROMAの、ハードコアにその独自性のみをかたくなに探求する姿は、孤高なるオプティカル伝導師のようで潔いよね。あと、サンプリングメインじゃなくモーショングラフィックスの流れから、エクスペリメンタルに進化した人たちもいつも注目してるよ。WIREで毎年一緒にやっているDEVICEGIRLSとか、GLAMOVEとかも素晴らしいと思うよ。もう彼らも大御所だよね。あと最近活動してないみたいだけど、FIXERはMAX使って独自のB-ISMを展開してたと思うし。あとやっぱり仲良しのBetaLand。もう8年くらい知ってるけど、彼らは毎年どんどんマジカルになっていってる。『FLOWERS OF LIFE』ってパーティーもオーガナイズしてる。BetaLandはVJだけではなく、パーティーシーンの時空を未踏のディメンションへ捩じ曲げるマジカルグルとしてもリスペクトしてる。あと、他社比社のメンバーでもあるHeart Bombは、何度か一緒にプレイしたこともあるけど、コミックスの効果線や爆破のアイコンをアフターエフェクツで1フレずつアニメートさせたり、スケルトゥーンはMUSTONEのLIVEペインティング上からイラレのベジェをリアルタイムで直接いじって、ベクター上でペイントしたり、世界的にみても誰も到達していないパフォーマンスをしてるよね。それから光Jや、10Kは、宇川フォロアーと見ているんだけど、どーでしょうか？

なんか彼らが遺伝子を継いでくれると思うとてもかわいい(笑)。あと、最近のエンライトメントのVJもすごくいいよね。プリンストンガのオールドスクールなTVセットもヤバイし。今年から他社比社と一緒にクラブ付きの「micro office」っていうオフィスを立ち上げるんだけど。そこではパーティーももちろんだけど、もっともっとVJの実験的な試みのみに焦点を当てて、深度3000メートル以上の壮大かつ過酷な映像の深海を開拓できないかと思ってる。

to an amazing result. The whole idea is spectacular. You create 3D movies out of JPEGs, and control these in real-time through a XYZ axis, using pads and a D-beam, just like an air synth. It's like playing music, but with visuals instead of sound. It's kind of an evolved version of the video synthesizers that artists like Nam June Paik and Stephen Beck were using back in the '60s. It's also similar to some machines from the '70s like the Scanimate and the EMS Spectre. This machine really is an invention.

——Any thoughts about the role of the VJ in the club? You wear that symbolic hat when you VJ, and it s always the first thing I notice.

I think that the club is a very primal and ceremonial space. The DJ is sort of the guru, who makes an effort to become possessed by the vibe of the crowd, and pumps music through a diamond needle onto the dance floor. DJing and VJing are both modes of expression that should be handled by people who have the ability to seduce the audience into an ecstatic trance. The sense of solidarity that envelopes the dance floor becomes food for the soul, bringing a wisp of bliss into the mundanity of everyday life. This is what I think. So, the VJ has to be a good translator for the DJ. One of the roles of the VJ is to translate the DJ's music into images. He or she has to render one language into another, just like a simultaneous interpreter. A translation that is too direct and literal is ineffective, and the whole essence is in involving the interpreter's personal taste here and there. The interactive relationship with the audience is also very important. Since the VJ's role is to stimulate the sense of sight, he is going to be transmitting a mass of information that has a certain directness which music does not have. This means that there is a danger of imposing limits on the imagination of the audience. On the contrary, music by nature does not limit the imagination. Once music has departed from the sender, interpretation is totally up to the recipient. Of course, the sender can attempt to express certain images in her mind through the music, but it still doesn't have a limiting effect. The audience dances along to the music, the DJ receives the vibes they emit, and responds by feeding back music. This kind of interactive cycle of communication is created on the dance floor. Everything here is vibration. When motion graphics are introduced into this cycle, there enters the possibility of limiting the imagination. Therefore, there is a need to form a relationship in which the three entities, the DJ, the VJ, and the audience, can produce a synergy that intensifies the vibe of the dance floor. I think this is what VJing is all about.

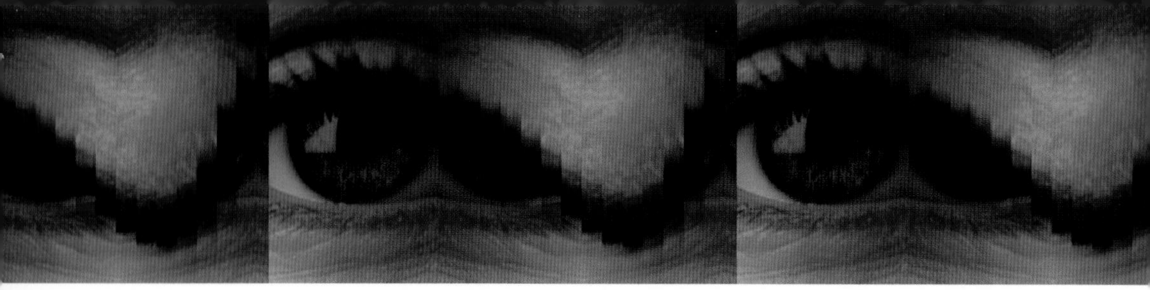

PROMOTION VIDEO

この数年の間に音楽のプロモーション・ビデオ（PV）が新たな表現手法として台頭してきている。2004年にはDirectors Labelよりミシェル・ゴンドリー、クリス・カニングハム、スパイク・ジョーンズの作品を収録したDVDもリリースされた。PVはエッジの効いたアイデアをベースにした視覚表現をポップマーケットに浸透させるための媒介となった。才能ある映像作家たちが、かつては一部の愛好家の目にしか止まることのなかった60〜70年代の実験映像のアイデアや速度を、進行形で発達し続けるテクノロジーを駆使して現代に呼び覚ました。新たな視覚的驚きやユーモアを5分足らずのストーリーに絡め、それを完成度の高い作品として発表する土壌が生まれた。それらの作品の中に見出されるのは凝縮された宇宙。僕らが日常で見逃しているディテイルと、スケール感のある想像力が合わさる着地点がそこに在る。

Born in the 1980s, the music video is recognized today as a comparatively new yet substantial mode of artistic expression. It has been especially prominent in the past few years, as collections of the works of popular music video directors have been released on DVD one after another. Music video has acted as an effective medium for allowing cutting-edge ideas to diffuse into the mass market. The ideas and kinesthesia of the experimental films of the 60's and 70's, which were back then viewed only by a handful of fans, have been resurrected into the present day by talented motion graphic artists through the application of technologies that are advancing day by day. A rich field has been cultivated to allow them to weave innovative forms of visual stimulation and wit into a five-minute narrative, and present it as formal work.

辻川幸一郎
KOICHIRO TSUJIKAWA

レコジャケから 映像へ

——映像を作るようになったきっかけを教えてください。

コーネリアスなどのミュージシャンと仲が良くて、もともとは彼らのグラフィックやレコードジャケットを作ったりしていたんです。それで、ある時、小山田圭吾くんにライヴで流す映像を編集してくれと言われて、映像を作りだすことにしました。

——映像の仕事はそれまで全くしたことがなかったんですか？

一度、ADで参加した以外はありませんでした。それなのに、小山田（圭吾）くんに頼まれて、しかも2、3週間後にそれを完成させなくてはならなかった。Macで作れるという話は聞いていたので、とりあえず秋葉原の電気店の店員さんにあれこれ教えてもらいました。ソフトの使い方なんかも「パソコンがうまく動かないんですけど」なんて言って、さりげなく聞き出してましたね。それが90年代の終わりごろのことです。

——平面から映像に移られて、アイデアや作業の仕方も変わりましたか？

今にして思えば、もともと平面のデザインもわりと映像的だった気がしますね。分解写真を使ったデザインや、ページをめくるとストーリーが展開するようなデザインを多く作っていました。美大では空間演出を専攻していたし、その後もデザイン会社に入っていたわけではなかったので、グラフィックの方もそもそも独学だったんですけど。

——当時、個人で映像の仕事をしている方は周りにいましたか？

そんなにはいなかったですね。映像を作ること自体、今ほど当たり前ではありませんでした。mini DVがまだ出始めたばかりのころで、映像を取り込んで編集するのも、プラグインや外付けの装置を整備しなくてはできないようなころでした。

——辻川さんを筆頭に、最近個人の映像作家が増えていますね。テクノロジーの発展によって、映像が写真やグラフィックデザインのように始めから終わりまで個人で作れる表現メディアになったことが影響していると思うのですが、その状況についてどう思いますか？

個人で作る映像と、ライティングやサウンドなど、ほかのメンバーと一緒に作る映像では、その目的も役割も違うような気がします。技術は発展してきて、いわゆるモーショングラフィックスのように、個人で作れるコンテンツが増えているのは面白いこ

From Record Covers to Motion Graphics

——What prompted you to begin creating motion graphics?

I was friends with musicians like Cornelius, and started out by making graphics and record covers for them. One day, I was asked by Keigo Oyamada (Cornelius) to edit some motion graphics for his concert, and that was the beginning for me.

——You had never done motion graphic work before that?

I had worked once as an assistant director, but I didn't have any experience other than that. For Oyamada's request, I had to complete the work within two or three weeks. I had heard that motion graphics could be made with a Macintosh, so I went to an electric store in Akihabara and kept asking the staff a load of questions. I would subtly find out how to operate the software by telling them things like "my computer isn't working properly."

——Was that around the end of the 90s ?

Yeah, it was around that time.

——Did the way in which you construct ideas and produce works change after you switched from graphics to motion graphics?

Now that I look back, I think that my graphic designs already had an inclination towards motion graphics. I often made designs in which a story would develop as you flipped the pages. I was majoring in spatial production during art school, and I didn't join any design companies after graduating, so my graphic designs were based on self-education.

——At the time, were there any other people around you who were working in independent motion graphics?

Not so many. Creating motion graphics wasn't such a common activity back then as it is now. It was when Mini DV was just being released. If you wanted to edit footage on your computer, you had to install several plug-ins and attach external devices.

——Recently, there has been a notable increase in the number of motion graphic artists working on an independent basis. I think it's because developments in technology are allowing for works to be produced from start to finish by the individual, just like in graphic design and photography. Do you have any views on this situation?

It's an interesting phenomenon how advancements in technology are allowing individuals to create motion graphic works. I have been creating works this way myself. However, I think that works

とだと思います。僕も、そうやって作ってきたから。ただ、集団で作る作品と単独で作る作品では、規模や役割が違ってきますからね。単純に、新しいジャンルが確立したということだと思います。

——映像を作っていく上で影響されたアーティストはいましたか？

もちろん、数え切れないくらいいます。映画はたくさん見てきたので、その影響はかなり大きいと思うし、小さい時から見ていたテレビ番組の影響も大きいと思う。本当に絞り切れませんけど、あえて言うなら、ティム・バートン。新作を見るたびに、すごく影響されているなって思います。ファンタジー系の映画は全般的に好きですね。それから、セサミ・ストリートやマペットショウをつくったジム・ヘンソンにはすごく影響されていると思います。

——ご自分で代表作だと思われる作品はどれですか？

やはり初めのころの作品ですね。代表作といえるかどうかは分からないけれど、初めのころの作品は初期衝動がそのまま出ていると思うので、やっぱり一番「素」に近いんじゃないんですかね。今でもそうだけど、コーネリアスのPVは自分が発展途上の時に作ったものだから、うまくない分新しいというか。具体的には『DROP』とか『TONE TWILIGHT ZONE』は、自分で編集までしているし、思い入れもあります。

実験の場としてのPV

——音楽というのは辻川さんの映像作りにとってどんなものですか？

PVを作る上では音楽は映画や芝居の脚本に近いですね。音楽を聞き込んで、その音楽に合わせた世界観だとか、テンポを作ったりします。音楽をベースにして、そこから映像表現としてどのような面白いことができるのかを考えます。

——90年代から、PVが表現のジャンルの一つとして台頭したと言われていますが、辻川さんはPVというジャンルをどのようにお考えですか？

以前は実験映画っていうジャンルがあったと思うんですよ。ズビグ・リプチンスキー、伊藤高志、トニー・ヒルに代表されるような映像表現です。何を描くかっていうことに先行して映像の技術的な追究をするような作品や、切り口だけで突き抜けている作品、いわゆる、実験映画的なアプローチの作品があったと思うんですね。それらの作

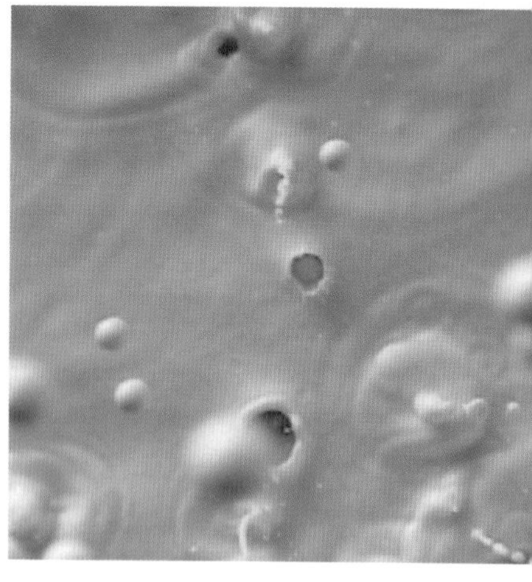

品って、一般の人たちがなかなか目にすることができなかった。それが、PVという枠を通してだと、意外と世の中にぽんと出てたりするんですよね。例えばミシェル・ゴンドリーのカイリー・ミノーグのPVは、実験映画の精神にものすごく近い作りの作品です。昔でいえばリプチンスキーの『Tango』のような作品ですね。以前は一部の限られた人たちにしか届かなかったそれらの作品が、PVになると誰もが見ることのできるポップなフィールドに送られる。だから、ほかのPVを見ていても「実験映画そのもの！」と思わせるものが多い

produced by the individual and those produced by a group have fundamentally different purposes and roles. When you work in a group, you can have other members handle the things like sound and lighting, so the scale of the project is often in a different realm than independent works. I think it s basically a matter of a new genre appearing onto the scene.

——Are there any motion graphic artists that have influenced you?

There have been many. I've been heavily influenced by the numerous movies that I've watched over the years, and also the TV programs that I've watched since I was a small child. It's really hard to narrow down, but if I had to choose one person, it would be Tim Burton. Every time I see a new film by him, I'm influenced greatly. Fantasy films are a genre that I take pleasure in watching. I've also received influence from Jim Henson, who created programs like Sesame Street and The Muppet Show.

The Music Video as a Field of Experimentation

——What is music to you, in terms of your practice?

In a way, music is to a music video what a script is to a movie or play. I concentrate on listening to the music, and try to create a world-image or a tempo that fits that music. I think about how I can use the particular audio track as a base for making an interesting motion graphic work.

——It's often considered that in the 90's, music video began to be taken seriously as a mode of expression. What are your thoughts on the this field?

There used to be a genre called experimental film, with people like Zbig Rybczynski, Takashi Ito, and Tony Hill. These works had a certain approach, for example, pursuing technical aspects before content, or having a concept strong enough to be remarkable in itself. Most of the time, these works were viewed by only a limited number of people, and didn't have a chance to reach the mass. But when the same kind of imagery is presented today through the format of the music video, it can reach the attention of popular culture very easily. For example, the Kylie Minogue video by Michel Gondry was a work that was very close to the spirit of the experimental film. It had similarities to Rybczynski's "Tango." When I'm watching music videos, I frequently see things that are practically identical with experimental film works. The time durations are often similar in the two fields, and so is the leeway of creative freedom. I think that's why similar-looking

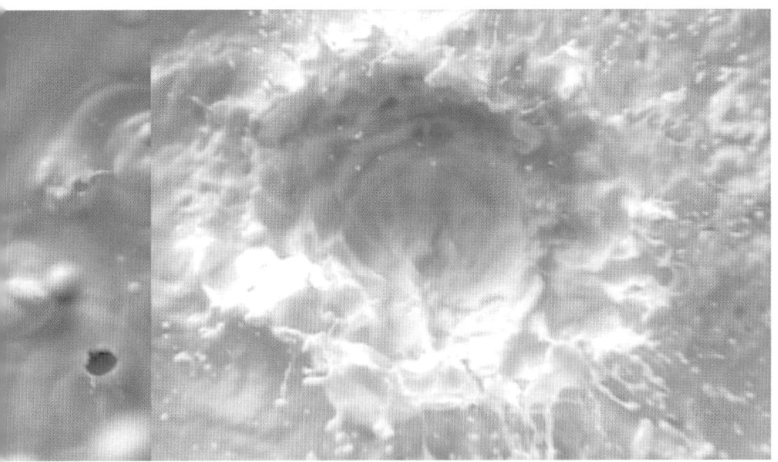

われたりしたんだけど、『Like a Rolling Stone』みたいなモーフィング表現というのは、PVでのみ観られる表現だったりします。最新技術というよりも、技術だけが目的の映像を、そのまま形にしても大丈夫な幅があるのがPVなんだと思います。映画やCMでは、本当の意味で最新の技術が使われていますね。逆にPVの場合は新しいかどうかということよりも、表現そのものが着地点になることが許されているジャンルなんですよ。新しいものというよりも、他のジャンルでは展開しづらいものもPVだったらOKになっているっていう、それくらいのことなんじゃないかと思います。

んですよね。長さとかも近いし、見せ方の自由度の幅も近かったりするので、似たような雰囲気のものが出てきやすいんだと思います。小山田くんなんかは音楽性そのものもそういうところと噛み合わせが良かったんでしょうね。まあ、結局PVにもいろいろあって、ひとくくりにはできませんが、僕にとってはPVは昔でいう実験映画みたいなヘンテコな表現が許されている、そういう可能性のあるジャンルですね。

——PVって最新技術が試される場所でもありますよね。タイムスライスとか、モーフィング技術とかもそうですし。

PVの場合、技術の発露や表現そのものでもっていける分、映画などに比べて試しやすいのだと思います。

『The Matrix』みたいなタイム・スライスは、他の映画でもCMでもPVでも使

——ご自身の作品の中で、PVじゃなかったら表現できなかったようなものってありますか？

例えばスケッチ・ショウの『ekot』のPVは、最初から最後までずっと白い波みたいなものを見せてるんです。ずっとその白い波を見てると、その動きが網膜に残るんです

works tend to appear. As for Oyamada, I think his style of his music had an affinity with this medium to begin with. There are many different types of music videos, so I really shouldn't be generalizing, but for me, music video is a field in which weird forms of expression are accepted, like the experimental films of the past, giving it lots of creative potential.

——Music video is also the field in which the latest technologies are experimented with, such as bullet-time and morphing effects.

Since the manifestation of a particular technology can be enough in itself for a music video to be an acceptable work, I think it's easier to try new things out than in a movie. Bullet-time as seen in "The Matrix" has been used in other movies and television commercials as well as music videos, but on the other hand, morphing effects as in "Like a Rolling Stone" are a technology that can only be found in music videos. It's not really a matter of testing the latest technology, because the most progressive ones are used in other fields like TV commercials and movies. Basically, the music video is a medium that has enough leeway to allow for the focus of a work to be on a particular technology in itself. So technologies that are difficult to incorporate into the works of other fields are easier to use in music videos.

——Within your own works, is there anything that could only have been realized as a music video?

In the music video I made for Sketch Show's "Ekot," white waves are displayed on the screen from start to end. As you keep staring at them, the movements of the waves become impressed on your retina. Then suddenly, an image of a flat plane appears on the screen for a moment, and the afterimage of the waves becomes visible, in a distorted form. It's an optical illusion, so it's a form of expression that deals with the physical aspect of the senses. I don't think I've seen this kind of thing outside of music videos. And also, it's a very simple thing, but I think that a work shaped by the complete synchronization of visuals and sounds is only possible in the realm of music videos.

——Between the late 90's, when you began creating music videos, and the year 2005, have you felt any changes happen in the motion graphics and music industries?

I was recently surprised to hear news that it's now possible to download motion graphics onto an iPod. This is really interesting. The cost of downloading just a song is 150 yen, and downloading a song that comes with a music video is 300 yen, so it's twice the price of the song itself. The music video originated as a

よ。それで、一瞬だけ平面の画像を見せた瞬間にそれまで見てた波の運動が目に残っちゃって、変形して見えるんですね。目の錯覚を見せるという、肉体感覚に訴えかける表現。それってPV以外ではまだ見られない表現だなって。あとは、もっと単純に、映像と音がぴったり合って成り立ってるという表現はPV以外ではありえないと思います。

——辻川さんがPV制作を始めた90年代後半くらいから2005年にかけて、映像業界や音楽業界の変化で、何が一番印象的でしたか？

最近一番びっくりしたのはiTMSで映像配信が可能になったということですね。あれは面白いと思いましたね。というのは、1曲150円程度でダウンロードできるものが、PV付きになると300円ぐらいっていう。つまり、PV付きの曲は、曲だけのものの倍の価格が設定されている。音楽のプロモーションとしての価値以外に、PV自体に商品としての価値が付けられているんです。プロモーションのために制作されたPVが売り物としてとらえられてきていて、そしてそんな風に配信されるようになったということが一番の大きな変化だと思います。その上でPVのディレクターが作っている作品が、プロモーション以上の評価を

受けてきているっていうのが面白いですよね。ただ、PVの制作者って、今は印税をもらえてないんですよ。そう考えると、150円のものを300円で売るためのコンテンツをつくっている自分たちって何なんだろうと思っちゃいますね（笑）。

——海外でも同じような状況なんでしょうか？

そうだと思います。だから、PVのディレクターって基本的にすごく苦しい仕事ではありますよね。楽しいからやるっていうのが、彼らがPVを作る一番の大きな理由でしょうし、僕の場合もそうでした。

CMとPV 2つの現場

——最近はCMのお仕事が多いですね。

そうですね。2005年はCMが中心でした。CMはPVと比べて、全然コミュニケーションの着地点が違います。クライアントさんがいて、メッセージや商品があって、それを伝えるための表現が二次的に存在しているっていう感じがします。PVよりも表

promotional appendage to music, but it's now being distributed as an article of commerce in itself. I think this is the biggest change that has occurred. It's not just about commerce; music videos are also receiving more artistic recognition than before. However, in the current situation, the authors of the music videos don't receive any royalties, even though their work doubles the value of a 150 yen commodity. This is why I sometimes have doubts about my job(laughs).

——Do you know what the situation is like overseas?

I think it's a similar situation. Generally, a music video director isn't a job that pays so well. The main reason why these people choose to keep making music videos is because they enjoy it.

——Recently, you've also been working on TV commercials.

Yeah, commercials were my main activity for the year 2005. When compared to music videos, the focus of communication is totally different. The client, the message, and the product come first, so the form of expression is a secondary factor, existing in order to communicate the more important things. For music videos, simply having a form of expression is sufficient enough to make the work an acceptable one, but in the case of commercials, you have to think about how the form of expression functions to communicate the product to the viewer. There's also a set timeframe, usually 15 or 30 seconds, and the things you can achieve within this frame is totally different from what you can do in a music video. Working within these constraints is a nice challenge. When you view a work that has a limit of 30 seconds, it becomes easier to grasp exactly how much of what is being realized within the work. Also, the strongest point of the TV commercial is the plentiful budget. This allows you to do things like take many cuts, or film on a well-made set, so the fundamental quality of the work can be set at a high standard. If the quality of the filming is high, it's possible to make an inspiring work even if the concept is commonplace.

Recently, I've been filming commercials for Yebisu Beer, under the motto "Yebisu: a beer with a bit of luxury." The theme of this work is to simply film as neatly as possible. We film on a very neat set, with very neat lighting and elegant women, all to make the beer look as nicely as possible. This work doesn't involve any revolutionary concepts. Because of a wide budget, we were able to make images that are refined and elegant to a great degree. The form of expression is very simple, but we were still able to do some deep filming. This kind of work is interesting in its own sense.

——Are there any fields you would like to

現の立ち位置が一歩後退していますよね。PVだと表現が一個あればそれですんじゃうんだけど、CMの場合はそれを伝えるためにどのように機能しているかっていうところまで考える必要がある。あとは30秒、15秒っていう尺の枠組みがありますよね。そういう尺の枠組みの中でできることっていうのはPVとはまるで違う。それらの制限がある分、ある種の面白さがあります。30秒っていう制限があるから、その中でどれだけのことをやっているかっていうのが見えやすくなりますからね。それから、CMで一番面白いと思うのは、バジェットがすごくあることですね。フィルムが回るから綺麗に撮れるとか、セットが作れるとか、そういう基本的な部分で体力があるから、映像の基礎体力もあがる。だから、普通のことをしても、映像が美しければ、グッとくるってところまで到達できるんです。最近の仕事で「ヱビス・ちょっと贅沢なビール」っていうコピーでヱビスビールのCMを撮っているんですが、そこでのテーマは、ともかくすごく綺麗に撮るということだけなんです。ものすごく綺麗なセットを使って、ものすごく綺麗な照明を打って、ものすごい美人を呼んできて、すごい綺麗に撮って、美味しそうに見せるっていう。変わったこと、とんがった表現っていうのは全くやってないんですね。ただ単に品がい い、だけどすごくお金をかけているからめちゃくちゃ綺麗とか。表現自体はシンプルだけど、すごく深く撮れる。それはそれで面白いですよ。

——辻川さんの中で、綺麗に撮るっていうのが基本にあるんでしょうか。例えばコーネリアスのビデオはどれをみてもシンプルで美しいですよね。

やってて楽しいことの一つではあるけど、基本にあるかどうかは分からないですね。逆に、映像は汚くてもいいと思うし。大切なのは、何をどう表現するかがシンプルに思い描けているかどうかだと思うんですよ。例えば『jackass』みたいなすごく危ないことを手持ちのカメラで撮って「やったー！」って騒ぐところを見せるのもそれはそれで楽しいと思うし。だけど例えば化粧品のCMだったりすると、女の子をどうやって綺麗に撮れるのかが目的になるわけです。要するに、どのような世界観で、何をやるかということをシンプルに決めることがCM制作の基本です。だから、綺麗に撮るというのはCMの場合だと多いですよね。

——CM以外に挑戦したいジャンルはありますか？

一生のうち一回は映画を撮りたいですね。ただ、先のこともすごく大事なんですけど、まずは現在進行している一つ一つの作品を大事にしたい。フレッシュなアイデアを、丁寧に形にしていきたいですね。

——映画撮るとしたらやはりファンタジーですか？

今の段階では、全然分かりません。実現の仕方としては、誰かと共同作業で演出を担当するという関わり方と、脚本から自分で書いて、もっとパーソナルに撮るという、その二方向ですね。そういうことができたら最高ですよね。男の子としては死んでもいいくらい(笑)。今でもすごく「幸せだな」って思うんですよね。セットとか作ってても、それが小学生の時に作っていたプラモだと思うと、こんな豪華なプラモデルってないじゃないですか。そう考えると、今の環境は本当に幸せですね。

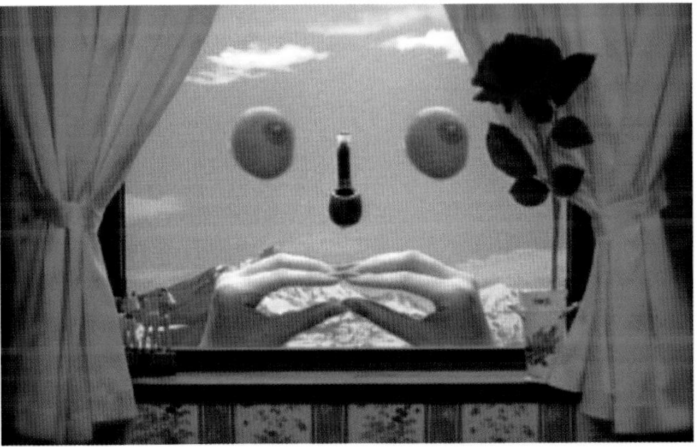

try working in besides commercials?

At least once during my lifetime, I would like to film a movie. But for now, I just want to concentrate on the works that I'm handling at the present moment, one by one. I want to shape fresh ideas into solid works.

——If you were going to create a movie, would you make a fantasy film?

I really can't decide at this moment. For the production process, I would either work with somebody else, allowing myself to concentrate on the artistic direction, or start from writing my own script and create the film in a more personal manner. It would be amazing if I had the chance to make a movie. I think it's something that every boy imagines at least once during his childhood. But even now, I feel that I'm a very fortunate man. When I'm creating a set, it's like playing with a toy, but on a greater scale. I feel happy for my current environment.

ANIMATION

アニメーションが手法として開発されてから随分たつが、作家たちのイマジネーションが作り出したその驚きは今も衰えることがない。それどころか、いまやアニメーションは日本が世界に向けて誇る一大ジャンルとなった。その第一人者であり、吉祥寺はスタジオ4℃にある一室で、昔話に出てくる鶴のようにその独特な世界観を、丹念に紡ぎ続けるアニメーション監督、森本晃司。その作品は、ありそうでなかった現実の新しいヴィジョンを照らし出した。テクノアーティストKENISHIIのアルバム『EXTRA』に提供されたイリュージョニスティックな光景の中を疾走するイメージに驚かれた方も多いだろう。奇怪で、狂っていて、でも愛くるしいほどのリアリティを持つ世界。そんな世界像が彼のどこから生み出されてくるのか。次なる作品へ向けて慌ただしく回転するスタジオ4℃のオフィスにてインタビューを行ってきた。

Animation makes drawings move. Sounds simple, but when this movement weaves a story, a living world emerges. When all goes well, the viewer's imagination can soar through this world. It's been a while since animation was first invented as a methodology, but the initial wonder is still kept alive within fantastical works that are pregnant with a pulsating feel of reality. You cannot spurn these works as things made for children. Koji Morimoto is an animation director that continually weaves this kind of wonder at Studio 4°C. His works throw light upon a raw vision of a reality that could have existed before our eyes but has not. You may have been one of the people who were astounded by his music video for Ken Ishii's "Extra," with its illusionistic imagery of speeding through streams of lights. It was mysterious and deranged, but felt real to the degree of being amiable. From where does this man spawn these world-images? We interviewed Morimoto at Studio 4°C, which was in full swing for an upcoming work.

森本晃司
KOJI MORIMOTO

仕事場に一升瓶

——森本さんがこの道に入られた出会いやきっかけとなった作品は何ですか?

中学校初めの頃かな、宇宙戦艦ヤマトを観て衝撃を受けた。もともとアニメーションは好きだったんだけど、アニメという存在を意識し始めたのはそれからです。最初は、アニメーションをどうやって作っているのかもさっぱりわからなかった。今でこそアニメ業界の詳しい本が出てたりするけど、うちは田舎だったし、あの当時そういう情報はなかったんです。でもそのうち、何本も好きな作品を観ているうちに監督やスタッフのクレジットなんかも見るようになってきて。例えば金田さんていう人が原画で入ってる回は面白いなとかね。その人ばっかりを追いかけたり、マニアックな見方をするようになっていきましたね。中でも『ガンバの冒険』の、演出家の出崎統が好きで「他にどんなアニメやってるんだろうな」って思ったら、自分の好きだった『家なき子』とか『宝島』とか『明日のジョー』とかをやってた。それで、彼がどこにいるか探したら当時のマッドハウスだったんです。じゃあ、「自分もマッドハウスに入れば出崎さんの作品に参加できるんだ」って思って。その当時、マッドハウスにはファンが会社を見学できる日があったんですよ。ファンの女の子たちがお弁当とか花を持って詰めかけてた(笑)。そのころ、アニメーターも人気があって「こんな派手な世界なのか! これはいい!」って思って入社したんですけど。僕が入ってからはそんなことはなくて(笑)。そういうこともあればいいなと思ってますけど。そのころ背景さんのところに行ったら一升瓶が置いてあって「飲むんですか?」って聞いたら「飲むよ。一緒に飲む?」って。酒飲みながら描いてたりして(笑)。その人の一番やりやすい環境というか、一番テンションのあがる状態で作業できたんです。もちろん、みんなが酒飲みたいから飲んでいいのかっていったらそうじゃなくて、飲んでだめになるんだったら飲ませられない。絵を描くこともそうだけど、自己管理できてないとダメ。飲んでもいいけどスケジュールは守らなきゃいけないから、そこで締め切り守れる人だったら飲んでもいいっていう感じでしたね。そこをはき違えたらいけない。でも、仕事っていうのは本当に好きな場所で好きなものに囲まれてやるのがベスト。そういう環境でしたね。

——すごく良い職場だったんですね。

そうなんです。ただ、あの当時は演出がやりたかったんだけど、なかなか機会がなかったり、発表する場が少なかったりしました。だからってそこで腐ったり、つまんないなぁって思ったりはしなかった。逆に今なら、若くてもチャンスや才能があればやれるような環境がある。そこで才能を発揮できれば楽しいだろうし、そうじゃなかったら早く見切りをつけられるだろうし。あとで、あれをやっておけば良かった

Animatrix © WarnerBros. Entertainment Inc.

The Site of the Production

——Were there any people or works that influenced you into entering the world of animation?

Around the beginning of junior high school, I saw "Space Battleship Yamato" for the first time and was captivated. I was watching animation even before that, but it was the first time an anime made a significant impression on me. At first, I had no clue as to how they were making those shows. Today, you can find detailed books about the anime industry, but back then, that kind of information wasn't lying around, especially in a rural area like where I grew up. But as I continued watching the programs that I was fond of, I eventually began checking the end credits. I would take note of things like, "it's always a cool episode when a man called Kaneda does the key drawings." I was keeping track of particular staff members, and viewed the programs in a way that a hardcore fan would.

I especially liked Osamu Dezaki, the technical director of "Ganba's Adventure." I discovered that he was also working on other animes I was a fan of, like "Ienakiko," "Treasure Island," and "Tommorow's Joe." I tried to find out where he worked, and it turned out to be Mad House. I figured that if I joined Mad House, I would be able to participate in Dezaki-san's works. At the time, the company had a day when fans could visit the studio. Girls would be coming over, bringing meals and flowers in their hands (laughs). Even the animators were popular. I joined the company thinking that I was entering a glittering lifestyle, but it was nothing like that once I began working there (laughs). I still wish it were.

——When you evaluate a person's talent, what kind of things do you look for?

I speak with the person, and try to find out how they think. For example, what they are thinking about when drawing a particular cut. When I am able to get an idea of how the person thinks, I may realize something, like how the guy would make a great technical director. This doesn't necessarily mean that they're going to want to become a technical director. Some people just like to draw.

——How about yourself?

I wanted to do technical direction right from the beginning. I wanted to draw the pictures that I like, onto a scene that I like. Even if there's a certain character you are good at drawing, that character comes to life only when it is put in a scene and situation that allows it to live out its potential. There are times when people select you for participation in a

とか後悔しないような環境を僕のほうが作らないといけないなって思ってます。たとえば、あのとき酒が飲めなかったから出来なかったとか。やりたいんだったらやればいいから。その人をどうやって伸ばすかっていう方法はいろいろとあるんだろうけど、道は開いてあげなきゃいけない。

Fluximation © MTV Networks

——才能を見極めるとき、森本さんはどんなところを見ますか?
話をしてみて、その人のものの考え方ですね。ひとつのカットに対してどういう思いで描いてるかとか。考え方を含めて聞いてみると、この人は演出向きだなとかいろいろ分かります。みんながみんな演出するわけじゃないですけどね。作画すること自体が好きな人もいるし。

——森本さん自身は?
僕は最初っから演出がしたかったんですよ。まず、好きな絵を自分が好きなステージで描きたいっていうのがあった。得意な絵があったとして、キャラクターが飛躍できる場とか状況があって初めてそのキャラクターを生かせる。本当に自分の絵が好きで抜擢してもらうこともあるとは思うけど、自分の絵の使い勝手は自分が一番よく知ってるから。だから、僕は作画と演出をくっつけてやってるんです。

——作画のやり方は演出によって変わっていくこともあるんですか?
もちろん。その逆もありますよ。

——絵がうまいだけじゃだめってことですか?
そうですね。絵を描くときの思考と、演出の思考とはちょっと違うかもしれないですね。あとは自分が絵を描かないで他の人に描いてもらうとしたら、自分はこんな絵は描かないけど演出的には欲しいなって思うときもあります。自分が絵を描かなくても、スケジュールとかやりたいことを効果的に表現できる方法を考えて逆算しながら、近道を探していく感じです。

——かなりのハードワークなんですか?
今は一週間事務所に泊まりっぱなしです。納期まで時間がないのも大変ですけど、制作時間があればいい作品ができるかっていうとそうじゃないんです。時間があれば多少見栄えがよくなるとかはあるけど、長い期間制作してると作品の本質が見えなくなることもあったりしますからね。

アニメ作家のリアル

——作品の本質の部分というのはどう判断するんですか?
それはコンテを切ったときにすでにできてますね。それがないとGOができない。すごく枚数が少なくても、チープでも、新しい何かがそこにあれば、それが見えた時点で、絵の作りは豪華でなくても自分の中ではOK。時間があって、もっと豪華なアニメーションになればなおさらいいですけど。でも、テクニックの中だけに留まった作業は確認作業でしかないし、そんな

work because they want you to draw for them, but I want to do both drawing and technical direction, because only I know how to handle my drawings in the most effective possible way.

——Are there times when your drawings become different because of the technical direction?
Yes, of course. Vice versa as well.

——Does that mean that it's not enough to just be good at drawing?
Yeah. The mode of thinking required for drawing and technical direction are a bit different. If I'm in a situation where I'm going to have somebody other than myself handle the drawings, I may choose a guy who's drawings are appealing in terms of technical direction, even if his drawings look nothing like mine. Even when I don't draw, I'm always searching for the most efficient path, taking consideration of factors like the schedule and the method in which I can effectively realize the things I want to express.

——Is it hard work?
Currently, I've been lodging in the office for a week now. It's tough when you're on a tight schedule, but just because you have lots of time, it doesn't mean you're going to be able to produce a quality work. You may be able to make the work look a bit more handsome, but there are times when a long production span causes you to lose focus from the essence of the work.

The Process of Making an Anime

——How do you judge the essence of a work?
It's already there by the time the storyboard is finished. If I can't see this essence, I can't start the production process. As long as there's something innovative, it's good with me, even if the work turns out a bit rough and unpolished. Of course, it would be ideal if there were enough time to turn it into a well-polished animation work, but operations that are confined within the realm of technique are nothing but acts of reconfirmation, and those kind of works quickly become things of the past. So basically, I don't want to make anything that I've already made. I want to make something that I've never laid my eyes on. When I'm commissioned to create a work, I'm often requested to make something that's like a variation on my past work, and I don't want to do that, but I can't just bring them something entirely new and be like, please accept this. I have to come up with something that will satisfy the clients even more than what they had expected. I personally enjoy those kinds of constraints.

のすぐに過去のものになってしまいますよね。だから、今までやったことはやりたくない。自分でも見たことのないものをやりたいんです。発注でも、過去の作品を参考にこうやってくださいっていう依頼がくるんですけど、過去にやったことはもうやりたくなかったりするじゃないですか。だけど全く新しいものを出して、これでお願いしますっていうんじゃなくて、それ以上に向こうが納得する何かを探さなきゃいけないと思います。発注者も納得がいくものを探すんです。そういう縛りに関しては、僕は好きですね。

——コンテは一人で作るんですか?
コンテの段階でこんな風にしたいなということが明確でないと、関わってくるスタッフに話ができなかったりするんで、まずは具体的なものを見せます。あと、コンテを作る作業は人に見られたくないんですよ。鶴の恩返しの鶴みたいな感じですね。悩んでる姿って見せたくないから。

——かなり集中力を要する作業ですよね。
悩んでるときって机についていればいいかっていうとそうでもなかったりしますね。気分転換に外に出て、公園をふらふらしたり。そうすると面白い発想が浮かんできます。吉祥寺の街の雰囲気とかが、好きなんで。もう10年くらいいますし。

——アニマトリックスの作品に出てくる町も、吉祥寺の雰囲気に近い感じがありますね。
あれは向こうが期待してたのとは違うんですけど、僕にはマトリックスの舞台が別にアメリカじゃなくてもいいじゃんていうのがあって。例えば、ガンダムでもメインの戦場があっても、東北のおじいちゃんとかおばあちゃんがテレビでガンダムのニュース見てるっていう風景って、たぶんあるじゃないですか。自分はそういうのが好きだなって。湾岸戦争だからって湾岸戦争行かなくても日本ではテレビの中ででもいいし、会話の中ででもいいと思うし。現地では大変なことになっているんだろうけど、アニマトリックスは一方そのころ、みたいな感じでやれたらいいかなって。だから、主人公も最初はじいさんばあさんにしようかなって思ってたんです。

——あの作品に出てくる風景って日常的なんだけどすごく不思議な風景でしたね。
自分の過去の作品だけど、『MEMORIES』のときとかはヨーロッパを舞台にしていたんだよね。だから、あれを境に外国の風景をやめようかなって思ったんですよ。フランスのロココ調とか資料を集めてきて、それを見て描くんですけど、リアルに近づけようとすればするほどリアルに見えてこない。自分がそこに住んでないからなんだよね。自分がロココの中に住んでないから、あのスケールとか冷たさとか匂いを分からないんですよ。リアルにすればするほどギャップが生まれて、なにやってるんだろうって。それで、自分の好きなものだったら広さとか質感をリアルに感じられるかなと思って日本を描こうって思った。あと、自分の好きな漫画作家のエンキ・ビラルって人がいるんですけど、ビラルの住んでいる街に行ったときに本当に彼の描くような街があった。なんだ、彼も近所を描いてたのかって思って。それを知って僕も日本に近所に憧れてるんだって気付いたんです。

——Do you create the storyboard all by yourself?
If the ideas I want to realize aren't definite by the time the storyboard is completed, I'm going to have trouble communicating to the staff who are involved, so I first present specific images to them. I don't want people to see me in this phase of production, because I don't like people watching me when I'm concentrating on my ideas.

——It sounds like a job that uses lots of brainwork.
When I'm concentrating, it isn't always best to be sitting at my desk. Sometimes good ideas come to me while I'm taking a break and wandering around the park. I especially enjoy the atmosphere of the city of Kichijyoji. I've been here for about ten years now.

——The cityscape that appears in your work for "Animatrix" kind of looks like Kichijyoji.

It was different from what the Animatrix people were anticipating, but I had this idea that the setting for The Matrix didn't necessarily have to be in America. Like in the world of Gundam: of course there's the main battlefield, but there could also be an old couple somewhere in rural Japan watching news coverage about the Gundam battle on their TV. I like this kind of setting. Just because there's a war in the gulf, it doesn't mean that you have to actually go to the Middle East in order to have a relationship with the war: you can see it on TV here in Japan, or hear about in some conversation. I bet it's an outrageous situation over there on the actual site, but for "Animatrix," I wanted to make something more along the lines of, "meanwhile in another location." In the beginning, I was actually thinking about making the protagonist an old man or woman.

——The scenery that appeared in that work seemed like it was from everyday life, but it also had a strange feel to it.
In one of my past works, the one for "Memories," the setting was based on Europe. While I was making that work, there was a phase in which I was sure that I would never draw the scenery of a foreign country again. I collected all these images of French Rococo, and drew the scenery based on these, but the more I tried to make it look realistic, the more it ended up becoming unrealistic. It's because I've never lived in such an environment, meaning I don't have a grasp of the scale, coolness, and atmosphere of it. When I made an effort to make it look real, the gap between my drawing and the real thing would proportionately

EXTRA © R&S Records/Beyond C.

大友克洋さんに出会ったときも、みんなダサいから日本を描かないでいるんだけど、日本の風景とか日本のおじいちゃんとかをかっこよく描いてる人だなって。それを見て、日本の価値観が変わった。日本人は短足でもかっこいいじゃん、かっこよく描けるんだって。こんなに日本人をかっこよく描いた人いないよなって思いましたね。彼は、みんなが蓋をしたいなぁって思ってるものを開いてる。人がかっこ悪いじゃんって思って形にできないものを描いてるんですよ。だから、描き方でかっこよく見せられたらいい。それを価値観としてもう一度提示できたらいいって思っていて。例えば今僕は、決めの絵じゃなくて中間のポーズで描きたいなって思ってる。人間の、力の抜けているふにゃっとした感じをかっこよく描きたいんです。

——確かに、人間のポージングをそういう風に描かれる方はあまりいないですね。
そうそう。みんなが描いてないから。どの本を見ても決めのポーズって似てるじゃないですか。こういうの描きたくないなって。誰もやってないからやりたいっていうのはある。自分が考えてたまんまの映画があったらもうやんないですよ。それだったら、自分は料理でも作ろうかなって思っちゃう。憧れてる人とか作品はあっても、「3割くらが好きであとはちょっと違うな〜」っていうのの積み重ね。それがあって「誰も作ってくれないなら自分で作る」っていうのもあるし。

コンピューターとテクノとアニメーション

——アニメーションにコンピュータを使い始めたのはどういったきっかけなんですか?
コンピューターが好きだからです。当時誰も使ってなかったっていうのもありますけどね。

——まだ一般的にアニメーションでCGが使われてない頃でしたね。
さすがに今ではどこでも使ってるんですけどね。あっと驚かせたいなっていうのがあって使ったんですけど。

——またKENISHIIの『EXTRA』のときは、テクノ文化の盛り上がりもあってすごくドキドキしたんです。
テクノが一番好きな音楽だったし。詞がないのがいいなって思っていて、詞がないからそこに話を乗っけて遊べるし、こんなに面白い音楽ないなって思っていて。日頃も

widen, so I didn't know what to do. I began thinking that if I drew the things that I was attached to, I would be able to make the scale and textures look real. So, I decided to draw Japan. There's a French comic author I admire called Enki Bilal, and when I once visited the town he lives in, what I found was a townscape that was just like the kind that appears in his works. I discovered that all he was doing was drawing his neighborhood. Through this experience, I came to realize that I actually had a yearning for the Japanese neighborhood. When I first met Katsuhiro Otomo, I felt that he was an author who was drawing the Japanese scenery and people in a stylish manner, while everybody else was avoiding to draw Japan because of it's unstylishness. My view of Japan changed. I was now able to think that even though the Japanese have a stumpy figure, it was possible to depict them in a cool way. I felt that Otomo was the first one who succeeded in this. He is an author who unlocks the things that everyone wants to conceal, and draws the things that others consider shameful and cannot draw. How good something looks depends on the way in which you depict it: this is the idea that I want to communicate to people. For example, what I'm trying to do now is to draw characters in deficient, halfway poses, instead of making them take ideal character poses. You can often find human beings in a flaccid, relaxed state. I want to depict this state in a stylish manner.

——I guess there aren't many people who draw character poses in that way.
Yeah. No one's doing this. In every book you look at, the poses are all similar. I don't want to draw like that. I want to do things that other people aren't doing. If there suddenly appeared a film that contained everything that I had ever imagined, I would quit this job and do something else, maybe become a chef. Of course there are authors that I admire, but when I view their works, I usually find one part of it interesting, and the rest banal. Viewing works is an accumulation of these kinds of experiences, and that's why I can motivate myself to make something: because nobody else is doing it.

Animation and Techno

——Why did you start using computers for your work?
Because I like computers. And at that time, people weren't using them so much.

——Yeah, it was still an age when CGs generally weren't used in animation.
Today they're used everywhere, but back then they weren't, and I wanted to surprise people.

テクノとかノイズとかクラシックとか聴いてて、絵が浮かんでくるんです。

――The Orbが好きというお話も伺いましたが。

The Orbは好きですね。彼らはほかの人たちとは違う世界を作ってる感じがする。聴いてみて、なんだ君たちそこで遊んでたんだって。

――自分の仕事と近いものを感じますか?

そうです。自分がやりたかったり気になることが、彼らを見ていて明確になる部分があるんです。これはまた別の作家の話ですけど、中・高・大学生のときに安部公房がすごく好きだった。彼が小説でやっているようなことをアニメーションでやりたいなっていうのがあって。彼の小説は、人間が棒になったり蓄音機になったりするんですね。そういう不条理なものが好きなんです。例えばここにあるコップが「今日辛いね」って言ってるとしますよね。リアルなおじさんが「今日辛いね」って言ってるのを誰もがそのまま見たくないでしょ。それはその年になれば分かることだから。コップとか小さい子にそういうことを言われたほうが面白い。その言葉を昔に自分が知ってたものだからドキッとするっていうことがあると思うんですよ。自分で鍵をかけていつの間にかしまい込んでしまっていたもの。小さいころ持っていたものをそのまま社会に持っていくにはきつ過ぎるから、95%はしまい込んでしまう。そして僕らは、その中の5%だけで生活してるんですね。あとはどれだけそれを引き出せるのか、昔かけた鍵を見つけてそれを開いたとき、絵の具を引いてカラーが生まれたときのような驚きが生まれるんです。

――作品を作る上でもそうですね。

全く新しいことなんて何もない。みんなが気付いてること、みんなが持っていて忘れているものに、絵を描いてる人間は気付いて引き出そうとするんです。映画でも、昔思っていたことや感じた何かを気付かされるから面白いし感動する。それで、何でそれを見つけられなかったんだろうって、くやしがるんです。

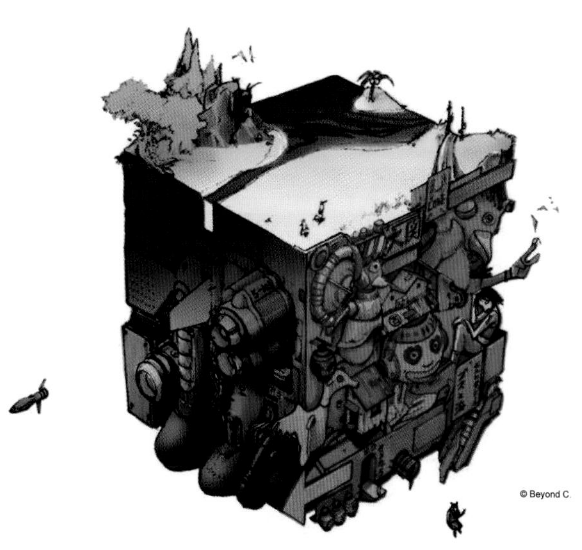

――The music video for Ken Ishii's "Extra" was very exciting for me because it appeared just around a time when techno culture was on the rise.

Techno was my favorite kind of music. I liked how there were no lyrics, so you could play around by putting your own imagined story onto the music. I thought it was a very exciting form of music. Even now, when I listen to music like techno, noise, and classical, images often emerge.

――I've heard that you're fond of The Orb.

Yeah, I really like The Orb. It feels like they create a world that is totally different from others. I listen, and I think, "oh, so you guys were playing in that place."

――Do you feel that there are similarities with your own work?

Yes. By listening to their music, the things I want to do and am attracted to often become clear. We try to carry into society the things we have when we are children, but it's too tough of a job, so we stow away 95% of it. We live our daily life with only the remaining 5%. So it's a matter of how much you can pull back out. When I was able to find the door that I had locked a long time ago, I opened it and was hit by a surprise that was kind of like when you apply paint and color appears.

――It sounds similar to creating a work.

There's no such thing as something completely new. Everybody has these things within themselves to begin with. An artist realizes this so he attempts to extract them. Movies are fun and they stir your emotions, because they allow you to realize things that you had felt or thought about in the past. You have to think, "why wasn't I able to find that first?"

INTERACTIVE

インタラクティブ・アートは、テクノロジーと密接に発展を遂げてきた。観客のアクションに対するリアクションにアーティストたちの意志を介入させる。受け手と送り手の双方向コミュニケーションアート。どこかアカデミックな毛色の強いこの分野に、ストリート的な感覚を加えられているのが exonemo の魅力だろう。彼らの作品は受け手と送り手の予定調和というだけでなく、送り手にとっての予想外のハプニングを引き起こす。既存のシステムや仕組みが壊れていく過程こそが彼らの作品なのだ。作品作りのすべての過程を公開し、制作作業を自らもオーディエンスとして楽しむ。それが exonemo のスタンスだ。ネットを主な活動の場としてとらえている彼らの、ほぼすべての作品は www.exonemo.com にアップされている。まずはそれらをチェックしてからこのインタビューを読んでいただきたい。

Interactive Art is a field that has developed hand in hand with technology. The user's action is met by a reaction in which the artist's will intervenes. It's a form of dual-way communication between the sender and receiver. In this field which often displays an academic inclination, Exonemo's works stand out for bringing in a subculturesque taste. Their works, which incorporate elements of chance, bringing unpredictability into the effects, are essentially subversions of existent systems and processes. Exonemo's stance is to openly display the production processes of the works, and to be able to enjoy the works themselves by becoming part of the audience. They consider the internet as their main location of activity, and most of their works can be experienced at [www.exonemo.com]. We recommend exploring their website before reading this interview.

エキソニモ　エ
EXONEMO　EX

ネットワークが発表の場

——exonemoが活動を開始したころの話を聞かせてください。

千房（千房けん輔） 僕ら2人は美大の時に友達になって。俺がデザイン科、彼女が彫刻科に通ってて、今みたいにコンピュータとも映像表現とも全く縁のない生活をしてましたね。彼女は旅行に行ったり、僕はスケボーにのめりこんで大会に出たり、ともかく全然勉強しないし、美大にいるのにアートとかも興味なくて。作品を作り始めたのって卒業してからで、学生時代の作品とかほとんどないんですよ。コンピュータも卒業してから使い始めたし。逆にインターネットに出会うまでは「なにか作ろう！」っていう気が起きなかったっていうか。やっぱ手で描くようなやり方だとスピードが遅いって思っていたのと、インターネットって作ってすぐに発表できちゃう、そのサイクルが自分に合ってたんですよ。

赤岩（赤岩やえ） インターネットももともと新しいテクノロジーとして積極的に使い始めたんじゃなくて。私がたまたま旅行へ行ったときに知り合った人が教えてくれたんですよ。大雪で成田空港で飛行機が足止めされちゃって、空港に泊まるはめになったとき、そこで偶然出会ったキャリアウーマン風の人と仲良くなって、その人がネットについて熱心に語ってくれて。「インターネットってボタン押したら外国なんだよね」って言われて(笑)。

——そんな時代でしたっけ？

赤岩 95年くらいですね。世間ではようやくビジネスとしてインターネットを使い始めたころだった。

千房 それで、大学卒業後、その人のところでバイト始めたんだよね。

赤岩 最初は「プログラミングは大変」なものって聞いていたんですけど。実際作業してみると、まずはソースをコピーしてペーストしながら作ってみたら「意外と簡単にできるじゃん」って思って、自分たちでも作ってみだしたの。作品を作りたいとかじゃなくて、ただ面白いからってことなんですけどね。

千房 世界でインターネットが使われ始めたころってまだネットの世界が試行錯誤していて、みんな実験的だったんですよ。会社のホームページに、会社の業務内容と何の関係もないミニゲームがあったりして、面白かった。

赤岩 そうそう。どのサイトもやたら地球儀を回してた。「インターネットで世界は繋がる!」みたいなイメージ。ネットは夢の象徴みたいな感じでね。

——exonemoを名乗ったのはいつごろなんですか？

千房 実際に名乗ったのは99年かな。そのときは相当悩んで、結局最後にポロっと出てきた「エキソニモ」って言葉で。この言葉に全く意味はないけど。展覧会に出展するときに便宜上名乗り始めたんです。

——ネットから映像表現に入ったっていうのは特殊ですよね。インターネットのスピード感っていうのがそれほど強烈だったんですか？

赤岩 作ってすぐに発表できるし。なにより完成したモノをあとから手直しできる、一度完成したモノに後から触れないのはつまらないし。完成品よりもプログラムで変わっていくものみせたいし。なにより紙じゃできないことをしたいんですよ。

千房 紙やプロダクトのように自分が完成しきってしまったものを作品にすると、どうし

— Please explain what the situation was like when you two began working together as Exonemo.

Sembo: We became friends during art school. I was in the department of design, and she was in the department of sculpture. Back then, we were leading lives that had nothing to do with computers and motion graphics like today. She often traveled, and I was into skateboarding and participated in competitions. I rarely studied, and even though I was in art school, I didn't have much interest in fine art. I began creating works after I graduated, so I barely have any works from when I was a student.

I started to use computers only after I finished school. Before I was exposed to the Internet, I really didn't have the motivation to make anything. I felt that drawing by hand was too slow of a process for me, so the cycle of being able to make a work and instantly present it online really suited me.

Akaiwa: People were telling me that programming was a very difficult activity, but I had a chance to try it out, starting from copying and pasting from a source. It didn't feel like something that was so hard, so Sembo and I began to make programs for ourselves. Not because we wanted to create a work of art or anything; it was just for fun.

Sembo: When the internet was beginning to be used by people around the world, everyone was trying all these experimental things online. You could go to some corporation's website and find a mini-game that has nothing to do with their business operations. That kind of thing was interesting.

The Internet as a Location for Presenting Works

—When did you begin introducing yourselves as Exonemo?

Sembo: I think it was 1999. We thought long and hard about our name, and decided to go with a word that finally appeared out of the blue, "Exonemo." It has absolutely no meaning. We had to choose a name because there was an exhibition we were going to participate in.

—It's rather uncommon to enter the world of motion graphics after working on works for the web. People that come from that field usually end up settling in either paper media or product design. Was the Internet and the accompanying sense of speed that intense?

Akaiwa: With the Internet, you are able to present your works right upon completion, and more importantly, you have the freedom to alter them afterwards. It's not fun if you're unable to retouch a work after it's finished. I would rather make something

ても飽きちゃうじゃないですか。ネット上で変化していくものに触ると、自分も観客の一人として新鮮に楽しめるのがいい。

——たとえば、ユーザーの方が投げかけたアクションに対応して、予測不可能なハプニングが起こる。そういう作品が多いですよね。
千房　作品はイコール"自分のためのエンターテインメント"でもあるから。僕らにとってのインタラクティブとは、「ボタンを押したら反応が返ってくる」という反射的な意味、つまり自動販売機的な意味ではなくて、むしろ僕らからの投げかけにユーザーの方からもアクションを起こせるようなそういうものが面白いと思います。インタラクティブって間（インター）が活性化（アクティブ）ってことだから自分と世界の間にあるものに意識的になるっていうことじゃないかな。映像でもなんでも僕らが興味を持つものは、ただ単に一方向的に情報を送り込んで終わりではなくて、実は人の意識の中でハプニングに対して編集を行っているということ、情報を受け止めたり、いらないと思って切り捨てたり、そういう自発性がポイントのような気がします。

——エキシビションなどに出始めたきっかけは？
千房　たまたま飲み会の席でオランダの映画祭のスタッフの人に出会って、作品をみせたんですよ。英語話せないから日本語で強引に「ねっ？ねっ？コレコレ！」って説明したんですよ（笑）。そうしたら2000年の「ロッテルダム映画祭」で、日本のゲームとかインタラクティブアーティストを取り上げる枠への出演オファーが来たんです。
赤岩　それから、いつの間にかエキシビションにたくさん参加するようになって。そのときは私たちがウェブ上で発表していた『DISCODER』っていう作品があったんですけど、それをアレンジして展示しました。キーボードにマウスを大量にとりつけて、（前ページ右上参照）そのひとつひとつでキー入力できるようにして、「Xどこ？Xどこ?」ってカルタみたいにウェブのURLを入力すると、そのページのソースコードに文字が入っていってページがどんどん壊れていっちゃうっていう仕組みになってて。これが最初のインスタレーションだったんですよ。

——こういった作品はアイデアを実現させることを前提として作りますか、それとも技術ありきで考えてますか？
千房　基本的にはアイデアが先で、それから

that keeps on changing than a completed work. Most of all, I want to try things that are not possible on paper.
Sembo: It tends to get boring if you're only making completed objects, like in paper media and product design. But when I'm interacting online with something that's constantly changing, I can become a part of the audience myself, and enjoy the work in a fresh manner.

——You produce many works in which a user's action is met by an unpredictable event.
Sembo: The works we create are all congruous with our own entertainment. For us, interactivity is not just about pressing a button and getting a reaction. It is more than a vending-machine-type reflex. We believe that it's more interesting when the user can perform an action as a response to our own action. Interactivity is about becoming aware of what is between the world and the self. In motion graphics or in any other field, the works that we find interesting are those that encompass more than a one-way transmission of information. The key point is a certain kind of voluntarity, like when an external event is covertly edited within the mind of the perceiver, or unconsciously making a choice between receiving a certain block of information and discarding it.

——When you are forming the ideas for these works, do you think about the technical aspect in parallel with the idea, or do you just let the idea roam free?
Sembo: Basically the idea comes first, and we think about how to realize it afterwards. But sometimes the idea is later affected by the technology, resulting in a transformation of the initial concept, and that's lots of fun.

——Even though most of Exonemo's works are mediated by a network, they have a peculiar low-tech, or maybe I should say lo-fi, feel to them.
Sembo: It's because we use basic technologies. I can't even imagine what the technology used in a high-end research facility could be like. Those kinds of things don't have so much reality for me. I don't like being future-orientated. Exonemo is shaped by the interaction between the systems that we toss out and the users, so we don't have much need for an artistic ego. I hope that Exonemo can ultimately become media itself.

——In the work you provided for Aichi Expo 2005 (Karadakarada, 2005) (image outside of text), your intervention was a minimal one in the form of an effect.
Akaiwa: Yes, we couldn't have made the work any simpler. We installed a Hi-Vision monitor at a square where people rest, and images of the people in front of the monitor

どうやったら実現できるかって技術的なものを考えて、でもやってるうちに技術に作品が突き動かされて、内容が変わってきちゃったり、それも面白いんですよ。

――exonemoの作品はほとんどがネットワークを介しているのに妙にローテクというかローファイな雰囲気がありますよね。

千房 身近なテクノロジーが多いっていうか。ハイエンドな研究所で作ってるような技術って実際想像もつかないし、僕らにとってリアルじゃないから。未来志向はあんまり好きじゃないんですよ。exonemoって僕らが投げかけたリアルなシステムの中にユーザーが入ってきて成立するから、あまりアーティスト的な我を必要としないんですよ。最終的にはexonemo自体がメディアになれたらなって思ってます。

システム破綻のクリエイティブ

――愛知万博に出展した作品『Karadakarada』(2005 / 左ページ図版参照)もexonemoはあくまでエフェクトとしての存在ですよね。

赤岩 あれは、これ以上ないくらいシンプルな作品ですね。万博に来たお客さんが一休みできるような広場にハイビジョンを設置して、モニターの前の広場の様子を固定カメラで映し出しているんですけど、広場にいる人の動きに合わせていろいろな画像と音のエフェクトがかかるって展示ですね。ハイビジョンってすごく処理が重くてできることの制限がすごくあって、だからベーシックだけど効きがいいものを作ろうって思って。みんな面白がって画面にむかってすごく変な動きしてましたよ。

千房 光が出てきたりストロークが出てきたりとか。超シンプルなインタラクティブものですね。だから内容はそんなに満足できてないし。ハイビジョンだからプログラムも自分で触り切らなかったんですよ。ハプニング的に広場っていう空間に介入できた点はすごくよかったと思いますよ。

赤岩 今回初めてプログラムを人に頼んでやってもらったんですけど、頼んだ人も"それ以上にやったら画面も画像も破綻する"っていうところまでは絶対にやんないのね。私たち一回破綻させてそこから形を整えるのが面白いって思うんですけど、そこがプログラマー側とは決定的に違っていて「もうちょっとやってくださいよ!」ってそういう駆け引きがあって。

千房 むこうはプロフェッショナルだからね。僕らは「パラメーター1から10のどれにしますか?」って聞かれたら「100!」って答えるけど、やっぱり機械の本来のスペックが破綻するような危険はみんな避けたがるから。でも会場の雰囲気は妙な感じで大人が走ったりとか。変な動きのおじさんおばさんを見ているこっちが面白かった(笑)。けどやっぱり万博の壁は厚かったね。

赤岩 厚かった。ハイビジョンっていうスポンサー企業の技術をみせたい訳だから、モニター壊れちゃったような映像がだめなのは分かりますけどね。

千房 関わっている人間の本能の中にあるワイルドさを風景の中に引きずり出したいなっていうのがあって。それを見たいっていうのがあるよね。僕は結構アウト・サイダーアートが好きで。アウトサイダー・アートって人からどう見られたいかっていう部分なしで、自分の欲望をガーッとはき出したモノだから、客観性がないから。僕らと同じものをみていても、彼らからすると全く違った印象のものだったりそこが強調されている。みんな同じようにコミュニケーションしてるって思ってるけど、他人から見れば全然ずれてたり。でも逆に根本的な、動物的なところではものすごく共感できたりする。そこが重要。

赤岩 人の欲望が素直に出せる場所や仕組みを作りたい。まずは自分がそこにいたいけど、他の人と共有できればもっと面白いことになるだろうなって。

千房 イギリスでの展示『SHIKAKU NO

would go through a camera and be displayed on the screen. We programmed various audial and visual effects so that they would correspond to the movements of the people. Hi-Vision uses lots of processing power, and it imposed heavy limits on what we could do, so we tried to make something that was basic yet effective. Visitors of the expo were doing weird movements and enjoying themselves in front of the installation.

Sembo: Effects like strokes and light would appear on the screen. It was a very simple interaction design, but we weren't too satisfied with the content. Since it was in Hi-Vision, we weren't able to build the whole program by ourselves.

Akaiwa: This was the first time we hired someone do the programming for us, but there were some decisive differences between the programmer and us. When we work, we like to first rupture the program and start building from there, but the programmer would not push the envelope of the images to their breaking point. We were telling him things like, "come on, just a little bit more!"

Sembo: That guy was a professional. If someone asked us, "where do you want that parameter between 1 and 10?," we would be like "100!," but most people want to avoid exceeding the aptitude of the machine. The atmosphere of the site was pretty nice. All these grown-ups were running around, and it was fun watching middle-aged men and women moving in strange ways (laughs). But unfortunately, the Expo was a hardheaded event.

Akaiwa: Yeah it was. What they wanted to do was to exhibit the Hi-Vision technology of the sponsoring corporation, so it's not so strange that they didn't want us to display images that looked like glitches.

Sembo: I want to release the untamed aspect of the user's instincts out into the landscape. I'm pretty fond of outsider art. Those artists go on creating without giving any thought to how they want others to view their works. It's a direct disgorging of the artist's desire, so there's no objectivity to it. Even if someone is looking at the same thing as me, he may be receiving a totally different impression. This kind of gap is often emphasized in the work of outsider artists, yet we are still able to heavily sympathize with the work at a primal, instinctive level. I think that's the important thing.

Akaiwa: I want to build a field or a mechanism where people can honestly release their desires. Foremost, I want to be in that place myself, but if I could share it with others, it would be even more fun.

Sembo: For our exhibit in Great Britain ("Shikaku no Mukou" 2005), we set up a room in which the lights and monitors all turn dark the moment a visitor touches the graphics tablet with a stylus pen. So right when you begin to draw a picture,

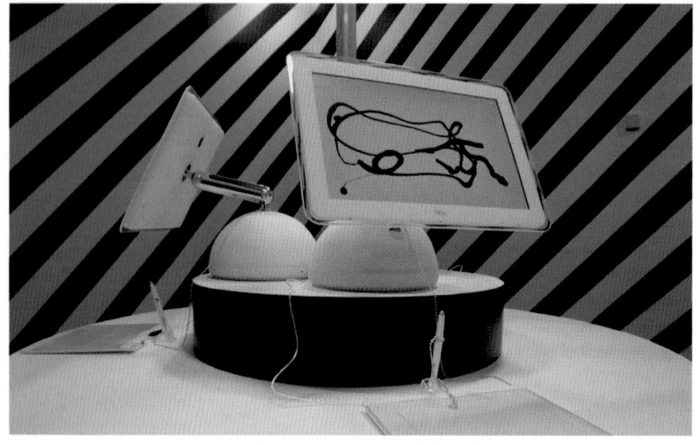

MUKOU』(2005) もホワイトキューブの中のペンタブレットをタッチすると部屋中の電気とモニターが真っ暗になるんですよ。絵を描こうとするといきなり視覚情報が奪われてしまうっていう仕組み。で、タブレットへのタッチに合わせて音が鳴り始めるから観客は適当に思いのままにガーッ筆を走らせちゃうんですよ。で、描き終わるとパッと自分の描いた絵がモニターに表示されるの。自分の行動と対面する。その時に気付いたんだけど、真っ暗になって音が鳴り始めるとみんな凶暴になるの(笑)。手が本能の向くままにガーッ書き殴ったり。その絵のような走り書きが、ネットを通じて世界中に配信されるわけですよ。

——exonemo の作品のほとんどはウェブにアップされているから展覧会を見逃したり、会場の遠くに住んでいる人も追体験できますよね。

千房　ウェブはいいですよ。人が好奇心のままに探索していくっていう体験をデザインできる。それこそインタラクティブに。インタラクティブって反応性が良くて思い通りに動かせたらそんなもの全然意味ないと思う。コンピュータの方向性として思い通りに動かせることが当たり前のこととしてあるじゃん。でも、その逆でコンピュータが邪魔をするのが創造的だと思うし、それがコンピュータの重要な仕事の一つ。

赤岩 コンピュータの仕事ね。そういえば前にフリッカーの実験をしたことがあるんですけど、その時たまたま遊園地でお土産に買ってきた小さい扇風機をプロジェクターのレンズの前に置いてみたら、ものすごい速さのフリッカーが巻き起こったんですよ。コンピュータじゃ絶対できない速さの点滅と質感がいとも簡単にアナログの力を借りて手に入ったんですよね。そのとき、何でもコンピュータでやろうとするのは間違いだってことをつくづく感じて。コンピュータに仕事させないっていうのも時には重要なのかも。ライブとかVJ の映像でコンピュータを使って映像を音とシンクロさせてるのってあるじゃないですか。コンピュータ使えば、例えば音量の変化なんかで簡単にシンクロさせることができるんだけど、人ってそういう風に音量だけで音聞いてないですよね。やっぱりコンピューターは音を信号としてしか聞けないから、そういう意味では物足りないなーって。そもそも「音と映像はシンクロしなくちゃいけないのか?」ってこと自体に疑問がありますけど。映像がオブジェみたいにポンって存在してもいいと思うし、コンピュータ使うにしてももっといろんなやり方あると思うんですよね。

千房　宇川(直宏)さんのVJ みたいに手でシンクロさせるっていうのはいいなって思いますけど。機械的にリズムに合うんじゃなくて、人間の解釈が入ってくるから、言語的な意味も出てくるし。

you suddenly lose all visual information, and sounds also start roaring from the speakers, so the surprised visitor will scribble something spontaneously. When she is finished, the drawing is displayed on the monitor, putting the visitor face-to-face with the result of her action. What I realized was that when the lights go out and noises start sounding, people become savage (laughs). Their hands become possessed by instinct and they draw ferociously. These drawings are then uploaded onto the Internet.

——It's nice how most of your works are online, so even if I miss an exhibition or live far away, I can still experience the work afterwards.

Sembo: Yeah, the Internet is great. You can design interactive experiences for users to explore freely. But if an interface's level of reactivity is too high, allowing the user to operate it smoothly at will, there's not going to be much meaning. Computers are assumed as being something that can and should be operated at will, but I think that a computer should also be obstructive. That's kind of what creativity is, and it's another important job of the computer.

Akaiwa: A job of the computer, huh. There was a time when we were experimenting with flickers. When we happened to put a small electric toy fan in front of the projector lens, an unbelievably fast flicker appeared. With the intervention of this simple analog device, we got a fluctuation speed and a type of quality that could never have been realized by using only a computer. From that experience, I learned that it's a mistake to try to do everything with the computer. I think that at times, it's important not to let the computer do its job.

——I guess that's where Exonemo's lo-fi feel comes from.

Akaiwa: You know how motion graphics and sound are often set into synchronization by a computer? You can see it at many concerts and VJ sets. It's easy to make the visuals correspond to the volume of the sound or whatever variable and achieve synchronization, but when people listen to music with their own ears, they are listening to much more than the volume. Computers can only interpret sound as signals, and sometimes that's not good enough. I actually doubt the whole concept of synchronizing sound and visuals. Is it really that necessary? I think it would be fine even if a motion graphic just existed as something like a sculpture. The ways of using computers don't have to be limited to the ways they are being used now.

Sembo: I think manual synchronization is interesting, like in Ukawa-san's VJ sets. Instead of just mechanically setting the tempo, human interpretation is brought into the process, so there is a semiotic aspect

赤岩　VJでも映像が音楽のサブになっちゃうんだとしたらVJなんていらないと思う。音楽だけで十分表現力があるのに、映像がその邪魔してるときってありますしね。だから、宇川さんが最近はVJ以外にフロア用のライティングをやってるって聞いて、妙に納得しましたね。プロジェクターの光以上にライティングの光ってその場を変える力があると思うから。

千房　以前、生西くんのVJを側でみていて、彼も激しく映像をスイッチングするから、画面がフリッカーみたいに点滅してたのを見て、映像って突き詰めると光なんだなって思いましたよ。フロアでの映像って結局光の演出で、その中で何が起きているかよりも、その枠が発光してるっていうことの方に興味がいっちゃう。光のフリッカーの方がフロアでは重要だったりしますしね。

――exonemoは、作品のネタばらしも積極的にやってますね。

千房　『VHSM : Video / Hack / and / Slash / Mixer』(2003) っていうインスタレーションでは3つのプロジェクターを全部ケージの中に入れて、中でプロペラを回して映像を点滅させて、さらに壁面で合成してるんですよ。人がその映像を横切ると影が3方向に複雑に絡んで、面白いことになる。映像の作品のようだけど、映像が生まれる瞬間を見せたかったから。普通ならプロジェクターも白い箱に隠すんだろうけど、あえて隠さないで中身が丸見えのケージにして見えるようにしてるんですよ。映像やるときも全部見せたいなって常に思っていて。あと、僕らが頭で考えてることだけをあまり大切にしたくないなっていうのがあって、自分が考えることには限界があるって思うから、こういう展示に向けて作業をしていて、やってるうちに内容が変わっていったり、広がっていくのは大歓迎なんですよ。作りながらフィードバックしながら変えていく。その過程をさらしている部分もありますね。

赤岩　大体考えた通りに作ってみると実際面白くなかったりすることがよくあるよね。無茶なプログラムをコンピュータにやらせてみたりするとコンピュータが暴走したりもするし、突き抜けたりする。そこで発見がある。

千房　自分たちのたどってきた道筋も同じで「インスタレーションや展示をやろう」って始めたわけじゃなくて、流れ流れてここまでたどり着いたって感じ。本当にすべて実験なんですよ。でもエンターテインメントでもある。他人と自分たちのためのエンターテインメント。

――ちなみにホームページのトップを開くとハードディスクが微かにチチチチ…リズミカルに処理音を鳴らすのは狙ってるんですか？

赤岩　しないよ？（実際に画面を見て）……本当だ。

千房　じゃあこれからは狙ってるって言おう（笑）。

involved.

Akaiwa: Your feelings and inner sensations can be expressed through using your body, even if a computer is mediating the flow. If the VJ's motion graphics are going to be submissive to the music, I don't think we need VJs. Music has enough expressive power by itself, and there are even cases in which the motion graphics hinder the effect of the music. So when I heard that these days Ukawa-san is not just VJing, but also doing things with the lighting as well, it made a lot of sense to me. Lighting is able to significantly affect the atmosphere of the space, probably even more than the light of a projector can.

——It seems that you guys actively reveal the mechanisms that lie behind your works.

Sembo: For an installation called VHSM ("Video/Hack/and/Slash/Mixer" 2003), we installed propellers onto three video projectors in order to make the projected images flicker, then put these projectors inside cages, and set the images so that they would be synthesized as they are projected onto the wall. When someone would walk in front of the images, the shadow of the person would complexly scramble in three directions, creating an interesting effect. It looks like a work emphasizing the content of the motion graphics, but what we really wanted to present was the instant that the motion graphics are born. I think normally the projectors would be hidden inside of white boxes or something, but we put them inside of cages that could be seen through (image outside of text), because we wanted to display what was going on inside. Another thing is, we don't want to place too much value on the thoughts and concepts that are inside of our heads. The things I conceptualize in my mind are under certain limits, and that's why I try to make use of the transformations of the content that take place during the production process. We are simultaneously building, receiving feedback from, and transforming the work. This process itself is something we try to express to the audience.

Akaiwa: When we create something in the exact same form it had while it was still an idea, the result is often not so interesting. But you can try other things, like making a computer perform some reckless program that causes it to go berserk and perform some unexpected action. Discoveries can be made from this kind of approach as well.

Sembo: Our career has also been like that. In the beginning, we weren't thinking about doing installations and exhibitions. We got to where we are right now by continually going with the flow of things. It's an experiment, and at the same time, it's entertainment. Entertainment for others and for ourselves.

VIDEO ART

映像のジャンルは今、多様化し、切り開かれつつある。そのなかで、高木正勝はその新しい領域を代表する存在である。その作品は、実写やアニメーションを越えた、動的な絵画とも呼ぶべきものだ。ノスタルジックな実写表現、コンピューターを用いたまばゆいばかりに鮮やかなエフェクト処理、そしてビジュアルによって表現される感情の連鎖、それらが織り混ざって彼の作品はできている。音に準じるのでもなく、ストーリーに準じるのでもない。それは、一枚の写真や絵画に集約されている記憶や感傷のように、完結している。いわば、それは時間軸を持った絵画といってよい。空間のなかに時間軸をともなって存在している作品、新しい映像表現の在り方がここにある。その在り方は絵画や写真を包括しながら進化していく、新たな表現の可能性を模索するものであるかもしれない。

Today, the field of motion graphics is rapidly diversifying and opening up to new possibilities. One of the most prominent artists of this new frontier is Masakatsu Takagi. His works intertwine nostalgic footage, vivid effects derived from digital technology, and images that manifest a succession of emotions. His visuals are not complimentary to music or to narrative: they are motion graphics of a genuine sort, luminously self-contained, like the sentiments and memories that are concentrated in a photograph or a painting. Takagi's work can be thought of as an extension of painting, but with a temporal axis embedded. Space and time naturally interpenetrate to materialize a new mode of visual expression. His practice continues to evolve, assimilating the essences of various fields of art.

高木正勝
TAKAGI MASAKATSU

クラブから美術館へ

――高木さんが音楽と映像という表現形態を選んだ理由はなんですか？

10代の頃にピアノを習っていましたが、当時は、どうやったら表現したいものを音楽で形にできるのか分からなかった。曲を作っても断片しかできなくて、きちんと終わらせることができなかったんです。その時に写真に出会って、その瞬間性と完結性に惹かれて、一気にのめり込んでしまいました。撮り続けていると、自分が撮りたいものが「映画のワンシーン」のような写真だということに気付いて、ビデオカメラで写真を撮るようになりました。その延長で映像を始めたのですが、今度は、映像でどうやったら作品が作れるのか分からなくなった。映画やミュージッククリップというのはあるけれど、何か違う形の映像が作りたかったんです。ミュージッククリップと違う形態の映像なんてすでにたくさん存在していたのですが、その時は情報が少なすぎて分からなかった。そんなある日、友人の青木孝允くんの音楽に自分の映像を付けてみたら、自分で作品と思えるものができ上がって、初めてやりたい映像が見えだしたんです。ただ、せっかく映像を作っても、最終的にどこで発表できるのか全く分からなかった。その時、近くの美術館で、生まれて初めて、映像が美術作品として展示されているのを見て衝撃を受けました。それまでは、絵画や彫刻しか展示されないものだと思っていたので非常に嬉しかった。美術館で映像を発表するという目標ができたんです。それからは映像制作に集中しだしました。音は青木くん、映像は僕という形でSILICOMという名前で二人で活動するようになりました。DVDにする話を頂いたり、クラブを中心に発表できる機会をたくさんいただけるようになって。2年間一緒に活動していたのですが、発表の場所がどうしてもクラブに限定されがちだったのと、2年間映像に集中して、ようやく映像で表現したい内容が具体的になって、自分で音楽を作るという必然性を否定できなくなった。それでSILICOMの活動を休止して、自分一人で映像と音楽を作るようになりました。コンピュータで作業をしていると映像を作るのも音楽を作るのも一緒だったんです。時間軸があるのも一緒だし、データの扱い方も構造もほとんど一緒だった。だからすんなり音楽も自分で制作できるようになりました。映像作品を中心に作っていたのですが、なぜか映像に付けていた音楽の方を先に気に入ってもらえて、ニューヨークやドイツのレコード会社から発表できるようになりました。そして、ギャラリーや美術館で映像を発表できる機会をもらえるようになって。今は、映像はそういったアートスペースでまず発表して、それをまとめてDVDにしたり、音楽だけの作品を作ってレコード会社からCDを発表したりしています。音と映像のライブをやったりもしているので、よく分からない肩書きになっていますが、映像も音も基本的には同じような感覚で作っています。

From the Club to the Museum

――What was the reason you chose music and motion graphics as your mediums of expression?

I was learning how to play the piano throughout my teenage years, but at the time, I didn't know how I could use music to give shape to the things I wanted to express. When I tried to compose, I could only make fragments, meaning I was not able to finish a whole song. During this period, I was exposed to photography for the first time, and I quickly got attached to the medium because of its instantaneity and completeness. As I kept on taking photos, I started to realize that what I really wanted to capture was a photograph that was like the scene of a movie, so I began taking photographs with a video camera. As an extension of this, I started creating motion graphics. However, I was again unable to make complete works, though it was motion graphics and not music this time. There were lots of movies and music videos around, but I wanted to make something that was different from these. In actuality, there were already many motion graphic works that took a different form from music videos, but I didn't know about them at the time because there wasn't enough information around. One day, I tried putting my motion graphics onto some music composed by my friend Aoki Takamasa, and what I got was something that I could finally perceive as a complete work. This opportunity allowed me to begin conceiving an image of the kind of motion graphics I really wanted to create. However, I didn't have a clue as to where I could ultimately have my works exhibited. Just around the same time, I happened to visit a local art museum, and I was amazed to find a motion graphic work exhibited there as a work of fine art. It smashed my preconception that only paintings and sculptures were exhibited at art museums, so I felt very happy. I now had the goal of exhibiting a motion graphic work at a museum. From then on, I concentrated on the production of my work. Aoki and I began to work together, under the name Silicom. We were given many opportunities to perform, mainly at clubs, and also to create DVDs. After working together for two years, Aoki and I put Silicom to a rest. One reason was because the exposure of our works was generally being limited to clubs. Another is because after two years of concentrating on motion graphics, I was finally able to specifically grasp the type of images that I wanted to express, and it felt natural to begin composing my own music as well. So from them on, I started creating both visuals and music by myself. Making music and making motion graphics are very similar processes when done on the

——美術館での映像作品の上映はどのような状況なのでしょうか？

美術界で映像というのは、数年前から当たり前の存在になっています。でも、美術館の展示スペースで映像を見せるとなると悩む部分もたくさんあります。例えば、プロジェクターやスピーカーなどの設備が弱かったり、音が響きすぎてしまったり。グループ展だと、他の作家の展示との兼ね合いもあって、照明を真っ暗にできなかったり、音量を小さくしないといけなかったり。空間自体を完全に作り込むような映像作品なら大丈夫かもしれませんが、映像そのものをきちんと見せるとなると苦労します。個人的には、5分間ある映像は、きちんと初めから5分間見てもらいたいと思っています。5分の作品なら5分間見てもらわなければ意味がない。そこに重きを置くと、どうしてもゆっくり映像を見れる空間を作ることから展示の準備を始めることになります。僕の映像の場合、じっくり映像に対して向き合える空間の方が好ましい場合が多いので。あと、どんな映像でも、性能の悪いプロジェクターで投影するとつまらなく見えたり、逆に高価な最新のプロジェクターを使ったらよく見えたりしてしまう。スピーカーも同じ。どういう機材が使えて、どういう空間で見せられるかというのは、作品のクオリティーに大きく影響してしまう大切な要素なんです。だから、機材や音響空間に対しても当然知識が必要になるんです。作品だけ持って行って、思い通りのクオリティーで流せるアートスペースはなかなかないと思います。テレビモニターやプロジェクターなど、映し出す大きさや雰囲気を自由に選べる分、ある一定の展示クオリティーを保つには映像制作とは別の知識や経験が必要になってくる。必ずしも映像作家が、映像空間のプロフェッショナルではないので、いろいろ戸惑うこともあります。これは映像に限ったことではないでしょうけど。だから、作品によってはきちんとした上映の仕方が最良の場合もあるのかなとも思います。例えば、映画館での上映というのも一つの在り方だと思います。映画館は、映像や音の適切な設備を最初から備えていますから。実際に、映画館で何回かやったこともありますが、映像がとてもキレイで感動しました。ただ見せ方は限られてしまうんですけれどね。アートスペースだと、投影場所一つとってもいろいろな方法を試せるので。映像プラスαの表現が可能になる。山口の情報センターなど、映像や音響に特化したスペースが増えてきているのでこれからが楽しみですね。

computer. The involvement of the time axis, the structure of the data, and the ways of handling the data are all nearly identical for the two. This is why I was able to compose my own music without difficulty. I was mainly focusing on my motion graphics, but for some reason, my music began attracting attention first, and I was able to release tracks from record labels in New York and Germany. I was eventually given the chance to exhibit my visuals at galleries and museums. Recently, I have been releasing my motion graphics at art venues first, and compiling them as DVDs afterwards. Also, I have been producing audio-only works, and releasing them from record labels in the form of CDs. I do live performances with both music and visuals, so I often wonder how I should describe my occupation to people, but the point is that I create both motion graphics and music in the same frame of mind.

——In what kind of ways are your motion graphic works exhibited at art museums?

Motion graphics in the art scene have been common since a few years ago, but there are still many difficulties that occur when exhibiting at art museums. For example, the projector or speakers could be too weak, or the sound could have too much reverberation. There are also constraints that are particular to group exhibitions, such as not being able to completely darken the lighting, or having to lower the volume of the sound, because these things could interfere with the display of the other artists' works. These constraints don't matter so much if your work involves creating the whole space in which your motion graphics are going to be shown, but if you're only working on the content of the motion graphics, there are bound to be difficulties. If I make a five-minute work, I personally wish for the viewer to watch the full five minutes from the beginning to end. There is no meaning unless the full clip is viewed. When this is prioritized, the preparation of the display must begin with setting up the space in a way that allows the audience to watch the work comfortably for a long duration. My works often favor this kind of space, so that the viewer can relax and go face-to-face with the motion graphics. Another thing is, in many cases, a motion graphic work will look boring when projected from a low performance projector, but appealing when using an expensive, state-of-the-art projector. The same goes for speakers. The type of equipment that you are able to use, and the type of space in which the work is going to be exhibited, are both important factors that are going to significantly affect the quality of the display. This is the reason why an artist producing motion graphics must also have knowledge of electronic equipment and spatial acoustics.

見て楽しいもの、良いものっていう風には考えていませんでした。自分のDVDは、あくまでカタログと言うか、画家でいう画集のようなものとして考えていて。DVDなので、美術館で発表するときもテレビで見るときも内容は同じなのですが、本当の作品は大きな画面で見たときの状態、という意識で作っています。大きな画面で見たときに、最大の効果が発揮できるように作っているので、是非、そういう状態で体験して欲しいと思っています。

——高木さんは、海外での活動も多いと思うんですけど、国によって作品のとらえられ方は違いますか？

海外の人からは日本人らしい作品だとよく言われますよ。そして、どちらかというと、手法やアイデアの部分に興味を持つ人が多い気がします。逆に日本で発表するとモチーフへの関心が強い気がします。でも作品の基本的な受け取られ方はそんなに変わらないです。

——まだ、高木さんが活動を始められた頃って、DVDっていうフォーマットもあまり一般的でなかった頃ですよね。

まだ映画のDVDですら、少ししか出てない時期でした。実際、当時はVHSでの発表も予定していました。僕自身、DVDプレイヤーを持ってなかったですから。いろいろなレコード会社を通してDVDをリリースしましたが、どのレコード会社にとっても初めての試みという感じでした。映像作品といっても今みたいに気楽に出せる感覚はあまりなかったんじゃないでしょうか。僕の場合、プロジェクターで投影された大きな画面で見てもらうことを想定して映像を作っていたので、テレビの画面で

映像と音の制作その手順

——制作の際に、テーマなどは最初に設定するんですか？

すごく大まかなテーマだけです。例えば「テーマパーク」とか「風」とか。そういうキーワードだけです。それも作りながらどんどん変わっていく。時々、絵コンテのようなものを描いたりもするんですけど、そういうものはほとんど使えない。あらかじめ考えたものをその通り作っていても楽しくないし、ただ再現しているような感じになってしまうので、作品にはならない。途中で偶然性が入ったり、自分の中で飛躍がないと作品にはならないんです。素材は

——As you often are active overseas, do you feel that people in different countries view your work in different ways?

In foreign countries, many people tell me that my work has a very Japanese style, and I feel that there are many who are interested in the techniques and ideas involved in the work. On the other hand, when I present my work in Japan, I feel that people are more interested in the motifs involved. However, there is generally not so much of a difference in how my works are received between different countries.

——You began your creative activities at a time when DVD wasn't such a common format yet, right?

It was a time when there were only a few number of movies available on DVD. I was actually planning to release works on VHS at the time, because I myself didn't own a DVD player. I did release DVDs through various record labels, but it was a risky venture for all of the labels. Unlike today, a motion graphic work wasn't something they could casually release. Even though I released DVDs, I was creating works presupposing that they would be viewed as projections onto a large screen, so I wasn't really thinking about motion graphics that would be interesting when viewed on a television screen. For me, my DVDs are something similar to a catalog, or a portfolio. It's a DVD, so it's going to have the same content whether projected on a screen at an art museum or displayed on a TV screen, but in my terms, my works are fully realized only when they are shown on a large screen. They are made to have the most effect when viewed in this kind of ideal situation, so I would be happiest if everyone could experience the images on a large screen.

The Process of Creating Visuals and Sound

——When you create works, do you establish a theme first?

Only a very rough theme. For example, just some keyword like "theme park" or "wind," but even those change as the production process advances. Sometimes I make a timeline sketch, but in most cases, they are unusable. Whenever I follow an initial plan, I cannot manage to create a solid work, as the result turns out to be something like a reconstruction. This method is not much fun either. It doesn't become a solid work unless there are elements of chance involved, and unexpected leaps in the production process. As for my material, I film anything whenever I feel like doing so. In most cases, I go to a place I've never been to in a foreign country for about three

思い立ったときに撮りためます。3週間くらい海外の知らない土地に行って撮影することがほとんどです。撮影しているときは、それがどんな映像作品になるのか全く考えずに撮っています。感覚的に反応するものだけ集中的に撮る。そうやって撮りためた素材から、テーマに合いそうなものを選んで、15秒くらいの映像を作ってみます。このときに同じ素材に対して何パターンも映像ができます。その中で実を結びそうな何かが見つかったら、その後は後戻りしないでどんどん続きを作っていくんです。でき上がった部分を何度も見ながら、その続きを作っていきます。終わりが分からないまま続けていくのですが、途中で必ず壁にぶち当たる。急に客観的になって、内容や手法、クオリティーに疑問が湧いてくる。それで作業が進まなくなるんですが、それを何とか乗り越えられたときに初めて作品になる気がします。映像を作る上でこの時期が一番辛くて、感覚的には錯乱状態というか、ふわふわしています。考えてるようで考えてないような。そういう自分で意識していない何かが出てこないと作品に仕上がらない。大体このときに、その作品に対する決定的なテーマみたいなのが分かり始めるんです。その映像で何がしたかったのかとか、もう少し具体的に分かり始める。そして、可能な限りそれを表現しようと一気に作り進めて行く感じです。最後に近づくと、もうそろそろ終わりだなっていう絵が自然にやってきて、映像に作らされている気分になります。音のことは考えずに映像だけを最初から最後まで作っていきます。その後、映像を見ながら音楽を作っていきます。映像は1日15秒くらいが限度なので、5分の作品だと1ヶ月ほどかかりますが、それにつける音は2、3日で仕上がります。ミュージッククリップの場合は音が先にありますが、映像の作り方は基本的に同じです。必ず前から順番に作ります。最近は、音楽だけの作品も作ったりするので、半年くらいの間隔で映像に集中する時期と音楽に集中する時期を分けています。バラバラにやると集中できない。音楽を作ると決めたら、今度は映像のことは全く考えません。二重人格みたいな気分です。

——高木さんの作品からは、ペインティングを映像でやっているような印象を受けます。

そう言われると、すごく嬉しいです。実は、一番興味があるのが絵画なんです。映像を作っていますが、世の中にある他の映像作品と自分の感覚がシンクロすることはあまりない。画集を集めたり絵画の展覧会に行ったりはするのに、写真とか映像にはそれほど興味がない。自分がやってる映像も、気持ちの上では、あくまで絵画の延長でやっている。絵は1枚の静止画だけど、そこにある感覚を5分間という時間の中でやっている。その5分の映像の中に1枚の絵を見たときの感覚を残したいと思う。自分は、絵を実際に描き始めたらキャンパスが真っ黒になるまで描き足してしまうタイプだけど、コンピュータでは、その筆で描くプロセスを時間や動きとして残せる。一つの絵ができ上がるまでに、可能性としての完成型が100個あったとしたら、100通り残したいって思ってしまう、タチの悪い人間なんです。100個は大げさですけれど、音楽でいうと、デモテープの状態に最高の魅力を感じてしまうのと同時にそれの完成型も聞いてみたいという、そういう極

weeks, and film the material for my work there. When I'm filming, I'm never thinking about what kind of motion graphics it could develop into. I just concentrate on capturing things that attract my attention. From these films, I choose something that seems to fit the theme I'm considering, and begin creating short movies of about 15 seconds or so, each of them a variation based on the same material. And within these short movies, if there's something that seems like it may give fruit, I keep on producing the rest of it without ever heading back. I continue the production process without knowing where it will end, but there always comes a phase of stagnation, in which I suddenly switch to an objective view, and become suspicious of the content, methodology, and quality of the work in progress. This phase is the hardest part of creating a motion graphic work, and my mind is in a sort of delirious and cloudy state during it. I find my self in these states where it seems like I'm thinking, when I'm really not. At this point, if something unexpected doesn't emerge from within me, the motion graphic isn't able to develop into a solid work. Also, during this phase, I begin to understand what the definitive theme of the work really is, and what it is that I specifically want to manifest through the work. So in an attempt to express this as much as possible, I work to push the production process forward.

——When I view your works, it feels as though you're painting with motion graphics.

That comment makes me very happy. What I am most interested in is actually paintings. I make motion graphics, but it is rare for my senses to synchronize with other motion graphic works in the world. I collect books of paintings and go to many painting exhibitions, but photography and motion graphics usually don't capture my attention. I feel that my motion graphics are an extension of painting. Through my works, I want to produce the same feeling that occurs when viewing a painting, though it is within a time frame of five minutes or whatever, instead of being a single still image. When I paint, I tend to apply so much paint that the canvas often ends up all blacked out, but when I use a computer, I am able to preserve the actual process of painting, as time and movement. If there are 100 potential ways a work could turn out, I'm the kind of person who would want to make all 100 of them. If we were talking about music, it would be like feeling the most attraction towards the initial demotape, but at the same time wanting to hear it in its completely finished state. Expressing this dichotomy in one work is not something that I am capable of doing in a painting, but I can do it using a computer, in the

端な感じです。それを一つの作品として見せるのは絵では僕にはできないけど、コンピュータで映像としてならできる。一枚の絵を描く過程を見せることを、映像の時間軸に組み込むというか。だから映像はスタートからゴールに向かって作りたい。そして時間を遡って手直しをしたくないんです。アイデアが生まれる段階や飛躍する段階、成長して形になる段階を一つの映像の中に残したいんです。

映像表現とコンピューター

——高木さんの作品は、コンピューターがあったからこそ生まれた表現ともいえますよね。

そうですね。ただ、見る人によっては技術的なところとか、そういうものが大きく見えてしまうのかもしれない。でも、自分にとってそういう技術的なことはあまり大切じゃないんです。例えば、どうやってこういう映像が作れるのか聞かれたとしたら、結構教えてしまったりします。コンピュータなので、同じ行程で作ったら同じものになると思われるかもしれませんが、実は無理なんです。もちろん同じようなものを作ろうと思ったら数秒くらいは作れるかもしれないけど、それが3分とか5分とかになると全く違うものになる。表現したいことによって、素材や技術を選ぶのであって、こういう素材や技術があるからこういうことをやろうというものではない。すべてが一致しないと作品にはならないし、意図的にやってもろくな結果にはならないものなんです。コンピュータで映像を作り始めて6年くらい経ちますが、ようやく絵筆のように扱えるようになってきたのかなと思います。

——技術が進み、映像表現がこれからどんどん個人のものになって、映像の世界も面白くなってきそうですよね。

そうですね。一昔前まで、映像作家の最終ゴールは映画みたいなとらえられ方が一般的だった気がしますが、こうやって個人でも映像を作れるようになると、映画だけが答えではないという感じになってきたのではないでしょうか。5分で表現できるものも2時間で表現できるものも、15秒の世界ですら一つの作品として広くきちんと受け取ってもらえるようになってきた気がします。制作者の顔が見えてきたというか、より多くの人に映像の作家性を見てもらえるようになった気がします。

form of motion graphics. It's like taking the whole process of a painting being created, and converging it into the time axis of the motion graphic. This is why I like to create a motion graphic work in a strict direction heading from the beginning to the end, without ever going back in time to fix something. Within one motion graphic work, I want to preserve all the phases of the production process, like the basic-idea-being-originated-phase, the new-elements-emerging-phase, and the development-into-a-solid-structure-phase.

Motion Graphics and Computers

——The nature of your work seems to be inseparable with the existence of the computer.

Some people might place their attention on the technical aspects of my work, but for me, technical matters are not so important. For example, if someone asks me how I made a certain work, I often explain how without hesitation. Some people may assume that since a computer is used, the same result would be producible if the same process is taken, but this is actually impossible. Of course, you might be able to create a few seconds of something similar if you tried, but when you attempt to create four or five minutes of images, it becomes something completely different. The techniques and material are chosen according to what it is you want to express, and not the other way around, in which what is expressed in the work is the result of the material and techniques used. The motion graphic doesn't become a solid work unless every element is in unity, and you can never get a good result if you create it in a manner of deliberacy. It's been about six years since I first started making motion graphics on the computer, and I feel like I'm finally starting to be able to use the machine in the same kind of way as a paintbrush.

——It seems that the world of motion graphics is going to become an exciting field as technology advances, and motion graphics as a medium becomes accessible on an even more individual basis.

I agree. Up until a while ago, it was common to think of the movie as the final goal for a motion graphic artist, but now that motion graphics can be produced by individuals, the movie isn't perceived of as being the only available destination. I feel that motion graphics of any duration, whether two hours, five minutes, or even fifteen seconds, are all beginning to be equally respected as complete works now. It also feels like more people now understand that there is an author behind each motion graphic work they see.

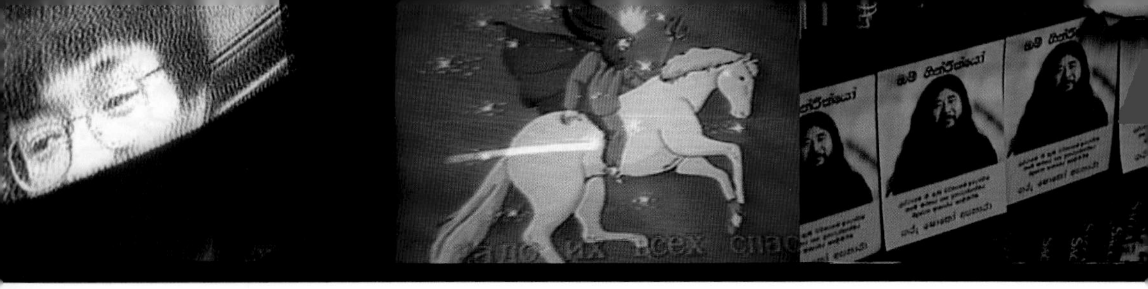

DOCUMENTARY

映像作家が個人の目線をメディアに定着させることができるドキュメンタリーというジャンルは、一様なテンションで一様な情報しか生産することのできないマスメディアに代わり、結果としてそれが作り出す印象とは全く別の、現実を映し出すことがある。森達也が手持ちカメラでオウム真理教の内側から彼らの人間像に迫る『A』、そしてその続編『A2』は、まさにそのようなドキュメンタリー作品である。マスメディアに慣れた僕らにとって、彼の作品はあまりにも生々しすぎるようにも思える。が、それ故に『A』はメディアの観客である私たちの世界に隠されているものを暴き出す。オウムという被写体に差し向けられたカメラのレンズは、現実のリアルな層を映し出しながら、マスメディアを通しては決して見ることのできない、私たち自身の姿をも映し出す。そう、『A』はまた私たち自身についてのドキュメンタリーでもあるのだ。

Due to a need for cumbersome apparatus and a wide budget, film and motion graphic media have had no choice but to be mass media. However, as high-performance recording equipment for personal use is successively released into the market, motion graphic production is now being opened up to independent creators as well. In the field of documentary, a filmmaker goes face to face with the reality that lies before him, and imprints his individual gaze onto the film. It is a media that has the capacity to depict a reality and a worldview that is wholly divergent from the leveled information provided to us by a levelheaded mass media. Documentary film director Tatsuya Mori's "A" and its sequel "A2" are such works. They focus in on the interior of the Aum Shinrikyo cult and the human beings involved. To our mass-media-accustomed-eyes, his works can seem unnervingly graphic, but this is precisely because the films unveil the things that are hidden in the world that we, a media audience, live in. The camera lens that gazes into Aum Shinrikyo captures images of a substantial reality, but it simultaneously captures what cannot be seen through the mass media, namely our own image. "A" is a film that documents us as well.

森達也
TATSUYA MORI

森
T
MO

ドキュメンタリーは一人称である

――森さんが自分自身でカメラを回し始めたというのは、どういういきさつだったんですか？

自分で撮影もするようになったのは、オウム真理教のドキュメンタリー『A』以降ですね。今でもそうだけど、基本的にテレビの撮影は「ENG」（Electronic News Gathering）っていう仕組みでやっている。要はテレビクルーです。カメラマンがいて、ビデオエンジニアがいて、という最小ユニットがあるんです。それが96年ぐらいに、デジタル撮影できる民生機が出てきた。ちょうど『A』を撮っている頃です。『A』の企画が、テレビで放送する予定だったのにダメになってしまって、それで「自分でやるしかない」と。それで、レンタルでデジタルカメラを借りてきて、見よう見まねで撮り始めたっていう。

――自分自身でカメラ持つことで作品は変わりましたか？

変わりました。作品もそうだし、僕自身が変わりました。テレビでは、カメラって人任せですよね。もちろんディレクターですから、ある程度指示はしますけど。自分で撮ることで一番気付いたことは、なんといってもカメラワークが主観ということですね。ズームとかパンていうカメラの表現は、要するに自分の感情表現なんです。今までは、それを人に任せていたんですよ。自分でカメラを持って撮ることで、何かをズームする自分に気付いた。あ、これは主観なんだなって。テレビって客観的で公正っていう幻想がある。で、僕もそれにすがってた部分もあった。でも実は、そんなものはないよ、と。映画やってる人はみんな知っていることなんだけど。僕はそれを、自分で撮影することでやっと気付いた。

――撮影している最中、『A』が作品としてテレビという枠の外で発表できるという確信はあったんですか？

ない、ない。最初のころは、フジがダメだったらTBS、TBSダメだったらNHKとかね。知り合いを訪ねて全部行った。それも、全部断られて。同時進行で撮影もしながら。それなら、じゃあ昔やってた自主映画しかないかってことになって。

――組織を離れることに抵抗はなかったですか？

全くなかったわけではないけれど、だいたいテレビ業界ってあんまり帰属意識がないからね。ディレクターでフリーの人はいっぱいいます。僕も契約する前はフリーでしたから。またフリーに戻るだけのことで。一般のサラリーマンが会社辞めるのとはちょっと感覚が違うかな。ただ、あちこち回りながら、これを発表したらテレビの世界で自分の居場所はないなと。それは感じましたね。恐怖というかあきらめというか。

――『A』はすごく情緒的な作品ですよね。

それは、僕の感情ですね。それを、『A』ではもう思いっきり全開にしようと思ったんです。

――それは撮ってるうちに？

撮ってるうちにですね。やっぱり自分でカメラ持ったことが大きい。カメラ持ってみて、客観なんてあり得ないと思った。テレビもそうなんですよ、あれも実は感情で作られているものなのに、それをどこかで客観的なものとして装ってる。であれば、最初からこれは主観ですよ、というのを画面にも刻み込みたい、と。

――『A』の中盤ぐらいで、撮影したテープを警察に届け出るかどうかを相談するシーンがありましたけど、撮影者である森さんがあそこでカメラのなかに登場して、そこからドキュメンタリーの雰囲気が変わり始めたような気がしたんです。

A Documentary is Written in the First Person

——Why did you begin filming with the camera yourself?

I began taking the camera into my own hands ever since "A," a documentary about the Aum Shinrikyo cult. When I direct TV programs, I operate in an "E.N.G." (Electronic News Gathering), which is just another name for a TV crew. It's a minimal unit that's comprised of people like a cameraman and a video engineer. In 1996, right around the time "A" was being filmed, a personal camera that could film in digital became available. The situation was, it was starting to turn out that "A" could not be aired on television contrary to the initial plan, so I decided that I would have to make it by myself. So, I rented the digital camera, and began handling the camera myself, learning how to use it along the way.

——By operating the camera yourself, has your work changed in any way?

Yes it has. My works have changed, and so have I. When you're directing something for TV, you let someone else handle the camera. Of course you give out directions to this cameraman, but it's still not you. The most important thing that I realized by operating the camera myself, is that camerawork is subjective. Zooming, panning, all those actions you can take with the camera are essentially emotional expressions. I can't believe I used to let someone else handle that for me. By holding the camera in my own hands, I was able to discover myself zooming into one thing and not another. I finally understood that it was a subjective process. We have this illusion that television is objective and neutral. So did I. But the truth is, it's false. Everybody creating movies already knows this. I was able to realize it only after inserting my own gaze through the finder scope.

——While you were in the filming process, did you have confidence that you would be able to present "A" somewhere outside of television?

Absolutely not. In the beginning, I just thought that if one station turned me down, I could go to the next. I went to meet people I knew in all of the stations, but every one of them turned me down. I was doing all this in parallel with the actual filming. I decided that my only option was independent film, just like I used to do in the past.

——Did you have any worries when leaving your company?

I can't say that I didn't have any at all, but in the television industry, people generally don't have so much sense of affiliation.

あの瞬間、映像を渡しても渡さなくても、どっちにしろ、作品は終わると思ったんです。渡せば、これはオウム擁護のレッテルが付くだろうし、渡さなければオウムとの関係性は終わっちゃう。じゃあ、どうすればいいのか。自分を被写体にするしかないな、と。テレビで、普通は、ドキュメンタリーに自分は出ちゃいけない。そういう不文律があるんですよ。自分も実際そう言われてきたし。絶対自分を出すなって。でも、あれが転機になりました。やむなく自分を被写体にしたことで。別に自分を出したっていいじゃん、と。

――テレビの世界で一人称を持つというのは難しいことなんですか？

難しいですね。というか、業界的にはやっちゃいけないことです。あと、徹底して分業なんです。音楽とかナレーションとかにしても、全部ディレクターとは別の人が担当する。編集が別の場合もあります。考えたらおかしいよね。音楽だって大事な演出のひとつの要素なのに、それを人任せにしちゃう。当たり前のようにね。テレビってそういうところありますよね、分業なんですよね。

――情緒には危険な部分もある意味あると思うのですけど。音楽にしても、世の中では誘導的な使われ方も多いですよね。

それを僕は否定しないです。プロパガンダですから、映像なんてものは。ただ、プロパガンダする主体を何にするかが問題だと思うんです。局とか会社とか民意とか政治とか、そういうものに依拠しちゃうことに僕はうなずけない。自分に依拠することが大事だと思う。簡単に言っちゃうと、ドキュメンタリーって、いろんな所を撮って、断片を寄せ集めて、自分の世界観を再構築するものなわけですよ。だから、『A』や『A2』は、事実の破片を素材に、「僕」が作った世界なんです。

変化しつつある世界

――森さんがそこまで、オウムに興味を持つ理由は？

やっぱり、あの事件で日本は大きく変わったと僕は思います。でもあの出来事自体は、どんどん風化してますからね。その流れに抗いたいと。変化が止まってればいいんだ

There are lots of freelance directors, and I was freelance too before I contracted. So it was nothing more than going freelance once again. It's a bit different from when a businessman quits his company. However, I did feel that if I ran around everywhere presenting this work, there wouldn't be a seat for me in the television industry. It was a feeling that was part fear, part resignation.

――I think "A" is a very emotional work.

Yes, those are my emotions. For "A," I made the choice to express them as much as possible.

――You made that decision while you were filming?

Yes, it was during the production process. Taking the camera into my own hands made a significant impact within me. I realized that objectivity was impossible. It's actually the same for TV as well. Those programs are created by emotions, but they subtly disguise it as being objective. So, for my film, I decided that I wanted to carve an expression of subjectivity into the screen right from the start, so that everyone would understand.

――Around the middle part of "A," there was a scene where you were discussing with the police about submitting tapes you filmed. You yourself entered into the scene for the first time, and it felt like the atmosphere of the film changed from that point on.

During that situation, I thought that whether I submitted the tapes or not, the work would be terminated either way. If I submitted them, the label of "Aum-supporter" would be placed on me, and if I did not, my relationship with Aum Shinrikyo would come to an end. So I was pondering about what I should do, and decided that the only choice for me was to become an object of the camera. Normally, in the world of television, you're not allowed to become part of the documentary. It's an unwritten rule, and it's what I was actually taught: that I could never appear on the camera. However, that one scene became the turning point for me. I made myself an object of the camera, thinking "why not?"

――So in the world of television, it's difficult to have a first-person perspective?

Yes, it is difficult. It's something the industry doesn't let you do. Also, the jobs are thoroughly divided. Whether it's music or narration, somebody other than the director handles all of these things. Even the editing is done by another person at times. It's strange if you think about it. Elements like music are an important part of the work, but you have to let someone else do it for you, as if it were a natural thing to do so. Television has that kind

けど、まだ続いてますからね。

——具体的に『変化』というのは？
セキュリティです。つまり、オウムによって不安とか恐怖みたいなものを強く刷り込まれて、その反動で、治安、身の安全を図りたいという流れができてきた。セキュリティ、つまり危機管理社会です。まあ安全を図ることはいいことなんですけど、その延長で統制が生まれてくる。だから、どんどん街に監視カメラがついて。人間ってそもそも、際限のない自由に耐えられないんです。怖くなっちゃう、自由であることが。で、もっと規制してほしいと。「ここから先はダメだよ」って標識があると、ここからこっちは安全だと同じですから。そこで人って安心できるんですよ。今、そういう社会になりつつある。この間の選挙でもそうですし、憲法も変わりそうですし。いろんなところに表れてきています。

——自民党がここまで圧勝するような時代になるとは全く思っていなかったですね。
そうだよね。でも、もっとすごいのが、一週間後の世論調査で「自民党がこんなに勝って不安だ」っていうのが7割強だったっていう。これはシンボリックですよ。じゃあ、誰が自民党に投票したんだって話です。だから、自分たちなんですよ、彼らを選んだのは。かつての日本にはファシズム国家の時期がありましたけど、ドイツ、イタリアと明確に違うのは、日本にはカリスマがいなかったんです。ドイツはヒットラーがいて、イタリアにはムッソリーニがいましたけど、日本にはいないんですよ。天皇や東条英機はカリスマとはちょっと違いますよね。日本の場合は何が求心力になったかといえば、民意です。みんなの意志なんです。つまり、デモクラシーなんですよ。デモクラシーが発動して全体主義になってしまった。日本はそんな、不思議な歴史を持つ国ですよ。それは、今についてもいえる。誰が悪いんだって、自分たちが悪いんです。そこに、気付いていない。

——作品を制作していて、日本の特殊性を感じることは多いですか？
特殊性というかね、たぶん全世界に同じことはあるんです。人間が持っている普遍的な部分だと思う。それが日本人は強い。そういう意味では、日本人は特殊なのかもしれないけど。特殊なんだけど、普遍的でもあるんですよ。まさしく9.11後のアメリカ

of inclination. The production process is divided.

A Changing World

——Why do you have so much interest in Aum Shinrikyo?
I think that Japan changed greatly because of that incident. However, the incident itself is being forgotten rapidly, and I intend to resist this trend. It wouldn't be a problem if the changes had stopped already, but they haven't, they're still continuing.

——Specifically, what kind of changes are you talking about?
Security. The subway sarin gas attacks have fiercely imprinted fear and anxiety into the minds of the Japanese. As a reaction, a trend has formed in which people desire more security and safety. It's basically a demand for a security management society. Of course, being safe is a good thing, but as an extension, regulation appears. This is why there are now so many surveillance cameras on the street. Human beings by nature cannot tolerate unlimited freedom. They become afraid of the fact that they are free. So they begin to request to be regulated. If there was a sign somewhere that had the words "do not go over to that side," it would be the same thing as saying that it's safe on this side, and that's when people can finally feel at ease. Right now, it's becoming this kind of society. The results of the recent election were a manifestation of this, and it even looks like our constitution is going to be altered. It's showing up in all kinds of places.

——I don't think anyone thought that it would suddenly become an age in which the Liberal Democratic Party wins by such a landslide.
Yeah. But what's even more unbelievable is that in a poll one week after the election, over 70% of the people said that they were worried about the LDP winning by such a wide margin. This is very symbolic situation. I mean, so then who is supposed to have voted for the LDP? It's themselves. Japan had a period of being a fascist state, but one thing that was different from Germany and Italy was that Japan had no central charismatic figure. Germany had Hitler, and Italy had Mussolini, but there was nobody like them in Japan. Emperor Hirohito and Hideki Tojo were not like them, they didn't carry the same kind of charisma. Instead, what became the centripetal force for Japan was public opinion. The will of the people. In other words, democracy. Democracy did its job, and somehow ended up becoming totalitarian. Japan is a country that has this kind of strange history. The same phenomenon is occurring today as well.

はそうなってきてます。それでも、たぶんアメリカはリカバリーするんですよ。みんなが自分勝手だから。日本の場合はね、なかなかリカバリーできない。いったんなってしまうと、周りと足並み揃えないといけないのかなとか、そういう意識が強いですからね。そうすると、どんどん違う方向に行っちゃってるのに、みんな内心変だなと思いながら、結局壁に当たるのか、崖から落ちるのか分からないけれど、そうなる。そういう歴史を繰り返していますからね、日本は。

カメラを通した人間関係

——森さんの作品は人間関係を重視されていますよね。カメラを回す前に事前に関係性をつくるといった準備をされていますけど、それは一般的なやり方なんですか？

よくドキュメンタリー撮る人は、人間関係が大事だって言うけど、人間関係良好じゃなくても、ドキュメンタリーは撮れるんですよ。原一男さんのドキュメンタリーなんかもそうだけどね。憎しみ合ってても、それはそれで撮れます。だから、必ずしも良好である必要はないと僕は思ってます。ただ、人間関係が険悪だと、単純に現場が、しんどいですけどね。

——カメラが存在しての人間関係というのは、どのような感じなんですか？

うーん、もちろん向こうは身構えますからね。撮る人、撮られる人によりますけど。僕はね、ちょっと挑発するんですよ。ちょっと怒らせる。で、人って面白いもので、怒りかけが一番素が見える。で、たまに距離を誤って、ほんとに怒らせてケンカになったりしますけど。

——実際に怒っちゃった場合はどうするんですか？

まあ、ケースバイケースで、修復できた場合もあれば、佐川一政という人を撮ったときは最後はケンカ別れで中断しちゃいました。

——ドキュメンタリーというのは、成立するか成立しないか、そこが難しい領域だなと思ったんです。ドキュメンタリーが作品として成立するというのはどういう点なんですか？

なんだろうね。直感だけど、ラストシーンが見えない場合は難しいかな。

——それは物語という意味ですか？

ドキュメンタリーもストーリーテリングですから、自分がエンディングをイメージできないとそれはちょっとやっぱり無理ですね。

——それを作りながら探していくという感じですか？

だいたい、そうですね。やはり、最初考えていたものとはだいたい変わっちゃいます。でも変わっちゃう分にはいいんだけど、分かんなくなっちゃったらダメですね。その分からなさを僕は信条にしているんだけれど、さすがにラストがないのはね。わけが分からなくなっちゃうからねえ。

——ラストが見える瞬間というのは、例えば

Who's to blame? Nobody but ourselves. We don't realize this.

The Camera and The Human Relationship

——Your works seem to place importance on human relationships. Before you start filming with the camera, you prepare by building a relationship with the person. Is this a common procedure?

People who make documentaries often say that a good human relationship is important, but in reality, you can make a documentary even if the relationship isn't a benign one. Kazuo Hara's films are a good example. Even if the filming side and the side being filmed despise each other, it's still going to be interesting in its own way. So I don't think that a good relationship is a necessity. The only problem is, if the relationships are conflictual, it's going to be a stressful environment during the filming.

——What are human relationships involving a camera like?

Well, it depends on the individual, but the person being filmed usually becomes tense. What I do is taunt them a bit, and make them feel a little annoyed. Human beings have interesting tendencies. They express their true selves the most when they're starting to become angry. But sometimes I misread the distance, and make them really angry, leading to a fight.

——What do you do when they actually get angry?

It's really case by case. Sometimes I can restore the relationship, but when I was filming a man called Issei Sagawa, production had to be suspended because we had a fight.

——If that happens, you can't make the film anymore?

No, I can't. For that film, I had a feeling that it wasn't going to develop into a solid work anyway, so I just thought, the hell with it. I didn't try so hard to restore the relationship.

——I have a feeling that the documentary is a genre in which there's only a thin line between being able to properly shape the work and not being able to.

Yeah, I guess so. This is just my intuition, but I think it's difficult if you don't have a vision of the final scene. A documentary is just a form of storytelling, so if you can't grasp a vision for the ending, it's going to be impossible to shape it into a solid work.

——Do you search for this vision in the midst of creating the work?

Yeah, most of the time. However, the final form of the ending usually ends up different from what I initially have in mind. There's no problem with this kind of changing, but

どういうときなんですか？　例えば『A』だったら。
やっぱり最後の電車の車窓です。あの時はあれが撮れて、ああ終わったって思えたんですよね。

——それを見越して、一緒について行ったんですか？
それは、ある程度はありましたね。たぶんこれで終わるんじゃないかなぁ、って。実際あの場でカメラを回しながら、ああ終われたなって思いましたけどね。

——それは自然とやってくるものなんですか、絵として？
親子の情愛というのは自分の中でのキーだったんですよね。それは荒木浩（オウム真理教の広報副部長、『A』の主人公）に何度も質問していたから、彼も「森さん撮りたいんだろうな」っていうのがあったから、行きませんかって声を掛けたと思うし。『A2』は、編集で終わらせました。分からなかった、終わりが。でも、『A3』があるからいいやと思って。

——『A3』の話はその時にはもうあったんですか？
要するにね、『A2』をふたつに分けたんですよ。だから使ってない素材がある。それは『A3』用にと思って。だから、それに加えて、もう少し追撮しようと思ってたんですけれど。本音言っちゃうと『A2』が不入りだったんです。それでショックでね。だから、『A3』という気分になれなくなっちゃって。

——じゃあ、『A3』制作の予定は、今のところない？
とりあえずはないですね。ただ、自分の中ではオウムについては3本撮りたいと思っていて。『A2』のラストは、to be continuedですからね。だから、いずれはやりたいと思ってるんですけど。

——森さんご自身は、どういう場所で表現していきたいというのはありますか、ドキュメンタリーなのか、映画なのか、テレビという世界なのか。
こういうジャンルがいいというのは、ほとんどないかな。どこでもいいのかもしれないですね。今は活字がメインです。だけど、ドキュメンタリーは撮りたいです。あとは、SFか恋愛映画を撮りたい。小説も書いてみたいです。

if it's a situation in which you "don't know" anymore, that's a big problem. When I make a film, I place value on the feeling of "not knowing," but the ending is a whole different matter, because "not knowing" how to end the film would lead to the whole work becoming one big perplexity.

——What it is like the moment you grasp a vision for the ending? For example, what was it like in "A"?
It was that final scene with the window of the train. As I was filming that scene at that actual location, A feeling that it was done emerged within me.

——Is it something that appears naturally? As an actual vision?
One of the key themes for me was the love between parent and child. Many times, I asked Hiroshi Araki (director of public relations for Aum Shinrikyo, and the protagonist of "A") questions concerning this theme. The reason he invited me to go with him was probably because he sensed that I would really want to film what would go on. For "A2," I had to construct an ending within the editing process, because I wasn't able to grasp a vision. I thought that it wasn't a big problem, since I was going to make "A3" anyway.

——It was already decided at the time that "A3" would be made as well?
Basically, I was planning to divide what I had for "A2" into two parts. So there was footage that I didn't use in "A2," and I was planning to use it for "A3." I thought I could tape some new footage as well, and put it all together into another sequel. However, to be honest, "A2" didn't attract much of an audience, and this was a big disappointment for me. So I couldn't motivate myself to start making "A3."

——So currently, there aren't any plans to make "A3"?
Not right now, but I want to make a trilogy of films about Aum. "A2" ends with a "to be continued" ending. So I intend to make a third film some time in the future.

——Do you have any preferences about the format in which you would like to be presenting your works? Whether documentaries, movies, or the world of television.
I don't have any preference of genre. I guess any kind of format is fine for me. Right now, writing is my main activity, but I do want to keep making documentaries. I also want to make a science fiction movie or a romance movie, and I want to try writing a novel as well.

映像作家 100人
クリエイティブ
ファイル

ARCHIVE OF
WORKS AND PROFILES OF
CREATORS

<u>001</u> ゼロスタジオ / 松川昌平
000STUDIO / SHOHEI MATSUKAWA

PROFILE
1974年金沢市生まれ。1998年、東京理科大学工学部建築学科卒業。1999年一級建築士事務所000studio主宰。個人をベースに活動しているデザイナーや、アーティストなどが同期（シンク）するためのプラットフォーム「Sync」の代表。2004年から、慶応義塾大学SFC環境情報学科非常勤講師。建築をベースとしながら、実空間と情報空間の連動をテーマに、映像をはじめ、さまざまなメディアを駆使しながら活動している。

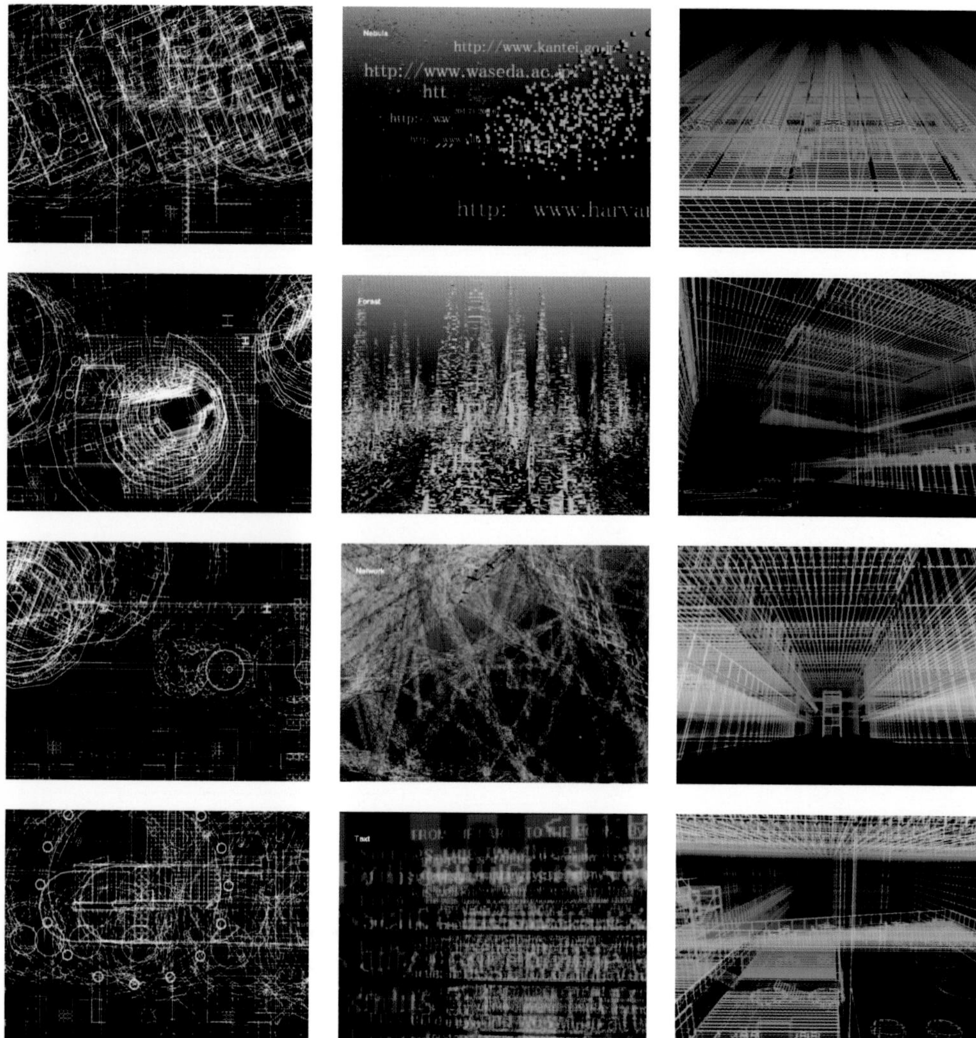

1　2　3

CATEGORY
Architecture

TEL / FAX
+81 (0) 3 5953 3575
—

E-MAIL
sho@000studio.com

URL
http://www.000studio.com/

TOOLS
PowerBook G4

Born in 1974 in Kanazawa, Japan. Graduated from Tokyo University of Science Department of Architecture. In 1999, Matsukawa founded the architecture office 000studio. He is also the representative of the collective "Sync." He has been a part-time lecturer at Keio University SFC Faculty of Environmental Information since 2004. Utilizing various media, with motion graphics playing a key role, he is creatively active with an underlying theme: the interaction between actual space and informational space.

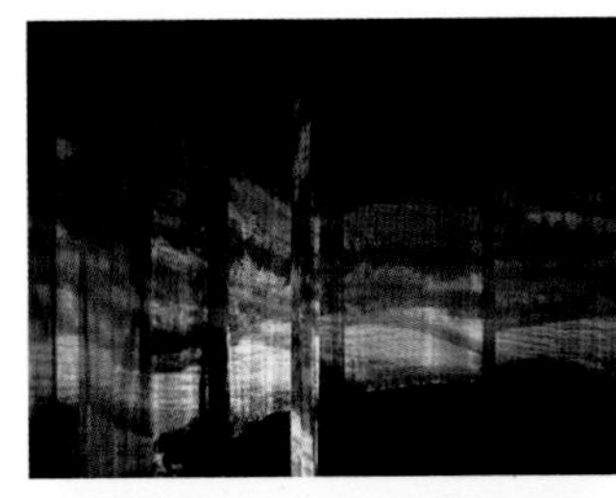

1
Exhibition - *Simulation* (Toyo Ito & Associates, Architects, 2000)
By 000studio and Ryoji Ikeda

2
Video Art - *GINGA* (Plannet Architectures, 1999)
By Plannet Architectures and 000studio

3
Exhibition - *Future University Hakodate* (RikenYamamoto & FIELD SHOP, 2000)
By 000studio and Daito Manabe

4
Exhibition - *NUNO* (NUNO Corporation, 2001)
By 000studio

5
Exhibition - *Simulation* (Toyo Ito & Associates, Architects, 2000)
By 000studio and Ryoji Ikeda

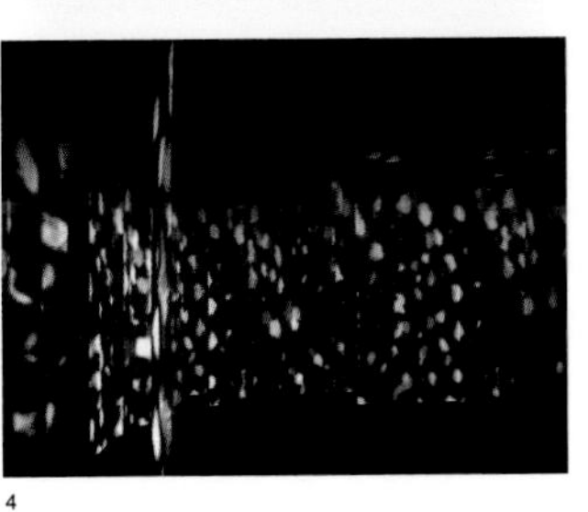

4

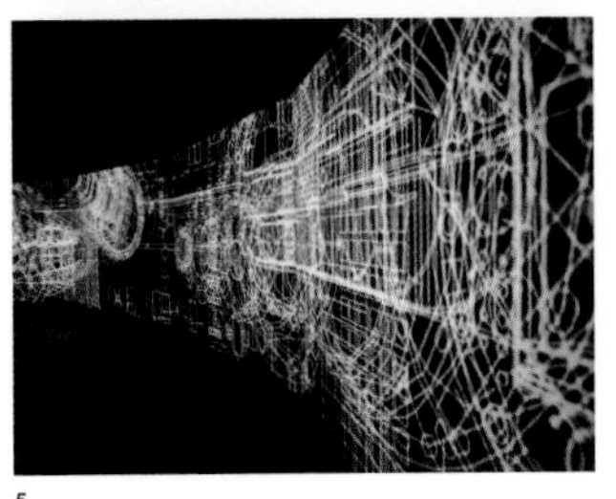

5

002 テンケイ / アウターリミッツ
10K / OUTERLIMITS Inc.

PROFILE

OUTERLIMITS Inc.のVJ。映像レーベル「STORY」主宰。90年代半ばに、生西康典、宇川直宏のVJに衝撃を受け、ソニーのビデオミキサー「XV-Z10000」を中古で購入するところからキャリアをスタート。2000年代に入り活動が本格化、感情を鷲掴みにするようなディープなパーティから、トラウマ級のエクストリームなライヴ、サイケデリックな持続音楽からドリーム・ミュージックまでと、ジャンル、形態を問わず、あらゆる現場に映像を提供している。

1　2

CATEGORY
VJ

TEL / FAX
+81 (0) 47 458 3615
—

E-MAIL
tokatsu_boyz@hotmail.com

URL
http://www.kinoco.com/mcsister/

TOOLS
Edirol V4 Video Mixer,
DVD Player, KAOSS PAD,
Sony Color Collector,
LD Player, VCR,
Sony Video Camera

The VJ of Outerlimits Inc.. Director of the film label "Story." 10K began his career by intuitively buying a second-hand Digital SEG XVZ-10000. His activities intensified after 2000. Whether he's at a deep party that grips your emotions, a live performance of trauma-level extremity, or surrounded by ever-sustaining sounds that take you to ecstasy, 10K provides visuals for any kind of situation, no matter the genre or form.

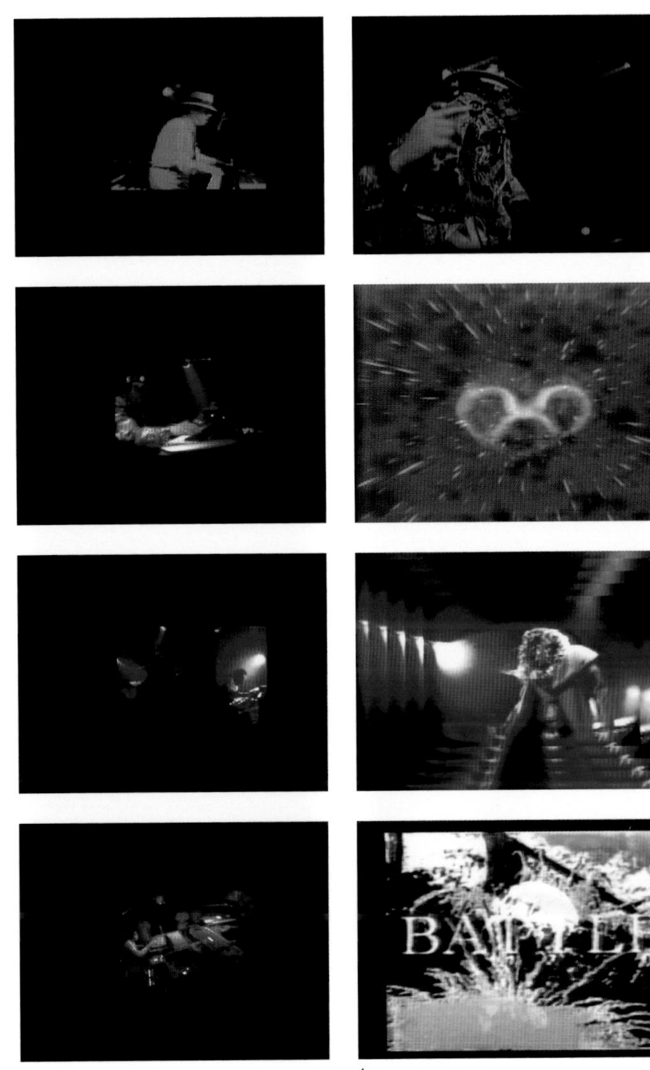

3

4

1
PV - ALTZ, *BOOGIE ALTZ* (時空 / LASTRUM CORPORATION, 2005)
Staring: BAKI3, YOSSY
Camera: kO-Op man

2
PV - FLYING RHYTHMS, *LIVE* (時空 / LASTRUM CORPORATION, 2004)
Camera: 高村弘次 Kouji Takamura (LASTRUM), 10K

3
NUDE JAZZ, *bonus live films* (Mary Joy Recordings, 2005)
Camera: kO-Op man
This movie collected in ALBUM "CYNODONTIA"

4
DVD - THE RAM: ΣLL:ZΣΣ, *GOTHIC FUTURISM* (Tri-Eight Recordings, 2005)
Camera: kO-Op man
This movie collected in DVD "Service Of Arms"

003 AC部
AC-BU

PROFILE
安達亨、安藤真、板倉俊介の3人が多摩美術大学在学中に結成した部活「AC部」。その濃厚でハイテンションなビジュアルを追求する創作活動がじわじわと注目され始め、大学卒業（2000年）後も活動を継続。NHK「デジタル・スタジアム」での年間グランプリ受賞を機に、テレビ、CM、PVなどで、メディアの隙間を狙って神出鬼没しながら活動の場を広げている。

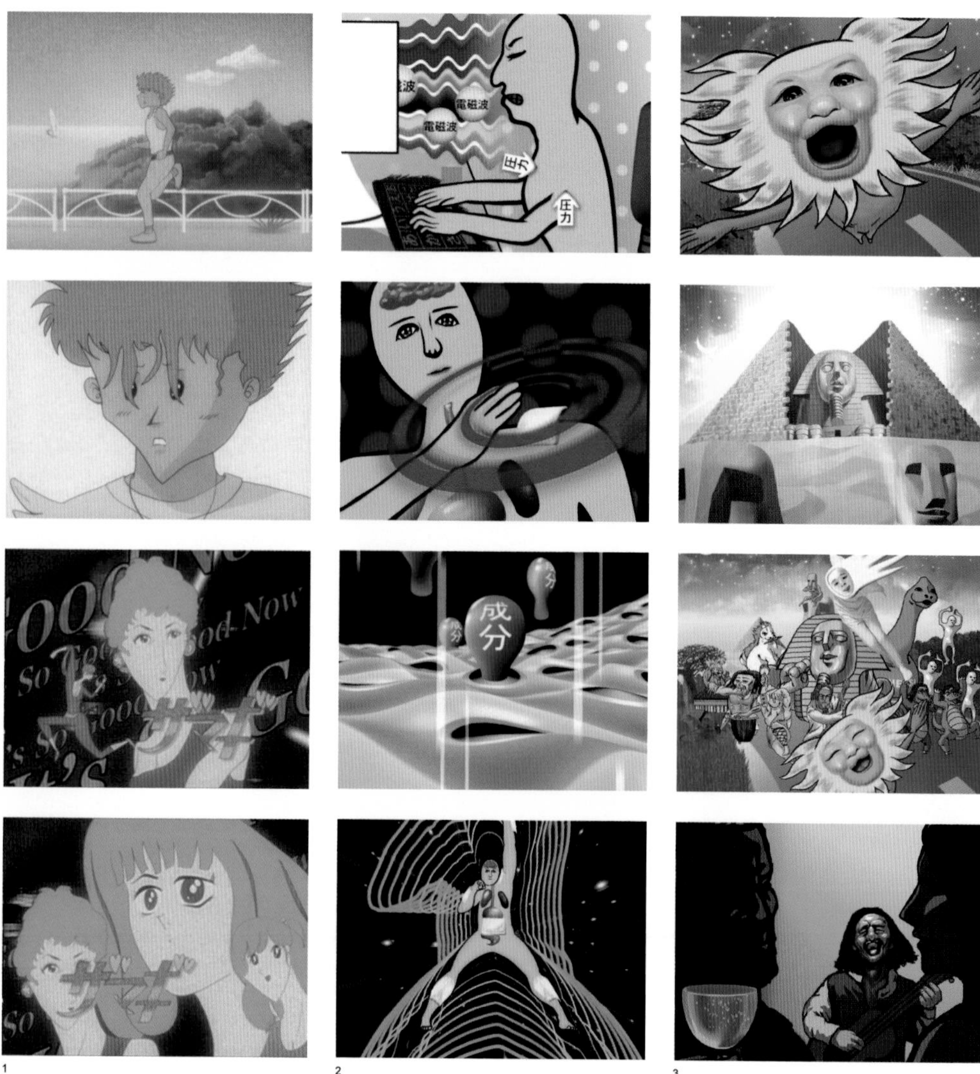

1

2

3

CONCEPT
ハイテンションで逃げ切る。

Hyperactiveness all the way.

CATEGORY
2D & 3D Animation

TEL / FAX
+81 (0) 42 481 8483

E-MAIL
info@ac-bu.info

URL
http://www.ac-bu.info

TOOLS
After Effects,
Photoshop,
Final Cut Pro,
Maya

AC-BU is a club that was originally created by Toru Adachi, Makoto Ando, and Shunsuke Itakura while they were attending Tama Art University. Their creative pursuit of dense and zealous visuals began to attract much attention, and the three members decided to continue the activities of the club even after they graduated in 1999. After being awarded the Yearly Grand-Prix of NHK's "Digital Stadium," they have been expanding their field of activity mainly in TV, commercials, and music videos, often making mysterious appearances in the niches of the media.

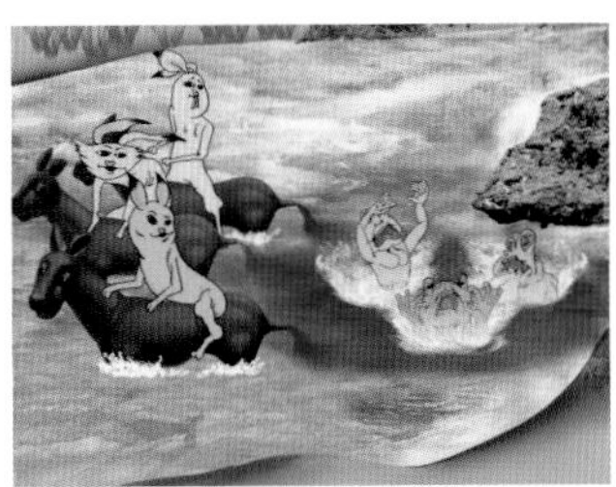

4

5

6

1 PV - ZAMAGI, 「い・そ・ぐ・な」 *It's So Good Now* (©R&C, 2005) Director: AC-BU, Music: ZAMAGI
2 PV - ZAMAGI, *Magical DEATH* (©R&C, 2004) Director: AC-BU, Music: ZAMAGI
3 Educational Song Video - Crocodile Papa, 「哲学するマントヒヒ」 *Tetsugaku Suru Mantohihi* (©NHK, 2003) Director: AC-BU, Music: Crocodile Papa
4 Short Animation - デジタルスタジアム Digital Stadium, 「鳥獣戯画~和風オリンピック〜」 *Choju GIGA*, (©NHK, 2003)
5 Short Animation - Sma STATION 「スマアニメ カッコいい男たち編」 *COOL GUYS* (©tv asahi, 2001)
6 Private Work - AC-BU, *Royal Dragon* (©AC-BU, 2003)

004 馬場 淳
ACCI BABA

PROFILE

1977年生まれ。鎌倉市出身。幼少時代より絵を描き始める。1985年に渡米、サンフランシスコへ移住。帰国後、慶応大学環境情報学部入学。2000年同大学卒業。イベントの映像演出、コマーシャル、ミュージックビデオを多数制作。2003年制作会社GH9を起業し現在に至る。近年は映画祭、国体などの大規模映像演出のほか、撮影用衣装の墨絵の描画や、短編アニメーションなどを手掛ける。Audio-Visualユニット、YAMABUSHI（http://www.yamabushi.com）の世界観構築・プレイヤーとして参加しており、国際的に発表を行い世界中から賞賛を得ている。

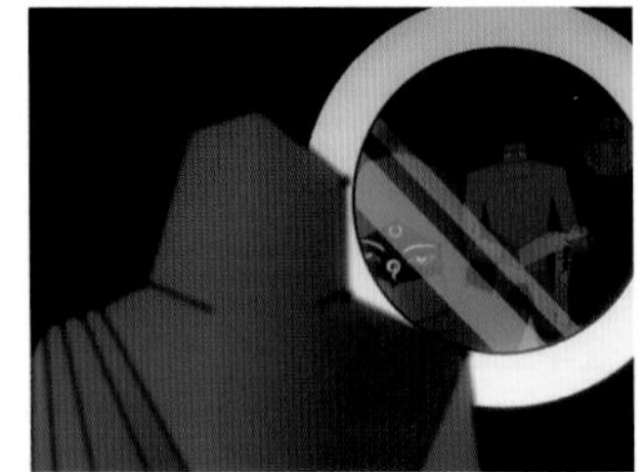

1

CONCEPT

森羅万象の「業」を具象化、ならびに「涅槃」の多面的な視覚化。アニメーション、実写、CGなどの技術手法は問わない。

The expression of “karma” which pervades the universe, and the multi-aspect visualization of “nirvana.” He does not limit himself to any particular technical methodology, whether animation, film, or CG.

CATEGORY
Animation, Program

TEL / FAX
+81 (0) 3 3493 1145
+81 (0) 3 3493 1145

E-MAIL
bishop@gh9.com

URL
http://www.gh9.com/accibaba

TOOLS
Brush and Japanese Paper,
Illustrator,
Photoshop,
After Effects,
Final Cut Pro

Born in 1977. Baba began drawing as a child. He moved to San Francisco in 1985, and after returning to Japan, he entered Keio University's Faculty of Environmental Information, which he graduated in 2000. He has produced motion graphics works for various events, commercials, and music videos. Recently, he has been involved in the production of large-scale motion graphic projects for film festivals and national sporting events, ink drawings for stage costumes, and short animation works. Baba participates in the audio-visual unit Yamabushi, whose works receive high acclaim around the globe.

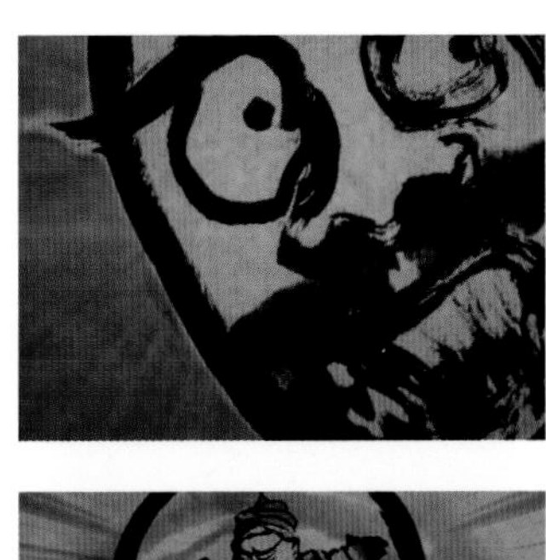

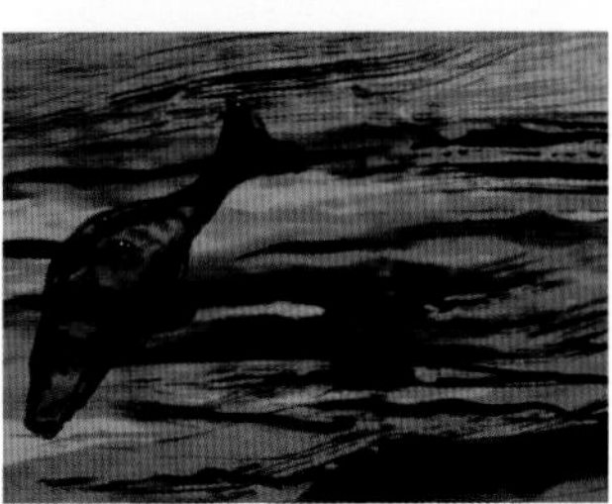

2

1
Original Work - *CORE*
(©GH9 Co.,Ltd., 2004-2005)

2
PV - ORANGER, *GOING UNDER*
(©GH9 Co.,Ltd. / Jackpine Social Club., 2003-2005)

005 アダプター ADAPTER

PROFILE
2003年、針谷建次郎を中心にデザイン集団ADAPTERを設立。スタイルをあえて固定しないグラフィックワークを基本に、アートディレクション、企画を展開中。また2003年よりヴィジュアルレーベル・NWBAの企画運営＆キュレーションを務め、2005年春からはヴィジュアルフリーマガジン「Public/image.」をスタート。2005年10月パリでSurface2Airがプロデュースする展示会「rendez-vous」に参加後、Surface2Airのショップで個展を開催した。

CONCEPT
常に新しい手法を試みる。

Always explore new methods.

CATEGORY
PV

TEL / FAX
+81 (0) 3 5779 7374
+81 (0) 3 5779 7374

E-MAIL
harigai@adapter.jp

URL
http://www.adapter.jp/

TOOLS
Photoshop,
After Effects,
Inferno

Born in 1977. Founded the design group Adapter in 2003. Harigai handles art direction and planning, with graphics of no determined style as his core activity. From 2003, he began to handle the planning, administration, and curation of the visual label NWBA, and in 2005, he started the free visual magazine Public/image.. In October of 2005, after participating in Rendez-vous, an exhibition produced by Surface2Air, he held a personal exhibition at Surface2Air's shop.

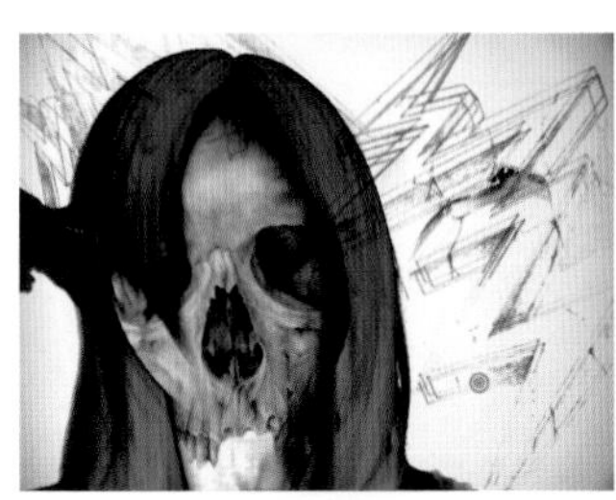

PV - Sachiko Mikami「相対形」*Soutaikei*
(©YAMAHA, 2005) Director: Kenjiro Harigai (ADAPTER),
Illustration: Manabu Honchu, Edit: KENEK JAPAN

006 エイジズ・ファイブ・アンド・アップ AGES5&UP

PROFILE
デザイナー・プログラマー。1997年ごろ活動開始。DIGITALOGUEにて、音を奏でるお絵描きソフト「PoPoRon」を発表し注目を集める。プログラム的な手法をベースにしながら、デジタルな玩具ともいうべきインタラクティブな作品の数々を制作。参加者のイマジネーションを掻き立てる独自のウィットを特徴とする。Webやi-modeスクリーン上でのインスタレーションなど、メディアを問わずに作品を発表しながら、インタラクティブな企業ロゴ、映像制作などを手掛けている。

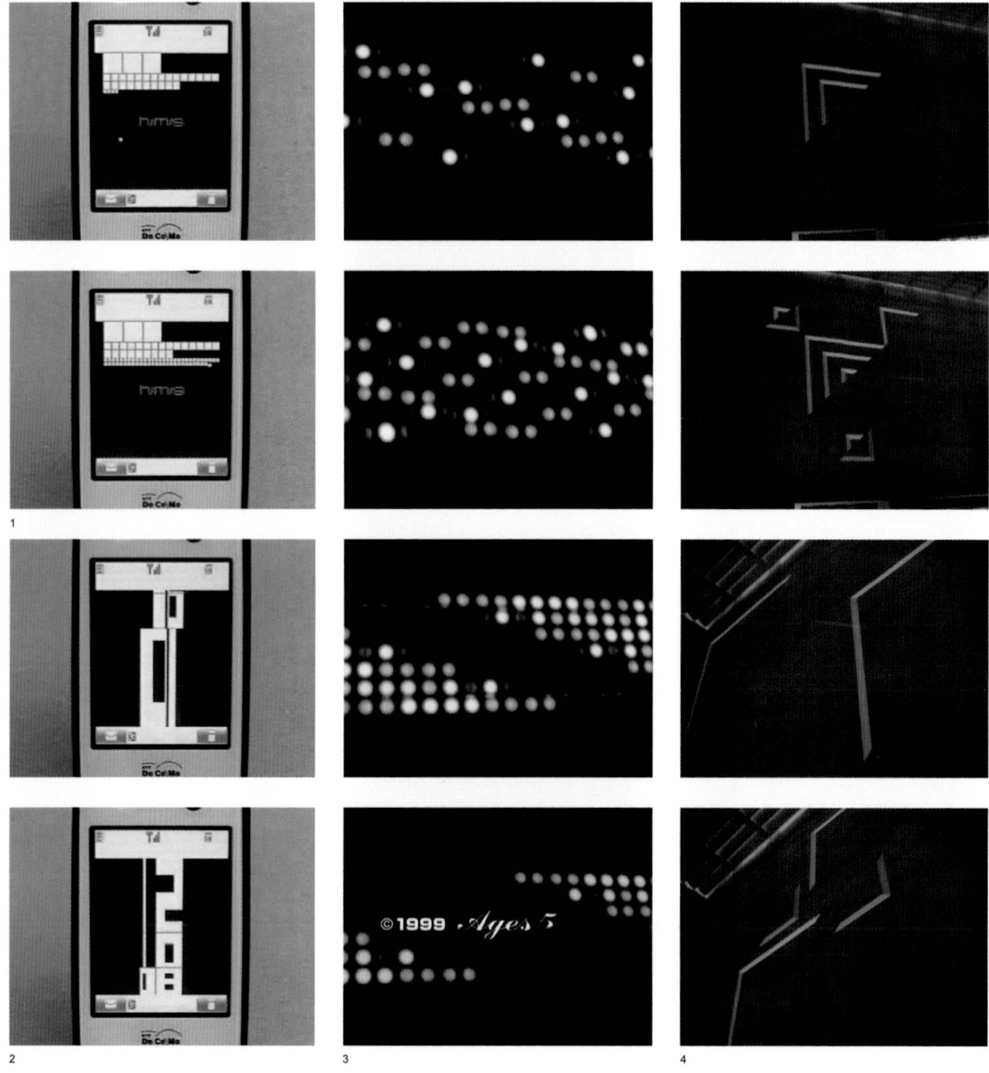

1
2
3
4

CONCEPT
知的玩具のようなひねりと分かりやすさと、対象年齢5歳以上を基本に作品を展開。

Develops works that have the understandability and novelty of a mind-toy, for ages 5 and up.

CATEGORY
Advertisement, Web

TEL / FAX
+81 (0) 3 5768 1893
+81 (0) 3 5768 1944

E-MAIL
mail@ages-five-and-up.com

URL
http://www.ages-five-and-up.com/

TOOLS
Proce55ing,
Director,
Flash,
After Effects,
Cubase

A design / programming project. They became active in 1997. Ages5&up attracted attention at Digitalogue, with thier release of "PoPoRon," a drawing software that plays musical notes. Using programming techniques, they produce many interactive digital toys, and thier works embody a certain wit that stimulates the user's imagination. They continually produce program-based works such as interactive corporate logos and motion graphics, for various media including the internet, i-mode, and on-screen installations.

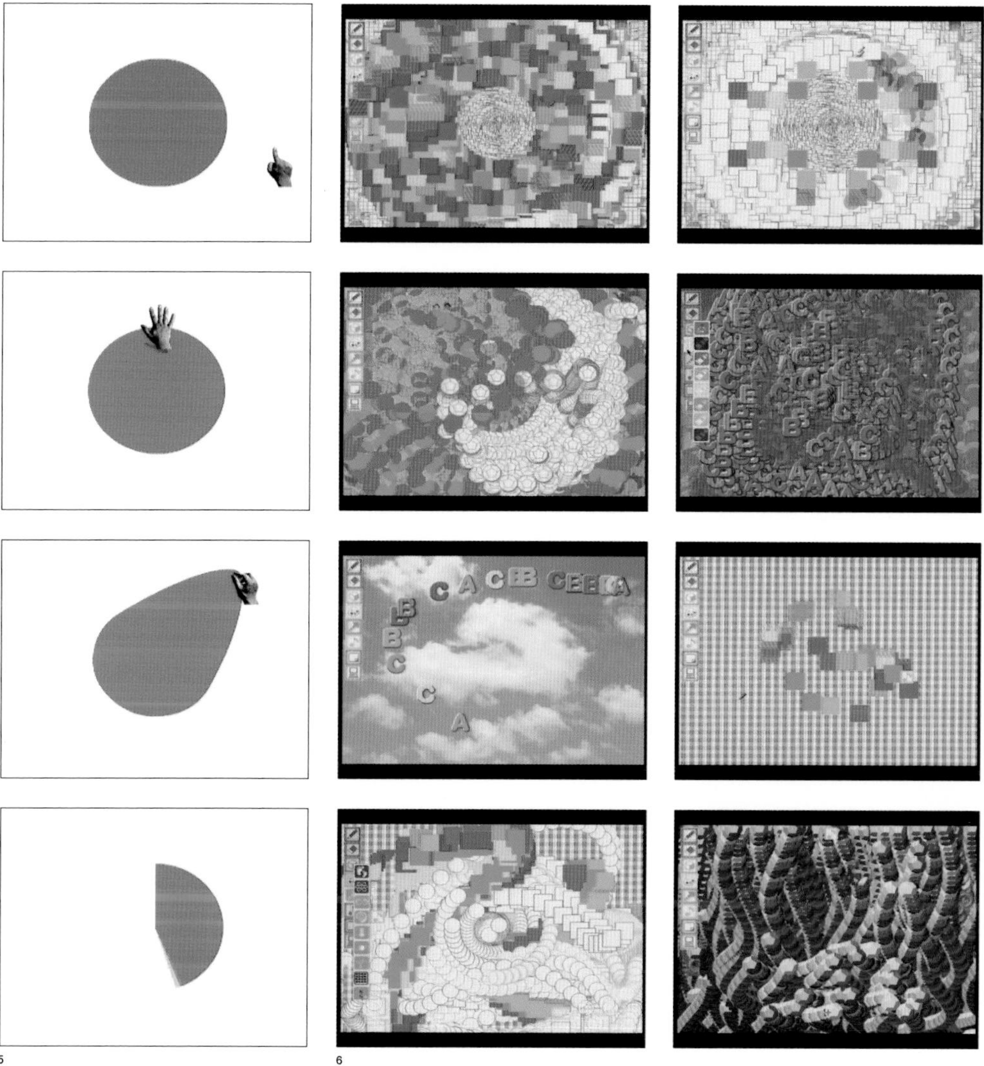

5

6

1 Aplication - *h/m/s* (Tachibana Hajime Design, 2001)
2 Aplication - *union_v* (Tachibana Hajime Design, 2001)
3 Video Art - *1999* (GASBOOK, 1999)
4 Instaration - *cell* (Mori Art Museum + TOHO CINEMAS Ltd., 2004)
5 VJ - *Japanese* (2004)
6 Aplication - *PoPoRon* (DIGITALOGUE, 1997)

007 亜妃子 AKIKO

PROFILE

1981年生まれ。漫画家である父の影響を受け、幼少のころより漫画やイラストレーションを描き始める。都立工芸高校グラフィックアーツ科に通いながら、現在の原点であるVJ活動や、挿画、フリーペーパーの制作を始める。2001年、桑沢デザイン研究所ビジュアルデザイン科入学。在学中に平面構成、色彩、Webデザインを学び、卒業後フリーデザイナーを経て、現在は制作会社にて音楽番組やWebコンテンツの映像制作を手掛けている。

1 5 2 6 3 7 4 8

CONCEPT

幻想的かつ陶酔感のある表現をもって、非日常のリアルを追求する。亜細亜の文化、女性の感性と神秘、人間と自然の調和が現在のテーマ。ものづくりの根本は影響しあいながら、共鳴していくこと。

CATEGORY
Video Art

TEL / FAX
090 7831 9324
+81 (0) 3 3855 6592

E-MAIL
akiko78@mac.com

URL
http://www.akikokika.jp/

TOOLS
Sony DCR-VX1000,
Power Mac G5,
After Effects,
Final Cut Pro

Born in 1981. Akiko began drawing manga and illustrations as a child, under the influence of her father who was a manga author. She drew illustrations, produced a free magazine, and was active as a VJ all while studying at Tokyo Metropolitan Kogei High School Department of Graphic Arts. In 2001, she entered Kuwasawa Design School Department of Visual Design. There, she studied plane composition, color, and web design. She became a freelance designer upon graduation, and now works at a production company, creating motion graphic works for music programs and websites.

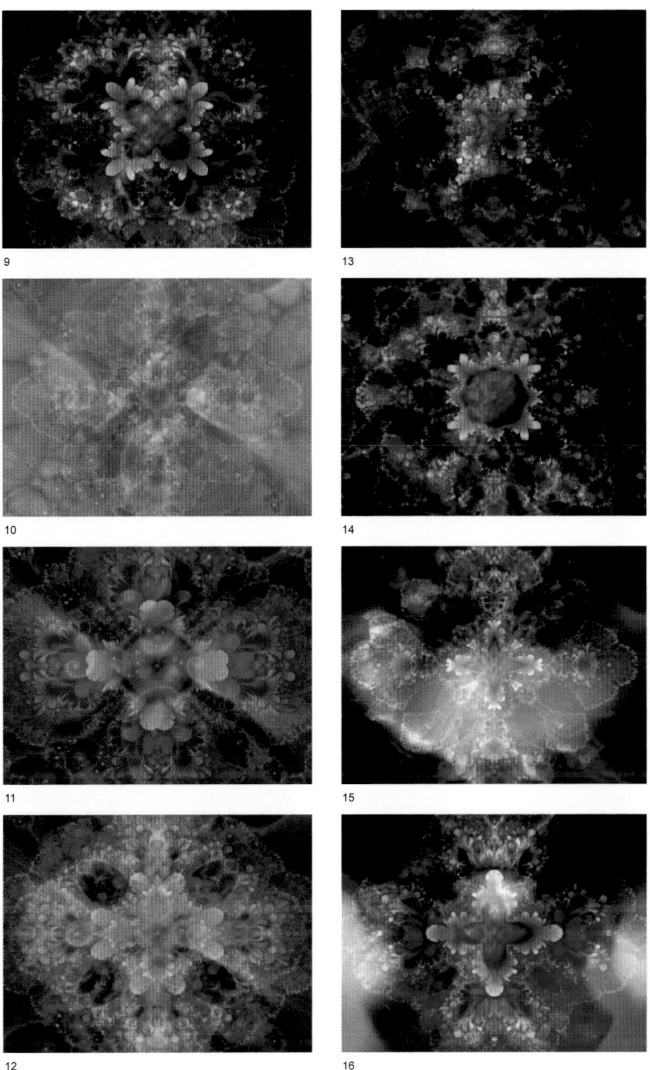

9 13 10 14 11 15 12 16

1-4
Video Art - *uminohana* (2004)

5-16
Video Art - *flower* (2004)

With an illusionistic and intoxicating style of expression, Akiko pursues the reality of the transcendental. Her themes are Asian culture, the sensibilities and spirituality of women, and the harmony of human beings and nature. The essence of her creative process lies in inter-influence and resonance.

008 手塚 敦 / フラヌール
ATSUSHI TEZUKA / FLANEUR

PROFILE

1969年長野県生まれ。美大入学を目指し上京するも、2浪の末に挫折。以後、独学にて今日に至る。その間、壁画や店舗内装を手掛けたり、ビデオアーティストのアシスタント、某劇団の舞台美術の職歴がある。そして、都内クラブでスライドショーやVJをしながら映像制作の道に進む。

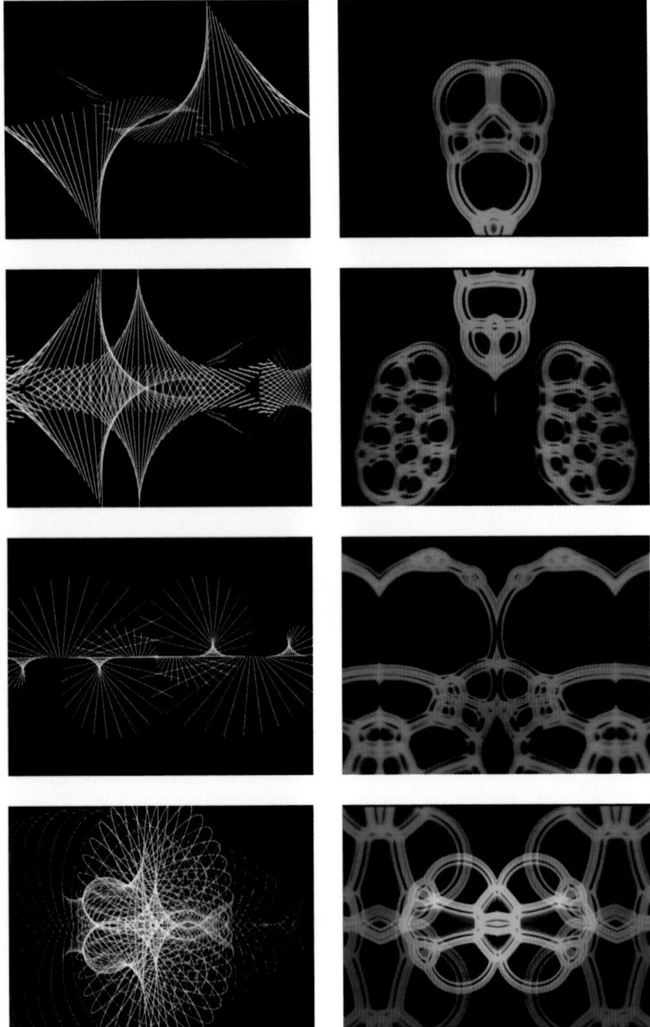

1　2

CONCEPT

Free Form. 計るものさしがないような、美しいものを作りたいと思ったりします。そして、写真を撮るのではなく、絵を描くように映像を描きたいと考えています。

Free form. To create beautiful things which cannot be measured by any ruler, and to create motion graphic works in a method more like painting than photography.

CATEGORY
CG Animation, PV

TEL / FAX
+81 (0) 3 3793 1488
+81 (0) 3 3793 1488

E-MAIL
flaneur555@yahoo.co.jp

URL
http://www.flaneur-studio.com

TOOLS
Windows, Mac,
DV Cam,
8mm Cam,
Illustrator,
Final Cut, Flash

Born on May 16, 1969, in Nagano Prefecture. Tezuka came to Tokyo in order to study at art school, but he gave up after being unaccepted two years in a row. He has been self-educating himself ever since. He has experienced various jobs such as mural painting, interior design, assistant to a video artist, and set design for a drama company. While he was doing slideshows and VJ sets at clubs in Tokyo, he got involved in motion graphic production.

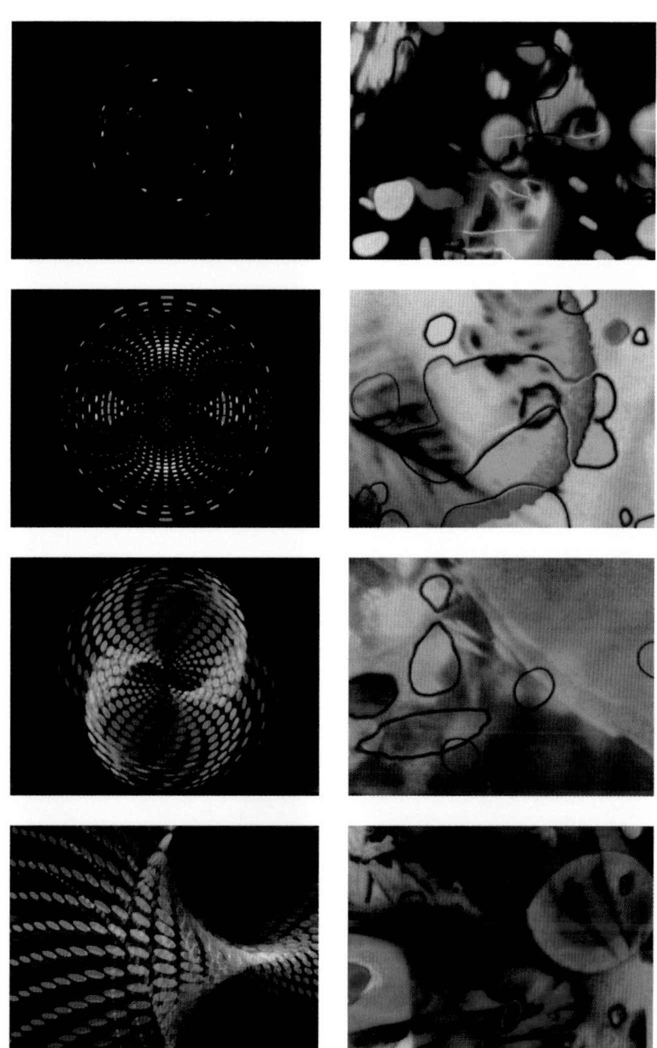

3

4

1
Study - *Stopping Time* (Atsushi Tezuka, 2001)

2
Study - *Bubbles* (Atsushi Tezuka, 2001)

3
Study - *Drop* (Atsushi Tezuka, Ueda, 1999)

4
Study - *Plant* (Atsushi Tezuka, Tora, 2000)

009 ベータランド
BetaLand

PROFILE

1998年8月アートフェスティバルBurningmanにて完全に覚醒＆結成、以来関西を拠点に全国350以上のパーティを創造するパーティフリークスVJ。V∞REDOMS、エゴラッピン、THE RAM:ΣLL:ZΣΣΣなどのライヴでもVJを務める。その活動は多岐に渡り、VJというスタンスを活かし、芸術的祝祭空間であるパーティ「FLOWER OF LIFE」を完全DIYでオーガナイズ。フライヤーや雑誌などでのグラフィックデザイン、味園ビル（大阪、千日前）の「MACAO」や「鶴の間」のような新しい形のパーティスペースのプロデュースにも大きく貢献している。2005年のBurningmanでは念願のVJを成功させた。

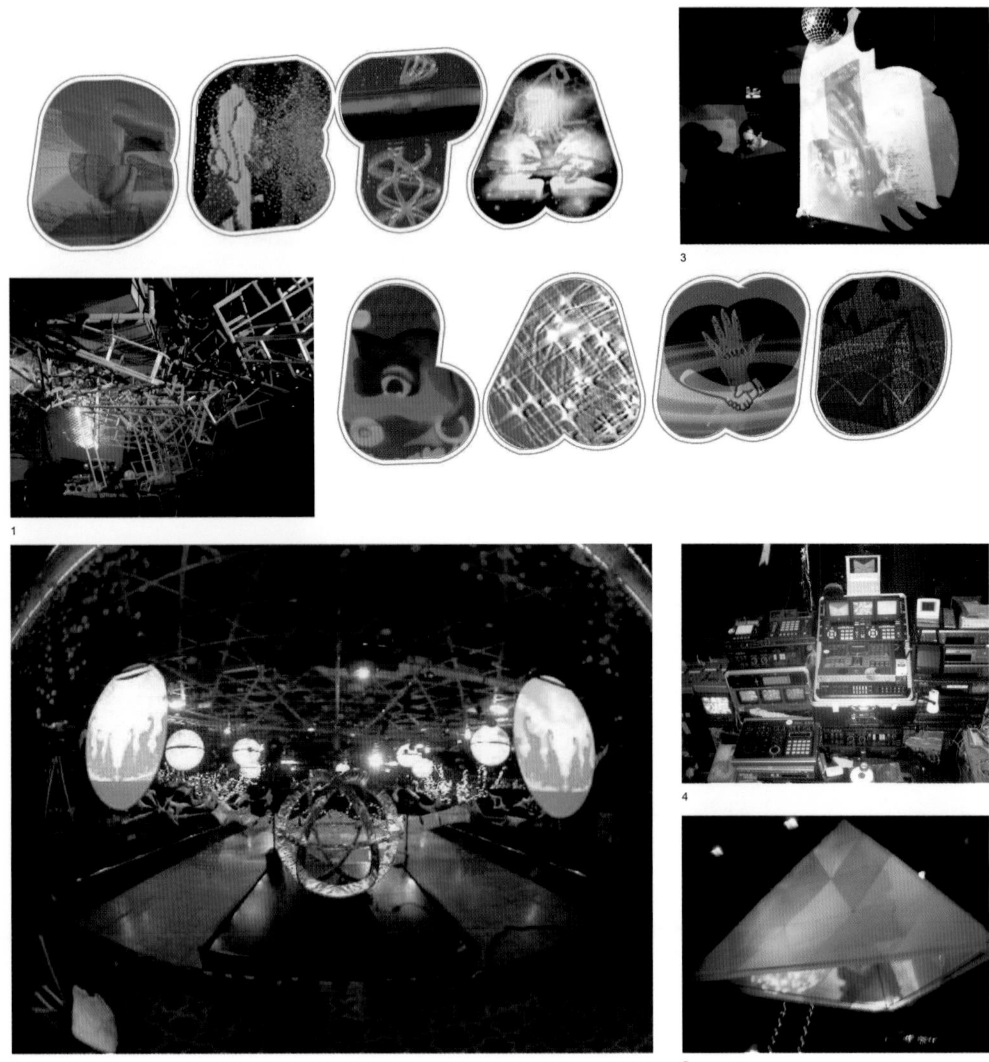

3

1

2

4

5

CONCEPT

音や空間そして人の形而上的なバイブレーションの表現、そしてVJプレイ中に思わぬ方行に遭遇してもそこで感覚を閉じず、その背後に隠れてるオラクルを受け入れミラクルに転じる。誰からも忘れ去られたり価値がないとされてるものに、独自の価値でポジティブエネルギーに昇華するリサイクルデリック感覚。

CATEGORY
VJ

TEL / FAX
—
—

E-MAIL
betaland@hotmail.com

URL
http://www.cwo.zaq.ne.jp/betaland/INDEX.html
http://www.flower-of-life.org

TOOLS
—

Betaland is VJ unit of party freaks, formed (and completely psyched out) at Burning Man in August 1998. Ever since, they have been creating sites of celebration at more than 350 parties, mainly in the Kansai area. They have VJed at the live performances of musicians such as Boredoms, Ego-Wrappin', and RAMM:ΣLL:ZΣΣ. They independently organize "Flower of Life," an artistic celebration event in which their stance as VJs is put into effect. In 2005, they were able to fulfill their desire by VJing at Burning Man.

1
VJ - *FLOWER OF LIFE presents EXTENDED*, MACAO (2004.01.11)

2
VJ - *FLOWER OF LIFE*, UNIVERSE (2002.12.31 - 2003.01.01)

3
VJ - *SUNFLOWER*, UNITED UNDERGROUND Tsuru no Ma (2004.04.17)
DJ: TERRETHAEMLITZ

4
VJ - *FLOWER OF LIFE VJ Booth*, MACAO (2005.09.23 - 24)

5
VJ - *FLOWER OF LIFE presents EXTENDED, pyramid screen*, Black Camber (2005.12.03)

6
Remix Movie - 「マインドゲーム」リミックス映像
MIND GAME Remix Movie (RENTRAK JAPAN CO.,LTD., 2004)

7
PV - *UFO ENCOUNTERS/BURNINGMAN '98&'99 feat AOA* (2000)

8
PV - OOIOO, *OPEN YOUR EYES, YOU CAN FLY* (2001)

9
DVD - RAMM-ELL-ZEE, *BATTLE STATION'S TARGETTING BATTLE STATIONS* (Tri-Eight, 2005)

10
CM - 「ニュースタイル・ハイ・キャバレー ユニバース」
New Style High Cabaret Universe (Misono, 2002)

11
PV - EGO WRAPPIN, *Manhole Syndrome* (TOY'S FACTORY, 2004)

12
Spot Played in Theater - EGO WRAPPIN, *Manhole Syndrome* (TOY'S FACTORY, 2004)

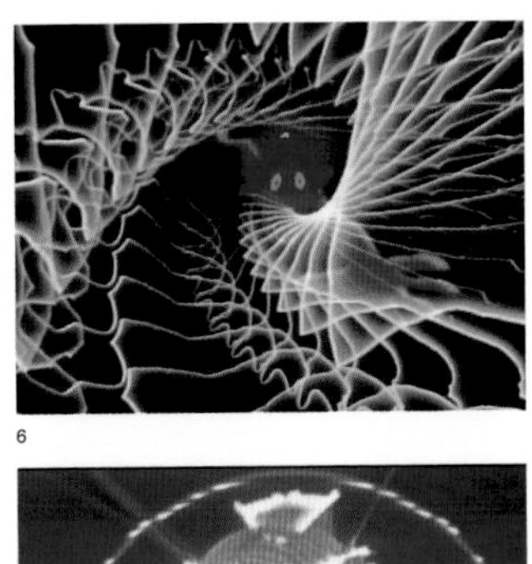
6

10

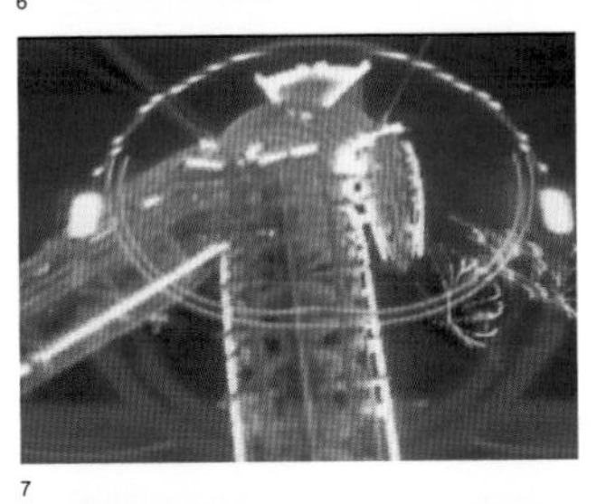
7

11

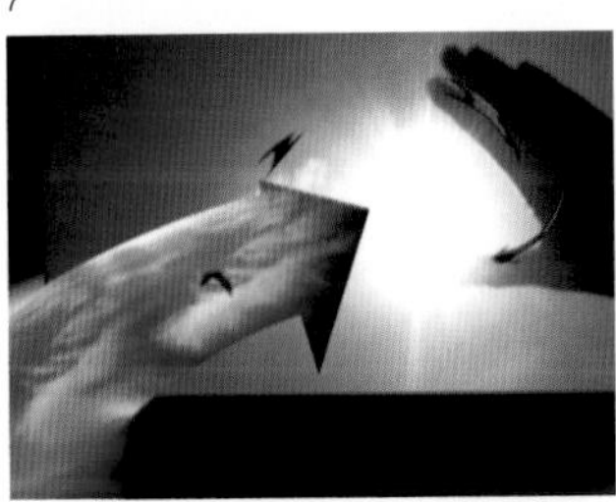
8

12

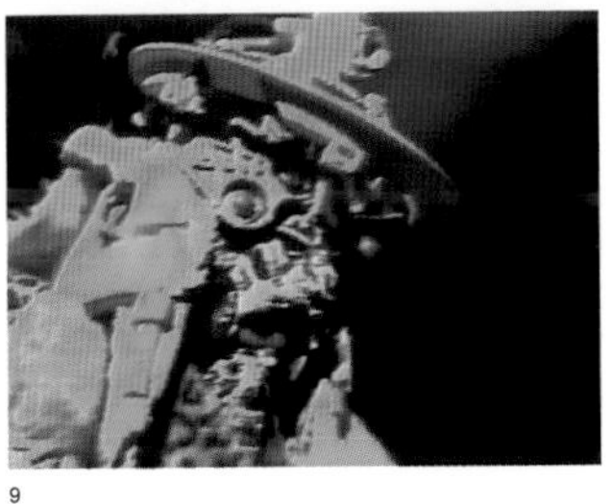
9

Through their visuals, Betaland expresses sound, space, and the metaphysical vibrations of people. Even if something unexpected happens during a VJ set, they don't close their senses, but accept the fate hidden in the background and turn the situation into a miracle. They have a "recychedelic" sense: through their own value system, they sublimate into positive energy those forgotten things that are believed to be valueless.

010

キャッチパルス
CATCHPULSE

PROFILE

1980年5月11日生まれ。zuinosinなどのPVを手掛ける。2005年からWEBTV (http://catchulse.tv/)をスタート。作品は、遊びの一部を切り取ることで自然と生まれる。制作の空間は、仲間が来たら自然と「精神と時の部屋」に早変わり。スキゾイドな現実にリアルタイムでエフェクト処理をし、切り取るスピードは「フラフラ」誌の編集に携わった一人としては異例のHighスピード。伸び縮みする睡眠時間は、本人ですら把握しきれていないほど。

1 5 9

2 6 10

3 7 11

4 8 12

CATEGORY
All Azimuths

TEL / FAX
—
—

E-MAIL
info@catchpulse.tv

URL
http://catchpulse.tv/

TOOLS
WinXP,
Photoshop,
Illustrator,
VEGAS,
LightWave, After Effects

Born in 1980. In 2005, he started a web TV stream (http://catchpulse.tv/). Catchpulse's works emerge naturally by clipping out parts of his recreation. When his friends arrive, he quickly turns into "The Room of Spirit and Time." The speed in which he cuts out and runs effects on his schizophrenic reality is extraordinarily fast for a man who has been involved in the editing of dizziness. His degree of dispersion, which even he himself is not fully aware of, manifests itself as stretches in sleeping time.

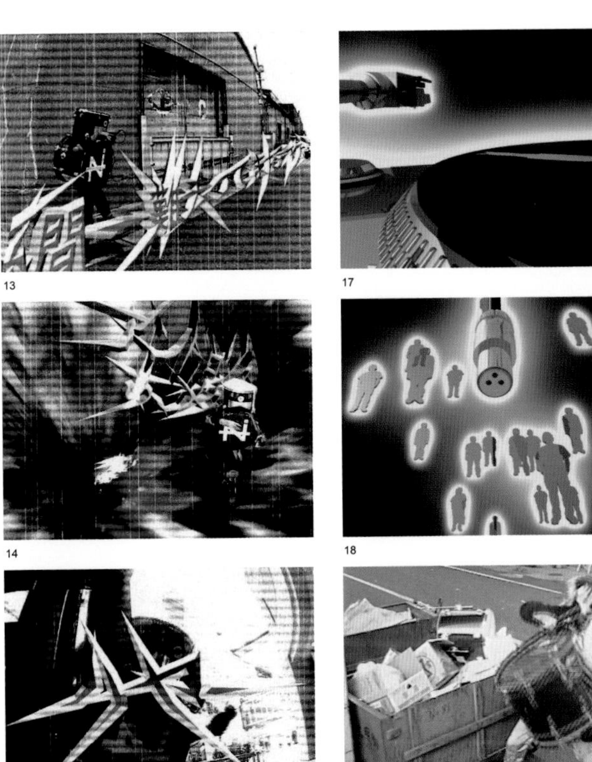

13 17 14 18 15 19 16 20

1-10
PV - *school oi (MUZIKHIZOMISSION ERSION)* (de-fragment, 2005)
By catchpulse, Tatuki Saito, cavilll (zuinosin) Artwork 土 babilll (ggow)

11-15
PV -「祭壇前最前列 2004 時ドラムスメーマン産まれる前」ZUINOSIN, *Saidanmae Saizenretsu 2004ji Drums Meiman Umarerumae* (2004)

16-20
PV - *100000000000000000PANIC!!!!!!! ZIGZAGMIX* (BRIDGE BOOKING, 2003)

011 キャビア CAVIAR

PROFILE

ディレクター２名、3DCG、2Dアニメーター３名、Flashアニメーター、スタイリストの計７名からなるクリエイティブチーム。NY ADC 銀賞。NYフェスファイナリスト3。文化庁メディア芸術祭優秀賞。ADC銅賞。RESFEST JAPAN オーディエンス・チョイス賞。RESFEST 2005 ワールドツアー参加など国際的活躍をみせる。

1　2　3

CONCEPT

Be FREE！　Be FRESH！

CATEGORY
CM, PV, TV, CG

TEL / FAX
+81 (0) 3 3791 9300
+81 (0) 3 3791 9310

E-MAIL
takeshi@caviar.ws

URL
http://www.caviar.ws

TOOLS
Mac, Windows,
3ds Max, Flash,
Final Cut Studio,
After Effects,
Photoshop, Illustrator

Caviar is a creative team composed of two directors, three 3DCG and 2D animators, one Flash animator, and a stylist. They have been awarded a NY ADC Silver Prize, an Excellence Prize at Japan Media Arts Festival, an ADC Bronze Prize, and an Audience's Choice Award at Resfest Japan. They have been three-time finalists at NY Festival, and have participated in Resfest 2005 World Tour.

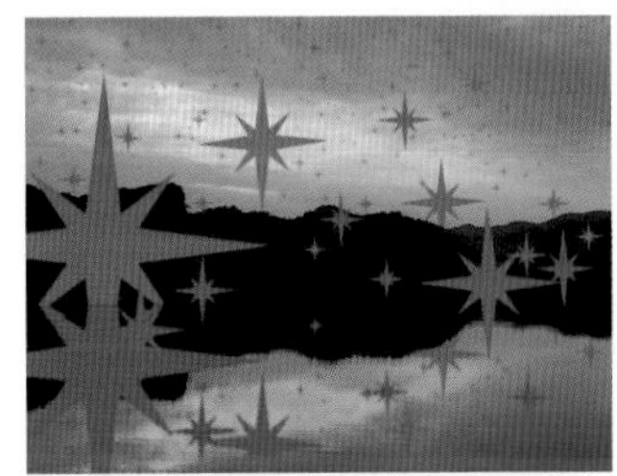

4

5

1
PV - YUKI, *JOY* (©Epic Record Japan Inc., 2005)

2
CM - *Visée Series* (©KOSÉ Corporation, 2005)

3
Promotion - *M5 Project* (US Coca-Cola, 2005)

4
Short Movie - *Ten Short Movies* (©Panasonic, 2005)

5
CM - *Freixenet* (©SUNTORY LIMITED., 2005)

<u>012</u> 松本 力 CHIKARA MATSUMOTO

PROFILE

1967年生まれ。1コマずつ手描きとビデオによるローテクのアニメーションを制作し、絵による映像表現を目指している。異ジャンルのアーティストとのコラボレーションも多く、ショーの演出のほか、演劇やダンス公演での上映など、幅広く活動。オルガノラウンジのライブにVJとして参加し、自身のアニメーションライブも継続して行っている。近年では、オリジナル映像装置「絵巻物マシーン」シリーズの展示や、商店街、学校、病院などで、同マシーンによるこどもたちとのワークショップを積極的に実施している。

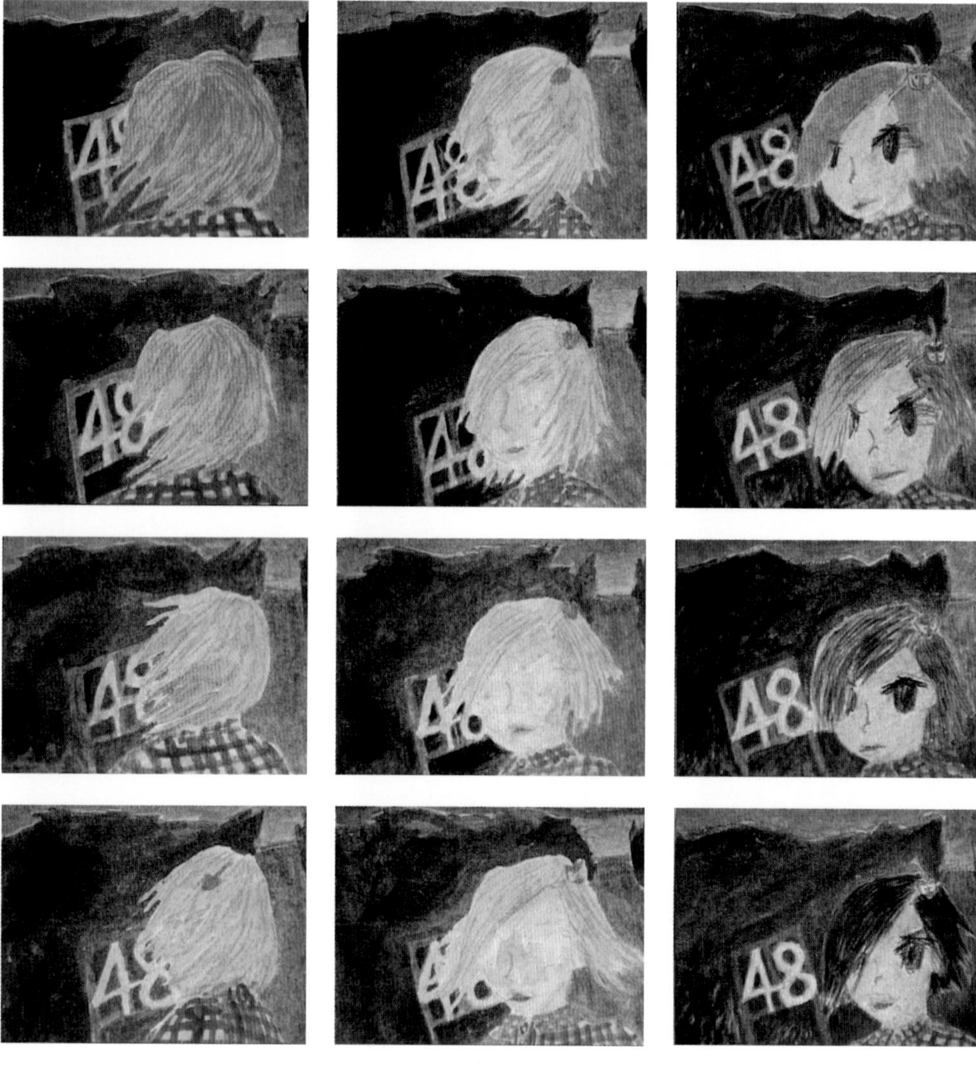

CONCEPT

目には見えないけれど大切なものや、たしかにあるものを観るために、手描きアニメーションという手法を用いて視覚化し、絵と絵の間にあるものを映像、または自作の映像装置「絵巻物マシーン」を用いて映し出す。

CATEGORY
Video Art

TEL / FAX
+81 (0) 3 3775 8430
+81 (0) 3 3775 8430

E-MAIL
teo_chikara@ybb.ne.jp

URL
http://www.takefloor.com

TOOLS
Fotovision FV-9,
Hi-Fi Stereo Video Cassette,
Recorder SR-5050,
Light Box,
PowerBook G4,
iMovie

Born in 1967. Matsumoto creates low-tech animation works using only hand-drawn frames and a video camera, and aims to produce motion image pieces composed of illustrations. He often does collaborative activities with artists of other fields, such as stage direction for shows, and screenings of his work at drama. Recently, he has been exhibiting a series of original visual devices, the "Emakimono Machine," in Japan and overseas. He has also been holding workshops for children, in which this machine is activated at various locations such as shopping districts, schools, and hospitals.

Video Art - 「48 のネオン」 *48 no neon* (2002)
Music "Cormworm" by Organ-o-rounge (Electronica)

Using the methodology of hand-drawn animation, in order to visualize those things which are significant but cannot be seen, those things which are certainly there.

Projecting those things that are in between drawings, using film and the original visual device "Emakimono Machine."

013 橋本大佑
DAISUKE HASHIMOTO

PROFILE

1977年生まれ。作画からアニメーション、ディレクションまでをトータルに行う、アニメーション作家・ディレクター。近年ではCMやOn Air Promotionなどの企画演出、CGアニメーションを主に活動。オリジナル映像作品「flowery」が2005年文化庁メディア芸術祭アニメーション部門優秀賞を受賞したほか、世界最大のデジタル映像フェスティバルonedotzeroやRESFEST、エジンバラ国際映画祭などにて招待上映された。

1

2

CONCEPT

毒々しいけど美しい、気持ち悪いけどかわいい、などのギャップがあるようなものを作ること。

To create works that involve opposing factors, such as unpleasant yet beautiful, or disgusting yet cute.

CATEGORY
Animation, Illustration, Live action, Motion Graphics

TEL / FAX
+81 (0) 3 5785 1780
+81 (0) 3 5785 1784

E-MAIL
post@picsco.net

URL
http://www.picsco.net

TOOLS
After Effects,
Illustrator,
Photoshop

Born in 1977. Hashimoto is an animation author and director who handles everything from the drawings to the animations and direction. Recently, he has been doing planning and direction for TV commercials and on-air promotion, and working on CG animation works. His original motion graphic work "Flowery" won an Excellence Award in the Animation Division of 2005 Japan Media Arts Festival, and was invited for screening at the world's foremost digital film festivals, Onedotzero and Resfest.

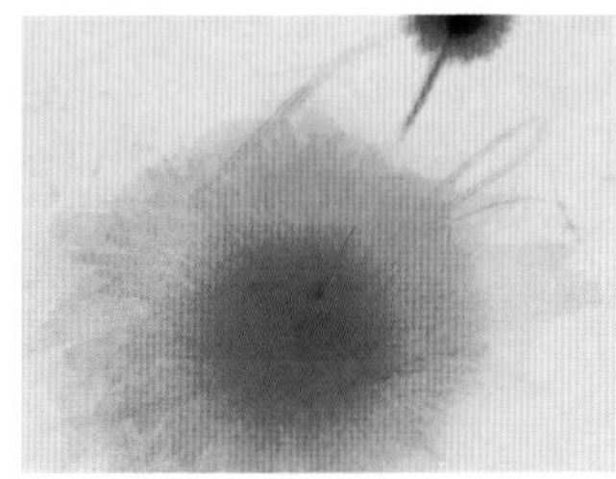

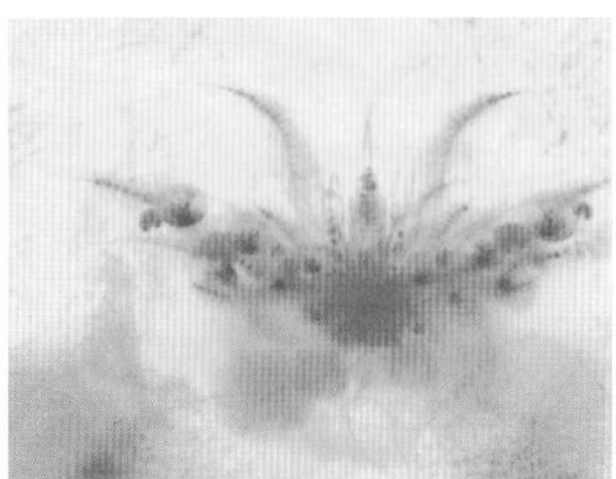

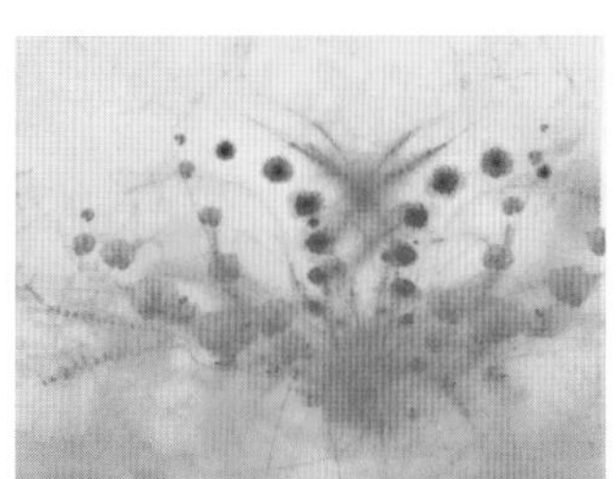

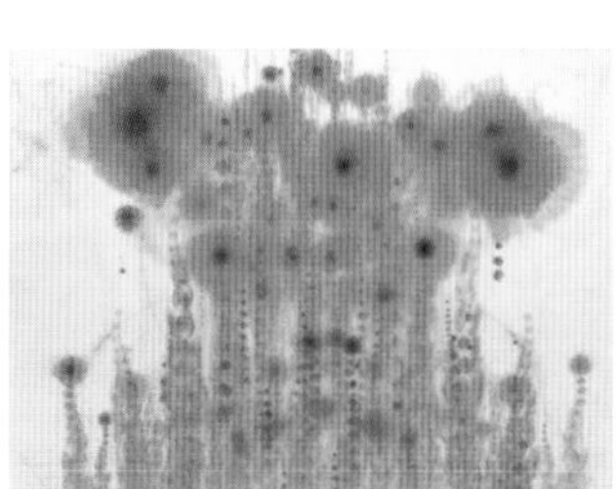

3

4

1
CM - ロッテ 小梅ちゃん「花の池篇」
LOTTE Koumechan, *Hananoike* (LOTTE, 2003)
Director + Animation: 橋本大佑 Daisuke Hashimoto
Producer: 寺井弘典 Hironori Terai
Productoin by P.I.C.S.

2
Station-ID - LaLaTV Station-ID「イメージ篇」（ジュピター・プログラミング, 2003）
LaLaTV Station-ID, *Image* (Jupiter Programming, 2003)
Director + Animation: 橋本大佑 Daisuke Hashimoto
Producer: 松居秀之 Hideyuki Matsui
Production by P.I.C.S.+WOW

3
Original Work - *flowery*
Director + Animation + Music: 橋本大佑 Daisuke Hashimoto
(©Daisuke Hashimoto)
2005年文化庁メディア芸術祭アニメーション部門 優秀賞受賞作品

4
Original Work - *respiration*
Director + Animation + Music: 橋本大佑 Daisuke Hashimoto
(©Daisuke Hashimoto)

<u>014</u>

北山大介 / オレンジ フィルムス
DAISUKE KITAYAMA / ORANGE FILMS

PROFILE
1975年兵庫県神戸市生まれ。1995年アニメーションスタッフルーム入社。1999年同社退社。1999年HELP! designにて映像部門HELP! films設立。2001年HELP!より映像部門を独立させorange filmsとしてスタート。

1　2　3

CONCEPT
Do It Yourself.

CATEGORY
PV, VJ, Station ID, DVD Contents

TEL / FAX
+81 (0) 3 3463 5596
—

E-MAIL
orange-films@nifty.com

URL
—

TOOLS
Final Cut Pro,
After Effects,
Illustrator,
Photoshop,
LightWave 3D

Born in 1975, in Kobe, Japan. Kitayama joined Animation Staff Room Corp. in 1995. He withdrew in 1999, and founded HELP! Films as a section of HELP! Design. In 2001, the film section went independent from HELP! Design, and became Orange Films.

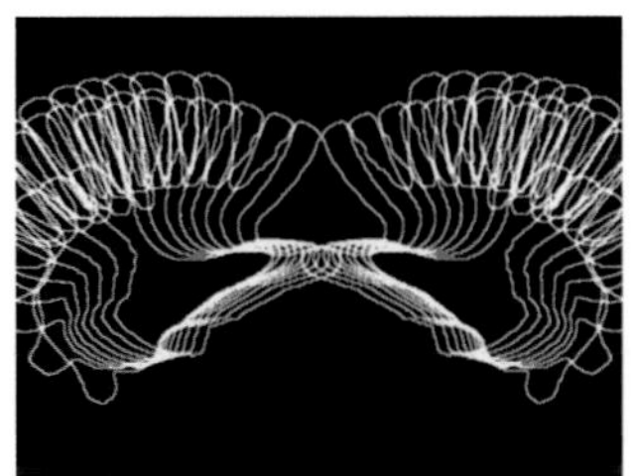

4

5

1
PV - HARCO, *Night Hike* (©Coa Records, 2005)

2
Openig Movie - *Foot!* (©J SPORTS Broadcasting Corporation, 2005)

3 PV - ANA「血湧き肉踊る」*Chiwaki Niku Odoru* (©compactsounds, 2005)

4 PV - STRAIGHTENER, *Against The Wall* (©TOSHIBA-EMI LIMITED, 2005)

5 PV - Cornelius, *Smoke* (©felicity + Polystar, 2003)

015 島田大介 / 四つ葉加工房
DAISUKE SHIMADA / YOTSUBA KAKOUBOU

PROFILE

1974年生まれ。京都芸術短期大学映像科卒業。在学中、日本の実験映像の第一人者である松本俊夫、伊藤高志に実験映像を学ぶ。卒業後、ロンドンとフランスに遊学し、なぜか現地でファッションモデルに転身し、パリコレ、CM、PVに出演する。その時に出会った写真家Jean-Baptiste Mondinoや映画監督Tarsem Singhの物作りに圧倒され、再び映像制作に目覚める。帰国後、谷田一郎のアシスタントディレクターを経て、2002年に独立。

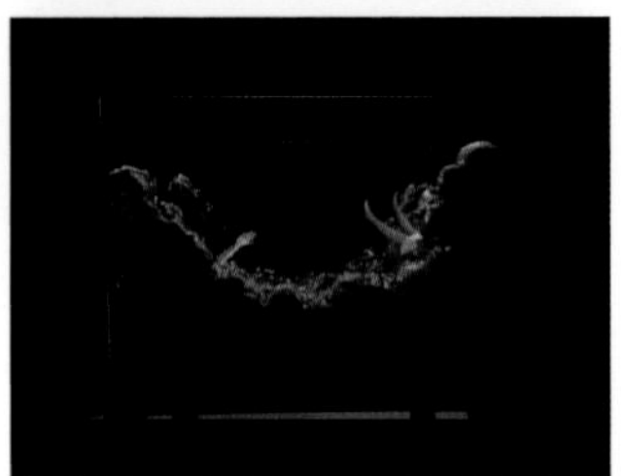

1

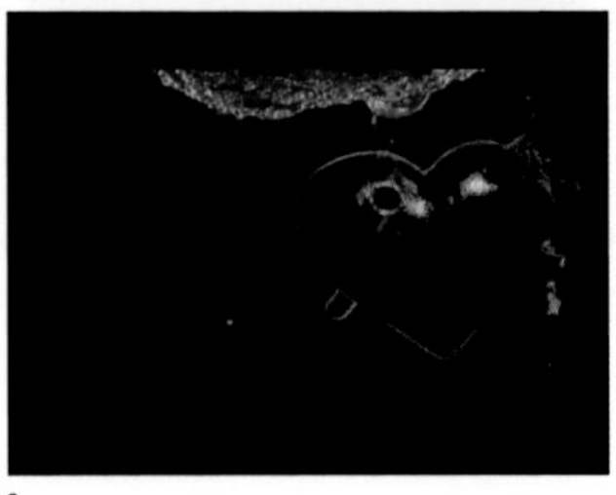

2

CONCEPT

幼少時代の記憶を再現すること。人間の内面や潜在意識の世界を表現すること。そのために、高度な技術を使った場合でも、あえてアナログ感を演出する。

To reproduce childhood memories, and to express the internal and subconscious realm of human beings. To do this, he creates an analog-feel even if using advanced technologies.

1
PV - Great Adventure, *ANY PLACE ROCKS*
(RESERVOIR RECORDS, 2005)
Producer: Masashi Watanabe
Director: Daisuke Shimada
Camera: Isao Okudaira
CG: Daisuke Honda
EED: Yoshitaka Sakaue
PM: Satoshi Arikawa
Production: MAZRI

2
PV - Kaera Kimura, *BEAT*
(COLUMBIA MUSIC ENTERTAINMENT, 2005)
Producer: Takashi Sugai
Camera: Susumu Takata
CG: Daisuke Honda
Light: Shinichi Hieda
Art: Mineko Yoneda
ST: Haruhisa Shirayama
H&M: Mihoko Fujiwara
EED: Shotaro Kamogawa
PM: Yuuki Minakami
Production: GUADELOUPE

CATEGORY
PV, CG, VJ

TEL / FAX
+81 (0) 3 3401 4578
+81 (0) 3 3358 3438

E-MAIL
info@qotori.com

URL
http://www.qotori.com/

TOOLS
Final Cut,
After Effects,
Shake,
Combustion

Born in 1974. Graduated from Kyoto Junior College of Art, Department of Film. There, Shimada was taught by Toshio Matsumoto and Takashi Ito, both pioneers of Japanese experimental film. After graduating, he studied in London and France, where he became a fashion model, and was featured in commercials, music videos, and the Paris Collection. During these experiences, he received much creative stimulation, and began working on motion graphics once again. After returning to Japan, he worked as an assistant director to Ichiro Tanida, and became independent in 2002.

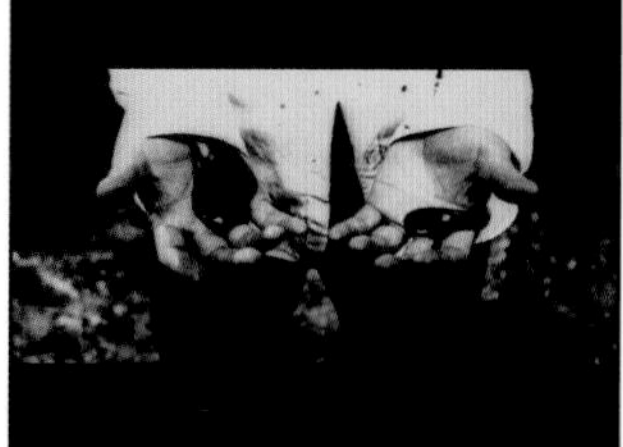

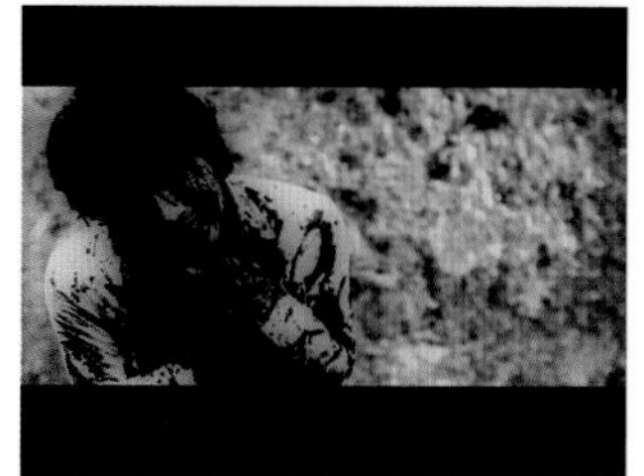

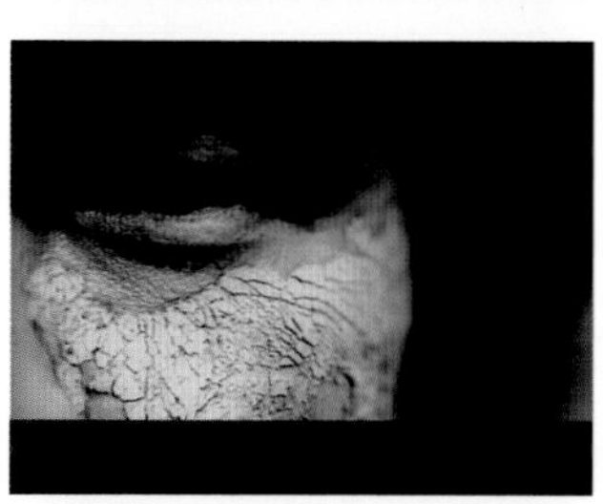

3

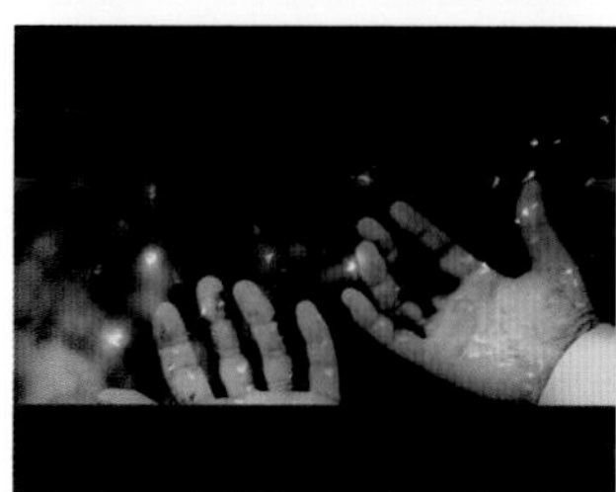

4

3
PV - Noriyuki Makihara, *traveling*
(Capitol Music Co., 2005)
Producer: Fumiyuki Yanaka
Director: Daisuke Shimada
CG: Yotsuba Kakoubou
PM: Akitoshi Yamada
Production: MAZRI

4
PV - Mr.Children, *Tenohira* (TOY'S FACTORY, 2003)
Producer: Masashi Watanabe
Director: Daisuke Shimada
Camera: Yuichiro Otsuka
Light: Keizo Ichimei
Styling: Tatsushi Sakai
H&M: Ayano Hashimoto
CG: Masaaki Tanabe
EED: Shotaro Kamogawa
Production: MAZRI

016 デラウエア DELAWARE

PROFILE

デザインを音楽する、音楽をデザインするスーパーソニックな4人組。NYのP.S.1/MoMAで展覧会&ライブ（2001年）、バルセロナのRASギャラリーで個展（2004年）、パリ・ポンピドーで開かれた「D-Day」（2005年）、そのほか、海外のカンファレンスや展覧会にも数多く参加している。これまでに音楽CDを6枚リリース。2004年夏、単行本「Designin'_in_the_rain」をバルセロナの出版社ACTARより刊行。横スクロールでおなじみのホームページ「FREEware/DELAware」は更新され続ける未完の作品。

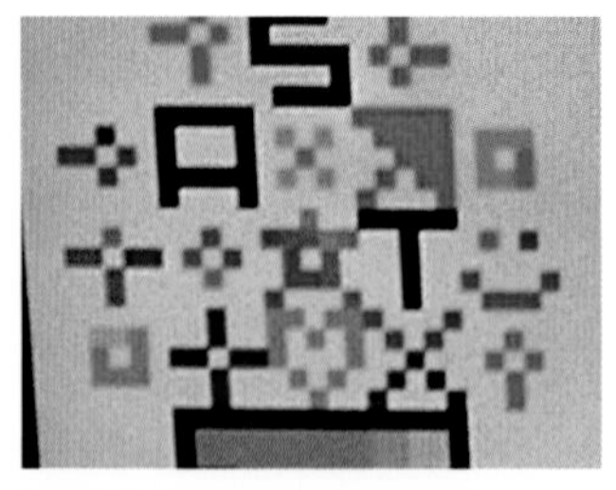

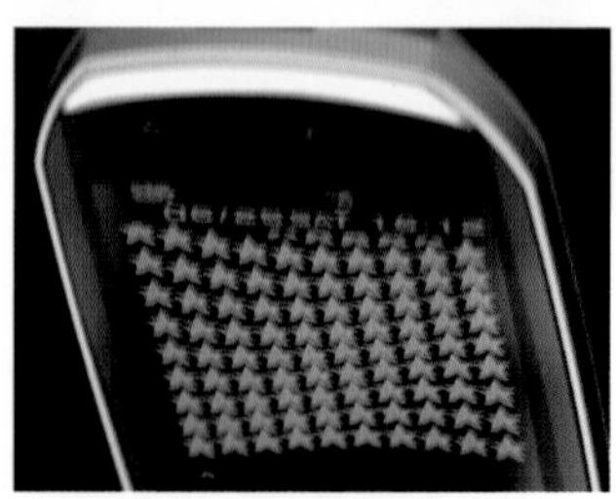

1

2

CONCEPT

Simple & Effective。一生懸命さぼる。

Simple & Effective.
Make a hard effort to play truant from work.

CATEGORY
Sound & Vision

TEL / FAX
+81 (0) 3 3409 4944
+81 (0) 3 3409 4944

E-MAIL
mail@delaware.gr.jp

URL
http://www.delaware.gr.jp

TOOLS
Director 5.0J,
GifBuilder,
Photoshop,
Simple Text,
Jedit, Sound Edit

A supersonic quartet that designs rocks and rocks designs. Delaware has participated in many exhibitions and conferences around the world, including exhibitions and live performances at New York's P.S.1 and MoMA (2001), A personal exhibition at RAS Gallery in Barcelona (2004), and "D-Day," held at Centre Pompidou in Paris (2005). They have released 6 music CDs so far. In Summer of 2004, Delaware released the publication "Designin'_in_the_rain" from the Barcelona publishing company Actar. Their side-scrolling website "FREEware/DELAware" is an uncompleted portfolio that is constantly being updated.

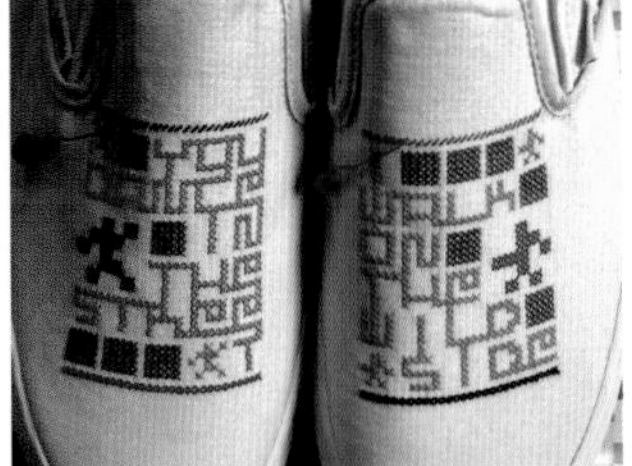

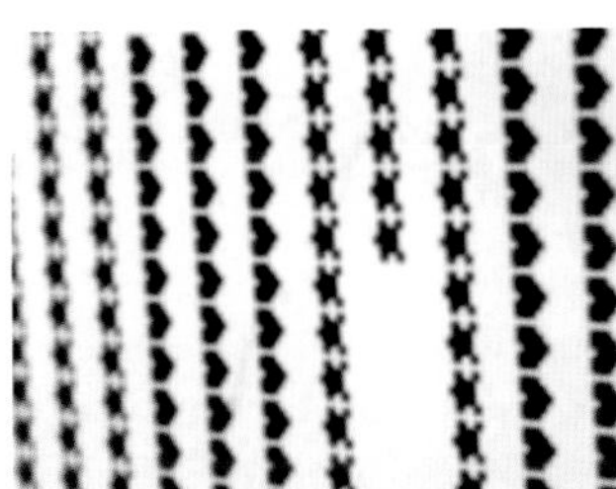

3

4

1
Exhibition - DELAWARE, *D-Day* (2005)
at Centre Pompidou Paris
DELAWARE with Takashi Yamaguchi

2
Live - DELAWARE, *Live! _Live!_ Live!* (2002 - 2004)
at AGI's International (Melbourne)
at IdN My Favourie Conference (Singapore)
at UrbanLenz (Tokyo)
at 33 meets Delaware Xmas (Tokyo)

3
ART - DELAWARE, *Sugo_Magazine* (2003)
at Sugo (Venis)

4
ART - DELAWARE, *Take_A_Walk_with_VANS* (2005)
VANS の展覧会 "Customize_Me" (Barcelona)

017 デバイスガールズ DEVICEGIRLS

PROFILE
VJ Workを主とする映像制作プロジェクト。1997年に映像インスタレーションからキャリアスタートし、翌年の長野五輪でのパーティでDJのTOBY氏と出会い、本格的にVJ活動に入る。フロアに根ざしたサービス精神溢れるダイナミックなプレイを本分とし、現在、石野卓球のレギュラーパーティー「STERNE」のVJを務めている。同氏がオーガナイズする日本最大の屋内レイブ「WIRE」ではメインフロアの映像を担当。さらに最近はロックバンドの大型LIVEツアーに映像演出として同行するなど活動の幅を広げている。

1 2 3 4 5 6 7 8 9 10 11 12

CONCEPT
その場その時にハマる映像、見て高揚するようなモノを作りたいといつも思っています。

To produce visuals that are adequate for the situation, and uplift the viewer.

CATEGORY
VJ

TEL / FAX
—
—

E-MAIL
info@devicegirls.com

URL
http://www.devicegirls.com/

TOOLS
Mac, Windows,
After Effects,
Premiere, LightWave,
Photoshop,
Illustrator

Device Girls is a motion graphic production project centered around V.J. Work. He began activity in 1997, starting with motion graphic installations, and began concentrating on VJing the next year, after meeting DJ Toby at a party for the Nagano Winter Olympics. He is currently a VJ for Takkyu Ishino's regular club event, "Sterne," and also handles the visuals for the main dance floor of "Wire," Japan's most massive indoor rave, also organized by Ishino. Recently, he has been widening his range of activities by doing things such as handling the visuals for a rock band's large-scale tour.

13 17 14 18 15 19 16 20

1-3
PV - RYUKYUDISKO, *ZAN (in waves)* (MUSIC ON! TV Inc., 2004)

4-8
VJ - *RYUKYUDISKO LIVE Visual Parts* (2004)

9-10
VJ - *DEVICEGIRLS VJ Visual Parts* (2005)

11
VJ - *TAKKYU ISHINO VJ Visual Parts* (2004)

12
VJ - *WIRE05 VJ Visual Parts* (2005)
By DEVICEGIRLS + HIDENORI HINO

13-18
VJ - *VJ Visual Parts* (2005)

19
VJ - *KAGAMI LIVE Visual Parts* (2005)

20
PV - KAGAMI, *Delight Head*
(MUSIC ON! TV Inc., 2005 / ©compactsounds, 2004)

018 ドラびでお DORAVIDEO

PROFILE

知的でストイックな作品が主流のメディアアートシーンの中、彼らの作品は粗野で下品そしてくどいぐらいのエンターテインメントである。2005年7月発売予定であった1st DVD「ドラびでお第一集」は、著作権侵害、名誉毀損、猥褻物陳列罪、図画法違反などのDVDで考え得る法律すべてに触れ、ギネス級の違反物と賞され発売直前に絶版。続く2nd DVD「ドラびでお第二集」も一瞬にして絶版になり、細心の注意を払い制作されたCD「ドラ!!ドラ!!ドラ!!われ奇襲に成功せり!!」も発売中ではあるが絶版は間違いないといわれている。

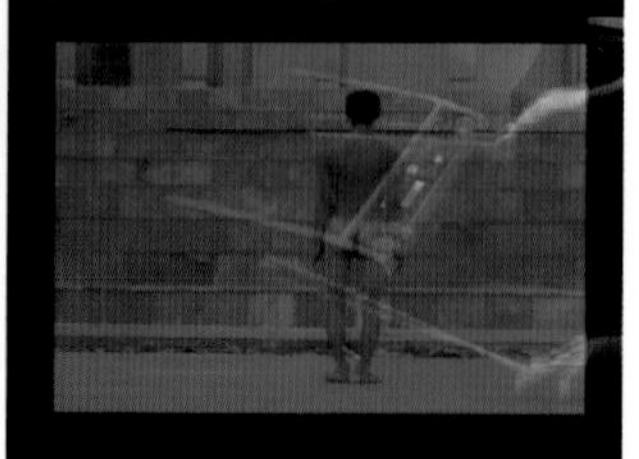

1

CONCEPT

ドラムセットを巨大なビデオデッキとして使用し、映像をコントロールするビデオ＆ドラムユニット。

A video and drum unit that controls images by utilizing a drumset as a large-scale video player.

CATEGORY
Drum

TEL / FAX
+81 (0) 83 927 1085
—

E-MAIL
dr.ichiraku@mac.com

URL
—

TOOLS
Roland TMC-6 Trigger MIDI Converter, Acoustic Drum Trigger RT-7K / RT-5S / RT-3T, Sampling Pad SPD-S, Kick Trigger KD-7, Pad PD-9, USB Audio/ MIDI Interface UA-25, Mac

In a media art scene where clever, austere works are the mainstream, Doravideo's works are entertainment of the purest kind: coarse, vulgar, and verbose. Their first DVD "Doravideo Daiisshuu," which was planned to be released in July this year, breached virtually every law that could apply to a DVD, including copyright violation, defamation, censorship violation, and violation of pictoral laws. Their CD "Dora!! Dora!! Dora!! Ware Kishuu ni Seikou Seri!!," currently available for sale, was produced with the utmost carefulness, yet it is said that this work will inevitably go out of print as well.

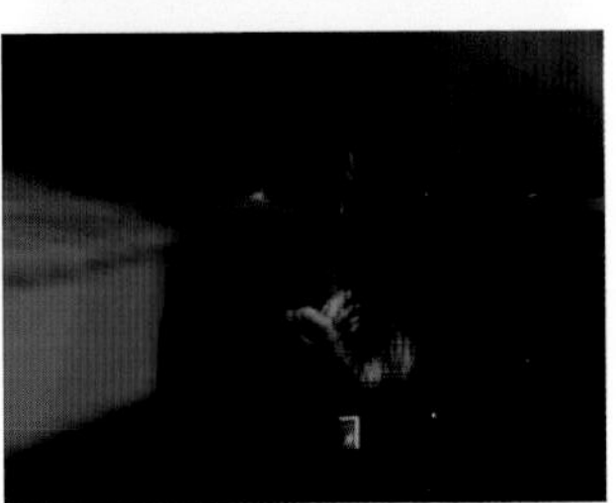

2

1
DVD -「ドラびでお第一集」*DORA VIDEO 1st Issue*

2
DVD -「ドラびでお第二集」*DORA VIDEO 2nd Issue*

019 エレクロトニック ELECROTNIK

PROFILE

中根ひろしと中根さやかによって2001年に結成されたデュオディレクターの映像チーム。撮影からCG、アニメーション、編集まで、すべての行程を二人で行う制作体制を基本としている。m-floの「prism」のPVをはじめ、これまでに数多くのPVを手掛ける。また、エジンバラ国際映画祭やRESFESTなど国内外のフィルムフェスティバルに出品し、高い評価を受けている。

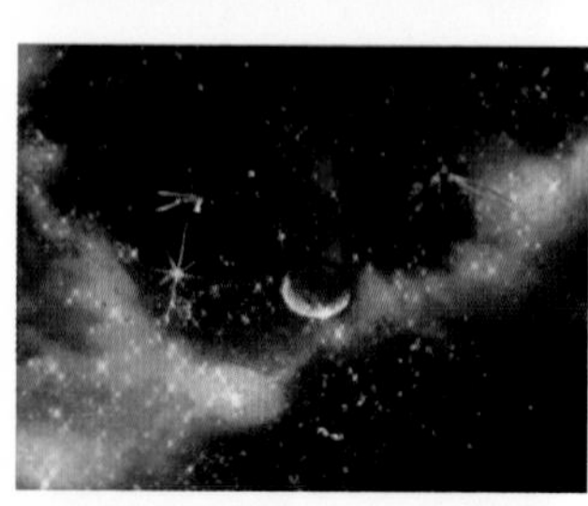

1

2

CONCEPT

アイデアの源泉はファンクやテクノなど、10代の頃から聞き続けている音楽。また、「宇宙」をイメージしたシーンはどの作品にも登場し、ELECROTNIK独特のファンタジーをつくり出す重要な要素となっている。

CATEGORY
PV, CM, Short Film, Title Sequence

TEL / FAX
+81 (0) 3 3705 3046
+81 (0) 3 3705 3047

E-MAIL
info@elecrotnik.com

URL
http://www.elecrotnik.com

TOOLS
Softimage XSI,
DPS Reality,
Digital Fusion,
After Effects

Elecrotnik is a dual-director motion graphics team that was formed in 2001 by Hiroshi Nakane and Sayaka Nakane. They handle every part of the production process by themselves, including shooting, CG, animation, and editing. They have made numerous music videos including M-flo's "Prism." The group has received high praise for submitted works to film festivals such as Edinburgh International Film Festival and Resfest.

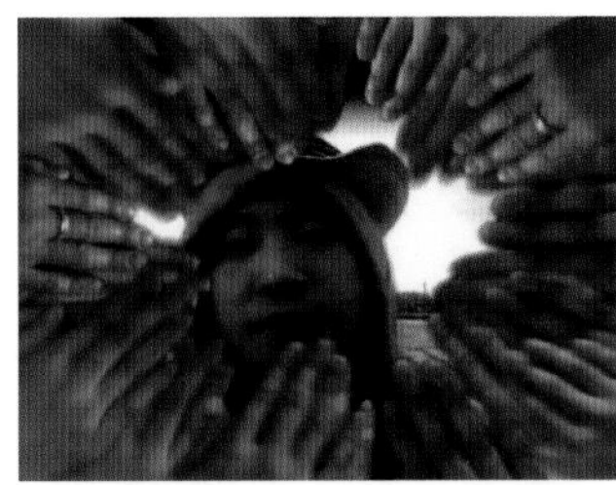

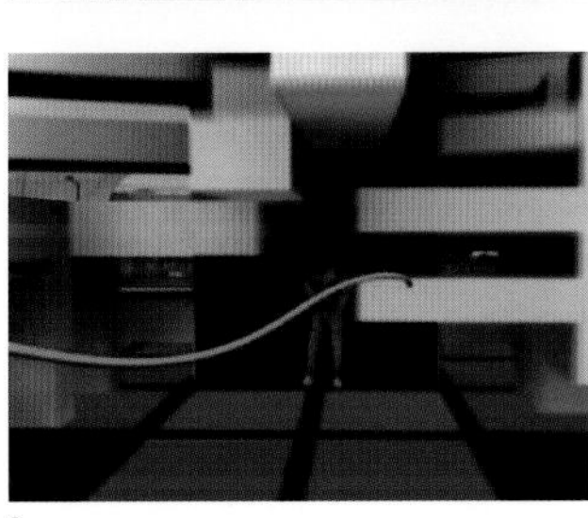

3

4

1
PV - m-flo loves LISA, *TRIPOD BABY* (avex inc., 2005)

2
PV - AUDIO ACTIVE, *Frozen Head* (beatink, 2003)

3
PV - BONOBOS, *THANK YOU FOR THE MUSIC* (Dreamusic, 2005)

4
DVD - *ZAMURAI TV* (SPACE SHOWER TV, 2005)
Staring: GAGLE, KENTARO, TUCKER

The source of Elecrotink's ideas are the music that they have been listening to since their teenage years, such as funk and techno.

Outer space is a theme that can be found in all of their works, and is an element that is a foundation of their original fantastic style.

020
エンライトメント
ENLIGHTENMENT

PROFILE
1997年結成。ヒロ杉山、三嶋章義、鈴木シゲルの3人からなるアーティスト集団。アートブック、フリーペーパーの出版や国内外での展覧会も多数。

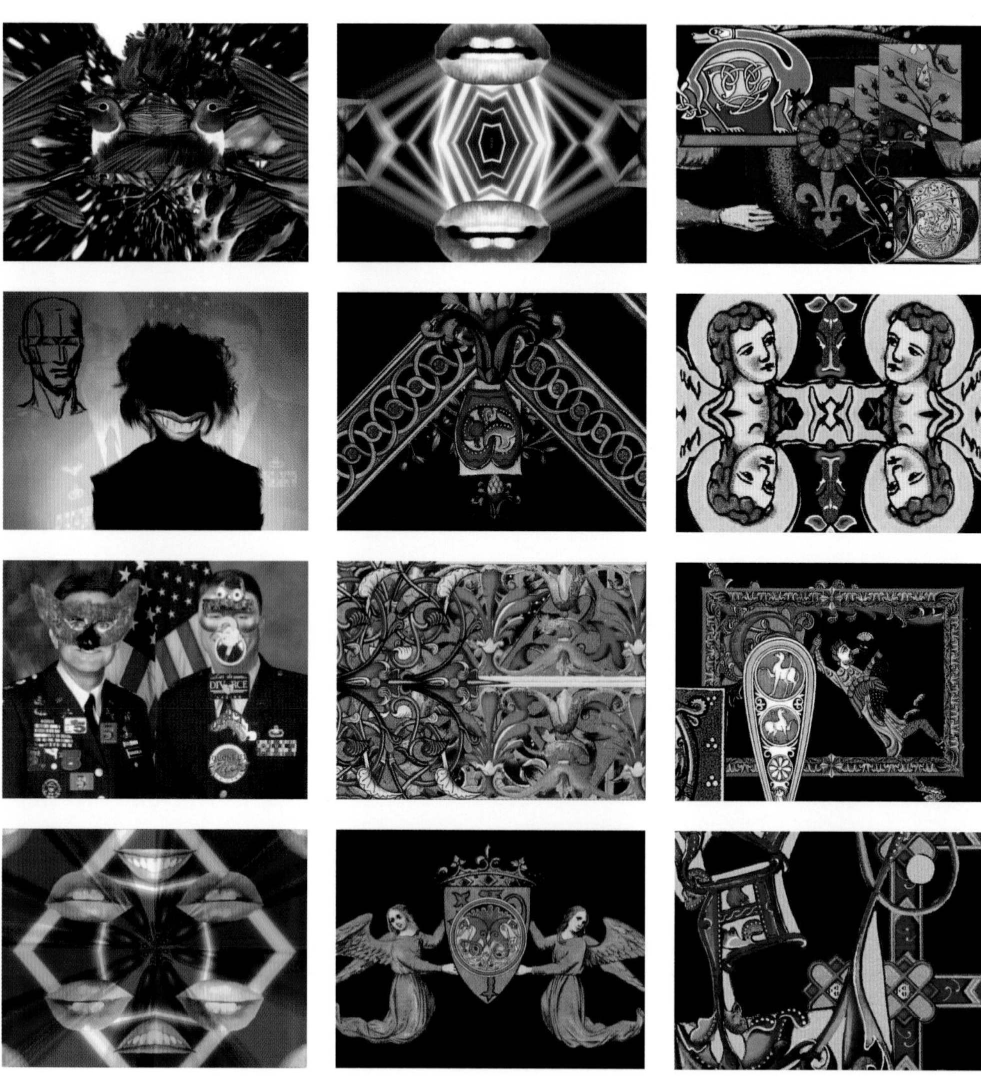

CATEGORY
PV, Art, etc.

TEL / FAX
+81 (0) 3 3705 5470
+81 (0) 3 3705 5471

E-MAIL
hs@elm-art.com

URL
http://www.elm-art.com

TOOLS
Illustrator,
Photoshop
After Effects,
Final Cut

Formed in 1997. Enlightenment is an artist group composed of Hiro Sugiyama, Akiyoshi Mishima, and Shigeru Suzuki. They have published many art books and free magazines, and have had many exhibitions within Japan and overseas.

Private Work - Enlightenment, *After Dark* (2004)

021 エキソニモ
EXONEMO

PROFILE

千房けん輔と赤岩やえによって1996年に結成されたアートユニット。以降、インターネット上で体験する作品を発表し始める。2000年には、国際的なメディアアート・コンペティションのアルス・エレクトロニカのネット部門でHonorary Mentionsを受賞。国内外の展覧会にも多数参加。現在の活動はネット上のみならず、インスタレーションやライブパフォーマンス、イベントプロデュースなど多岐に渡る。ソフトとハードを分け隔てることなくハッキングと遊びの感覚でメディアをゆがめる。活動拠点は東京及びexonemo.com。

1
Art - *VHSM: Video / Hack / Slash / Mixer* (2004)
3台のプロジェクターの照射光をプロペラで遮り、重ねて投影される映像にランダムな要素を加える。初台のICCで展示されたインスタレーション。（インタビューページP.37参照）

This project intends to add random elements to images projected on top of one another by cutting off irradiated beams from three projectors by propellers. This installation was exhibited at ICC (Intercommunication Center) in Hatsudai, Tokyo. (Read their interview on P.37)

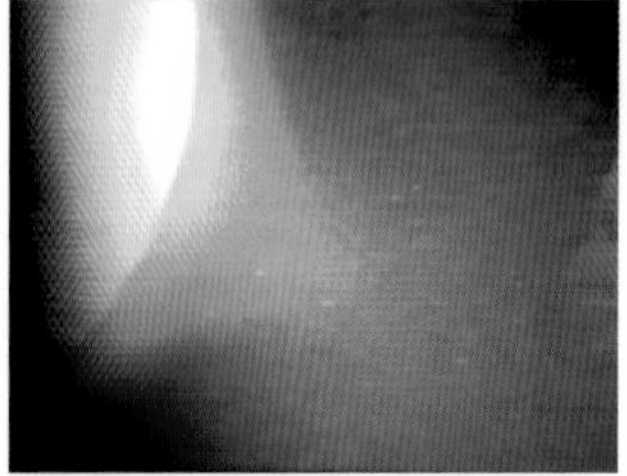

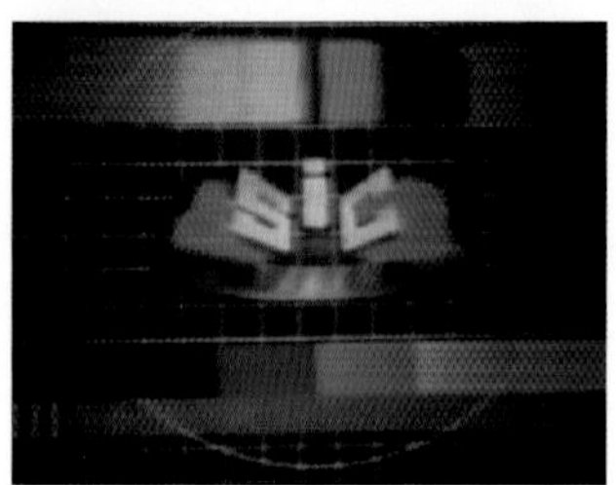

1

2
Art - *RGB F__CKER* (2003)
広島市現代美術館で開催されたエキソニモ展「new FUNKtion」で発表され、現在でもexonemoのウェブ上で公開されている「rgb f__cker」。会場に訪れた人やネットからの参加者が作ったさまざまなフリッカーパターンが次々と大画面で映し出された。

First exhibited at Exonemo's exhibition "new FUNKtion" held at Hiroshima Contemporary Art Museum, this "rgb f__cker" is still being exhibited on their website. At the venue, various flickering patterns generated by participants (including ones online) were projected on a large screen.

CONCEPT

リアリティと変化し続けること。

Reality and constant change.

CATEGORY
All Media Hacking

TEL / FAX
—
—

E-MAIL
mail@exonemo.com

URL
http://exonemo.com/

TOOLS
Laugh,
Anger,
Text Editor

An art unit formed by Kensuke Senbou and Yae Akaiwa in 1996. Exonemo has been presenting works that are experienced through the internet. In 2000, they received an Honorary Mentions award in the internet branch of ARS Electronica, an international media art competition. They have also participated in many exhibitions within Japan and overseas. Many of their current activities take place in various situations other than the internet, including installations, live performances, and event producing. The base locations of their activities are Tokyo and exonemo.com.

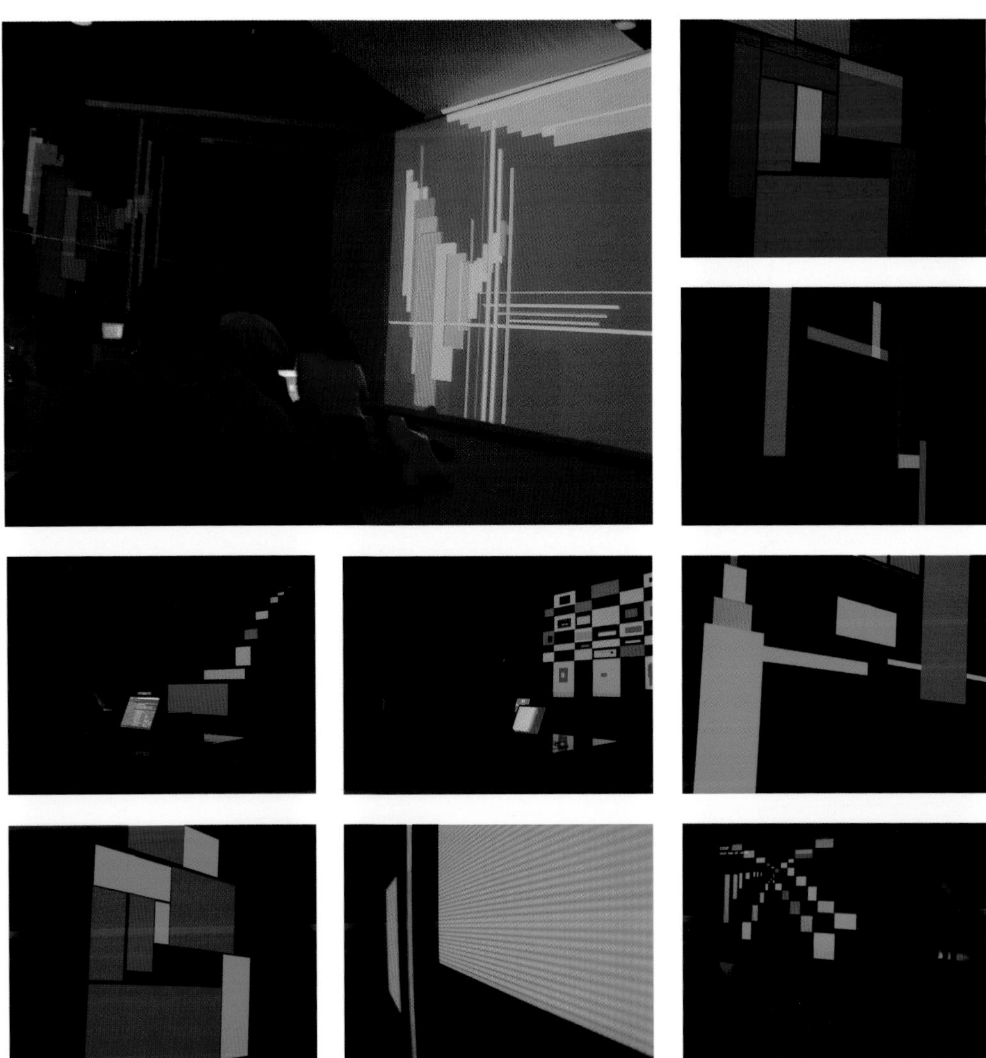

2

022 フクーピィ / キュウオブキュウ fc∞py / QofQ

PROFILE

1973年2月6日新潟県生まれ。琉球ランド在住ミラクルイメージナビゲーター。1996年より感情の赴くままにさまざまなシーンを撮影し、TV番組やPVなどの制作に携わる。1997年にy∞coとエクスペリメンタルドリーミーユニットQofQ結成。絵本的世界をライブに取り入れるスタイルで、めくるめくalterated toy musicの世界を表現。また、パーティオーガナイザー・ラジオ番組ナビゲーター・DJ・VJ・コラージャーなど、多彩な顔もあわせ持つ。2003年より活動拠点を東京から沖縄へ移し、光と音と人が奏でるミラクルヴァイヴスを追究し続けている。

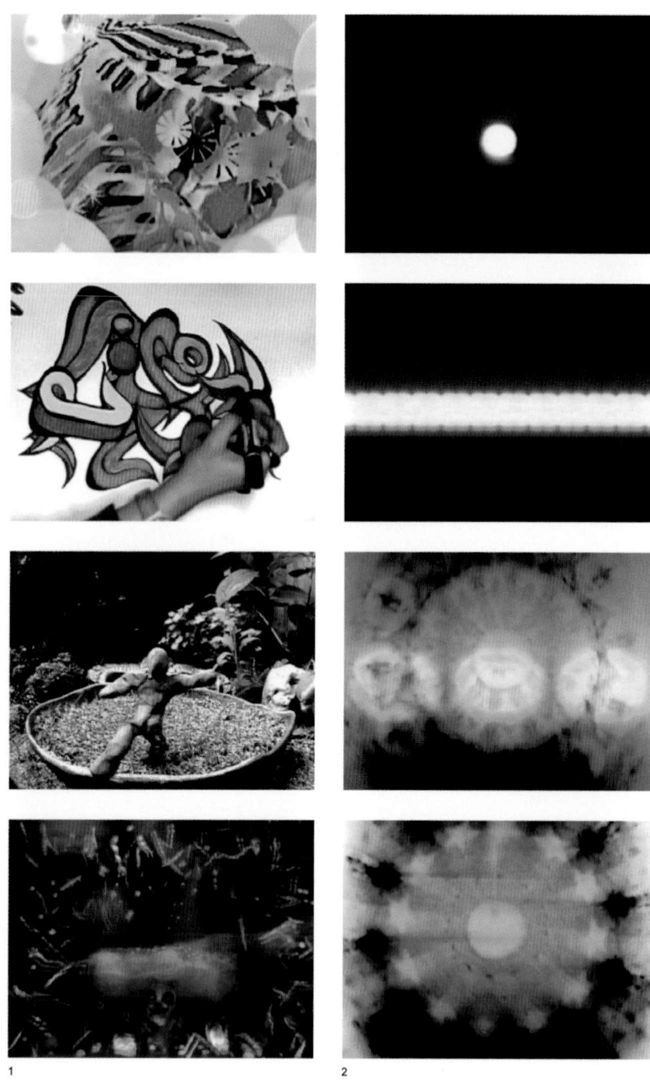

1

2

CONCEPT

その時出会ったもの（光、音、人、etc）とその瞬間に感じたことに自分とカメラをシンクロさせて撮影し、その連続したイメージたちから生まれた物語を紡いで作品をつくる。

Images are captured by the cameraman synchronizing with the camera, the things they encounter (light, sounds, people, etc.), and the feelings that occur towards these things. These continuous images are spun into stories.

CATEGORY
—

TEL / FAX
—
—

E-MAIL
fcoopy@QofQ.com

URL
http://www.QofQ.com

TOOLS
—

Born on February 6, 1973, in Niigata, Japan. fc∞py is a "miracle image navigator" residing in Okinawa. In 1996, she began filming numerous scenes following her whim (live performances, parties, everyday life, etc.). In 1997, together with y∞co, she formed the "experimental dreamy unit" QofQ. They depict a dazzling world of "alterated toy music," with a style that incorporates the universe of children's picture books into their live performances. She moved from Tokyo to Okinawa in 2003, and continue to pursue the miraculous vibes produced by light, sound, and people.

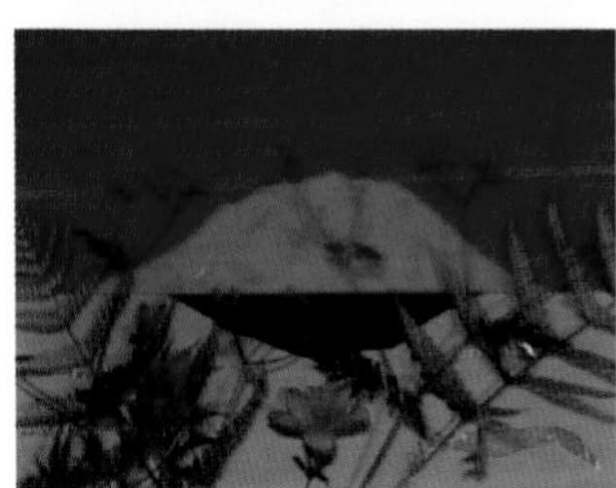

3

4

1
TV - *Chi Chi 5 MILK* (MusicLink, 2000)
Director: fc∞py
Kirie: 川路
Graffiti: 37A
Soil&Water: 土門
Doll: ファニマルマニュファクチュア
Edit: 鎌田将孝

2
PV - Museum of Plate, *F#* (Museum of Plate, 2000)
Director: fc∞py

3
PV - OOIOO, *Kila Kila Kila* (APE SOUNDS, 2003)
Director: fc∞py + Shoji Goto (eagle design)
Cooperation: 片山宏明, 船引亜樹, 立川晋輔, 大嶋明英

4
Animation - *MOMO* (東南植物楽園 Southeast Botanical Gardens, 2004)
Director: fc∞py
Kirie: マドモアゼル朱鷺 Mademoiselle Toki
Edit: MILLER

023 ギフト GIFT

PROFILE

雑誌「+81」のDVD制作を経て、2001年よりフリーとして活動したのち、2005年gift設立。放送番組や DVDパッケージ 、Station IDなどの映像制作、ディレクションに携わる一方、グラフィック、エディトリアルデザインも手掛ける。

CONCEPT

映像的でないこと。平面やグラフィック的な考えを映像化する。

Motion graphics that are not so film-like, but more from the viewpoint of graphics and 2D design.

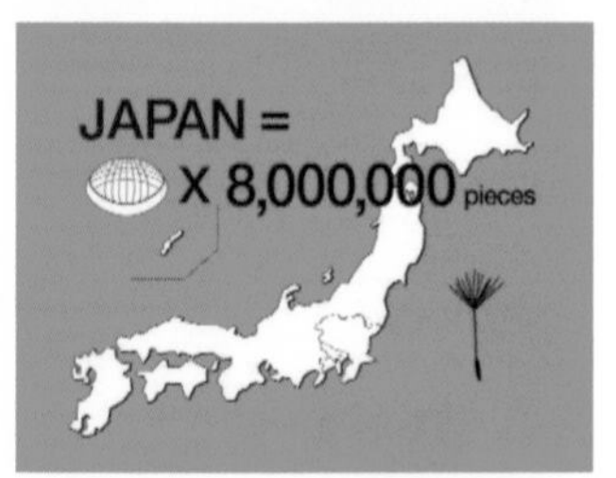

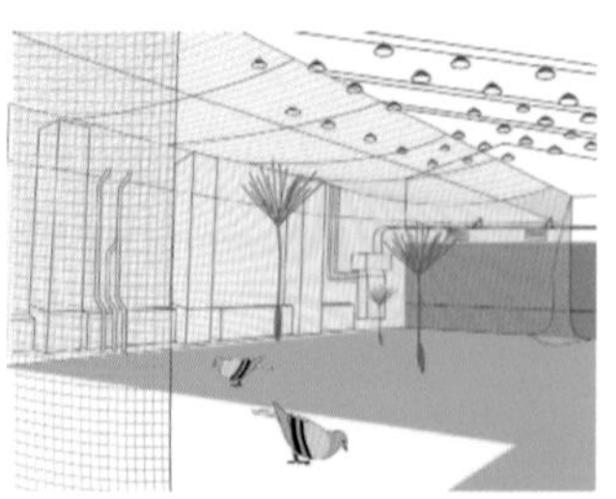

IdN
MY FAVOURITE
CONFERENCE
2004
HOOK ON YOUR
FAVOURITES!

1

2

CATEGORY
CG Animation, PV

TEL / FAX
+81 (0) 3 5768 5204
+81 (0) 3 5768 5205

E-MAIL
info@gift-for.co.jp

URL
http://www.gift-for.co.jp

TOOLS
After Effects,
Premiere

Gift was founded in 2005 by Hideki Saijo, after he produced a DVD for the magazine "+81," and worked freelance beginning from 2001. Gift handles projects such as DVD packages, motion graphics production/direction for TV programs and station IDs, and also graphic and editorial design.

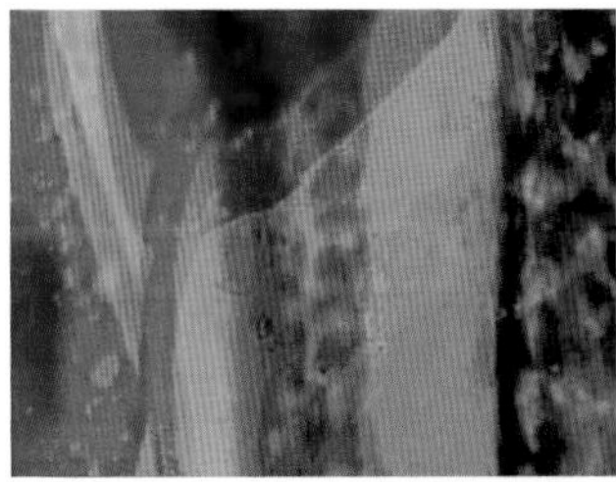

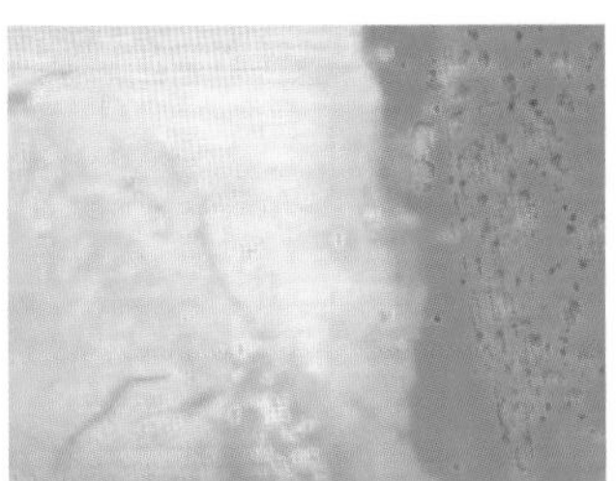

3

4

1
Promotion - *ALLRIGHTSRESERVED for Press*
(©ALLRIGHTSRESERVED, 2005)

2
DVD Opening Movie - *IdN My Favourite Conference*
(©IdN / Nowonmedia, Inc., 2004)

3
Promotion - *Leno Promotion Movie*
(©YAMAHA MUSIC FOUNDATION / asovina, 2005)

4
Opening Movie -*Shinseido Music Treasure*
(©SPACE SHOWER TV, 2005)

024 ゴーモーション GO MOTION

PROFILE
武蔵野美術大学卒業後、Walls art+design社にてTAG Heuer社のアートディレクションを行う。そのほかにも、シャネル、ジバンシー、Victorinoxのウインドウディスプレイやセリーヌ、メリルリンチ、AOLのパンフレットデザイン、ディスプレイ、プロダクトなど幅広く手掛け96年に独立。rudesignを立ち上げ、Web制作、映像制作（GO motion）と活動の幅を広げる。

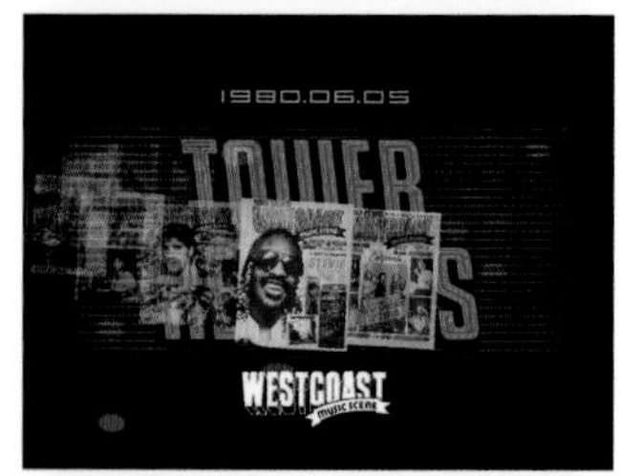

1

2

CONCEPT
Motion & Groove
言葉とは違うかたちで感じ伝えるコミュニケーション。

Motion & Groove. Communication that is received and sent in a different form than words.

CATEGORY
Print, Web, Motion Graphic

TEL / FAX
—
—

E-MAIL
yuta@rudesign.jp

URL
http://www.rudesign.jp
http://www.kinet.or.jp/kits/mt/

TOOLS
Mac,
Photoshop,
Illustrator,
Final Cut,
Motion, Seift 3D

After graduating from Musashino Art University, Yutaka Kitamura joined Walls Art+Design, and handled art direction for Tag Heure. He has produced a wide variety of works in fields such as display design and product design. Examples are window displays for Chanel, Givenchy, and Victorinox, and pamphlet designs for Celine, Merrill Lynch, and AOL. He went independent in 1996, and founded Rudesign, where he handles Web design and motion images (Go Motion).

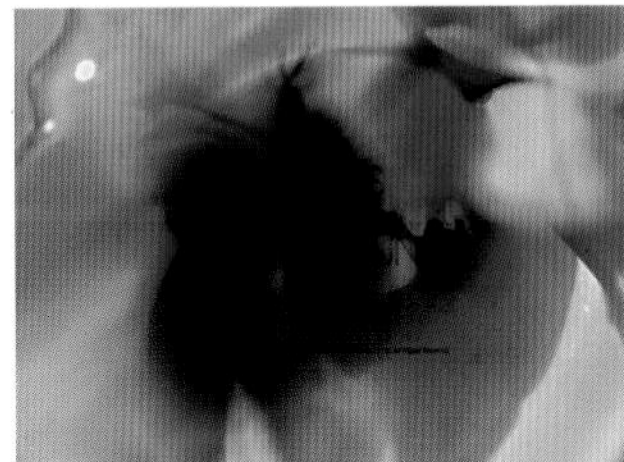

3

4

1
DVD -「バナナマンのシャブリなコメディ / 337 拍子、足しちゃった」*Bananaman's Chablis Comedy / 337 byoushi Tashichatta*
Director: GO motion
(©CLUBKING CO., LTD. 発売元：東北新社 TOHOKUSHINSHA FILM CORPORATION, 2005)

2
CM - *Tower Records Bounce.com* (TOWER RECORDS, 2001)
Director: GO motion

3
Concert Movie - PornoGraffitti 6th Live Circuit, *74ers* (2004)
Director: GO motion

4
Opening Motion - *Seeds & Ground WEB* (Seeds & Ground, 2005)
Director: GO motion, Kaoru Inoue

025 グルーヴィジョンズ GROOVISIONS

PROFILE
1993年以降、グラフィックを中心にプロダクト、インテリア、ファッション、ムービーとさまざまなデザインを行うデザイングループ。タレント「Chappie」の所属事務所。

1

2

3

4

5

6

7

8

9

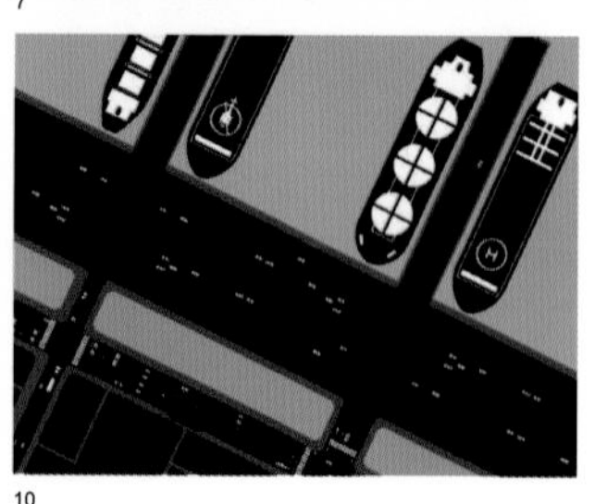
10

11

12

CONCEPT
エンターテインメントとして成立するものを心掛けている。

To produce works that can function as entertainment.

CATEGORY
PV, CM, Animation, Web

TEL / FAX
+81 (0) 3 5723 6558
+81 (0) 3 5723 6356

E-MAIL
grv@groovisions.com

URL
http://www.groovisions.com

TOOLS
Final Cut Pro HD,
After Effects 6.5J,
Photoshop CS,
Illustrator CS

Since 1993, GROOVISIONS is a design group whose core activity is graphic design, but also includes interior design, fashion, and film. They are the agency of the performer “Chappie.”

13

1-3
CM - *ALL IN ONE* (THE NISHI-NIPPON CITY BANK, LTD., 2005)
CD: Takao Ito
DR: GROOVISIONS
CH: GROOVISIONS
M: Gakuji Matsuda (CUBISMO GRAFICO)
PL: GROOVISIONS + Takao Ito + Toshiyuki Hidari
C: Toshiyuki Hidari
Pr: Kenichiro Ueda
Production: GROOVISIONS + Dentsu Kyushu + T&E

4
CM - *Rikunabi NEXT* (RECRUIT CO., LTD., 2005)
CD + P + C: Michihiko Yanai
PR: Hitoshi Ookuwa
Director + CG: GROOVISIONS
M: Fantastic Plastic Machine
NA: Marin
PM: Tetsuya Furuta
A&P: KAZETOROCK + Spoon

5-6
PV - Halfby, *Rodeo Machine* (SECOND ROYAL RECORDS, 2005)

7-9
Artwork - *GRV2196* (Station navi) (Expo 2005 AICHI JAPAN) at EXPO 2005, AICHI, JAPAN, EXPO PLAZA, EXPO Vision
CD: Spiral / Wacoal Art Center

10
Artwork - *GRV1778* (DesignEXchange Co., Ltd., 2002)
M: Yukihiro Fukutomi "rebel / console pt.1~pt.4"

11
PV - chappie, 「水中メガネ」 *Suicyumegane* (Sony Music Entertainment Inc., 1999)

12
PV - pizzicato five, *lesson 3003* (Nippon Columbia,1998)

13
PV - RIP SLYME, *GOOD JOB!* (©Warner Music Japan, 2005)
Producer: Fumiyuki Yanaka
Production: MAZRI

026 本木秀明
HIDEAKI MOTOKI

PROFILE
2003年より「ZOUNDS」という音の生態系をテーマとしたプロジェクトを始動。ザウンズという楽器生物が、音を通じてコミュニケーションをはかり、ほかのザウンズや環境と接触しながら、多様な音を作り出し成長・進化していく。将来的には音によるコミュニケーションツールとして、ネットワーク空間へと展開することを視野に入れている。基本的に自分がイメージした世界は、自分で作るという制作スタンスをとる。その作品は、RESFESTやOPTRONICAなどに招待され、海外での評価も上昇中。

1

2

CONCEPT
画を聴く、音を観る。

Listen to images, view sounds.

CATEGORY
CG Animation, PV

TEL / FAX
—
—

E-MAIL
motoki@zounds.tv

URL
http://zounds.tv

TOOLS
Windows, Mac,
LightWave, Premiere Pro,
After Effects, Photoshop,
etc.

In 2003, Motoki began "ZOUNDS," a project centering around the theme of: an ecosystem of sounds. In it, musical organisms called ZOUNDS not only communicate through sound, but also invent an abundant variety of sounds through interaction with the environment and each other, to grow and evolve. The project may even enter into network space and develop there in the future, as a communication tool based on sound. Motoki's stance is to create the things which he himself imagined, by himself. His works have been exhibited at events such as RESFEST and OPTRONICA.

3

1 PV - RYUKYUDISKO, *CHURAZIMA* (MUSIC ON! TV, 2005)
Director + CG: 本木秀明 Hideaki Motoki
2 PV - Rays, *MOONFLOWERS* (HORIZON / liquid recordings, 2004)
Director + CG: 本木秀明 Hideaki Motoki
3 Original Work - *ZOUNDS* (2003)
Director + CG: 本木秀明 Hideaki Motoki
Music: 松前公高 Kimitaka Matsumae

027 稲葉英樹
HIDEKI INABA

PROFILE

2004 年 Nike Women's アジアキャンペーン広告、2005 年 LEVI'S RED 広告、relax 誌の iPod 表紙など数多くのグラフィック作品を制作。映像分野では GAS や DVD「AUDIOVISUALJAPAN」などのムービーディレクションを手掛ける。GRAPHIC DESIGN NOW（TASCHEN）の表紙や、ドイツ red dot award '04 で best of the best 賞を受賞するなど、海外での活躍もめざましい。

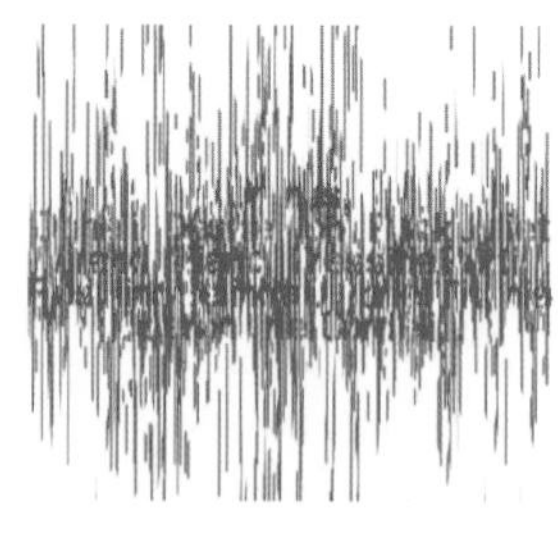

h i De k i
in a b a

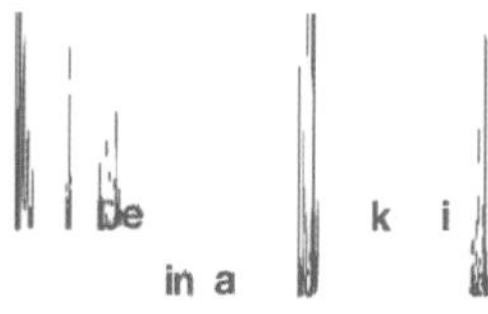

Uranus,
Ophelia Desdemona Puck Juliet
Miranda Bianca Cressida Portia
Rosalind Belinda Umbriel Titania
Oberon Ariel Cordelia.

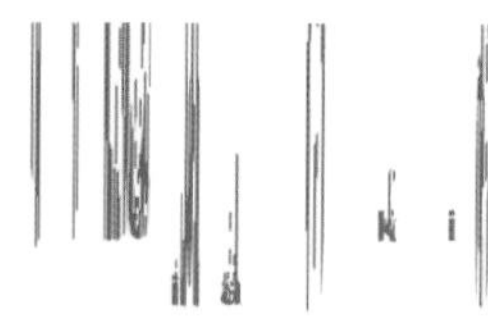

Uranus,
Ophelia Desdemona Puck Juliet
Miranda Bianca Cressida Portia
Rosalind Belinda Umbriel Titania
Oberon Ariel Cordelia.

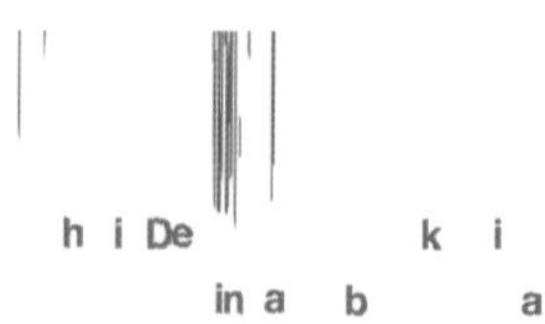

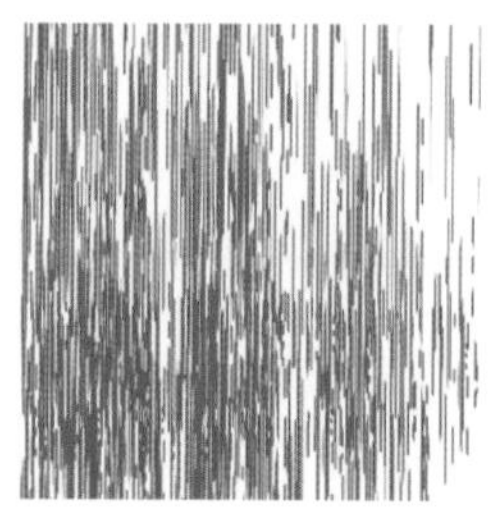

CATEGORY
Art

TEL / FAX
+81 (0) 3 3321 1766
+81 (0) 3 3321 1787

E-MAIL
user@hidekiinaba.com

URL
http://www.hidekiinaba.com

TOOLS
Gutte Two,
Ichitaro,
Ram Doubler

Inaba has created numerous graphics such as Nike Women's '04 Asia Campaign Advertisement, Levi's Red '05 Advertisement, and the cover of relax magazine's i-pod issue. He has held a personal exhibition, NEWLINE. In the field of motion graphics, Inaba has directed the title sequences for GAS and AUDIOVISUALJAPAN. His graphic design works have appeared on the cover of TASCHEN popular publication Graphic Design Now, and have been chosen for the red dot award '04 Best of the Best award in Germany.

Maritima Olga
Victoria Ludmilla Bellona
Polyxena Kreusa Miriam Ute
Shaposhnikov
Bowell Feodosia Nerthus
Goberta Scythia.

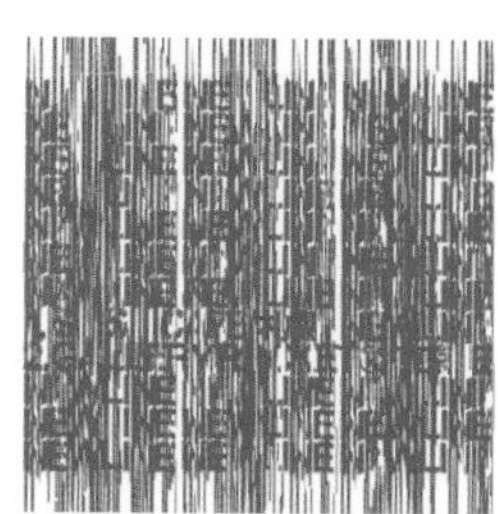

Maritima Olga
Victoria Ludmilla Bellona
Polyxena Kreusa Miriam Ute
Shaposhnikov
Bowell Feodosia Nerthus
Goberta Scythia.

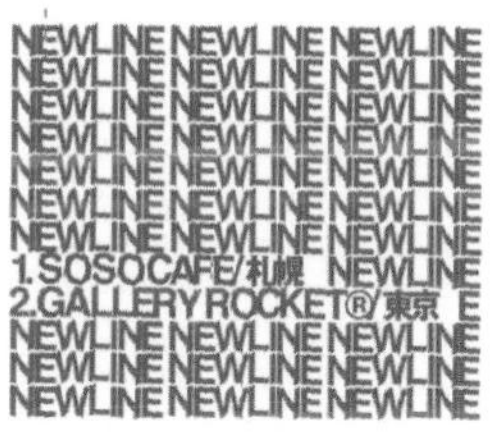

Art - *NEWLINE / Burst Helvetica*(©Hideki Inaba, 2004)
Art Direction + Design: Hideki Inaba
Movie Authoring + Design: Masanori Izumi

028 田中秀幸 / フレイムグラフィックス
HIDEYUKI TANAKA / FRAME GRAPHICS

PROFILE
多摩美術大学グラフィックデザイン学科卒業。フレイムグラフィックス代表。グラフィックデザインやキャラクターデザイン、またビデオクリップ、CM のディレクション、テレビ番組、ゲームのアートディレクションなどの映像制作を行っている。

1

2

CONCEPT
問題は何もない。

No Problem.

CATEGORY
CG Animation, Music Video

TEL / FAX
+81 (0) 3 5459 1122
+81 (0) 3 5459 4477

E-MAIL
info@framegraphics.co.jp

URL
–

TOOLS
Illustrator,
Photoshop,
After Effects,
SI,
Softimage XSI

Graduated from Tama Art University, Department of Graphic Design. Tanaka is the director of Flame Graphics. He creates works of graphic design and character design, and also works in various fields of motion graphic production such as music videos, TV commercials, TV programs, and art direction for video games.

3

4

1
CM - *Giant Bra* (LAFORET HARAJUKU, 2001)

2
Animation - 「OH! スーパーミルクチャン」 *Oh! Super Milk Chan*
(©FG, SSNW, SPLX, RTK, ADV)

3
CM - *SKI Campaign* (JAPAN SNOW PROJECT, 2005)

4
PV - DJ TASAKA, *Speaker Typhoon*
(Ki/oon Records, 2005)

029 光J
HIKARU J

PROFILE

2000年結成。映像作家・グラフィックデザイナーなどで構成されるVJ・映像制作ユニット。主にVJ、PVディレクション、TV番組のCG、映像インスタレーションなどを手掛ける。TVサンプリング＋googleリサーチ主体のアナログかつイリーガルな発狂VJスタイルで、イベント後にオーガナイザーに怒られている姿が印象的な若者の集団。

CONCEPT

純なラヴ/勇気/ドリーム/冒険/ヴィクトリー/青春/SF/オカルト/R.I.P.などを題材とした、ウルトラ・バブルガム・ポップ・ヴィジュアル制作

Ultra-bubblegum-pop-visual-production, with themes such as pure love, courage, adventure, victory, teenage years, S.F., occult, and R.I.P..

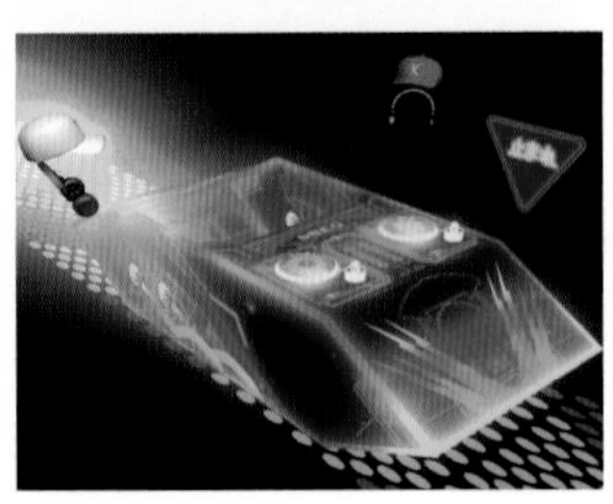

CATEGORY
VJ, PV, Promotion, TV

TEL / FAX
+81 (0) 3 3712 0181
+81 (0) 3 3712 0181

E-MAIL
hikaruj@mount-web.com

URL
—

TOOLS
Final Cut Pro,
3ds Max,
After Effects,
Illustrator,
Photoshop

Formed in 2000. Hikaru.J. is a VJ/motion graphics production unit, composed of motion graphic authors and graphic designers. They mainly handle such things as V.J.ing, music video direction, CGs for T.V. programs, and motion graphic installations. They are a group of young men who can often be found being scolded by event organizers because of their illicit, analog, and insane V.J. sets, which are based on T.V. sampling and Google.

PV - DJ KOHNO (from Ketsumeishi) & DJ TATSUTA,
「お客様が神様です」 *Okyakusama ga kamisama desu*
(©Dreamusic Inc., 2005)
Director: Hikaru J (Munechika Sasao)
Producer: Katsunori Odagiri + Satomi Fukuda
Graphic: Hikaru J (Masuhiro Yamada), mount (Daisuke Nishihara)
3D Animation: Hikaru J (Munechika Sasao), NABE(Rice Field)
2D Animation: Hikaru J (Yuki Hasegawa)

030 小池 光
HIKARU KOIKE

PROFILE
グラフィックデザイナー・デジタルコンテンツデザイナー。デザイン会社サルブルネイを経て1997年に独立。主にActionScriptを使ったFlashのサイト構築デザイン。CD-ROM「Jungle Park」でAMD Award '96優秀作品賞及びBest Visual Designer賞受賞。

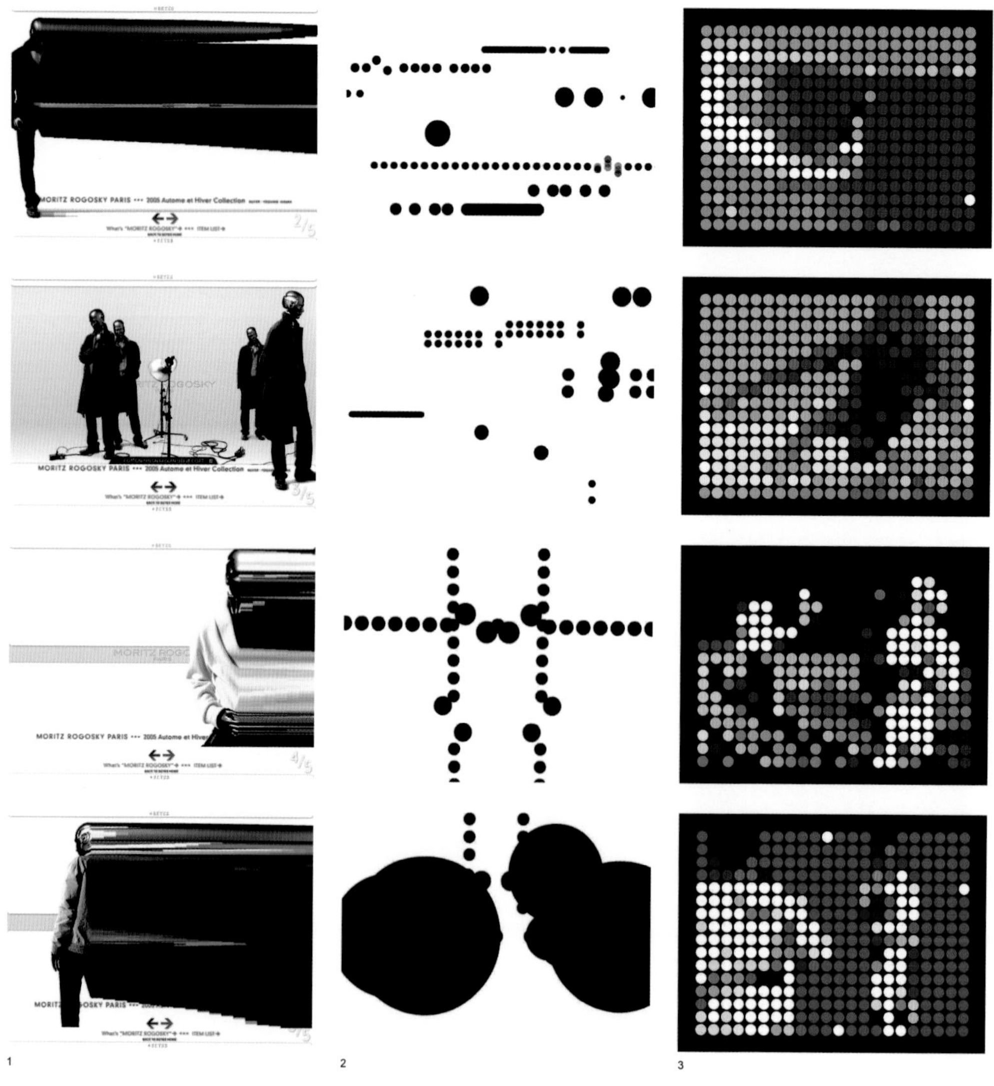

1 2 3

CONCEPT
何かイイ感じに。

Making the Image of pleasant.

CATEGORY
Web

TEL / FAX
+81 (0) 3 3410 5401
—

E-MAIL
00hikaru@d1.dion.ne.jp

URL
http://www.marmalade-wafer.com

TOOLS
Flash,
Illustrator,
Photoshop

A designer of graphics and digital contents. Koike went independent in 1997 after working for the design company Saru Brunei. He mainly handles website design using Flash and ActionScript. For his CD-ROM "Jungle Park," he was awarded the AMD Prize and Best Visual Designer at AMD Award '96.

4

1
Web Flash - *BEYES : Moritz Rogosky* (BEYES, 2005)
Photo: Tomoo Nozawa

2
Edicational Movie - 「うごく【絵】じてん -ピアノ-」
moving [picture] encyclopedia (NHK, 2004)
Director: Masaki Fujihata
2D Animation: Hikaru Koike
3D Animation: Sora Matsumoto
Music: Yasuo Higuchi

3
Private Work - *Dot Slasher* (1999)
Music: Delaware

4
Installation - *DANBOXEL01 -images moving interaction-* (KDDI Designing Studio, 2005)
Artists: Projectors(Ichiro Higashiizumi, Hikaru Koike, Kentaro Fukuchi), DGN(Daito Manabe, Motoi Ishibashi)

031 井口弘史 HIROSHI IGUCHI

PROFILE

1973年生まれ。個人プロダクション「THE BWOY」、柴垣英治とのプロジェクト「THE POTATO」などを使い適材適所（或いはその逆）に発信中。

1

2

CATEGORY
—

TEL / FAX
—
—

E-MAIL
—

URL
—

TOOLS
CONTAX T VS Digital

Born in 1973. Iguchi works both independently as "The Bwoy," and together with Eiji Shibagaki as "The Potato." He always puts the right thing in the right place.

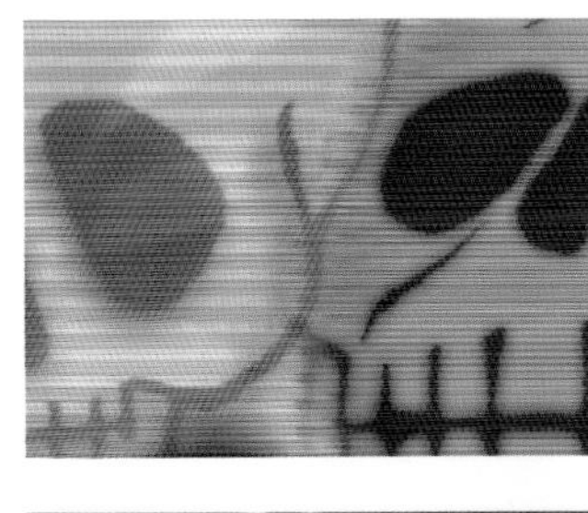

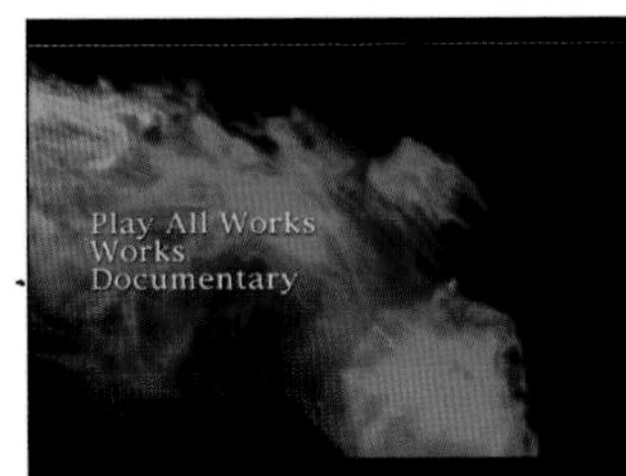

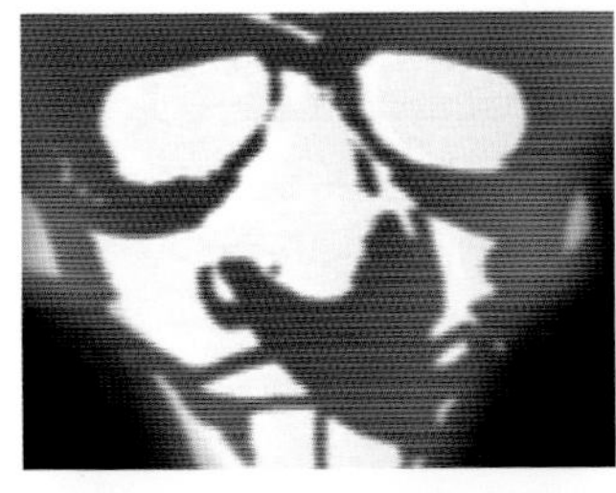

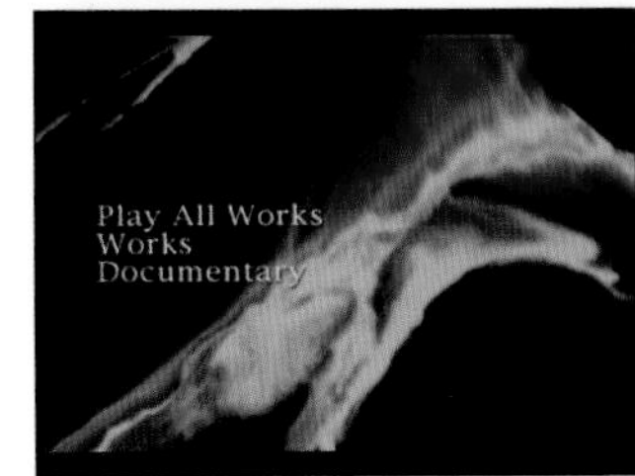

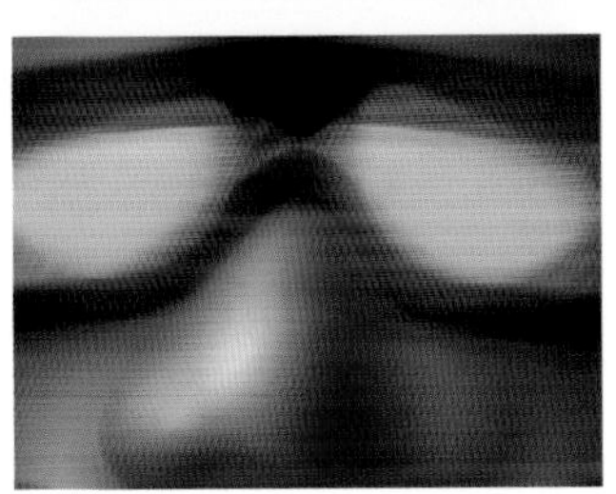

3

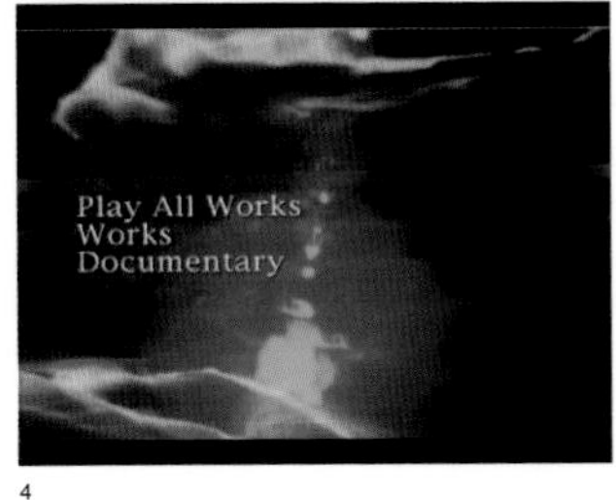

4

1
Art - *HELL* (2002)

2
Art - *Inside* (2005)

3
Station ID - *GANG STA*, (©SPACE SHOWER TV, 2001)
Music: Illreme

4
DVD Opening - *SOUND × VISION Opening Movie*, (©Gas As Interface Co., Ltd., 2004)

032 木津裕史 / エムティーヴィージャパン
HIROSHI KIZU / MTV JAPAN

PROFILE

1976年福島県生まれ、大阪育ち。1999年京都芸術短期大学映像専攻科卒業。在学中、伊藤高志に師事し実験映像の面白さと映像制作の心得を学ぶ。2001年夏、MTV JAPAN入社。番組の宣伝スポット、パッケージ、On Air Promotion などの映像を多数手掛ける。

CONCEPT

サウンドに対して映像をいかにカッコよく刻み、編集するのかが重要。精神面では、常に身の程を知り、ダークサイドの立場からテーマを考える。女の子は可愛く演出する。

The most important thing is how to edit and cut up the visuals corresponding to the sounds in a cool way. As for the mental aspect: to know your limits, and contemplate various themes from the standpoint of the darkside. Make the girls in your work look pretty.

1

2

1
Title Movie - *MTV WORLD CHART EXPRESS* (MTV JAPAN, 2003)
Director + Editor: Hiroshi Kizu
AD: Kentaro Fujimoto
CGI Director: Masaaki Matsumoto
CGI Animator: Takeo Furutani
Flame Editer: Mitsuhiro Kanaya
Sound: Soichi Terada
Voice: Srage
MA Mixer: Kohei Takagi

2
Opening Movie - *MTV COOL CHRISTMAS* (MTV JAPAN, 2004)
Director + Editor: Hiroshi Kizu
AD: Tsuyoshi Hirooka
Camera: Yoshinobu Yoshida
Light: Koji Furuyama
VE: Shinya Mayuzumi
CG: Hitoshi Kimura
Sound: Soichi Terada
Model: Aoi Miura
Stylist: Naohiro Matsunoshita
Hair + Make: Eiichi Ikeda
Production Manager: Midori Hibino
Producer: Shigeru Agari

CATEGORY
Music, Nerd, Youth

TEL / FAX
—
—

E-MAIL
—

URL
http://www.mtvjapan.com/

TOOLS
After Effects,
ableton Live,
Avid Media Composer,
AKAI professional MPC2000XL

Born in Fukushima Prefecture, Japan in 1976, and raised in Osaka. Graduated from Kyoto Junior College of Art, Department of Film. While a student, Kizu developed a taste for experimental film, and studied the methods of film production under Takashi Ito. In Summer of 2001, he entered MTV Japan. He has handled things such as packages, and numerous motion graphics works for on-air promotion and commerical spots for MTV programs.

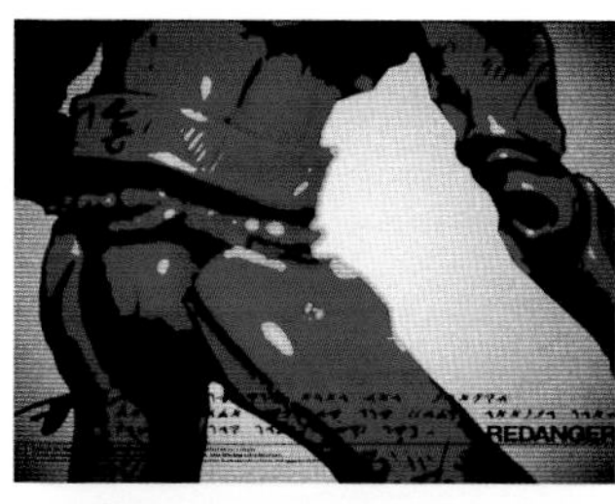

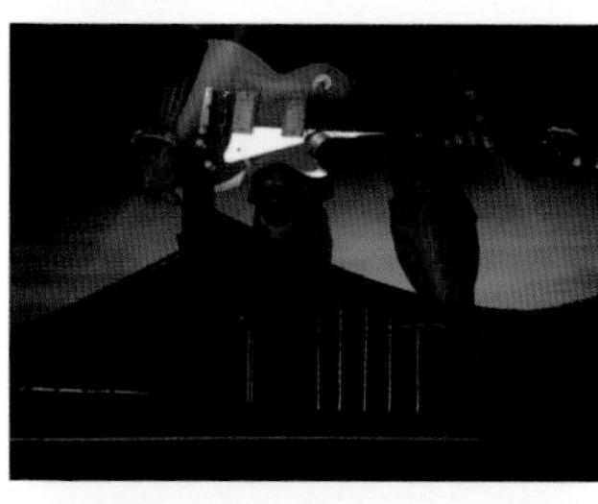

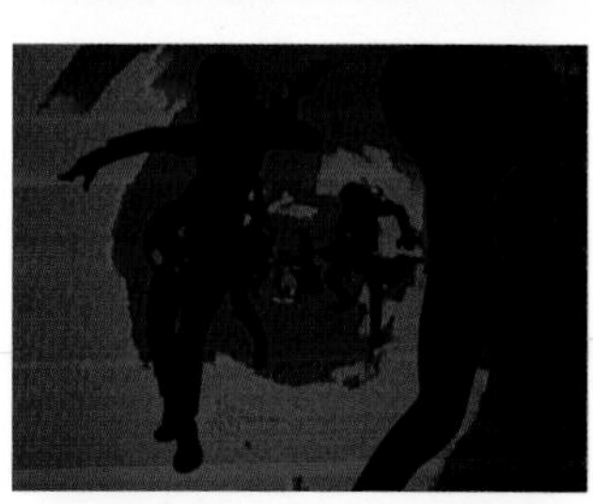

3

4

3
Opening Movie - *MTV THE SUPER DRY LIVE 2005 "REDANGER!!"* (MTV JAPAN, 2005)
Director + Editor + Sound: Hiroshi Kizu
Character Design + CG: Junji Okubo
Graphic Design: Kentaro Fujimoto
REDANGER CGI: spice inc.
3DCG: Takumi Shiga
Flame Editer: Mitsuhiro Kanaya
Camera: Sakuma Shinji
Choreographer: Seishiro Fujimoto
Sound: Yoshiaki Tanaka, Junji Kamatsuka
Voice: Baraki
MA Mixer: Kohei Takagi
Production Manager: Midori Hibino

4
Tune In - *MTV's LIVE SELECTION* (MTV JAPAN, 2003)
Director + Editor + Sound: Hiroshi Kizu
Character Design: Shu Ishihara
Logo Design: Kentaro Fujimoto
Voice: Baraki
MA Mixer: Kohei Takagi

033 中尾浩之 HIROYUKI NAKAO

PROFILE
1968年生まれ。日本大学芸術学部放送学科卒。1998年MTV Station IDコンテストグランプリ受賞。2000年カンヌ広告祭におけるニューディレクターズショーケース（サーチ＆サーチ主催）で世界の新人監督8人に選ばれる。2004年Short Shorts Film Festivalにて短編映画「ZERO」がグランプリ含むトリプル受賞。2005年クレモンフェラン映画祭International部門にノミネートされたほか、カンヌ国際映画祭ショートフィルムコーナーにも出品。

1

2

CONCEPT
壮大かつ普遍的なテーマを、現代的なモチーフや個人の物語を使って、いかに躍動感あふれる映像で描写するかということ。

To depict majestic and universal themes as visually dynamically as possible, while using contemporary motifs and personal narratives.

CATEGORY
Live action, Livemation (live Action + Animation), Script

TEL / FAX
+81 (0) 3 5785 1780
+81 (0) 3 5785 1784

E-MAIL
post@picsco.net

URL
http://www.picsco.net

TOOLS
Premiere,
Photoshop,
Director

Born in 1968. Graduated from Nihon University College of Art Department of Broadcasting. In 1998, Nakao won the MTV Station ID Contest Grand Prix. He was chosen as one of the eight most prominent new directors in the world, in Cannes Lions 2000's New Director's Showcase (hosted by Saatchi & Saatchi). In 2005, his work was nominated for the International Competition at the Clermont Ferrand Film Festival, and his work was also submitted to the Cannes International Film Festival Short Film Corner.

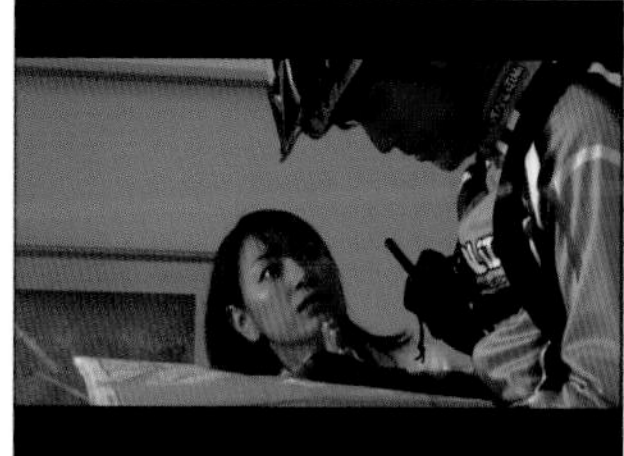

3

4

1
Short Movie - *trainsurfer* (©MTV Japan Inc. / P.I.C.S. / Hiroyuki Nakao, 2003-2004)
Director: 中尾浩之 Hiroyuki Nakao
Producer: 松居秀之 Hideyuki Matsui
CG: JINNI'S Animation Studios, 山本倫裕 Norihiro Yamamoto
Music: 戸田色音 Irone Toda
Production by P.I.C.S.
2004年文化庁メディア芸術祭審査員推薦作品

2
Short Movie -「スチーム係長」
Steam Kakarichou (©テレビ東京 TV TOKYO / P.I.C.S., 2005)
Director: 中尾浩之 Hiroyuki Nakao
Producer: 寺井弘典 Hironori Terai
CG: 山下裕智 Hirotomo Yamashita, 佐藤広大 Kohdai Sato, JINNI'S Animation Studios
Production by P.I.C.S.

3
PV - 氣志團「族」
Kishidan, *ZOKU* (TOSHIBA EMI LIMITED, 2004)
Director: 中尾浩之 Hiroyuki Nakao
Producer: 下田伸貴 Nobutaka Shimoda
Camera: 小川 幹 Miki Ogawa
Light: 野村泰寛 Yasuhiro Nomura
CG: Image
Production by P.I.C.S.

4
Short Film -「ザ・シークレットショウ」
The Secret Show (©Pacific Voice Inc. All Rights Reserved., 2005)
Director + Script: 中尾浩之 Hiroyuki Nakao
Camera: 小川 幹 Miki Ogawa
Light: 野村泰寛 Yasuhiro Nomura
Music: 戸田色音 Irone Toda
Production by P.I.C.S.
2005年 Short Shorts Film Festival スカラシップ監督作品

034 谷田一郎 / ジョン・アンド・ジェーン・ドォ
ICHIRO TANIDA / JOHN AND JANE DOE INC.

PROFILE

1965年東京生まれ。1994年にCGと音楽をリンクさせたCD-ROM作品「UNDER GROUND A TO Z SO OUT」で独自の世界観を表現し、注目を浴びるようになる。CG制作の経験を生かしユニークなキャラクターをCMに取り入れた「ラフォーレ グランバザール」のシリーズを皮切りに、CMディレクターとしての活動が始まる。現在は年間30本以上のCMの演出を担当し、谷田の手掛けたCMを目にしない日はない。近年、木彫りを多数制作。常に彼の手は休まることなく動き続けている。

1

2

CATEGORY
CM

TEL / FAX
+81 (0) 3 3499 4608
+81 (0) 3 3499 4604

E-MAIL
jjd@jjd.co.jp

URL
http://www.jjd.co.jp

TOOLS
—

Born in Tokyo in 1965. In 1994, Tanida began attracting attention for his unique worldview expressed in "UNDERGROUND A to Z: So Out," a CD-ROM linking music and computer graphics. He became a TV commercial director starting with the "Laforet Grand Bazaar" series. Today he oversees more than 30 commercials each year, and not a day passes without one of his commercials being aired. In recent years he has also created numerous sculptures in wood. He is constantly at work, never allowing his creative hands to rest.

3

4

1
CG - *COPET*

2
CM - 「KIRIN のどごし生」 *KIRIN Nodogoshi Nama* (KIRIN BREWERY CO., LTD.)

3
CM - 「ラフォーレ グランバザール」 *Laforet Grand Bazer* (LAFORET HARAJUKU)

4
Exhibision - *KITTY EX*

035 今井トゥーンズ IMAITOONZ

PROFILE

1971年生まれ。デザイナー・イラストレーター・コミックアーティスト。1995年MTV「TOP OF JAPAN」のOPアニメーションを皮切りに、サントリー「C.Cレモン」のCM、NIKE PRESTOのPRアニメーション、KENISHIIのPV、ReebokとのIMAITOONZコラボレートシューズなど、多方面に作品を提供。アニメーション作品が国内外の映画祭に招待出品されたほか、企画・原作・キャラクターデザインを務めた中編アニメ映画「DEAD LEAVES」(松竹配給)も公開。2005年には東京上野の森美術館の「GUNDAM～来るべき未来のために～」展に作品を出品した。

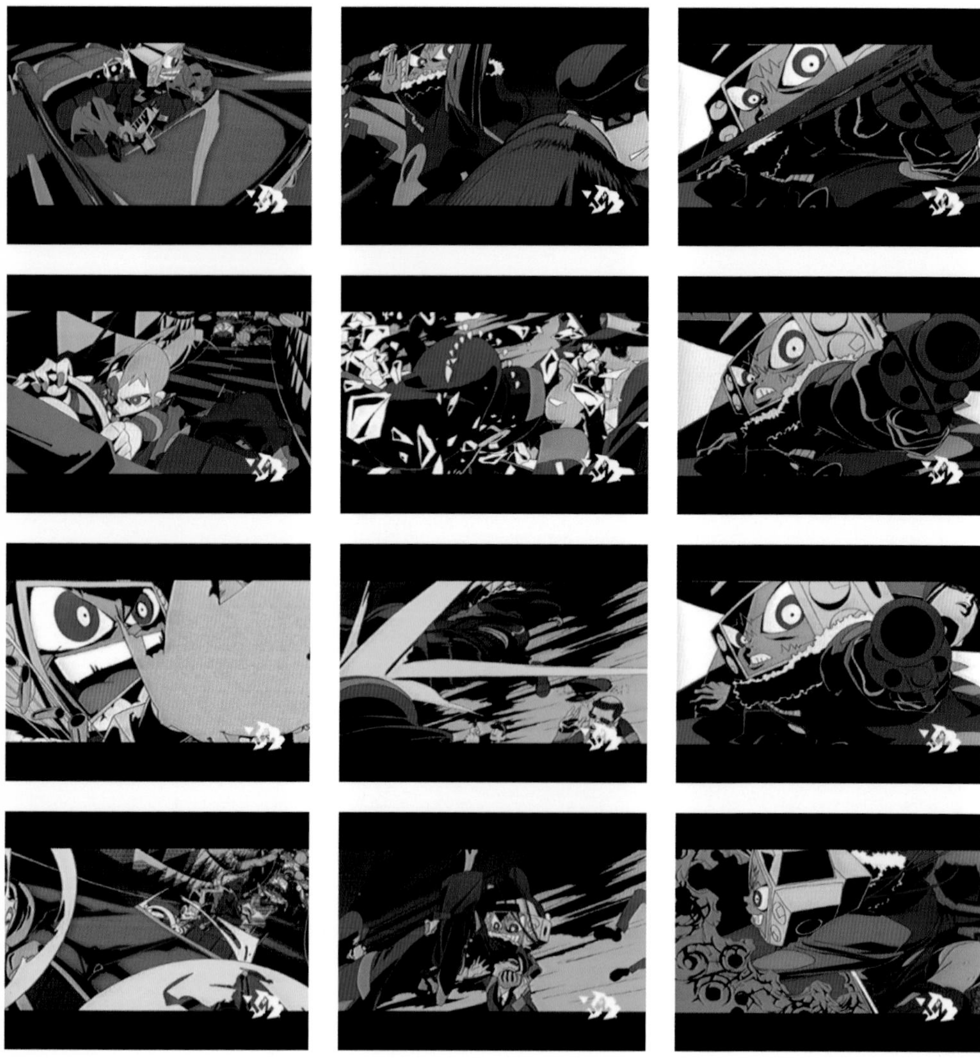

CONCEPT

日本から海外、そしてまた日本へと伝染して行く「MANGA」を記号として捉え、新しい造形美、表現の抽出をコンセプトに活動する。

Manga, which transmits from Japan to overseas and back to Japan again, is grasped by Imaitoonz as a symbol, as he produces works through the concept of: the extraction of a new compositional aesthetic and a new form of expression.

CATEGORY
Everything

TEL / FAX
+81 (0) 3 5430 1181
—

E-MAIL
info@imaitoonz.com
info@philspace.com

URL
http://www.philspace.com (phil co., ltd.)
http://www.imaitoonz.com

TOOLS
Photoshop,
Painter,
Final Cut,
Premiere

Born in 1971. A designer, illustrator, and comic artist. He has produced works for various fields, including an OP animation for MTV's "Top of Japan" in 1995, A TV commercial for Suntory "C.C. Lemon", a PR animation for Nike Presto, a music video for Ken Ishii, and an Imaitoonz collaborative shoe with Reebok. His animation works have been invited for presentation at overseas film festivals, and the animation movie "Dead Leaves" has been released, in which Imaitoonz handled the planning, original story, and character design.

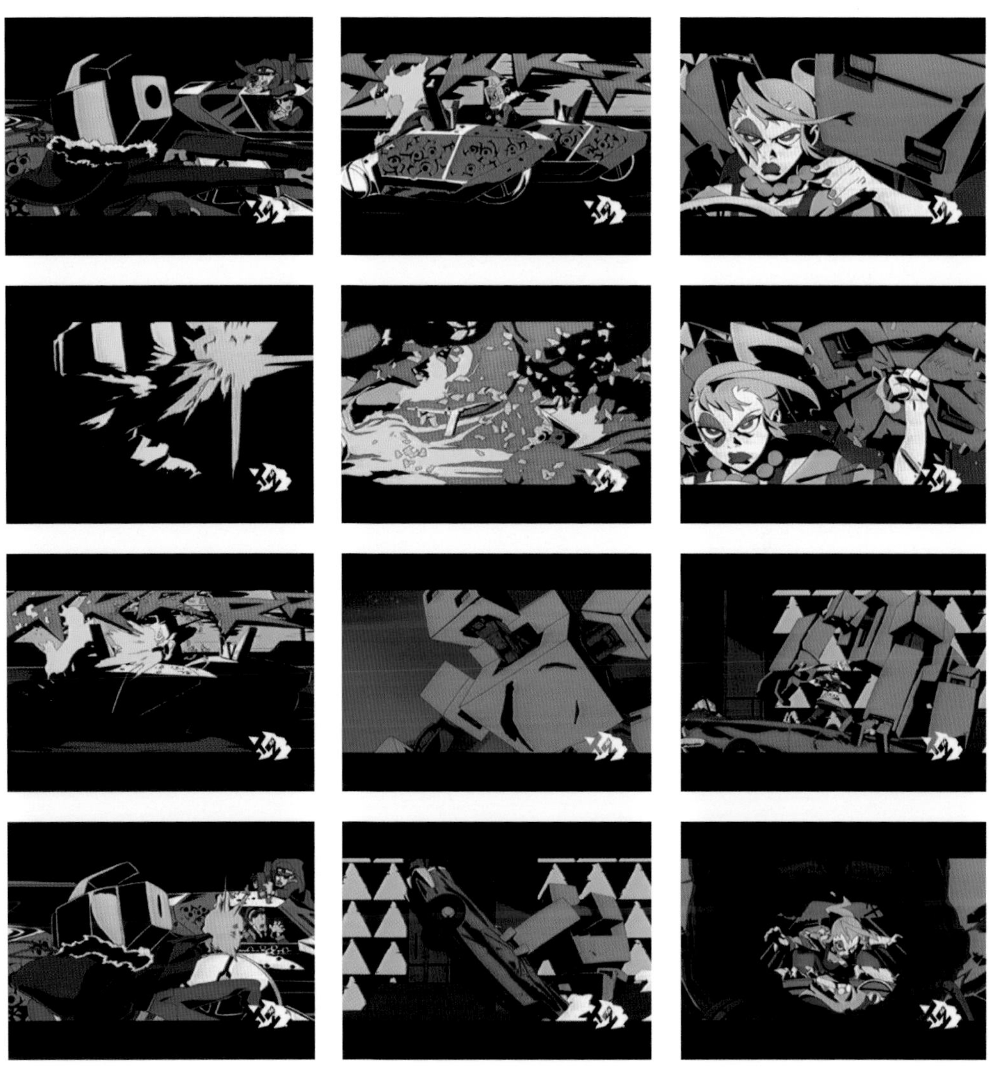

Animation Movie - *DEAD LEAVES*
(©Production I.G / MANGA ENTERTAINMENT, 2004)
Supervision: Hiroyuki Imaishi
Plan + Character: Imaitoonz
Producer: Katsuji Morishita
Production: Production I.G

036 西郡 勲 ISAO NISHIGORI

PROFILE
1974年生まれ。文化学院高等部美術科在学中に、CGを駆使したVJを始める。1995年MTV Station IDコンテストグランプリ受賞をきっかけにMTV JAPAN入社。現在はPV・CMなどの映像作家として、クリエイティブプロダクションP.I.C.S.所属。SIGGRAPH、PROMAX&BDAなどで受賞多数。2004年文化庁メディア芸術祭アニメーション部門優秀賞、SICAF Animated Film Festival（韓国）審査員賞受賞ほか。

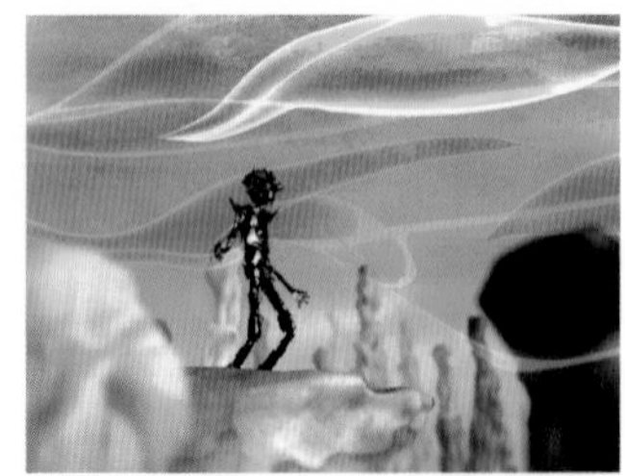

1

2

CONCEPT
感覚を刺激する様な、印象に残る作品づくり。

Creating works that stimulate the senses, and make a deep impression upon the viewer.

CATEGORY
Live action、3DCG

TEL / FAX
+81 (0) 3 5785 1780
+81 (0) 3 5785 1784

E-MAIL
post@picsco.net

URL
http://www.picsco.net

TOOLS
LightWave 3D,
Photoshop,
After Effects

Born in 1974. While Nishigori was attending Bunka Academy High School Department of Fine Art, he began VJing using CGs. After winning the grand prix at 1995 MTV Station-ID Contest, he entered MTV JAPAN. Currently, he handles music videos and TV commercials at the creative production firm P.I.C.S.. Nishigori has won numerous awards at competitions including Siggraph and Promax&BDA. He has also won such awards as an Excellence Prize in the Animation Division of 2004 Japan Media Arts Festival, and a Juries' Award at South Korea's SICAF Animated Film Festival.

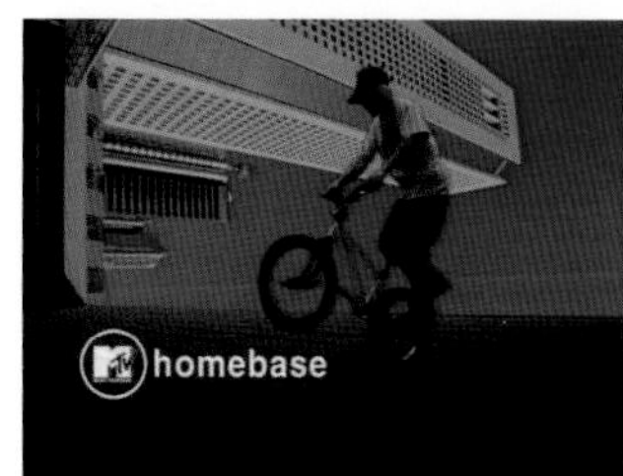

3

4

1
PV - ACIDMAN Short Film「彩 -SAI-（前篇）/ 廻る、巡る、その核へ」ACIDMAN Short Film, *-SAI- / Revolving...to the core*（東芝EMI TOSHIBA EMI LIMITED, 2004）
Director + CG: 西郡勲 Isao Nishigori
CG: 米澤拓也 Takuya Yonezawa, 伊藤まゆみ Mayumi Ito
Producer: 松居秀之 Hideyuki Matsui
Production by P.I.C.S.
2004年文化庁メディア芸術祭アニメーション部門 優秀賞受賞作品

2
PV - ACIDMAN, *SOL*（東芝EMI TOSHIBA EMI LIMITED, 2005）
Director + CG: 西郡勲 Isao Nishigori, 米澤拓也 Takuya Yonezawa
Producer: 松居秀之 Hideyuki Matsui
Production by P.I.C.S.

3
CM -「リバー・オブ・ミュージック篇」*River of Music*（アイリバー・ジャパン iriver Japan, 2005）
Director + CG: 西郡勲 Isao Nishigori
Camera: 小林基己 Motoki Kobayashi
Light: 古屋達也 Tatsuya Furuya
A&P: 大広+ピクニック・アド Daiko Advertising Inc. + PICNIC AD

4
On Air Promotion - *MTV home base / pure music package* (2000)
Director + CG: 西郡勲 Isao Nishigori
Producer: 松居秀之 Hideyuki Matsui
DP: 河津太郎 Taro Kawazu
Gaffer: 中川大輔 Daisuke Nakagawa
Productin by P.I.C.S.

映像提供：MTV JAPAN

037 出雲重機 IZMOJUKI

PROFILE

出雲重機＝大久保淳二。1974年東京都生まれ。専門学校職員、漫画家アシスタントを経て現在フリー。キャラクターデザインからイラストレーション制作、グラフィックデザイン、映像制作、アートディレクションなど多方面に活動中。

CONCEPT

あり得ないモノが日常空間に現れる。そんな非現実的状況でありながら、現実でありうるという説得力を持たせること。今回掲載された作品は、MTV JAPANの木津裕史の力を借りて、過去に制作した作品（静止画）の世界観を映像化したもの。

An impossible object appears in everyday space: even in this kind of unreal situation, Ookubo aims to visually persuade the viewer that it is in fact possible. In the work presented here, he turned the world of the pictures he had created in the past into a motion graphic work, with the help of Hiroshi Kizu of MTV Japan.

CATEGORY
PV, Station ID

E-MAIL
information@izmojuki.com

TOOLS
Photoshop

TEL / FAX
+81 (0) 3 3791 7882 (Rare Drop)
+81 (0) 3 3791 7882 (Rare Drop)

URL
http://www.raredrop.jp
http://www.izmojuki.com

Born in 1974, in Tokyo. Ookubo is currently freelance, after experiencing jobs such as working at a college and working as an assistant for a manga author. He is currently active in various fields, including character design, illustration, graphic design, motion graphic production, and art direction.

Station ID - *ARAKAWA strikes!!!* (©MTV Japan Inc., 2004)
Director + Editor: Yuji Kizu (MTV JAPAN)
Concept + Design: Junji Okubo (IZMOJUKI)
CGI: Joji Hayashi (SPICE Inc. / www.spice-inc.co.jp)
Composite: Noriko Ishihara (SPICE Inc.)
Cordinator + Logo Design: Kentaro Fujimoto
Picture: Juri Watai
Production Management:
Midori Hibino (MTV JAPAN)
Cam: Yuji Kizu, Noriaki Tanaka, Yusuke Kiki, Ryuichi Negishi, Kazuya Okamoto
Music: Noriaki Tanaka, Yuji Kizu
MA: Kohei Takagi (Video-Tech)
Voice: Maya Sakamoto
Staring: Seisiro Fujimoto, Kodama Takayoshi, Yusuke Kiki, Ryuichi Negishi, Kazuya Okamoto

038 影山二郎 / 右脳事件
JIRO KAGEYAMA / unou-jikenn inc.

PROFILE
広告制作を中心とした企画・演出ユニット。2003年に制作活動を開始する。映像ディレクターを中心に、シナリオ、デザイン、音楽、Webと、全方位的な企画・演出・プロデュースを行う。活動領域はコンテンツ制作のみならず、プロダクト企画やCIデザイン、イベントプロデュース、広告プロモーション企画の立案・演出まで多岐にわたる。右脳事件の活動の主体は「企画」に起因するものであり、あくまでもその実現ツールとして「コンテンツ演出」を行うことによって、「芸術性」と「商品性」を高い次元で融和させた創作活動を実現している。

CONCEPT
「Live creation」。企画から最終的な演出・プロデュースまで、プロジェクト単位でのコンセプト・メイクを最重要視することで、常に先進的、かつ包括的なクリエイティブを行っている。

"Live creation." By prioritizing the concept-making of each project, from the planning to the final presentation and producing, Kageyama constantly performs creative activities that are progressive and comprehensive.

1

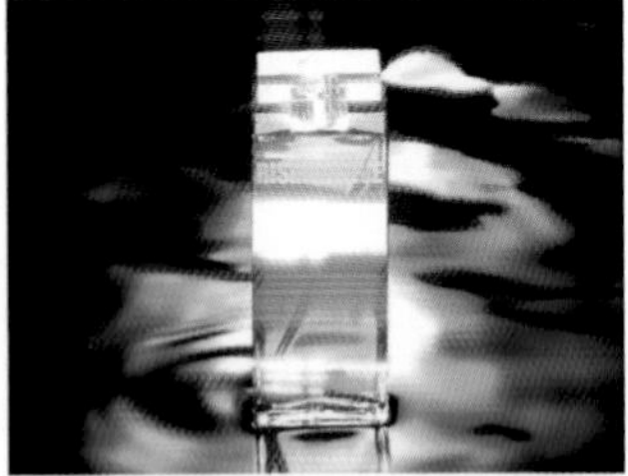

2

CATEGORY
AD, PR, Documentary,
Motion Graphics

TEL / FAX
+81 (0) 3 3405 2061
+81 (0) 3 3405 2062

E-MAIL
info@unou-jikenn.com

URL
http://www.unou-jikenn.com

TOOLS
Sony DSR-450WSL,
Sony DSR-PD150,
Sony DSR-50,
Final Cut Studio,
Shake, After Effects,
Illustrator, Photoshop

A planning and direction unit, specializing in advertisement production. Formed by members who were active in fields such as the organization and direction of stage performances, regional invigoration projects, and the organization of advertising/PR events. Unou-Jikenn became active in January of 2003, with a base of commercial motion graphic production. In November of 2004, they became a corporation. They perform multidirectional planning, direction, and producing, with motion graphic direction as their key activity, but also handle things such as scenarios, design, music, and websites.

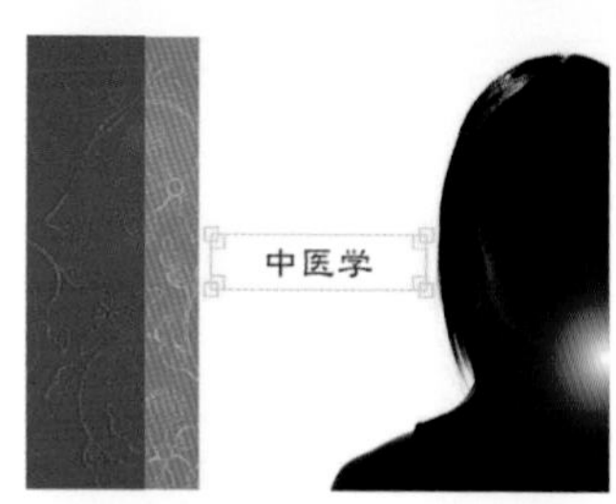

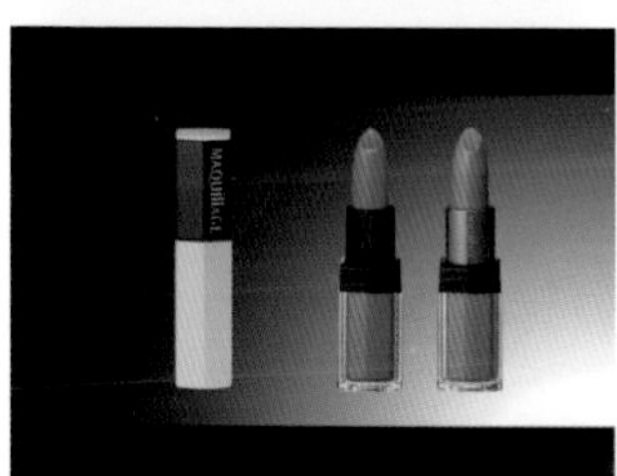

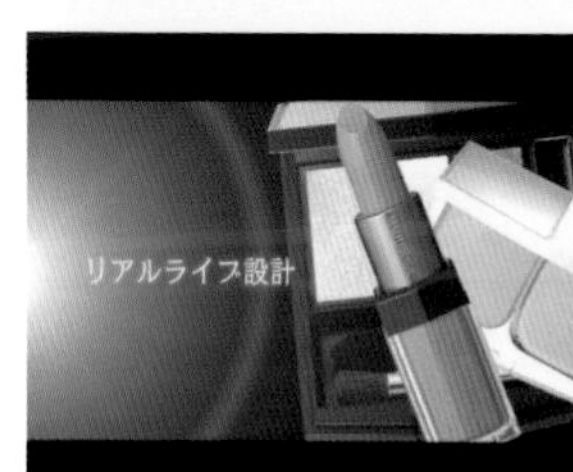

3

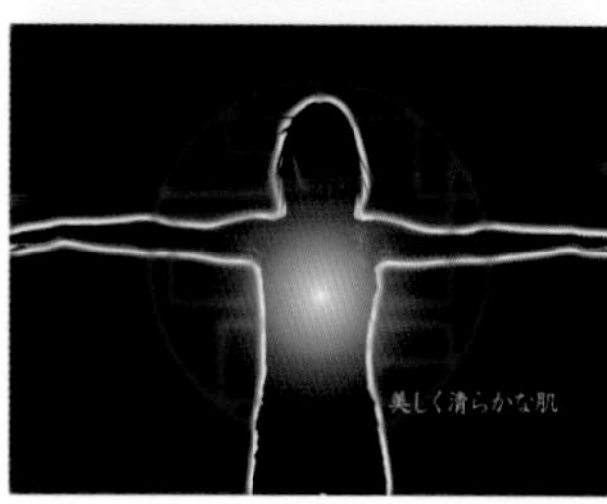

4

1
Opening Movie - *BAKU2004* (©BAKU, 2004)

2
PR Video - *RISINGWAVE*
(©FITS Corporation K.K., 2004)

3
VP - 資生堂「マキアージュ」
Shiseido, *Maquillage* (©Kadobeya, 2005)

4
VP - 資生堂「シノアドア」
Shiseido, *Sinoadore* (©Kadobeya, 2004)

039 堀切 潤 / ポータブルコミュニティ
JUN HORIKIRI / PORTABLE[K]OMMUNITY

PROFILE

1975年、愛媛県松山市生まれ。2000年からportable[k]ommunity、もしくはソロとして、高密度の音と映像をリアルタイムに構築・交錯・展開させるパフォーマンス、インスタレーションを国内外で発表し始める。既成、自作を問わず、ソフトウェア、ハードウェアが内包するバグの中に暴力的かつ繊細な美を発見し、その可能性を作品化していく。

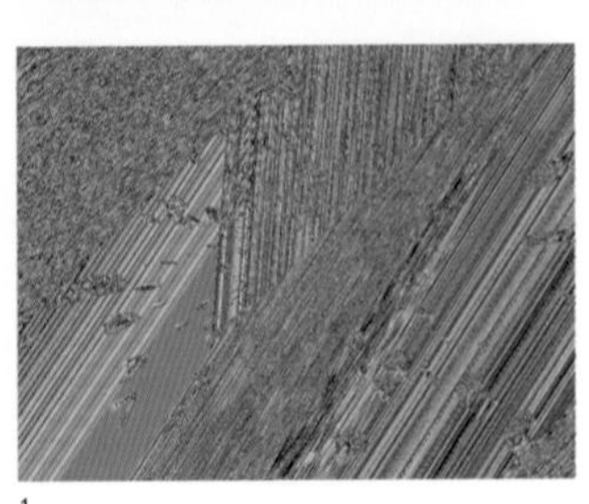

1

2

CONCEPT

技術をオペレートするのではなく技術と戦うことにより、フルデジタルな表現でありながら再現不可能な一回性の表現を獲得することにある。

By conflicting with technology instead of merely operating it, he aims to create works that, even though are fully digital, have an unreproducable once-ness.

CATEGORY
Art

TEL / FAX
090 9556 1136
—

E-MAIL
jun-horikiri@jpn.ac
portablekommunity@hotmail.com

URL
http://www.junhorikiri.com

TOOLS
Mac OS 9.2 + OS X,
Max / MSP4.1 + Nato.0+55

Born in 1975, in Matsuyama, Japan. Since 2000, Horikiri has been presenting performances and installations around the globe that construct, interlace, and develop high-density sounds and visuals in real-time, either as a solo artist or through the unit portable[k]ommunity. He discovers a destructive yet delicate beauty within the bugs that are inherent in various software and hardware, whether self-made or ready-made, and develops their potential into works of art.

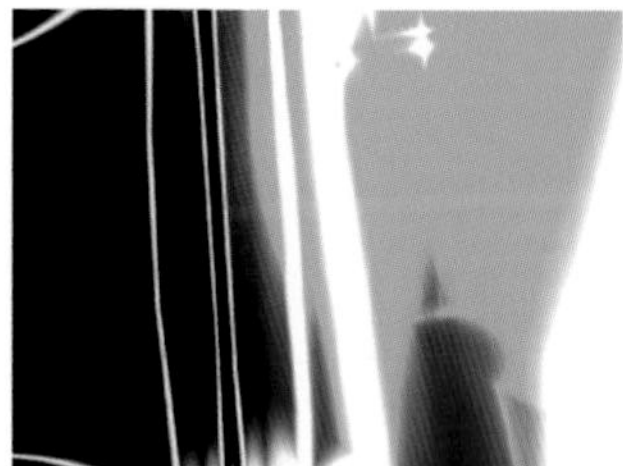

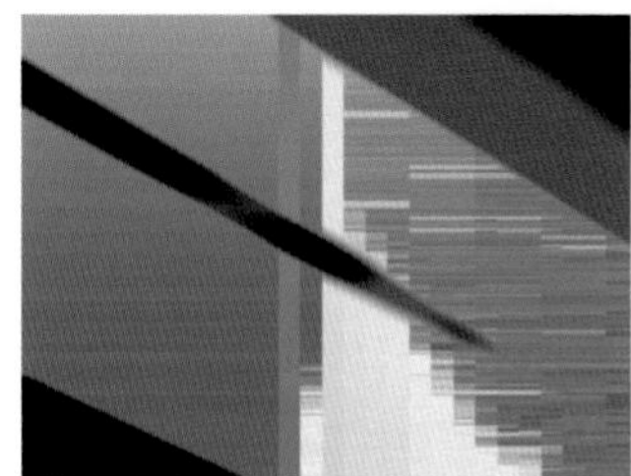

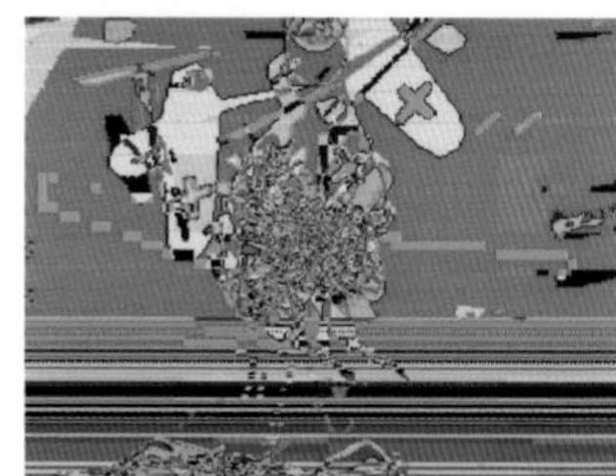

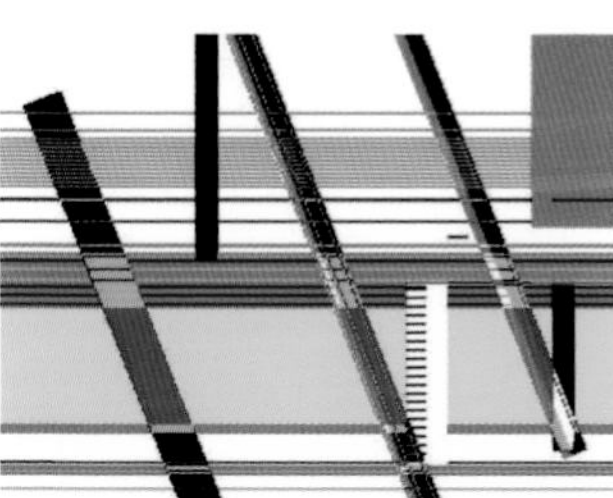

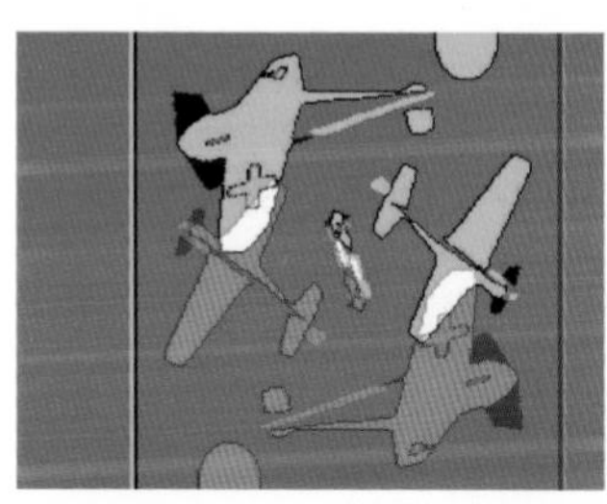

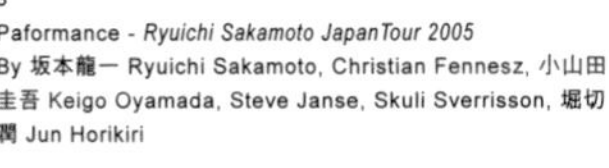

1
Paformance - *anti-format* (SPACE SHOWER TV, 2004)
By DJ klock, 堀切潤 Jun Horikiri

2
Exhibition - *AudioVisual work, setp11or today* (金沢21世紀美術館 21st Century Museum of Contemporary Art, Kanazawa, 2005)
By 堀切潤 Jun Horikiri

3
Paformance - *Ryuichi Sakamoto JapanTour 2005*
By 坂本龍一 Ryuichi Sakamoto, Christian Fennesz, 小山田圭吾 Keigo Oyamada, Steve Janse, Skuli Sverrisson, 堀切潤 Jun Horikiri

4
DVD - *portable[k]ommunity DVD* (Sónar 2003, SónarCinema, 2003)
By 堀切潤 Jun Horikiri, 澤井妙治 Taeji Sawai

3

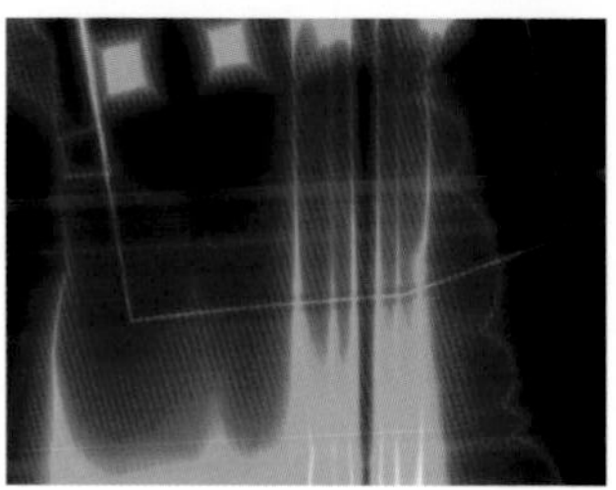

4

<u>040</u> ジュウリョク JURYOKU

PROFILE
2004年、WOW所属のデザイナー中路琢磨、水野祐佑、工藤薫でクリエイティブユニットJURYOKUを結成。2004年製作「The Poetry of Suburbs」でRESFEST 2005ワールドツアーにノミネート。graf、Yoshio Kuboとのコラボレーションによる最新作「fit-ment」ではインターフェイスに反応し、レイアウトが無限に変化するリアルタイムモーショングラフィックス作品を制作。インタラクティブ性を意識した新しいビジュアルデザインの可能性を示した。

1 2 3 4 5 6 7 8

CONCEPT
設定したテーマを個々の世界観に置き換え、融合し、新たな表現を生む。ジャンルや手法にとらわれない幅広い新しいビジュアル表現を目指す。

CATEGORY
Movie, Graphic,
Realtime Motion Graphics

TEL / FAX
+81 (0) 3 5775 0055
+81 (0) 3 5775 0056

E-MAIL
juryoku@w0w.co.jp

URL
http://www.w0w.co.jp/juryoku

TOOLS
Quartz Composer,
3D Studio MAX,
Cinema 4D,
After Effects,
Final Cut Pro

In 2004, the creative unit "Juryoku" was formed by Takuma Nakaji, Yusuke Mizuno, and Kaoru Kudo. Juryoku's work from 2004, "The Poetry of Suburbs," was nominated for the Resfest 2005 World Tour. Their new work "fit-ment," a collaboration with Graf and Yoshio Kubo, is a real-time motion graphic work in which the composition goes through infinite changes as it reacts to an interface. It presents the possibilities of a new type of visual design that focuses on interactivity.

9, 10, 11, 12, 13, 14, 15, 16

1-6
Original Work - *The poetry of suburbs* (2004)

7-12
Original Work - *fit-ment* (2005)

13-16
Original Work - *Botanica* (2005)

Creating new forms of expression by displacing certain themes with individual worldviews, and fusing them. JURYOKU aims to produce new visual forms of expression that are not caught up in any particular genres or methodologies.

041 タナカカツキ
KATSUKI TANAKA

PROFILE

1966年大阪生まれ。京都精華大学美術学部（現芸術学部）ビジュアルデザイン学科在学中に小学館新人漫画賞を受賞、マンガ家デビュー。フルCGアニメ「カエルマン」制作・発売を機に、映像の世界へも仕事の幅を広げる。また、インターネットラジオ「デジオナイト」（http://dedionight.com/）を開局するなど活動のジャンルは多岐にわたり、笑いの中にときおりのぞかせるノスタルジックで美しい世界観はほかに類をみない。著書に「バカドリル」「オッス!トン子ちゃん」（扶桑社）などがある。

CATEGORY
Manga

TEL / FAX
—
+81 (0) 3 5773 8067

E-MAIL
ka2ki@kaerucafe.com

URL
http://www.kaerucafe.com

TOOLS
Power Mac G4,
After Effects,
Photoshop

Born in Osaka in 1966. Tanaka debuted as a manga author while attending Kyoto Seika University's Faculty of Art, by being awarded Shogakukan's Rookie Manga Author Award. He began working on motion graphics after the production and release of the full CG animation work "KAERUMAN." His activities span through various fields, e.g., he has his own internet radio station "Dedionight" (http://dedionight.com). Tanaka's works display implicit elements of nostalgia and beauty within a base of humor. Examples of his publications are "Bakadoriru" and "Ossu! Tonko-chan."

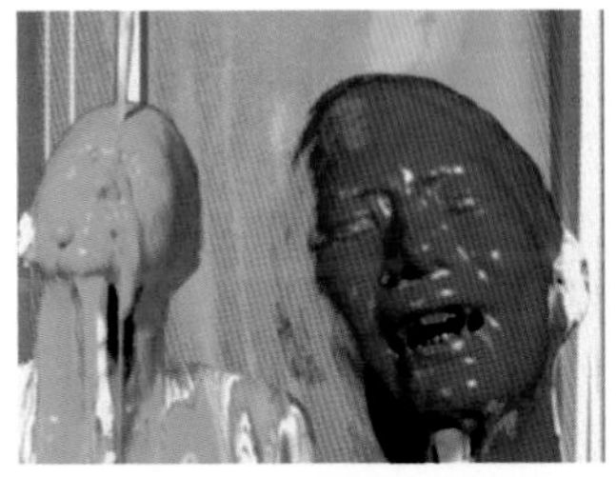

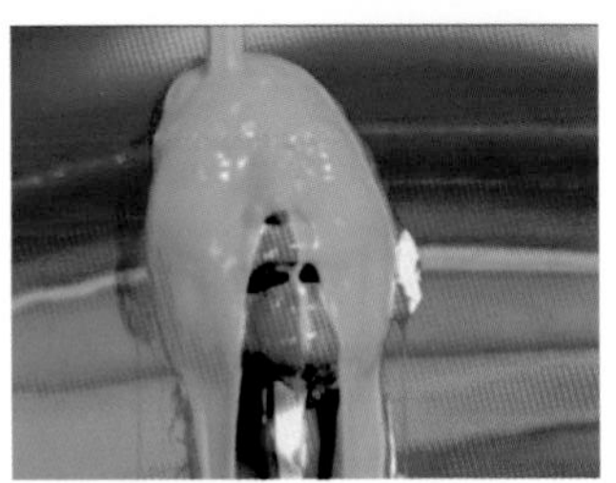

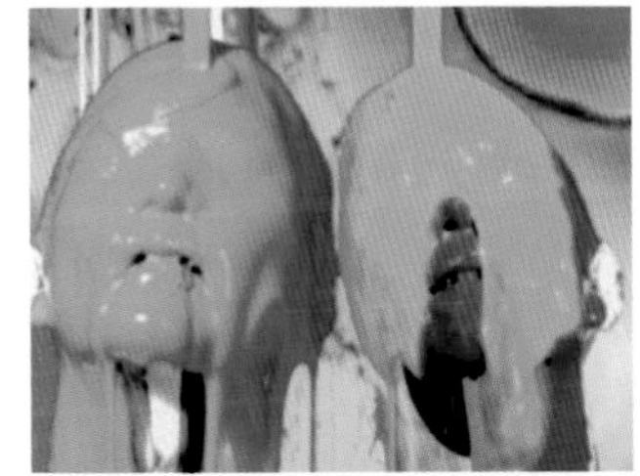

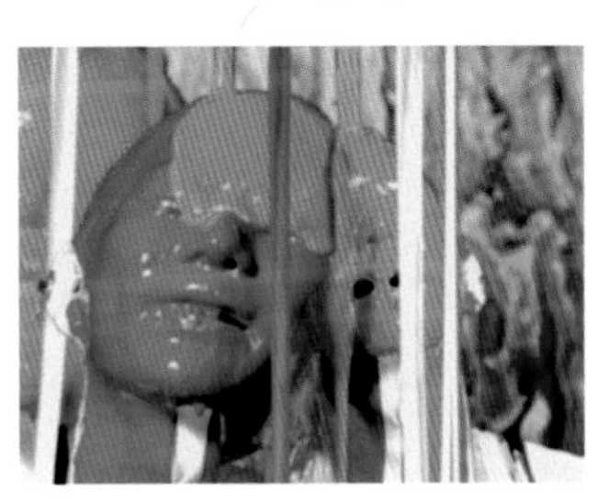

DVD -「赤ちゃんジングル 3」*akachanjingle3*
タナカカツキ DVD「赤ちゃん」(DDD DVD) に収録
it records on a DVD Katsuki Tanaka "Akachan" DDD DVD
(©Katsuki Tanaka / icca / DDD Manufacture committee, 2005)

042 若野 桂 / ガール・スタジオ
KATSURA MOSHINO / GIRL STUDIO

PROFILE

1968年生まれ。1980年代後半からCDジャケットのイラストレーションをはじめ、ミュージッククリップ、ナイキのバスケットボール世界キャンペーンCM、ソニーのAIBO第三世代のプロダクトデザインなどを手掛ける。2002年、現代音楽家の竹村ノブカズの音楽に8ヶ月かけて映像を付けた9分45秒のショート・ムービー「SIGN」は、シカゴの最も先鋭的なレコードレーベルであるTHRILL JOCKEYから発売された。この作品は、世界各国で反響を呼び、スペイン、イタリア、アメリカ各地の映画祭に出品され、上映されている。

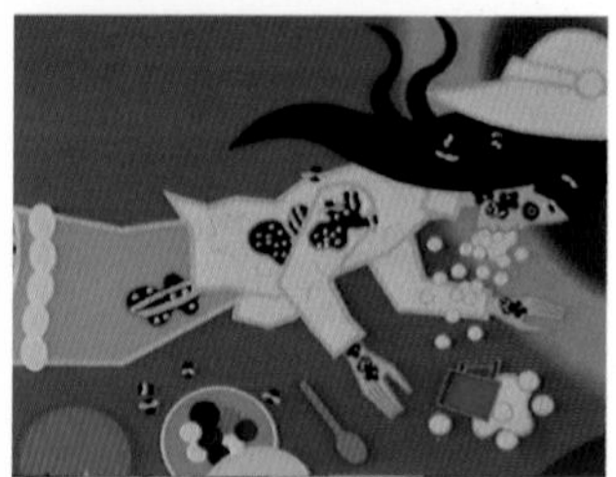
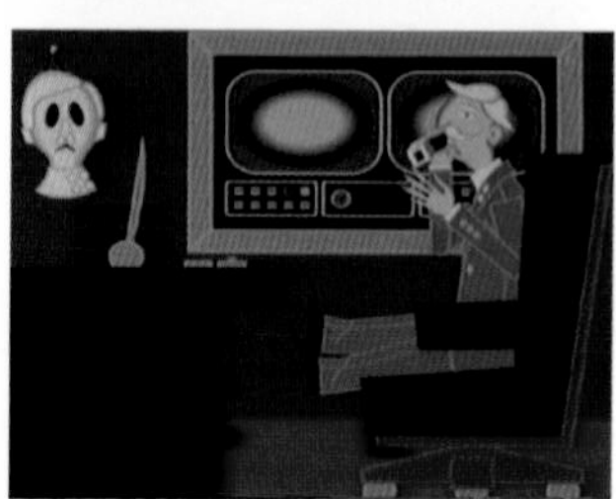

1

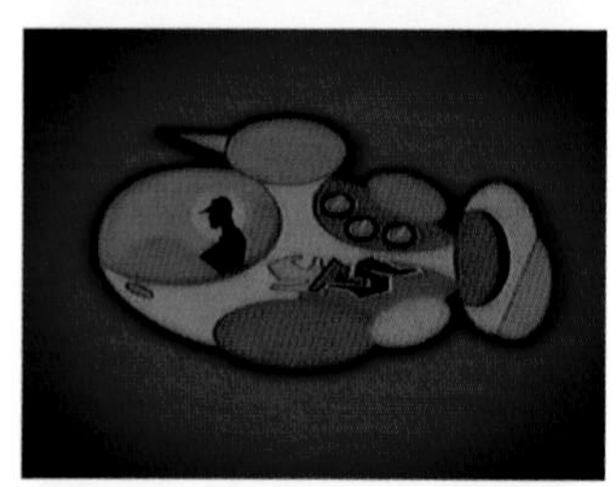

2

1
Short Movie - *SIGN* (2001)
Story + Continuity + Character Design + Animation + Edit : Katsura Moshino
Music: Nobukazu Takemura

2
PV - DJ YAS from KAMINARI KAZOKU, *SUBMARINE* (ENTOTSU RECORDINGS, 2000)
Director: Katsura Moshino
Director Of Photography : Hiroshi Inukai
Animation: Katsura Moshino
Editor: Katsura Moshino
Music: DJ-YAS (KAMINARI KAZOKU)
Editing Studio: IMPACT

CONCEPT

自分自身や関係者が10年後に見て、「あー死にたい」と思わなくてよい作品。

Producing works that will not become objects of creative disillusionment in ten years time.

CATEGORY
Character Animation (Short Movie), CM, PV, VJ

TEL / FAX
—
—

E-MAIL
rawcom@infoseek.jp

URL
http://girlstudio.at.infoseek.co.jp

TOOLS
Mac, Smoke,
After Effects,
Illustrator,
Photoshop,
Digital HD Camera

Born in 1968. Beginning from the late 1980's, Moshino has handled projects such as illustrations for CD covers, music videos, a TV commercial for a worldwide Nike basketball campaign, and the product design of the third generation Sony Aibo. "Sign," a 9 minute 45 second film in which Moshino spent eight months creating the visuals for a track by the musician Nobukazu Takemura, was released from Chicago's most progressive record label Thrill Jockey in 2002. This work received global acclaim, and was submitted to and screened at many film festivals, including ones in Spain, Italy, and the U.S..

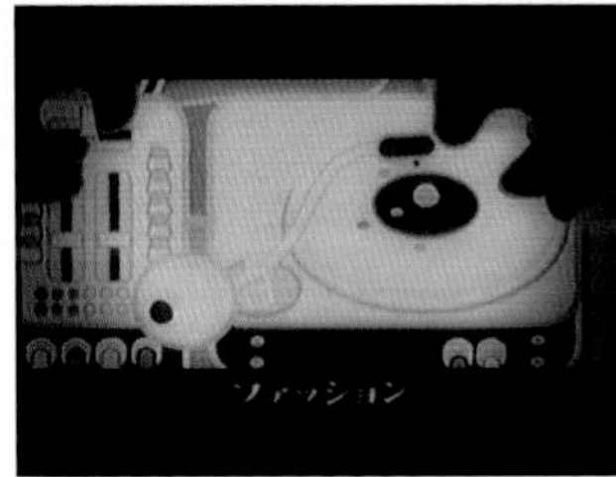

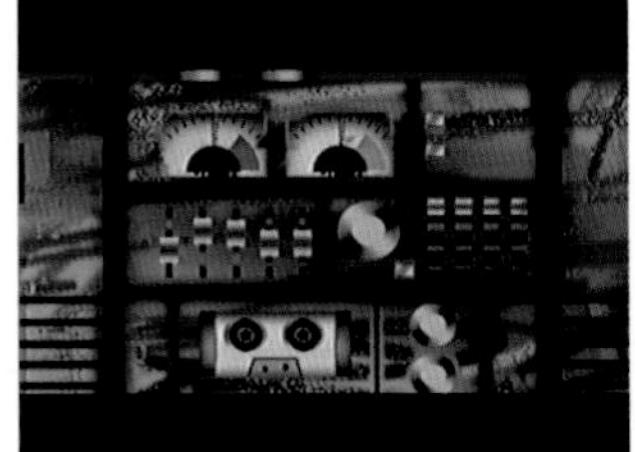

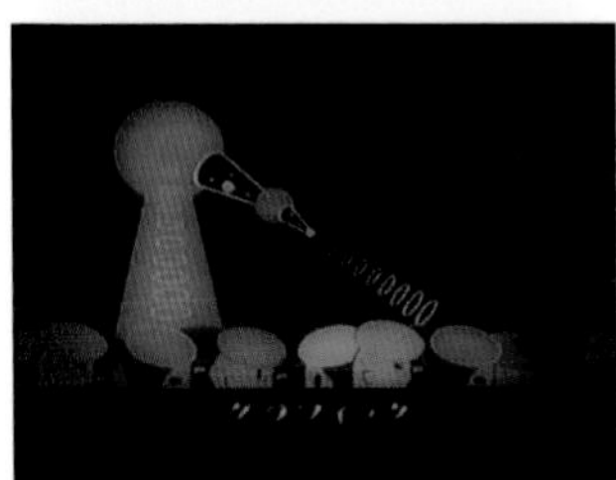

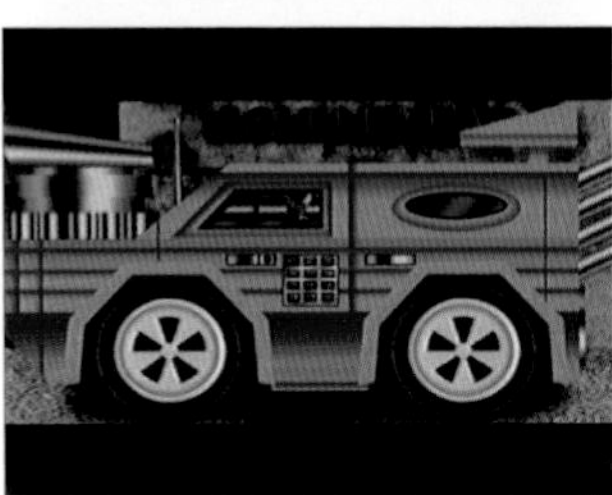

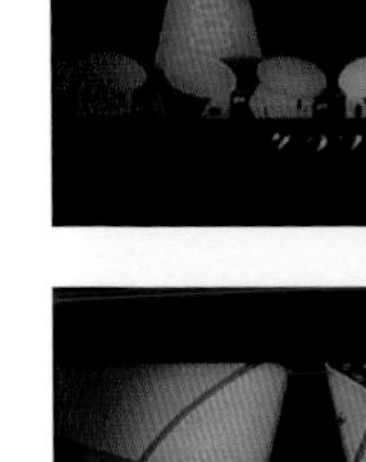

3 4

3
CM - 東京モード学園「一つ目の宇宙人編」
TOKYO MODE GAKUEN, *one eyed alien*
(MODE GAKUEN, 2000)
Director: Katsura Moshino
Animation: Katsura Moshino
Music: DJ KRUSH
Editing Studio: SONY PCL
Agency: HAKUHODO Inc.

4
PV - nobodyknows+,「ココロオドル」*Kokoro Odoru*
(Sony Music Entertainment Inc., 2004)
Director: Katsura Moshino
Animation: Katsura Moshino
Editing Studio: Digital Tank
Music: nobodyknows+
Shooting Studio + Lighting Staff: Naoya Hatta from HEAT
Director of Photography: Hideo Fujiwara
Video Engineer: Shin Hasegawa (GRAN)
Shooting Coordination: Digital Tank
Model Coorporation: Central Japan
Dance: Rose Hips
Styling: CHISA
Break Dance: top up production
Software Coorporation: Adobe Systems Incorporated

043 カワイオカムラ KAWAI+OKAMURA

PROFILE

岡村寛生（1968 年京都市生まれ）と川合匠（1968 年大阪市生まれ）が京都市立芸術大学大学院在学中の 1993 年に結成したユニット。結成当初はペインティングを主としたインスタレーションを表現手法としたが、1997年の個展を機に映像へシフトし、近年はアニメーションが主となっている。2005年「第1回アンダー 10 ミニッツデジタルシネマフェスティバル」グランプリ受賞。

CONCEPT

風刺、滑稽、新しい笑いとその教訓。虚と実の間にある「リアル」をテーマにしたコメディー。さまざまなイメージの集積と無限連鎖が錯綜しながらも絶妙に構成された、ビジュアル・ビート。

Satire, humor, and a new comedy along with its lessons. Comedy that picks up, as a theme, the “real” that lies between the imagined and the actual. A visual beat that is exquisitely composed in the midst of the jumble of infinite chains and many collected images.

1

2

CATEGORY
Animation

TEL / FAX
+81 (0) 75 771 0559
+81 (0) 75 771 0559

E-MAIL
kawaiokamura@yahoo.co.jp

URL
—

TOOLS
Panasonic AG-DVC30,
CASIO QV-3500EX,
Power Mac G4,
Premiere,
After Effects

A unit formed by Hiroki Okamura (born in 1968, Kyoto) and Takumi Kawai (born in 1968, Osaka) while they were students at Kyoto City University of Arts Graduate School. Kawai+Okamura originally made installation works with painting as the main medium, but after their personal exhibition in 1997, they shifted to motion graphics. Their main method of expression has recently been animation. In 2005, they won the grand prix at the "1st Under 10 Minutes Digital Cinema Festival. "

3

4

1
Short Movie - *Head Wrest-3001 Series*
(©Vermilion Pleasure Night, 2001)
Staring: Tomonari Mihara, Masanobu Yanobe, Naniwa no Torayan

2
Short Movie - *Ficfion Drill* (2002)
Voice: Shirou Gou
Co-Writer: Toshiro Kimura
Costume Production: Yoko Nishikawa

3
Short Movie - *AIRS* (2005)
Voice: Shirou Gou
Co-Writer: Toshiro Kimura
Costume Production: Yoko Nishikawa
Assistant Director: Takao Machiba

4
Short Movie - *Ficfion7* (2004)
Voice: Shirou Gou
Co-Writer: Toshiro Kimura
Costume Production: Yoko Nishikawa

「ヘコヒョン7」を含む「Under 10 minites Digital Cinema Festival」の優秀作品を収録したDVDがエイベックス・マーケティング・コミュニケーションズから発売中。

044

森野和馬
KAZUMA MORINO

PROFILE

1966年静岡県生まれ。1998年 ストライプファクトリー設立。世界最高峰のCG学会、SIGGRAPHにおいて、1993年から2005年までに10本の作品で入賞を果たす。数々のCMや、サントリー、日テレなどのモーションググラフィックス、KENISHIIや井上陽水のプロモーションビデオなどを手掛ける。プロダクトデザイナー石井洋二との照明・椅子の制作、アーティスト田中千絵とともに立ち上げたモノブランド「ラインワークス」など、さまざまな商品の企画作成も手掛ける。最近では愛知万博「瀬戸日本館」1階の総合ディレクターやニューヨークフィルムフェスティバルのオープニング映像を担当。

1　2　3

CONCEPT

時代に色褪せない作品づくり。

Creating works that do not fade with the age.

CATEGORY
Short Movie, PV, CM

TEL / FAX
+81 (0) 3 5772 3540

E-MAIL
kazuma@stripe.co.jp

URL
http://www.stripe.co.jp

TOOLS
Windows, Mac
Maya, Softimage, Studio MAX,
After Effects, Shake, Premiere,
Final Cut Pro, Photoshop, Illustrator

Born in 1966 in Shizuoka, Japan. He founded Stripe Factory in 1998. At Siggraph, the world's foremost CG conference, Morino received awards for ten of his works between 1993 and 2003. He has worked on numerous projects including TV commercials for Canon and Rikunabi Next, motion graphics for Suntory and Nippon Television Network, and music videos for KENISHII and Yosui Inoue. Recently, he was the general director of the first floor of "Japan Pavilion Seto" at Expo 2005 Aichi, Japan.

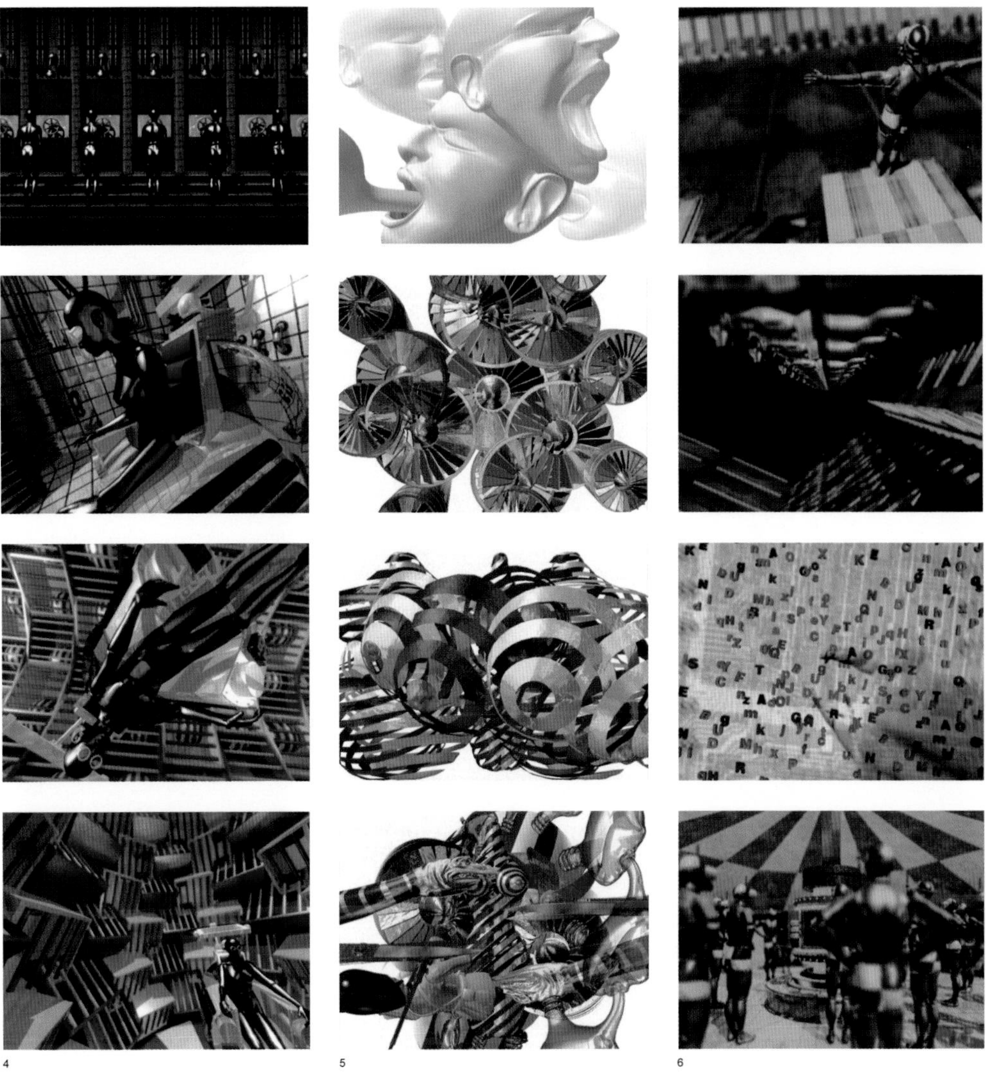

4

5

6

1 PV - 井上陽水「花の首飾り」
Yosui Inoue, *Hananokubikazari* (FOR LIFE MUSIC ENTERTAINMENT, 2001)
2 PV - KENISHII, *AWAKENING* (70Drums, 2002)
3 Original Work - *Runners* (1997)
Music: 薄井由行 Yoshiyuki Usui
4 Opening Movie - *Electronic Museum* (NHK, 1997)
Music: 薄井由行 Yoshiyuki Usui,
CG Animator: 沼沢良典 Yoshinori Numazawa
5 Original Work - *Free-Quent Objects* (1995)
Music: 薄井由行 Yoshiyuki Usui
6 Opening Movie - *Motion Graphics 97* (1997)
Music: 薄井由行 Yoshiyuki Usui

045 北岡一哉 / エディトリアル KAZUYA KITAOKA / EDITREAL

PROFILE

80年代半ば、西麻布にあったP.PICASSOという名のクラブでDJ活動を行う。90年代初期に、スペースシャワーTVという音楽chTVを設立。周りのDJたちが世の中に音を出すにあたり、ビデオの必要性とともに必然的にビデオ係を担う。そして、現在に至る。

1

2

3

CONCEPT

その事について考えた時の最初の閃き、思いつき。

The initial flash of inspiration and the ideas that occur when thinking about something.

CATEGORY
PV

TEL / FAX
—
—

E-MAIL
kazya8100@hotmail.com

URL
—

TOOLS
Mac

Kitaoka used to D.J. in the mid 80's at a club in Nishi Azabu called P. PICASSO. In the beginning of the 90's, he founded the music T.V. channel SPACE SHOWER TV. As other D.J.s emitted sounds into the world, Kitaoka was led to take care of the need for the visuals, and continues to this day.

4

5

1
PV - silent poets, *Suger man* (featuring Terry Hall)
(TOY'S FACTORY, 1998)

2
PV - Small Circle Of Friends, *HEADPHONE LOVER*
(SKYLARKIN, 1998)

3
PV - CHAR, *MUSTANG*
(EDOYA RECORDS, 1995)

4
PV - United Future Organization, *Spy's Spice*
(UNVERSAL, 1996)

5
PV - PEACE FORCE, *Mr. FREEDOM cd-extra*
(BMG, 1996)

046 黒坂圭太 KEITA KUROSAKA

PROFILE
1985年、壁面や岩肌を素材にした抽象映像でデビュー。さまざまな手法を用いた短編アニメーションを数多く制作。CM、漫画、イラストなども手掛け、MTV Station ID「パパが飛んだ朝」は国際的にも高く評価された。1999年から長編アニメ映画「緑子」を制作開始、現在も続行中。個展やワークショップなどの活動も積極的に行う。レティナ国際映画祭（1993）、アヌシー国際アニメ祭（1998）、BDA 国際デザイン賞（1998）、オタワ国際アニメ祭（1998）、オランダ国際アニメ祭（1998）などをはじめ受賞多数。

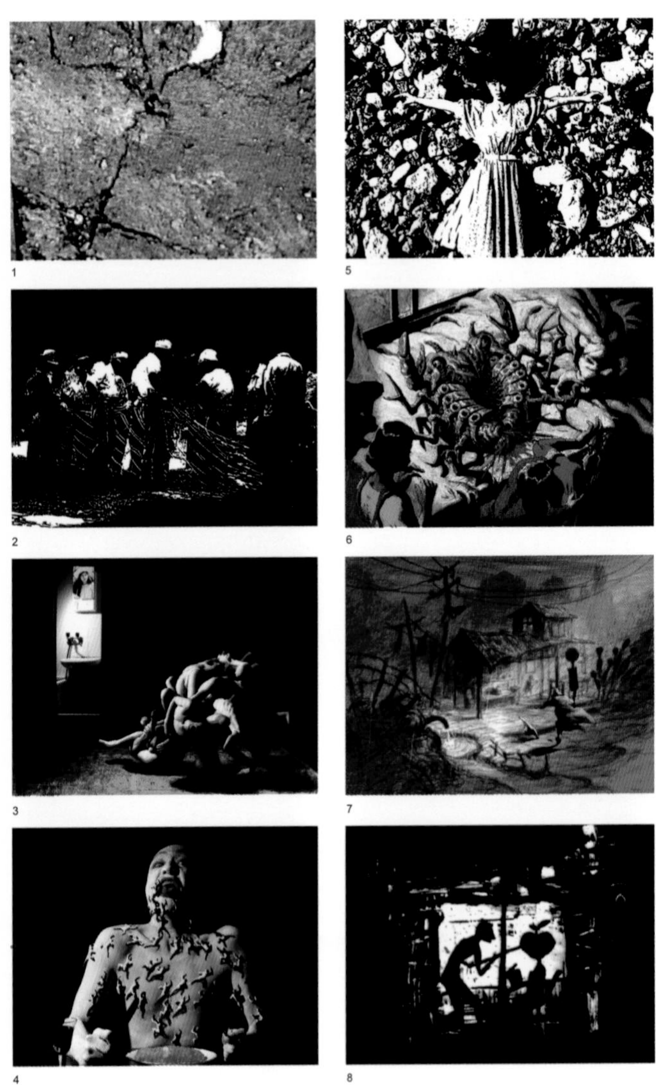
1 5 2 6 3 7 4 8

CATEGORY
Animation, Art

TEL / FAX
+81 (0) 3 5920 3454
+81 (0) 3 5920 3454

E-MAIL
—

URL
—

TOOLS
—

In 1985, Kurosaka debuted with his abstract motion graphics that used walls and the surfaces of stones as material. He has created numerous short animation works, using diverse techniques. His fields of work include T.V. commercials, manga, and illustrations. "Papa ga Tonda Asa [The Morning that Papa Flew]," the MTV Station ID. that he created, received international acclaim. He also actively holds exhibitions and workshops. He has won many awards at events including Annecy International Animation Festival '98, BDA International Design Awards '98, Ottawa International Animation Festival '98, and Holland Animation Film Festival '98.

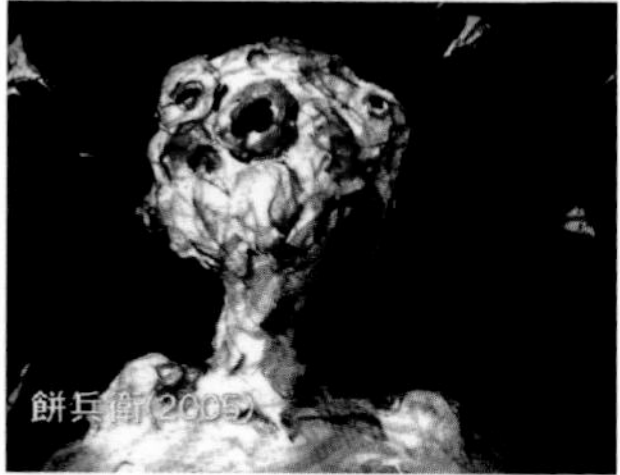

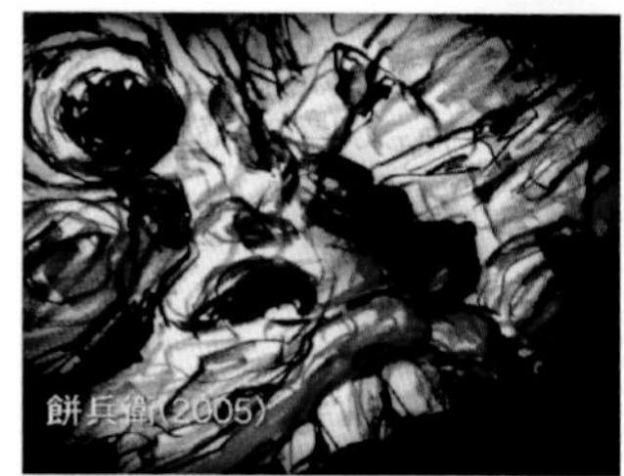

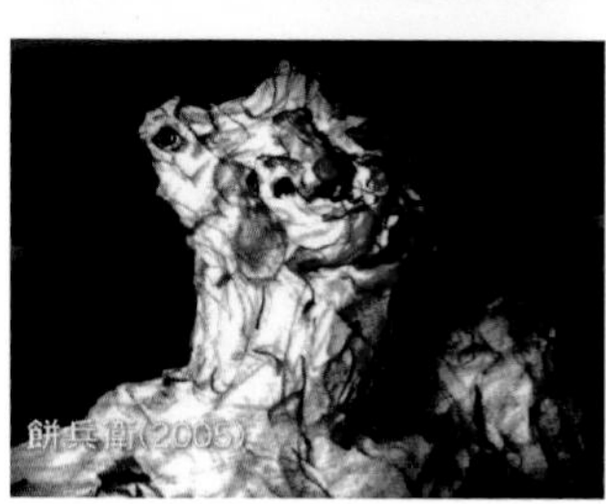

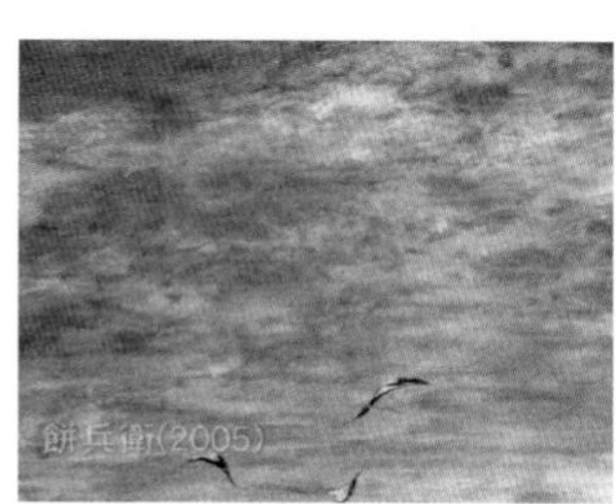

9

1
Animation - 「変形作品第２番」 *TRANSFORMATION No,2* (1984)

2
Animation - 「海の唄」 *SONG OF OCEAN* (1988)

3
Animation - 「個人都市」 *PERSONAL CITY* (1990)

4
Animation - *ATAMA* (©MTV Japan Inc., 1994)

5
Animation - 「春子の冒険」 *ADVENTURE OF HARUKO* (1991)

6
Animation - 「パパが飛んだ朝」 *THE DAY MY DAD FLEW* (©MTV Japan Inc., 1997)

7
Animation - 「冬の日」 *WINTER DAY* (©IMAGICA entertainment, 2003)

8
Animation - 「壁男」 *WALL MAN* (2004)

9
Animation - 「餅兵衛」 *MOCHIBE* (2005)

047 横井 謙 KEN YOKOI

PROFILE
1976年千葉県出身。大学卒業後CG専門学校へ。在学中に友人と制作した映像作品「Landscape Laundry」をきっかけに、個人で映像制作活動を始める。2D、3Dや、実写ビデオなどを用いて制作。NHK-BS2「デジタル・スタジアム」に2001年度入賞。RESFEST 2001 RESMIX SHORT#2で上映。森アートミュージアム主催のYVAI（ヤング・ビデオ・アーティスト・イニシアチブ）で佳作入賞。デジタルコンテンツグランプリ2002「新しい才能」の部入賞。布袋寅泰「DOBERMAN DVD」(2003)でミュージックビデオ制作。

1

2

3

4

5

6

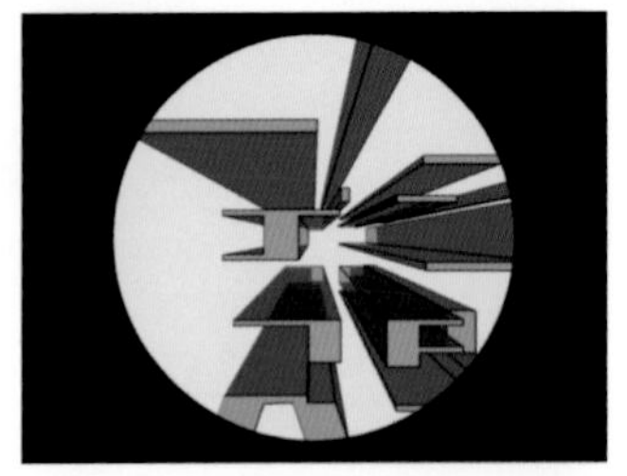
7

8

CATEGORY
Alternative, Free Style

TEL / FAX
070 6524 2929
+81 (0) 47 386 8687

E-MAIL
info@free-yokoi.com

URL
http://www.free-yokoi.com

TOOLS
Windows,
DV Cam,
Maya,
After Effects

Born in 1976, in Chiba Prefecture, Japan. After graduating from university, Yokoi entered a CG school. There, he made the work “Landscape Laundry” with a friend, and he has been producing motion graphics ever since. As material, he uses 2D images, 3D images, and footage. He won an award in NHK-BS2's “Digital Stadium” in 2001, and his work was screened at RESFEST 2001 RESMIX SHORT #2. Yokoi won an award in the “New Talent” section at Digital Contents Grand Prix 2002. He produced the music video for Tomoyasu Hotei's “DOBERMAN DVD” (2003).

1-2
Original Work - 「2Fスナッカー」 *2F Snacker* (2002)

3
Opening Title - 「デジスタ・アウォード2002」 *Digital Stadium Award 2002*
(NHKエンタープライズ NHK ENTERPRISES, 2002)

4
Opening Title - 「デジスタ・アウォード2005」 *Digital Stadium Award 2005*
(NHKエンタープライズ NHK ENTERPRISES, 2005)

5
Original Work - *bay No.3* (2004)

6
Opening Title - 「デジタルアートフェスティバル東京2003」 *Digital Art Festival* 2003
(NHKエンタープライズ NHK ENTERPRISES, 2003)

7
BGV - 「デジタル・スタジアム・2005年」 *Digital Stadium 2005*
(NHKエンタープライズ NHK ENTERPRISES, 2005)

8
Original Work - 「ミュージックビデオのための試作」 *Making for trial purposes for music video* (2003)

9
Opening Title - 「送ってみよう!・ケータイ俳句」 *Okuttemiyou! Mobile Haiku* (NHKエンタープライズ NHK ENTERPRISES, 2004)

10-11
Original Work - *Landscape Laundry* (2001)
Co-production: Naoki Takenaka

12-13
Original Work - 「M市とC市とG町の戯画」 *Modern Chouju Giga* (NHK, 2003)

14
Original Work - 「フォトグラファーとの共同制作作品」 *Joint production work with photographer* (2005)
Photo: 近藤要 Kaname Kondo

15
BGV - 「スーパーカー・ライブ (TV放送 BS2)」 *Super Car Live*
(NHKエンタープライズ NHK ENTERPRISES, 2003)

16
BGV - 「デジタル・スタジアム・2005年」 *Digital Stadium 2005*
(NHKエンタープライズ NHK ENTERPRISES, 2005)

9

13

10

14

11

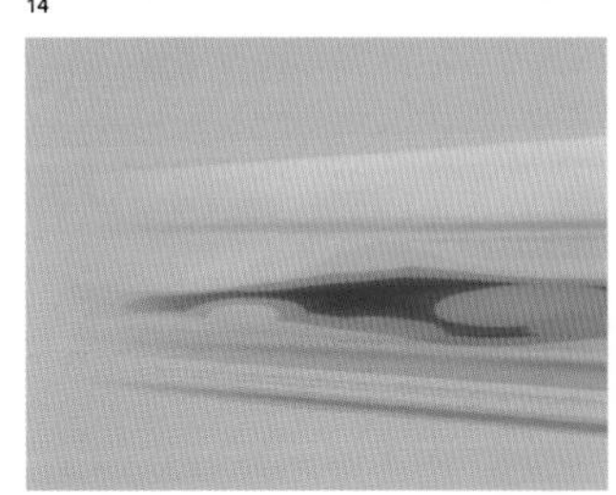

15

12

16

048 辻川幸一郎
KOICHIRO TSUJIKAWA

PROFILE

1972年生まれ。1993年よりレコードジャケットのデザイナーとして活動を開始。代表作品は、コーネリアス、SKETCH SHOW、UAなどのプロモーションビデオ、資生堂「HAKU」、NTT東日本、パルコのCMなど。世界15カ国以上をツアーするグローバルなデジタルフィルムフェス・RESFESTでは、自身で監督したコーネリアスのPV「DROP - Do It Again」が2002年ミュージックビデオ部門オーディエンスチョイスアワードを受賞。TRAKTORやミシェル・ゴンドリーを抑えての日本人アーティストの受賞として話題に。

CONCEPT

好奇心。何かを発見しながら作ること。どのような世界観の中でどのようなことをやっていくかという枠組みをシンプルに決めて、それを追究する。

Curiosity. Discovering something while creating something. To set a simple framework of what kind of things to do within what kind of worldview, and pursue this.

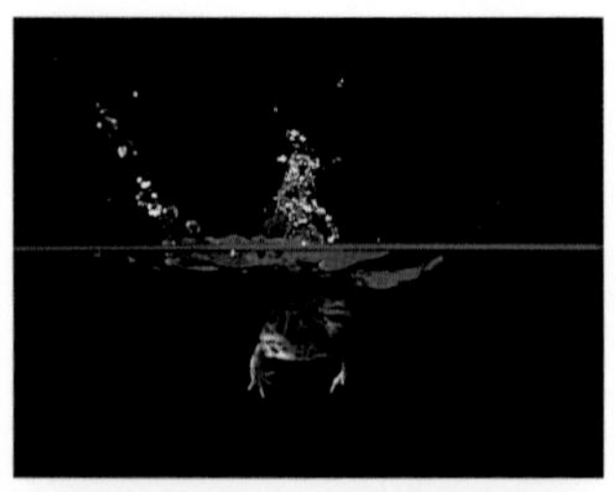

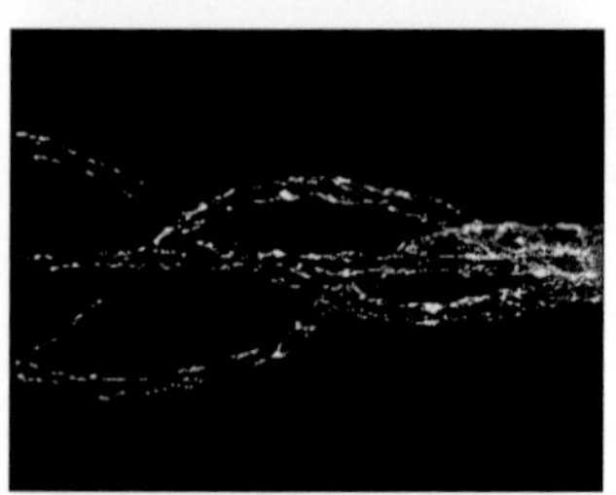

1

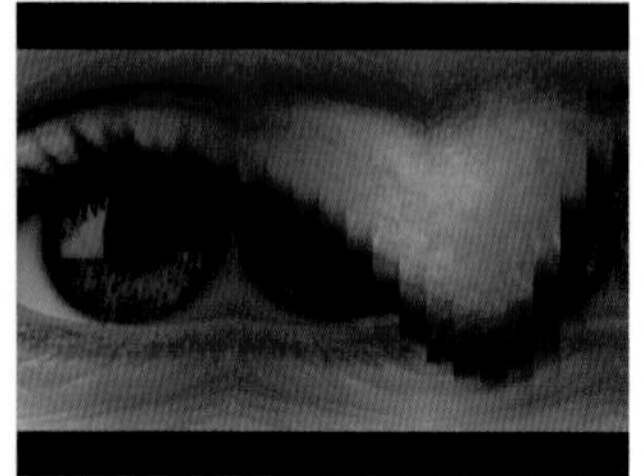
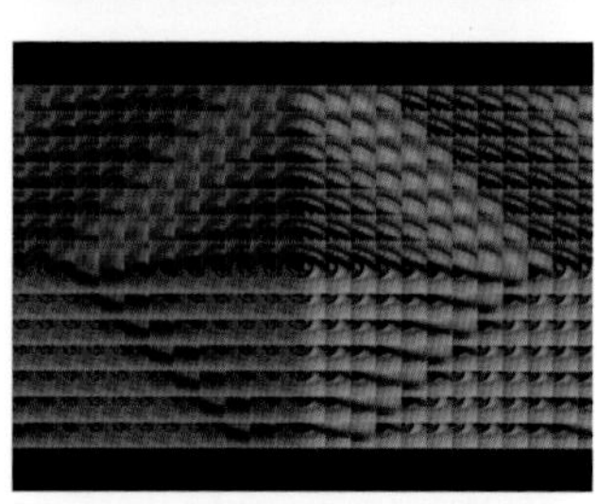

2

3

CATEGORY
PV, CM

TEL / FAX
—
—

E-MAIL
jick01@mac.com

URL
—

TOOLS
After Effects

Born in 1972. Tsujikawa began his creative activities in 1993, as a designer of record covers. Some of his representative works are: music videos for artists such as Cornelius, Sketch Show, and UA; works for Shiseido Haku, NTT East; and a T.V. commercial for Parco. At Resfest, a digital film festival that tours over fifteen countries, Tsujikawa's music video for Cornelius "Drop - Do it Again" won the Audience's Choice Award in 2002, winning over such powerhouses as Traktor and Michel Gondry.

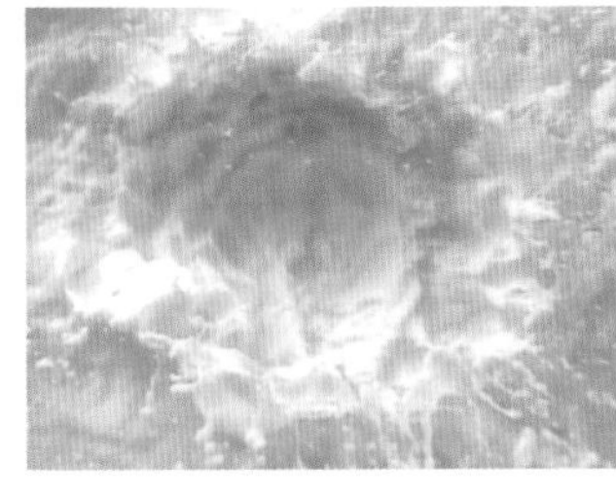

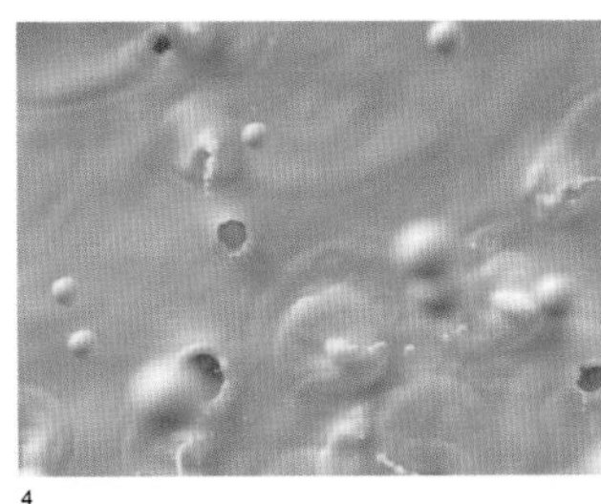

4

6

5

7

1
PV - Cornelius, *Drop* (Polystar, 2002)

2
Short Film - *eyes* (Getty Images, 2004)
Music: Cornelius

3
PV - Cornelius, *TONE TWILIGHT ZONE* (Polystar, 2002)

4
PV - SKETCH SHOW, *EKOT* (daisyworld, inc., 2003)

5
PV - SKETCH SHOW, *MARS* (daisyworld, inc., 2003)

6
CM - 資生堂「HAKU」Shiseido, *HAKU* (Shiseido Co., Ltd., 2005)

7
CM -「エビス・ちょっと贅沢なビール」*Yebisu Beer* (SAPPORO BREWERIES LTD, 2005)

049 森本晃司 / スタジオ4℃
KOJI MORIMOTO / STUDIO4℃

PROFILE

1959年生まれ。大阪デザイナー学院卒。監督・アニメーター・演出家。1989年、STUDIO4℃創設メンバーとして活動を開始。そのオリジナリティあふれる独特の世界観及び映像スタイルには定評がある。自身の音楽的趣味を大いに発揮したKENISHIIのミュージッククリップ「EXTRA」で一躍脚光を集め、以降「サバイバル2.7-D」「永久家族」「音響生命体ノイズマン」「MEMORIES（彼女の想いで）」「ANIMATRIX（BEYOND "O"）」などの先鋭的な映像作品を次々と生みだしている。

1

1
Animation - *ANIMATRIX, Beyond*（©STUDIO4℃, 2003)

2
Mobile Movie - Utada × Koji Morimoto, *FLUXMATION*
(©STUDIO4℃, 2005)

3
CM -「永久家族」*ETERNAL FAMILY*
(©STUDIO4℃, 1997-1998)

4
Animation -「次元ループ - SOS レスキュバージョン」
Dimention Loop (©STUDIO4℃)

CATEGORY
CG Animation, PV

E-MAIL
—

TOOLS
—

TEL / FAX
—
—

URL
http://www.studio4c.co.jp

Born in 1959. Graduated from Osaka Designers' College. Morimoto is a director, animator, and producer. He began his creative activities in 1989 as a founding member of Studio 4°C. He receives continuous acknowledgement for his highly innovative worldview and style. Morimoto was first exposed to the spotlight for creating the music video of Ken Ishii's "Extra," and later for other cutting-edge works such as "Survival 2.7," "Eternal Family," "Noiseman Sound Insect," "Her Memory (a chapter of MEMORIES)," and "Beyond (a chapter of ANIMATRIX)."

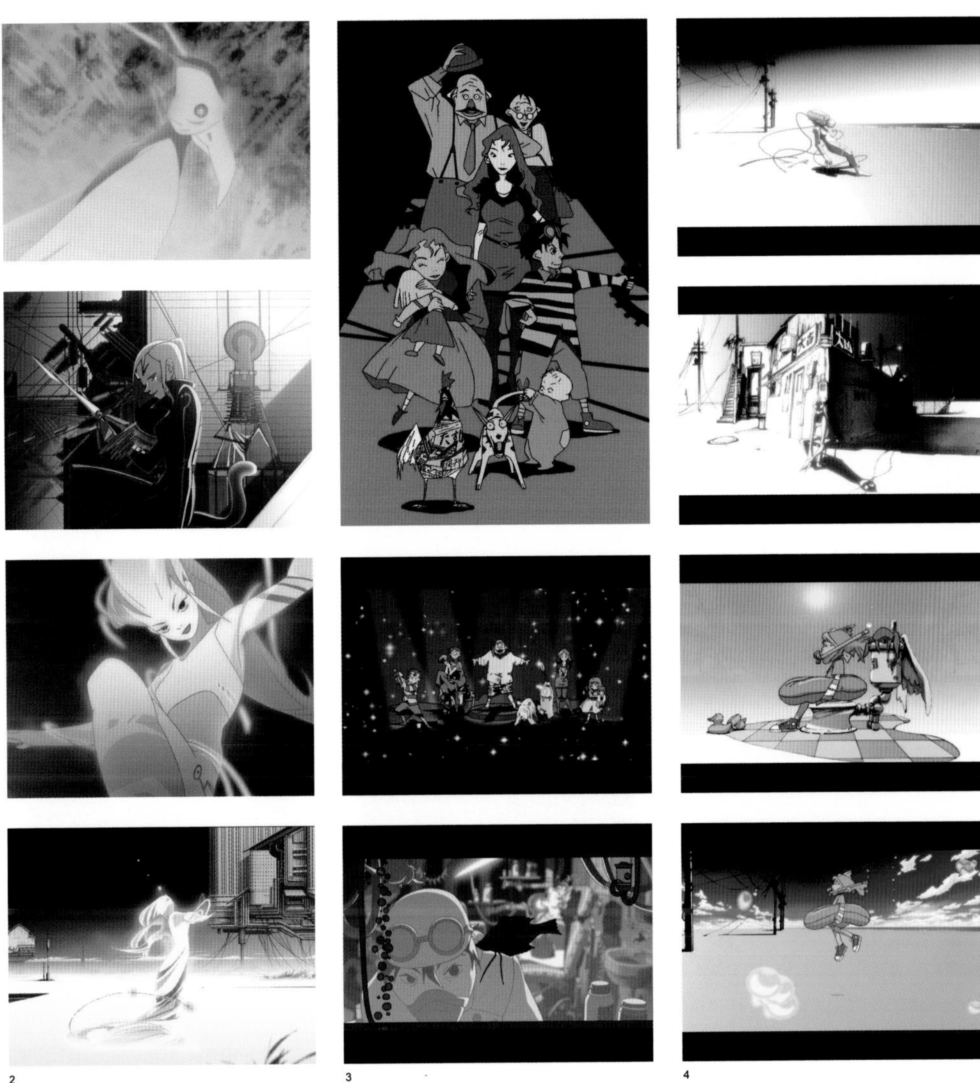

2

3

4

050 西田幸司 KOJI NISHIDA

PROFILE
1976年生まれ。アートディレクター・WebデザイナーとしてRAKU-GAKI（http://raku-gaki.com）を中心に活動し、Web上で個人作品、クライアントワーク、広告などを展開。最近は他ジャンルの人たちとのコラボレーションや紙媒体、映像媒体にも興味を持ちつつ活動中。2004年にはWebのアカデミー賞といわれるTHE WEBBY AWARDを受賞（日本人初）。テレビ朝日「スマステーション4」ジャパニーズインザワールドやNHK教育テレビ「情報A」などにも出演。

1

2

CONCEPT
グラフィックにユーザーのアクションに呼応した動きを付けることで、見ている人が関わる事が出来る「インタラクティブグラフィック」をコンセプトに制作している。

CATEGORY
Web Design, Graphic

TEL / FAX
—
—

E-MAIL
nishida@raku-gaki.com

URL
http://raku-gaki.com/

TOOLS
Power Mac G5,
Flash 8,
Photoshop,
Illustrator,
3ds Max

Born in 1976. Active as an art director and web designer, Nishida exhibits both personal and commissioned works on the internet. Recently, he is developing an interest in paper media, motion graphics, and collaborating with people from other fields. In 2004, he was the first Japanese to be awarded the Webby Award, often referred to as the Academy Awards of the internet. He has appeared on television programs such as the corner "Japanese in the World" of TV Asahi's "Sma STATION-4," and NHK Educational TV's "Jyouhou A."

1
Website - *Strange Ga Rhythmom* (Strange Ga Rhythmom, 2003)
(http://sgr.jp/)
Design + Graphic + Flash: Koji Nishida
Illustration: Masaki Yokobe

2
Website - *arteligent christmas* (MORI BUILDING CO., LTD., 2004)
Motif: Jonathan Barnbrook
Design + Flash: Koji Nishida

3
Website - *YAZAWANOWHERE vol.1* (YAZAWA'S DOOR, 2005)
(http://www.yazawa.ne.jp/ynh/ynh001/)
Creative Direction + Art Direction: Kashiwa Sato, Design + Flash: Koji Nishida
Graphic Design: Yoshiki Okuse
Photograph: Shoji Uchida
Produce: Ken Kiuchi

4
Website - *EIGHT THE PROJECT* (Macromedia, 2005)
(http://eight8.jp/)
Direction: Yujiro Kaizawa
Art Direction + Graphic + Design: Koji Nishida, Illustration + Design: Tarout
Flash: Hisayuki Takagi
Flash: Takeshiro Umetsu
Movie: Minoru Tanaka
Produce: Hikaru Seto

3

4

He produces work under the concept of "interactive graphics," in which the user can interact with graphics by triggering animations that are allocated and programmed to correspond to the user's actions.

051 山村浩二
KOJI YAMAMURA

PROFILE

1964年名古屋市生まれ。1983年東京造形大学絵画科非具象コース卒業。同年、ムクオスタジオ入社。1989年ムクオスタジオ退社後、アニメーション作家としてフリーに。1993年ヤマムラアニメーション設立。2002年「頭山」がアニメーション映画祭の最高峰、アヌシー2003（仏）で日本人としてはじめてグランプリを受賞、また第75回アカデミー賞短編アニメーション部門にノミネートされ、全米で公開される。こちらも日本人として初の短編賞のオスカー・ノミネートとなる。国際アニメーションフィルム協会（ASIFA）日本支部理事、日本アニメーション協会（JAA）理事、東京造形大学客員教授。

CONCEPT

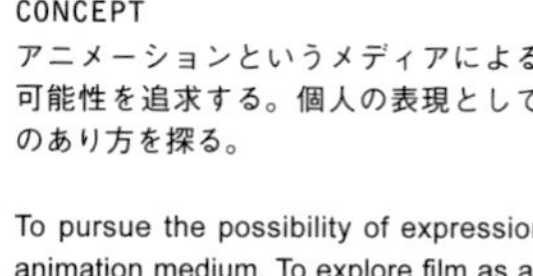

アニメーションというメディアによる表現の可能性を追求する。個人の表現としての映像のあり方を探る。

To pursue the possibility of expression in the animation medium. To explore film as a form of personal expression.

1

2

CATEGORY
Animation

TEL / FAX
—
—

E-MAIL
yam@jade.dti.ne.jp

URL
http://www.jade.dti.ne.jp/~yam/

TOOLS
Photoshop,
Final Cut Pro,
RETAS! PRO

Born in Nagoya, Japan in 1964. In 1983, Yamamura graduated from Tokyo Zokei University after studying painting there, and entered Mukuo Studio in the same year. After leaving the studio in 1989, he started working as a freelance animation artist, and eventually founded Yamamura Animation Inc. in 1993. His work "Mt. Head" (2002) was awarded the Grand Prix in Annecy 2003, the foremost animation festival in the world. It was also nominated for the 2003 Oscar, in the category of Short Films - Animation, and was screened all over the United States.

3

4

1
Animation -「カロとピヨブプト」*Karo & Piyobupt*
(©Yamamura Animation, 1993)

2
Animation -「年をとった鰐」*The Old Crocodile*
(©Yamamura Animation, 2005)

3
Animation -「バベルの本」*Bavel's Book*
(©Yamamura Animation, 1996)

4
Animation -「頭山」*Mt. Head*
(©Yamamura Animation, 2002)

052 空気モーションググラフィックス KOO-KI MOTION GRAPHICS

PROFILE

1997年12月設立。福岡を拠点に日本、韓国、台湾などの仕事を行う。主にTVCM、番組オープニングタイトル、Station IDなどを企画・演出・制作する。BDA、クリオ、ロンドン広告賞、IBA、NYフェスティバル、アドフェストなど受賞多数。

1

2

3

4

5

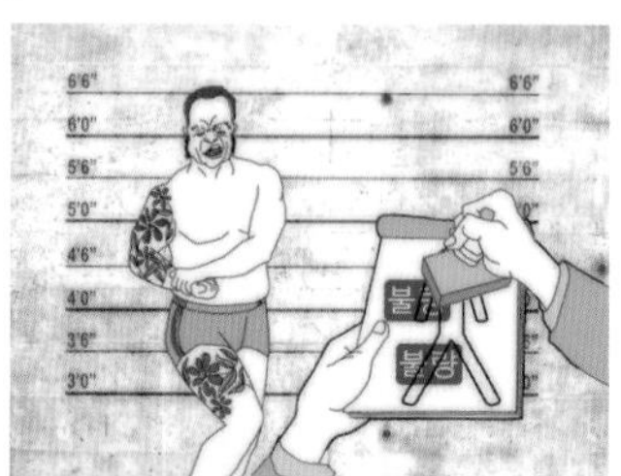

6

7

8

1
On Air Packag - *SSS* (SPACE SHOWER TV, 2004)
Director: Kee.J.Cuon

2
Station ID - *LIFE* (SPACE SHOWER TV, 2003)
Director: 竹清 仁 Hitoshi Takekiyo
Animator: 新田健士 Kenji Nitta

3
On Air Package - アテネオリンピック2004民放共通オープニング *Athens the Olympics 2005 Commercial broadcast common opening* (民放連 National Association of Commercial Broadcasters in Japan, 2004)
Director: 竹清 仁 Hitoshi Takekiyo
CG Director: 田中賢一郎 Kenichiro Tanaka

4
CM - e-maのど飴「ガクトロイド」*Gacktroid*
(UHA味覚糖 UHA mikakuto Co., Ltd., 2005)
Director: 江口カン Kan Eguchi

5
CM - *MIZUNO WAVE* (ミズノ MIZUNO, 2005)
CG Director: 田中賢一郎 Kenichiro Tanaka
Animator: 高村 剛 Tsuyoshi Takamura, 竹野智史 Satoshi Takeno

6
On Air Package - *DO THE RIGHT THING*
(MTV Korea, 2005)
Director: Kee.J.Cuon
The Asia Image Apollo Awards 2005 Best PSA ファイナリスト

7
Original Work -「替え玉」*Stand-in* (2004)
Director: 江口カン Kan Eguchi
SHORTS SHORTS FILM FESTIVAL 2004 福岡にて上映
SantaFe×shockwave.com Internet Shortfilm Festival 2005 AtomFilms 特別賞受賞

8
On Air Package - *MTV CHART* (MTV JAPAN, 2004)
Director: 竹清 仁 Hitoshi Takekiyo
Animator: 村上ヒロシナンテ Hirosinante Murakami, 新田健士 Kenji Nitta

CONCEPT

作品とそれに携わるスタッフによってさまざまだが、とにかくエンターテインメントすること。

It depends on the work and the staff involved, but in any case: to make entertainment.

CATEGORY
CM, Station ID, Animation, CI, On Air Package, GAME Opning Movie

TEL / FAX
+81 (0) 92 533 3270
+81 (0) 92 533 3271

E-MAIL
koo-ki@koo-ki.co.jp

URL
http://www.koo-ki.co.jp

TOOLS
—

Founded in Dec. 1997. Koo-ki Motion Graphics are based in Fukuoka but also work in Korea and Taiwan. They mainly plan, direct, and produce projects such as TV commercials, opening titles of TV programs, and Station IDs. They have won numerous awards in competitions such as BDA, Clio Awards, London International Advertising Awards, IBA, New York Festival, and Asia Pacific Adfest.

9
Original Work - *NINJA GROOVY* (カートゥーン ネットワーク ジャパン Cartoon Network Japan, 2005)
Director: 竹清 仁 Hitoshi Takekiyo
Animator: 村上ヒロシナンテ Hirosinante Murakami

10
GAME - *WCCF* (SEGA, 2003) オープニングCG映像担当
Director: 白川東一 Motohiro Shirakawa
2004 BDA design AWARD (New York) 金賞

11
GAME -「マリオブラザーズ 20th Anniversary」*SUPER MARIO BROTHERS 20th Anniversary* (任天堂 Nintendo, 2005)
Director: 木綿達史 Tatsushi Momen
Animator: 髙村 剛 Tsuyoshi Takamura

12
GAME -「きみのためなら死ねる」*Kiminotamenara shineru* (SEGA, 2004)
Director: 白川東一 Motohiro Shirakawa
オープニングCG映像担当

13
CM - 資生堂「ピエヌ」Shiseido, *PN*
(CG Supervise: 酒向桂輔 Keisuke Sako)
Animator: 村上ヒロシナンテ Hirosinante Murakami
(資生堂 Shiseido Co., Ltd., 2005)

14
Original Work - Mr.デニロー *Mr. Deniroo* (2005)
Director: 木綿達史 Tatsushi Momen
Animator: 髙村 剛 Tsuyoshi Takamura

15
CM - *ROLLING DOOR* (台湾セブンイレブン 7-Eleven Taiwan, 2005)
Director: 竹清 仁 Hitoshi Takekiyo
Animator: 村上ヒロシナンテ Hirosinante Murakami, 竹野智史 Satoshi Takeno

16
CM -「とんがらし麺」*Tongarashimen*
(日清食品 NISSIN, 2005)
Director: 江口カン Kan Eguchi

9

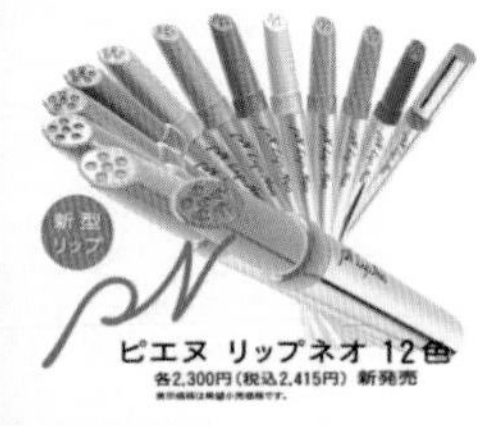

13

10

14

11

15

12

16

053 小野浩太
KOTA ONO

PROFILE

1971年生まれ。映像のライブMIXにより、VJやビデオアートなどの分野で、主にその場限りの作品をマイペースに発表している。アナログ機材を複数使用し、映像素材を幾重にも組み合わせる手法が特徴的。その手法により生み出される、まるで万華鏡の中を覗き込んだかのような世界観は、有機的でミニマムな美しさを持つ。また、ハプニングなどの事象を直接映像に混ぜ合わせることにより、より異形な映像世界を映し出している。

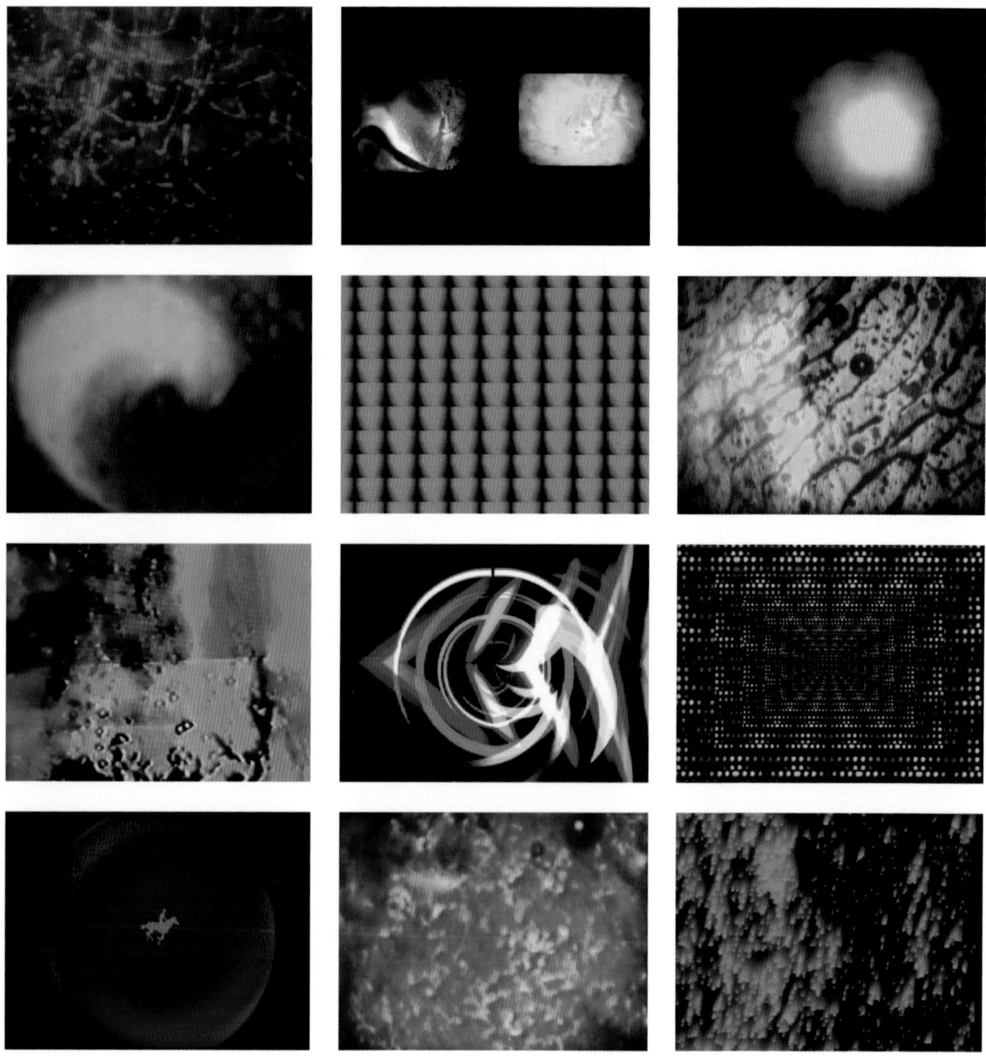

CONCEPT

頭の中にあるフワフワ、モヤッとしたものの映像化。それを媒介として音や見ている人との言葉を用いない脳の対話。

The visualization of the amorphous and blurry things in his head. With this as the medium, he aims to set up a non-verbal mental dialogue with the music and the audience.

CATEGORY
Abstract Movie

TEL / FAX
080 3024 7958
—

E-MAIL
kouta@xf6.so-net.ne.jp

URL
http://www014.upp.so-net.ne.jp/book_life/

TOOLS
Futek Digital Video Mixer MX-1,
Sony DCR-VX1000,
Various Lenses and Filters,
Cathode-ray Tube TV,
VHS Video, Premiere, After Effects

Born in 1971. Ono presents on-the-site works at his own steady pace in the fields of VJ and video art, in which he mixes motion images live. The way in which he utilizes numerous analog machinery and layers images over one another is unique. From this methodology emerges an organic and minimal aesthetic which can be compared to the inside of a kaleidoscope. In addition, by mixing in real-time occurrences into his visuals, his works achieve the depiction of a world that is like none other.

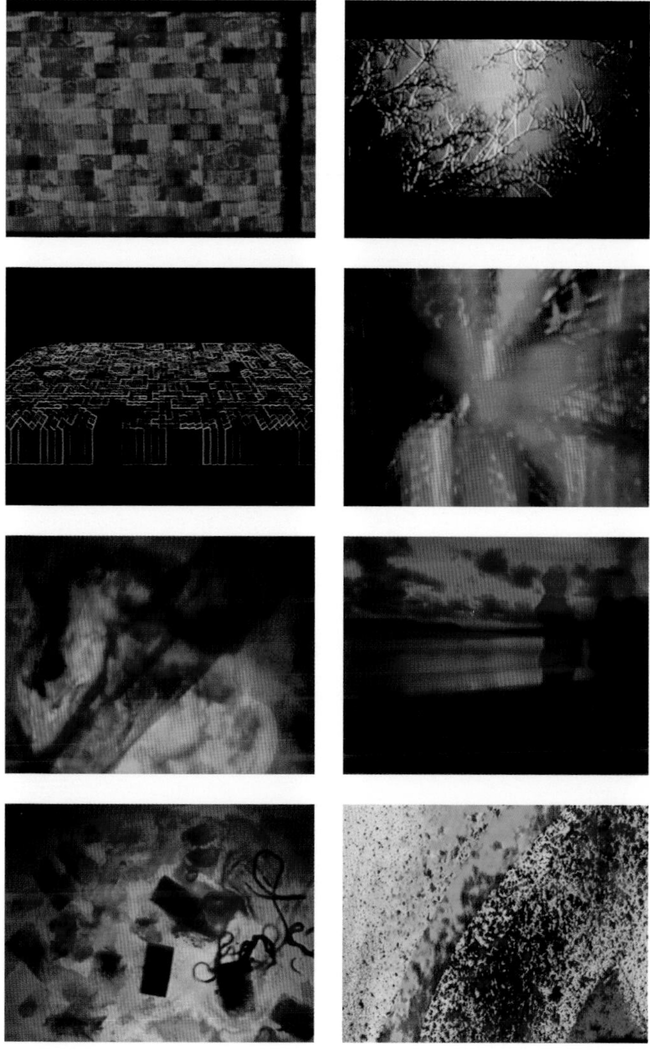

Original Work - No Title
(©kota ono, 1999-2005)

054 加藤久仁生 KUNIO KATO

PROFILE

1977年4月24日生まれ。多摩美術大学グラフィックデザイン科卒業。大学在学中に制作した作品で国内のアニメーション賞を獲得。卒業後、2001年に㈱ロボット入社。現在は同社のコンテンツ部アニメーションクリエーターチームROBOT CAGEに所属。テレビ番組、Webアニメーション、スポットCMなどさまざまなアニメーション作品を手掛けている。

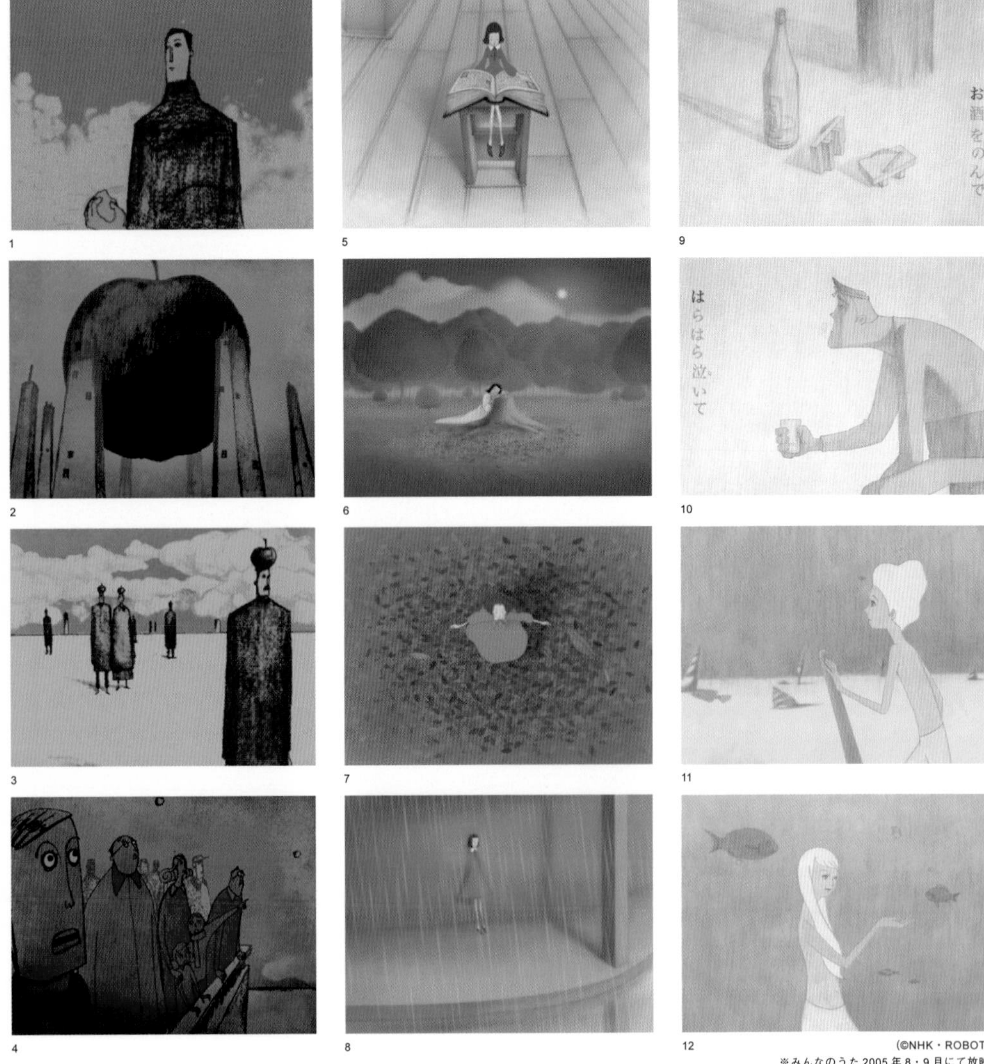

1 2 3 4 5 6 7 8 9 10 11 12

(©NHK・ROBOT)
※みんなのうた2005年8・9月にて放映

CONCEPT

作る絵は、なるべく手描きの感覚の残る、アナログな質感を目指しています。

Creating images that have an analog texture and a hand-drawn feel.

CATEGORY
Animation

TEL / FAX
+81 (0) 3 3760 1247
+81 (0) 3 3760 1248

E-MAIL
char-anim@robot.co.jp

URL
http://www.robot.co.jp/charanim/index.html
http://kiteretsu.robot.co.jp/kunio/index.html

TOOLS
Power Mac G5,
Photoshop,
After Effects,
Flash

Born on April 24, 1977. Graduated from Tama Art University, Department of Graphic Design. Kato received a domestic animation award for a work he produced while still a student. Upon graduation in 2001, he joined Robot Communications Inc., and is currently a member of Robot Cage, an animation creators team within the company. He handles animation works for diverse media such as T.V. programs, web animation, and spot commercials.

1-4
Animation - *The Apple Incident* (2001)
Director + Animator: 加藤久仁生 Kunio Kato

5-8
Animation - *MY LITTLE LOVER WEB ANIMATION "FANTASY"* 全5話 (2003)
Director + Animator: 加藤久仁生 Kunio Kato
Animater: 森川耕平 Kouhei Morikawa, 飯島有 Yu Iijima
Music: 小林武史 Takeshi Kobayashi
(©烏龍舎 Oolomg-sha Co., Ltd. · ROBOT)

9-10
Animation - おはよう *O HA YO U* (2005)
Director + Animator: 加藤久仁生 Kunio Kato

11-12
Animation - NHKみんなのうた「セルの恋」
NHK Minna no Uta "Seru no Koi" (2005)
Director + Animator: 加藤久仁生 Kunio Kato
Composition: めけて Mekete
Song: 中川晃教 Akinori Nakagawa
Producer: 飯野恵子 Keiko Iino
Animater: 森川耕平 Kouhei Morikawa, 飯島有 Yu Iijima, 博多哲也 Tetsuya Hakata
Production: NHKエンタープライズ NHK ENTERPRISES

13-19
Animation - 或る旅人の日記　全6話 WEB ANIMATION
Aru Tabibito no Nikki 6 all stories (2003)
Director + Animator: 加藤久仁生 Kunio Kato
Music: 近藤研二 Kenji Kondo
Producer: 日下部雅謹, 松本絵美 Emi Matsumoto
SE: 日高貴代美 Takayomi Hidaka (ONPa)
Production: ROBOT
shockwave.comサイト内で公開
(©ROBOT)
2005年1月ジェネオンエンタテイメントよりDVD発売

20
Animation - 或る旅人の日記「赤い実」
Aru Tabibito no Nikki "Akaimi" (2004)
Director + Animator: 加藤久仁生 Kunio Kato
Music: 近藤研二 Kenji Kondo
Producer: 日下部雅謹, 松本絵美 Emi Matsumoto
SE: 日高貴代美 Takayomi Hidaka (ONPa)
Animater: 森川耕平 Kouhei Morikawa, 真取輝和Terukazu Matoi, 亀島耕 Kou Kameshima
Production: ROBOT
或る旅人の日記 DVD収録
（発売元：ジェネオンエンタテイメント）
"Aru Tabibito no Nikki" DVD collection (Published by Geneon Entertainment)
(©ROBOT)

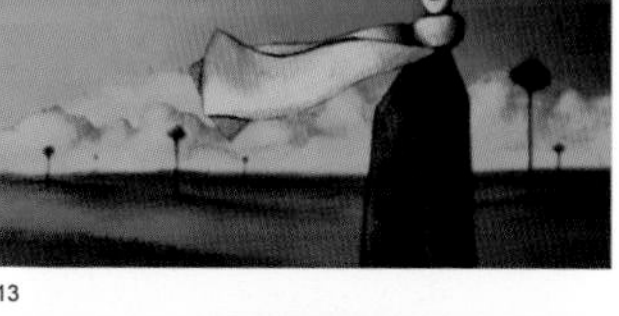

13

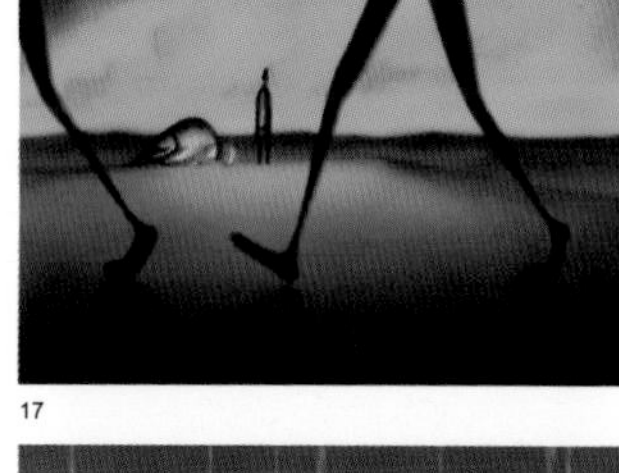

17

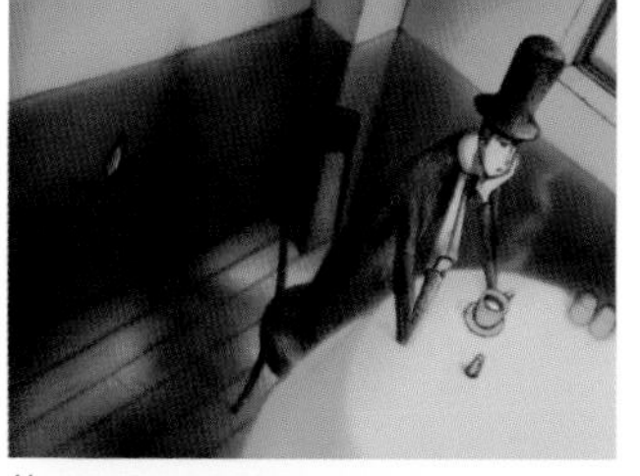

14

18

15

19

16

20

055 ランリュウ LANRYU

PROFILE
1978年生まれ。「power of film」の意思のもと、ビジュアルアートコミューン「合掌-gassyo-」を立ち上げる。被写体が放つ力を極限まで引き出す映像表現を追求した、ライブプロジェクションを展開。その後、坂本龍一主催アフガニスタンチャリティーへの出演をきっかけにコンセプチュアルな作品制作へと移行。DVD「lifepack」は、モンゴルの草原からありふれた日常の1コマまで、世界を旅して切り取ったイメージの数々によって綴られ、文字通りライフをコレクトしてパッケージした作品となっている。

CATEGORY
Food, Clothing, Housing, Art

E-MAIL
lifepack@apple.ac

TOOLS
—

TEL / FAX
+81 (0) 3 3794 6772
+81 (0) 3 3794 6772

URL
http://www.lifepack.jp

Born in 1978. Under the concept: "power of film," Lanryu founded the visual art commune "Gassyo." They pursue to unleash to the extreme, the energy that the object of the camera emits. Lanryu's work started becoming more conceptual after being involved in an Afghanistan charity project headed by Ryuichi Sakamoto. 1st DVD "lifepack" in 2004 was released. Lanryu's visual poetry is composed of the many images that he cropped throughout his worldwide travels, from the grassy plains of Mongolia to the elements of everyday life. Just like the title, it is literally a package of collected life.

DVD - *lifepack* (2004)
Directer: lanryu
Music: KINKA, kontrajaz, Uhyo,
江戸からかみ砂子 Edo karakami sunago by Genki
Ticket Illustration: Sato Yoshiro

<u>056</u>

ルドビック・グザスデラ
LUDOVIC XASDERA

PROFILE

1972年生まれ。東京を拠点に活動する、マルチメディアアーティスト。フランスに生まれ、4年間サンフランシスコを活動の拠点としたのち、東京へ移住。コンピュータやビデオなどのニューメディアと、ペインティングやタブラパーカッションなどの伝統的な手法を織り交ぜながら制作される作品は、彼独自の芸術言語として強度を持つ。異なるメディアを交錯させながら、さまざまなアーティストとのコラボレーションによる作品制作を行うことで、常に新しい表現手法を創造し続けている。

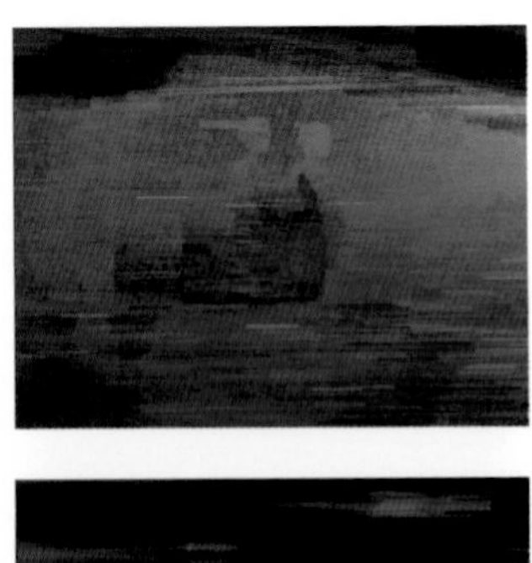

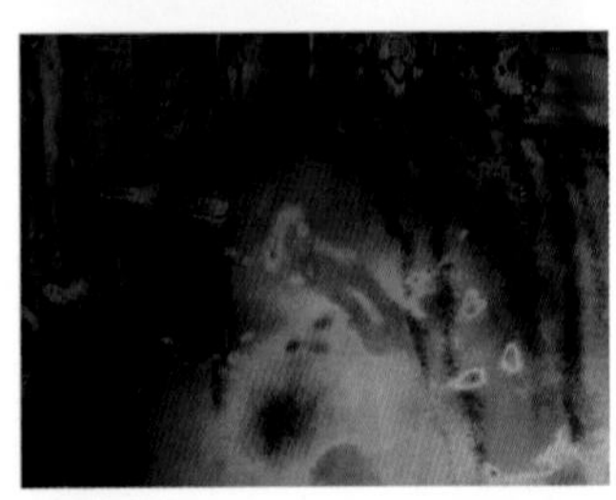

1

2

CONCEPT

観る者に、比較的意識的な自己探求へと進んでもらうために、それ独自の時間、空間、質量、そして言葉の参照点を備えた別のリアリティーを見せる。

Show a different reality with its own time, space, matter and narrative referentials, so that the audience/viewer can proceed to a more or less conscious self-exploration.

CATEGORY
Video Art

TEL / FAX
—
—

E-MAIL
ludo@xasdera.com

URL
http://www.xasdera.com

TOOLS
After Effects,
ArKaos VJ,
Ableton Live

Born in 1972. Xasdera is a multimedia artist based in Tokyo. He was born in France, and after being active in San Francisco for four years, he moved to Tokyo. His works, which weave together new media such as computers and video, with more traditional forms of expression such as painting and Tabla percussion, achieve the intensity of a highly unique artistic language. He perpetually produces a new expressive methodology by interconnecting different media and collaborating with other artists.

3

4

1
Original Work - *Joey's song*
Music: R. Schrock

2
Original Work - *Segments*
Music: R. Schrock

3
Original Work - 「たけやぶやけた」 *Takeyabu yaketa*

4
VJ - *VJ Image*

057 マジック・コバヤシ
M.MAGIC.KOBAYASHI

PROFILE

1969年長野県生まれ。1994年日本大学芸術学部美術学科ビジュアルコミュニケーションデザイン卒業。1994年メイウェル入社。1997年退社。1997年横尾忠則と石川次郎の事務所、スタジオ・マジック設立に参加。1999年までいくつかの横尾忠則作品にデザイナーとして関わりCDパッケージ、広告、グッズなどを制作。1999年ソウルマークデザインオフィス主宰。広告制作、CI、エディトリアル、パッケージデザイン、フォトディレクションなどマスを対象にしたグラフィックデザインを主軸としながらプライベートワークを制作し続けている。

1　　2　　3

1 Improvisation Sculpture - *DRUNK TOWER / ASAKUSABASHI DRUNK TOWER RETURNS +301*（2004）
2 DVD - *Super Star Series / Solid Society* (©Gas As Interface Co., Ltd., 2001) Artists: Yasunori Ikunishi, Yasunori Kakegawa, kuknacke Feat. m.magic Kobayashi
3 DVD - *Super Star Series* (©Gas As Interface Co., Ltd., 2001) Artists: Yasunori Ikunishi, Yasunori Kakegawa, kuknacke Feat. m.magic Kobayashi
4 Art - GUNDAM GENERATION FUTURES, *Breath upon the Universe / Breath in the Universe* (©SOTSU AGENCY CO., LTD / SUNRISE + ©2005 Ikunishi Yasunori × Kakegawa Yasunori × kuknacke × shu × m.magic Kobayashi × Tetsuya Nagato)
Artists: Ikunishi Yasunori, Kakegawa Yasunori, Kuknacke, shu, M.Magic Kobayashi, Nagato Tetsuya

CATEGORY
CG Animation, PV

TEL / FAX
090 9979 0204

E-MAIL
magickobayashi@hotmail.com

URL
http://www32.ocn.ne.jp/~magic_kobayashi

TOOLS
FinePix F10,
NV-MX2000
Illustrator,
Photoshop,
After Effects, Final Cut Pro

Born in 1969, in Nagano, Japan. In 1994, Kobayashi graduated from Nihon University College of Art, Department of Fine Art, majoring in visual communication design. In 1994, he entered Maywell corp., and withdrew in 1997. In the same year, he participated in the foundation of "Studio Magic," the office of Tadanori Yokoo and Jiro Ishikawa. In 1999, he began directing Soulmark Design Office. While commercial graphic design works are his base activity, which include advertisement production, CI, editorial design, package design, and photo direction, he continuously produces private works as well.

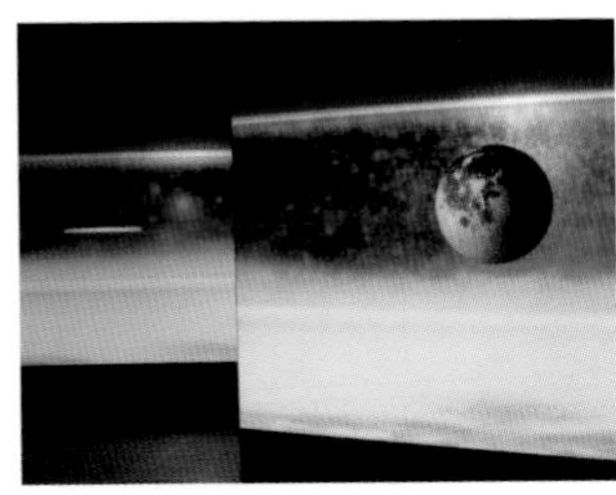

4

マジックコバヤシは正確な意味では映像作家ではない。映像は表現のひとつでしかなく、そのほか写真、ペインティング、グラフィック・デザイン、インスタレーションなどさまざまなカタチをもって彼は作品を残し続ける。マジックコバヤシはいったい何者なのか？彼の表現を読み説く上で重要なのは「記憶とループとねじれ」。大酒飲みである彼は、飲酒中に記憶を飛ばすことも多いが、オート・パイロット・モード中は、シラフ時以上に彼のマインドは激しく化学反応を起こしているのだ。それは、周囲の人間や環境を巻き込み「ハプニング」という目に見えるカタチで現れる。彼は、ギリギリで狂気を正気で押さえ込み、デジカメ、カムコーダーなどの記憶装置でそのハプニングを記録する。そして、記憶と記録をオーバーダブさせ、加工し作品に落としこむ。過去の世界はマジックコバヤシの中でねじれ、まだ見ぬ新たなカオスが、作品として表現されるのだ。

彼の作品で興味深いのが2004年9月に行われた体験型インスタレーション作品「DRUNK TOWER RETURNS」だ。廃業した居酒屋をスクワットし、そこでは東京のクリエイターが大集結し、一週間、狂乱の宴会が催された。一つのスクリーンでは前日記録された宴会の模様が上映され、それを肴に酒を飲むオーディエンスの様子は、さらに録画され、同時にリアルタイムでもう一つのスクリーンに映される。前日の映像を写すカメラの映像は連凧のように重なり合い、グループも日を追うごとにねじれ、圧縮されスパイラルを描いてゆく……。観客は宴会を楽しむと同時に、マジックコバヤシにサイコダイブしている、という非常にスリリングで実験的な作品であった。

マジックコバヤシの作品は見ていて楽しいものである。彼にとって、大好きなお酒は、あくまでも媒介であり、すべての表現に通底するのは、つるつるでピカピカのピュアさと暖かなユーモアなのだ。DVD作品「SUPER STAR SERIES」にわかりやすく、それを見て取ることができる。ビョーク、風船おじさん、ピカード艦長、横尾忠則、岡本太郎など、彼が敬愛するスターたちの顔を、それぞれ約30ものレイヤーに分解し、星をちりばめて、銀河に浮かぶポートレイトとして再構築した映像作品である。星たちは、ひとつひとつが宇宙の記憶の断片を表すメタファーであり、それらが時と共にねじれてゆく過程の、ある瞬間にSUPER STARは生まれる、というのが裏のストーリーだ。「記憶とループとねじれ」そして「恒久性」の視覚化を試みた、マジックコバヤシの意欲作である。それを包み込むのが「スターが星になった」さりげないトンチなのだ。この手法の一部は、「GUNDAM GENERATION FUTURES」に出展された「Breath upon the Universe」「Breath in the Universe」の2つの作品に受け継がれている。

「A・R・T」という3文字の言葉は歴史的に言えば、物体の継承であり、論議をはじめるきっかけとなるもの。自身のピュアな感動をもって周囲の事象を記録し、創作を続ける彼は、本来の意味で「アーティスト」たる存在なのかもしれない。
（文：星野一樹）

058 石浦 克 / ティー・ジー・ビー・デザイン
MASARU ISHIURA / TGB design.

PROFILE
1975年東京生まれ。グラフィックデザイナー・アートディレクター・武蔵野美術大学非常勤講師。CDジャケット、ファッション、プロダクト、TOY、映像、音楽、オーガナイズなどを手掛ける。ミュージックビデオのディレクターとして、RESFESTワールドツアー、ASIAN AMERICAN FILM FESTIVAL（USA）、シアトル国際映画祭、サウンド・アンシーン映画祭など数々のフィルムフェスティバルでノミネートされている。

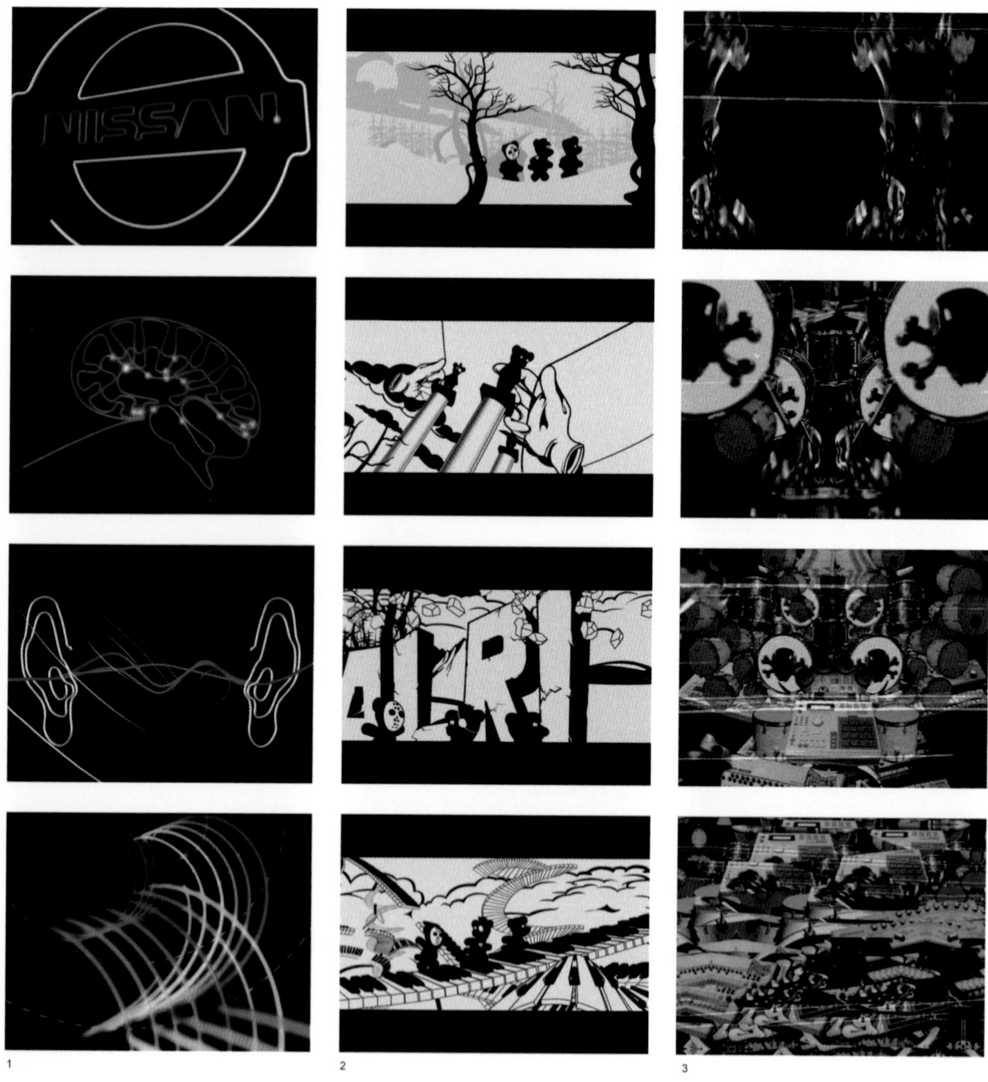

1　2　3

CONCEPT
さまざまな異分野の表現をグラフィックデザインの延長としてとらえてデザインする。

Designing with the notion that the visual expressions of many different realms are all extentions of graphic design.

CATEGORY
PV, Promotion

TEL / FAX
—
—

E-MAIL
ishiura@tgbdesign.com

URL
http://www.tgbdesign.com

TOOLS
Illustrator,
Photoshop,
Final Cut Pro,
Inferno

Born in 1975 in Tokyo. A graphic designer, art director, and part-time lecturer at Musashino Art University. His activities include the designs of CD covers, fashion, products, toys, motion graphics, music, and event organization. As a music video director, he has been nominated at a number of film festivals including Resfest world tour (USA), Asian American Film Festival (USA), Seattle International Film Festival, and Sound Unseen Festival.

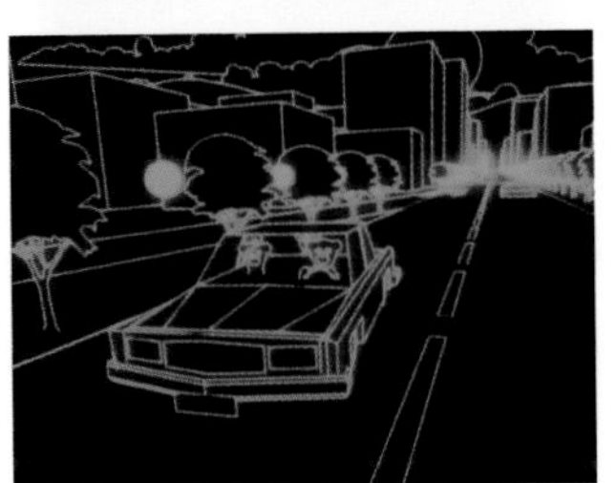

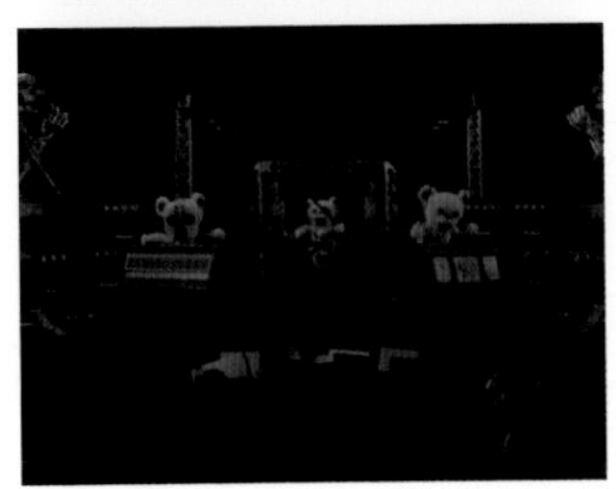

4

1
Promotion - *NISSAN DESIGN perceived Quality Design Department*
(©NISSAN DESIGN, 2003)
Director + Motion Graphics: Masaru Ishiura
Producer + Concept: François Bacon
Illustrator: Takaho Inoue
3D Animation: Takashi Kaiga
Editor: Kotaro Takano

2
PV - CUBE JUICE, *EXPLOSION*
(©Victor Entertainment Inc., 2002)
Director + Illustration: Masaru Ishiura
Producer: Junichi Tanaka
Animation: Itsuo Ito
3D Animation: Hiroyuki yabe

3
PV - COM.A, *Lights, Camera, Hallvcination: COM.A*
(©ROMZ record & TGB design., 2005)
Director + Motion Graphics: Masaru Ishiura
Edit: Tanaka, Shimoyama

4
DVD - CUBE JUICE, *cube world -music is our message?-*
(©Victor Entertainment Inc., 2003)
Director + Illustration: Masaru Ishiura
Screen Writer: Kotaro Tenmyo (PAVLOV)
Plastic Art: Tetuya tamanoi
Animation: Itsuo Ito
3D Animation: Hiroyuki yabe
Edit: Kotaro Takano
Producer: Junichi Tanaka
Remix works: logan, new stench
Character Design: TGB design.

Licensed by Victor Entertainment,Inc.
Produced+Manufactured+Distributed by Nowonmedia, Inc.

<u>059</u> 明鏡止水
MEIKYOSHISUI

PROFILE
1972年生まれ。グラフィックデザイン、映像制作、フィールドワーク、磐座・ペトログラフの研究など、幅広い活動を行う。その作品には、古来よりつちかい受け継がれてきた精神性を現代の手法を用い実践するという一貫した思想が貫かれている。プロジェクトを進める際のプロセスや契約期間に生まれた結果にアートを生かし、心の教育とリクリエーションを担う。

1　2　3

CONCEPT
「△」: 山（自然）をテーマとするライフワーク。代表作として、「カミ」: 日本各地の森をテーマにした作品、「磐座」: 日本各地の巨石・巨岩をテーマにした作品、「ア∞ウ」: コマイヌ（阿吽）が見てきたモノ、「今と昔」「男と女」「オトナとコドモ」「戦争と平和」などをテーマにした作品などがある。

CATEGORY
Art

TEL / FAX
+81 (0) 3 5430 6418
+81 (0) 3 5430 6418

E-MAIL
m_meikyoshisui@ybb.ne.jp

URL
—

TOOLS
AG-DVX100
Final Cut

Born in 1972. Meikyoshisui's activities are rich in variety, ranging from graphic design and motion graphic production, to fieldwork and research of Iwakura and Petrographs. Throughout his work flows a current of personal ideology which concerns a spirituality that has been cultivated and inherited from ancient times, and how this can be expressed through contemporary methods. He aims to contribute to the education and recreation of the mind, through injecting art into the process of developing a project, and the results that are produced within the production period.

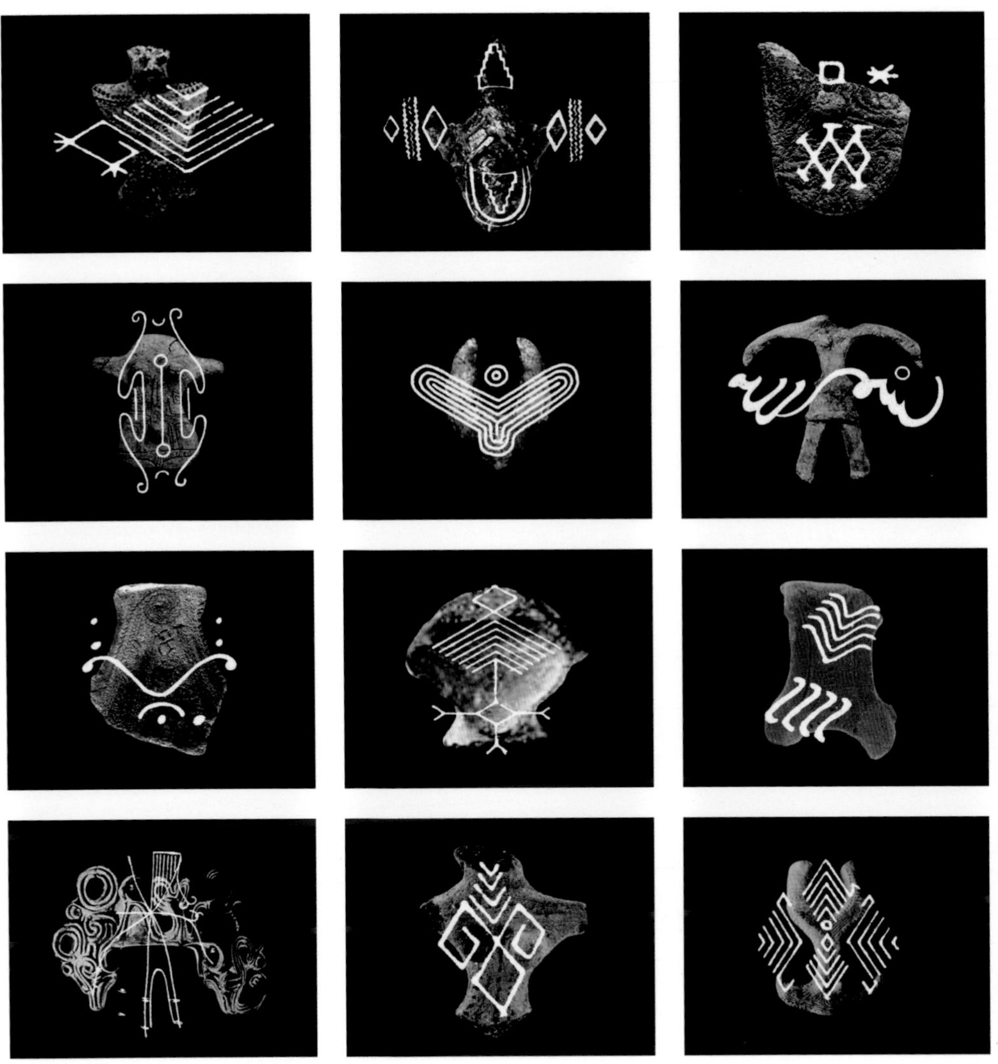

4

"△": a lifework with mountains (nature) as the theme. "Kami": A representative work dealing with forests in various areas of Japan. "Iwakura": A work dealing with huge stones all over Japan. "A∞U": The things that the Komainu [stone guardian dogs] have seen over the ages; various pieces with themes such as "present and past," "man and woman," "adult and child," "war and peace."

1 Art -「カミ」*Kami*
2 Art -「磐座」*IWAKURA*
3 Art -「カミ」*Kami*
4 Art -「無題」*No Title*

060 michi / 石多 未知行
michi a.k.a. MICHIYUKI ISHITA

PROFILE

1974年生まれ。映像＋空間演出アーティスト。2001年、アーティストのコラボレートを中心とした「ku-ki」というイベントを結成。その中で演出を手掛けたことから、自ら映像制作にも参入し、映像アーティストとしての活動を開始する。映像をスクリーンへ投影することから、光としての扱いをより強め、自在に空間を支配する新たな表現へ昇華させている。2005年8月、スパイラルホールで自らプロデュースした「conscious ー意識ー」公演では、映像空間を中心にした新しい世界を提示し反響を呼ぶ。映像の進むべき次の世界を探求し、そこへ踏み込んだ表現は各界で高い評価を得ている。

1

2

CONCEPT

映像をスクリーンやモニターで見るための表現ではなく、3次元的で感覚に訴える表現を方法とする。複数のプロジェクターを使用した、視界に収まらないスケールの映像と空間表現により、視覚を超えたコミュニケーションを試みている。説明的な答えのある表現ではなく、抽象性の中に問いや対話を求め、観る者の感覚をクリエイトさせることを意識の中心において活動している。

'michi' uses motion graphics not as something to be seen on a screen or monitor, but as a sensuous three dimensional form of expression. By producing spaces that cannot be contained within one person's view, through the use of multiple projectors, he attempts to create a form of visual communication that transcends the sense of sight. 'michi' focuses on producing works that, within a frame of abstraction, require the audience to mold their own senses and construct questions, thus inducing a dialogue, instead of providing a form of expression that contains a preconceived explanatory answer.

CATEGORY
Space Production,
Live Performance

TEL / FAX
+81 (0) 3 3366 9210
+44 (0) 79 1429 2120 (UK)

E-MAIL
michi@michiyuki.net

URL
http://michiyuki.net

TOOLS
PowerBook G4, Edirol V4 Video Mixer, DVD Player, DV Camera, After Effects, FUSE Media Projector, FUSE Visual Console

Born in 1974. A motion graphics and spatial production artist. In 2001, 'michi' started "ku-ki", event based on collaborations between artists. He began his creative activities at this event, where he participated in direction and motion graphic production. By treating projected motion graphics as streams of light, instead of projecting them onto flat screens in a conventional manner, they are sublimated into a new form of expression that freely dominate the space they reside in. In August of 2005, "conscious -ISHIKI-", a performance produced by 'michi', was held at Spiral Hall. It received much acclaim from various fields, for presenting a new type of environment centered on motion graphics.

3

4

1
Art Live - *sound+dance+visual vol.4*, BankART1929 YOKOHAMA (2004.6.19)

2
Art Live - *Electric Love Station*, Bar TUNE / Motion Blue Yokohama (2005.3.27)

3
Art Live - *michi produce "conscious -ISHIKI-"*, SPIRAL HALL (2005.8.27)

4
Art Live - *sound+dance+visual vol.5*, BankART1929 馬車道ホール (2004.11.28)

1-4
photo by nohomi

061 ミズヒロ・サビーニ MIZUHIRO SAVINI

PROFILE

1968年東京生まれ。1995年からteevee graphicsに参加。ミュージシャンとしても活躍する映像作家。暖かみのある色彩が特徴的な、モンドでストレンジなアニメーション映像を得意とする。フリーのディレクターとして数々のCM、ミュージックビデオ、番組タイトル、Station IDなどを手掛ける。主な仕事に、奥田民生、ACO、audio activeなどのPV、ロッテ「紗々」のアニメーションCMなどがある。最近はVJとしても活動中。

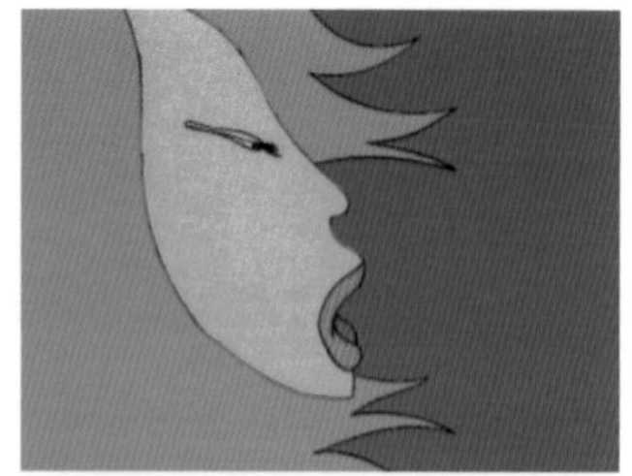

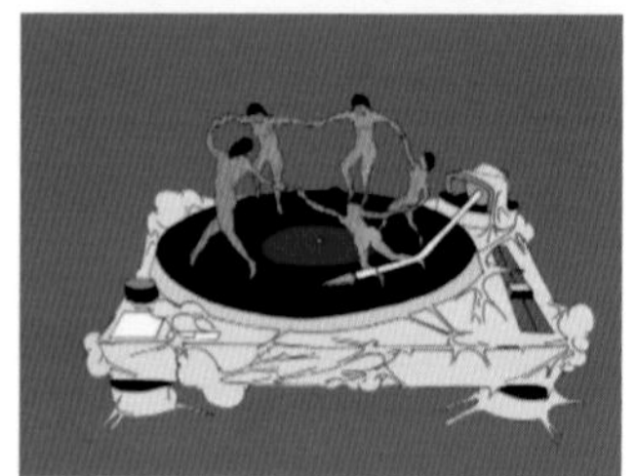

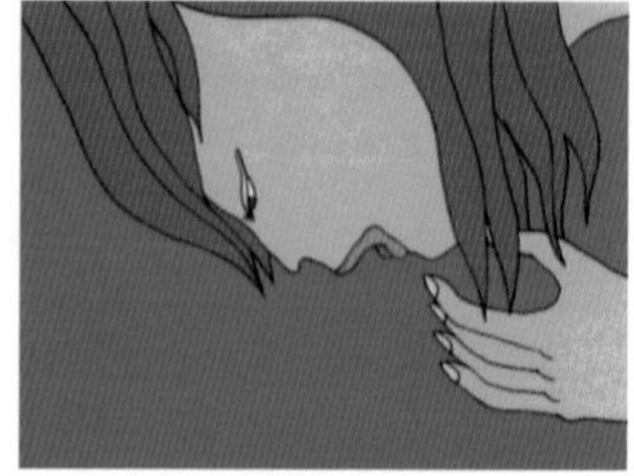

1

2

CONCEPT

常にユーモアとキテレッツィーなアイデアを持って仕事をしたい。

To always work with humor and bizzare ideas.

CATEGORY
Animation Director

TEL / FAX
+81 (0) 3 3400 6455
+81 (0) 3 5468 7048

E-MAIL
mizuhiro@desco.tv

URL
http://www.desco.tv

TOOLS
Windows,
After Effects,
Illustrator,
Photoshop,
LightWave 3D

Born in 1968. Participated in TeeVee Graphics from 1995. Savini is a motion graphic artist who is also active as a musician. He excels in unusual, non-categorizable animation, with warm coloring. As a freelance director, he has handled numerous TV commercials, music videos, TV show title sequences, and TV station IDs. Some of his representative works are music videos for Tamio Okuda, ACO and Audio Active, and an animation commercial for Lotte's chocolate line Sasha. Recently, Savini has also been active as a VJ..

1
Original Work - *Sleeper's Rag* (Teevee Graphics, 2005)
Director+ Animation+Music: Mizuhiro Savini

2
Original Work - *puls to puls* (Teevee Graphics, 2001)
Director + Animation+Music: Mizuhiro Savini

3
CM - *AiDEM* (AiDEM Inc., 2005)
Director + Animation + Music: Mizuhiro Savini

4
Station ID - *Space Shower TV Station ID* (SPACE SHOWER TV, 2001)
Director + Animation + Music: Mizuhiro Savini

3

4

062 野田 凪
NAGI NODA

PROFILE
アートディレクター・映像ディレクター・アーティスト。デザイン集団「宇宙カントリー」主宰。ラフォーレ、ナイキ、サントリー「ラテラテ」、パンダのAIBOなどの広告や、YUKI 、宇多田ヒカル、スネオヘアーなどのPV・CDジャケットを制作。hanpandaの生みの親。最近では海外のミュージックビデオ、TVアニメ「ハチミツとクローバー」のオープニングタイトルも手掛ける。東京TDC賞、東京ADC賞、NYフェスティバル銀賞、NYADC賞GOLD・SILVER・Distiinctive Meriなど数々の賞を受賞。2006年からはロサンゼルスのPartizanに所属。コカコーラワールドキャンペーンのCMディレクターを務める。2月にはギンザ・グラフィック・ギャラリーにて個展が開催される。

1

2

3

CONCEPT
女性の感性で創る独特の世界観。

An original worldview created by the sensibilities of a woman.

CATEGORY
PV, CM, Short Film

TEL / FAX
—
—

E-MAIL
mailinfo@uchu-country.com

URL
http://www.uchu-country.com/
http://www.hanpanda.com/

TOOLS
—

An art director, motion graphic director, and artist. Noda is the head of Uchu-Country. She has handled works such as advertisements for Laforet, Nike, Suntory Latte Latte, and Lon Lon, the panda-type Aibo, and also music videos and CD covers for Yuki, Utada, and Suneo Hair. Recently, she has worked on music videos for musicians from overseas, and the opening title of the animation "Honey and Clover." She has won numerous awards including Tokyo TDC award, Tokyo ADC award, silver prize at NY Festival, and gold/silver/distinctive merit for NY ADC. Noda is the creator of Han Panda.

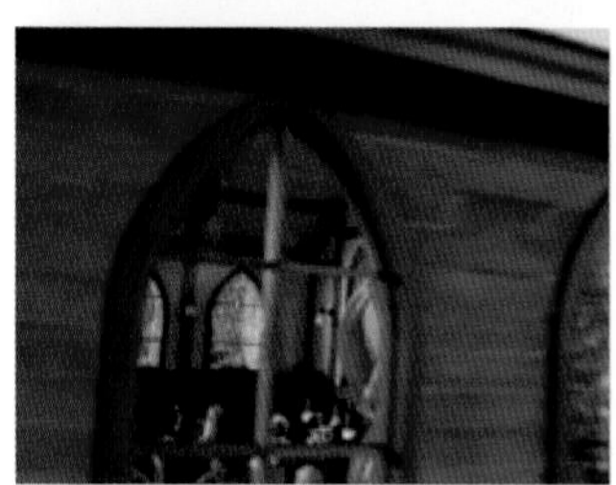

4

5

1
Fitness Video -
For Being Appraised As An "ex-fat Girl" (2004)

2
PV - YUKI, *SENTIMENTAL JOURNEY*
(©Sony Music Entertainment Inc., 2003)

3
CM - *LAFORET Butterfly Ribbon*
(©LAFORET HARAJUKU, 2002)

4
CM - *LAFORET Wedding*
(©LAFORET HARAJUKU, 2003)

5
CM - *A Small Love Story About Alex & Juliet*
(©Francfranc, 2003)

063 生意気 NAMAIKI

PROFILE
1970年ニュージーランド生まれのデイヴィッド・デュバル・スミスと1966年イギリス生まれのマイケル・フランクによるクリエイティブ・ユニットとして1997年に活動を開始。ナイキやエドウィンなどのアパレルのCMやミュージシャンのPV、CDジャケット、ステージデザインを手掛ける。また、「GANGOO」展、東京オペラシティ・アートギャラリー＆バービカン・アートギャラリー「JAM: 東京—ロンドン」展、原美術館「2×2」など、個展やグループ展多数。

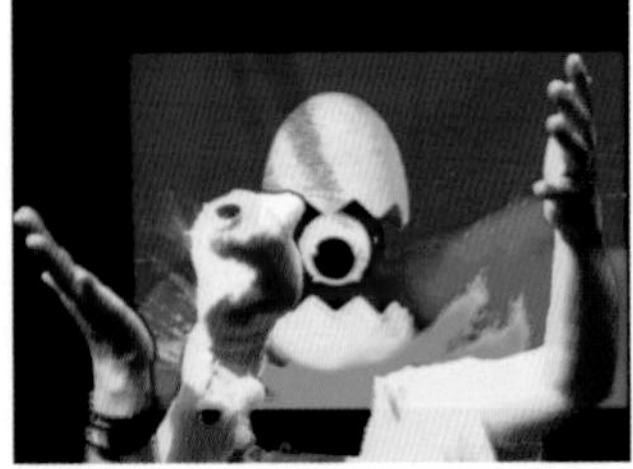

1

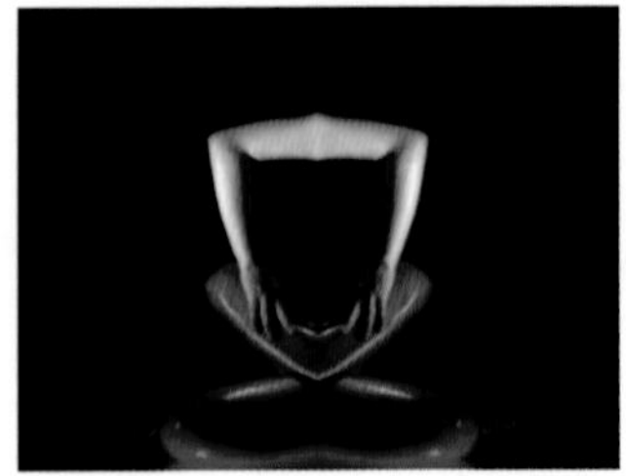

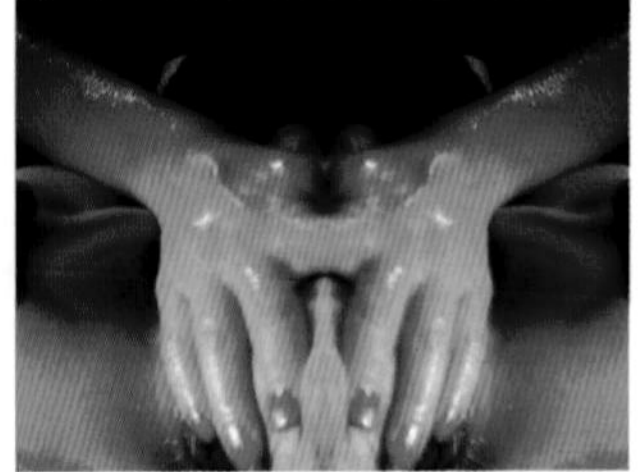

2

CONCEPT
グラフィック・ミュージック、ダンシング・ピクニック、無料食物フィルム、それとドラマチック積み肥ワークショップ。

CATEGORY
Installation, PV, CM, Graphic Design

TEL / FAX
+81 (0) 3 5733 0048
+81 (0) 3 5733 0049

E-MAIL
mail@namaiki.com

URL
http://www.namaiki.com/

TOOLS
The internet,
bread products and string.

Namaiki is a creative unit formed in 1997, by David Duval-Smith who was born in New Zealand in 1970, and Michael Frank who was born in Great Britain in 1997. They have handled projects such as TV commercials for apparel brands including Nike and Edwin, and produced music videos, CD covers, and stage designs for musicians. They have exhibited their works at many personal and group exhibitions, such as "Gangoo" and "2x2," both held at Hara Museum of Contemporary Art, and "JAM: Tokyo-London," held at both Tokyo Opera City Art Gallery and Barbican Art Gallery,

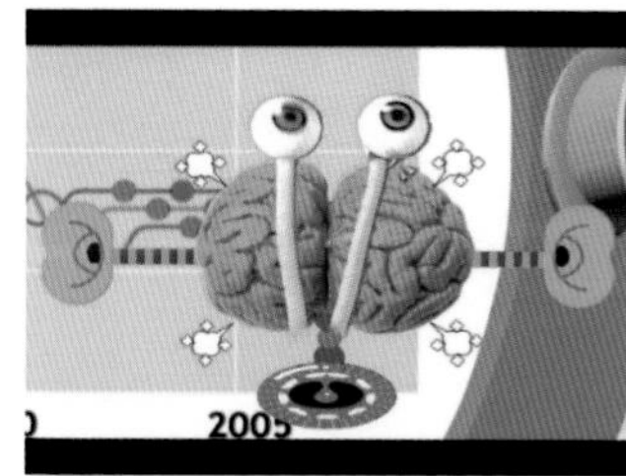

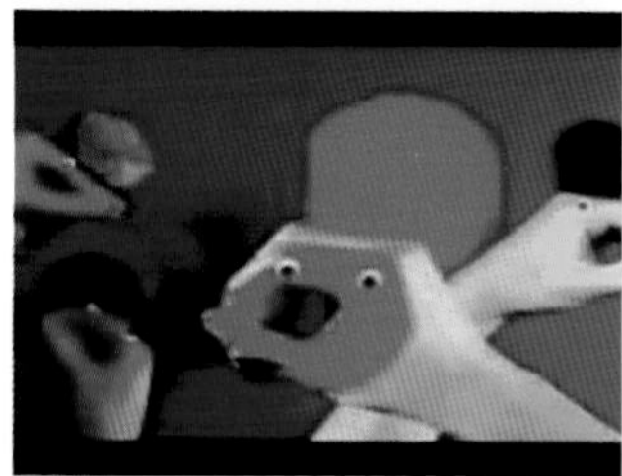

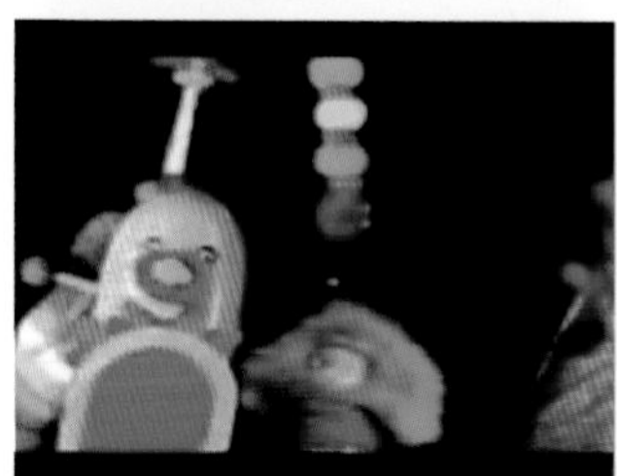

3

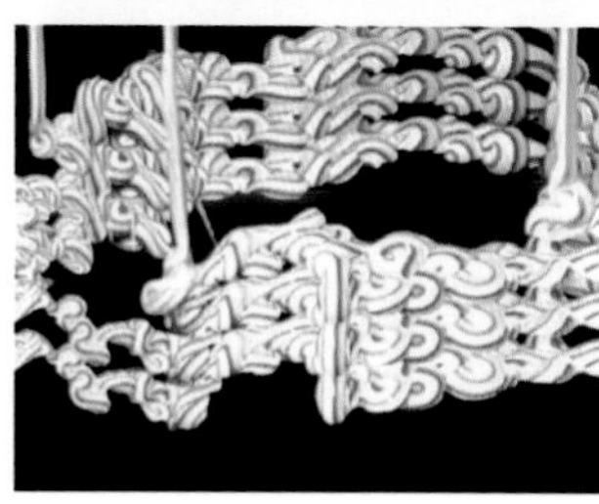

4

1
Installation - *Waku Waku TV* (National Museum of Ethnology, Osaka / special exhibition "More Happy Everyday"「きのうよりワクワクしてきた。」, 2005)
Left to right: Yae (exonemo), Mari (Namaiki), Soshun and Tame (Black Bath), Mako (Strange Kinoko)

2
PV - Yasuyuki Okamura and Takkyu Ishino, *Come Baby* (©Ki/oon Records Inc., 2002)

3
Title sequence - *MTV Video Music Awards Japan 2005* (MTV JAPAN, 2005)

写真提供: MTV JAPAN

4
DVD - GAS DVD, *Whiter hair, softer teeth* (2002)
Released by Gas As Interface Co., Ltd.
Distributed by Nowonmedia, Inc.

We're all in this boat together.
A.R.S.E (agricultural research super extraordinary)

Graphic music, dancing picnics, free food film and dramatic compost workshops.

064 河瀬直美 / 遷都
NAOMI KAWASE / SENT

PROFILE

1969年奈良市生まれ。自主映画「につつまれて」（1992）「かたつもり」（1994）が、1995年山形国際ドキュメンタリー映画祭をはじめ国内外で注目を集める。劇場映画デビュー作「萌の朱雀」（1996）で、1997年カンヌ国際映画祭カメラドール（新人監督賞）を史上最年少受賞。その後、「火垂」（2000）、「きゃからばあ」（2001）「追憶のダンス（2002）、「沙羅双樹」（2003）などを発表、ヨーロッパを中心に世界各地で映像個展を開催し、高い評価を得る。また、CM演出、小説、エッセイなどジャンルにこだわらず表現活動を続ける。現在、命の誕生をテーマにした新作「垂乳女-Tarachime」を仏アルテ社と共同制作中。

1

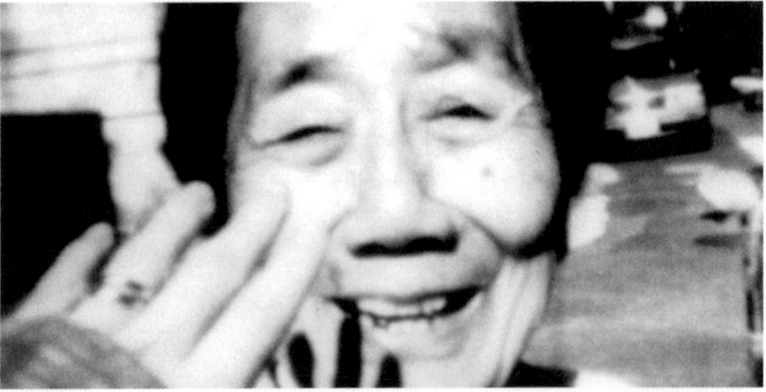

2

3

1

Documentary -「につつまれて」*Embracing* (1992)

戸籍謄本と写真を手がかりに、一度も会ったことのない父親探しの旅に出る。当時23歳の河瀬直美が "生まれながらの孤独" と向き合い、真っ直ぐなまなざしと生身の声で迫る、緊迫の40分。

With only a transcript of the family register and a photo to guide her, the 23-year-old Kawase goes on a journey to find her father who she has never met. It is a tense forty minutes, in which she faces her lifelong solitude, and approaches it with her straight gaze and raw voice.

Production Company: Sent Inc. + Kumie
Director: Naomi Kawase
Photography: Naomi Kawase

2

Documentary -「かたつもり」*Katatsumori* (1994)

「につつまれて」から2年、河瀬直美は育ての親である "おばあちゃん" と暮らす日々を8ミリフィルムで紡いでゆく。家族とは血縁とは何かという根源的な問いをさらに掘り下げる。大切な畑仕事であるエンドウ豆の生長を通して描かれた日常のあたたかさが見る者を魅了する。

Two years after "Embracing," Kawase captures with 8mm film, her everyday life with the "grandma" who has raised her. She further deepens the question of what kinship and blood is. The attractive warmth of everyday life is depicted through the growth of the crops in the string bean field.

Production Company: Sent Inc.+Kumie
Director: Naomi Kawase
Photography: Naomi Kawase

3

Fiction -「萌の朱雀」Suzaku (1996)

舞台は奈良県西吉野村。過疎化が進むこの村で、鉄道の建設工事が中断されて15年。建設に携わっていた父親が、ある日8ミリカメラを手に出かけたまま帰らぬ人となった。この地を愛し互いを想う気持ちとは裏腹に、残された家族たちは一家離散を余儀なくされる。河瀬の演出は、父親の死を受け止めようとする家族の痛切な想いを、そこに舞い降りた "朱雀" の視点で、残酷なまでに淡々と捉えている。

The stage of this film is Nishi-Yoshino Village, in Nara Prefecture. In this village facing depopulation, it has been fifteen years since the construction of the railroad has come to a halt. The focus is on a family who must leave the village that they love and also each other, because the father, who was formerly participating in the construction, left the house one day with a 8mm camera in hand, never to come back alive. Kawase captures the emotions of the family, who try to accept the death of the father, through the detached perspective of the legendary bird "Suzaku."

Production Company: WOWOW + BANDAI VISUAL CO.,LTD.
Director + Screenplay: Naomi Kawase
Photography: Masaki Tamura
Music: Masamichi Shigeno
Sound: Osamu Takizawa
Cast: Jun Kunimura, Machiko Ono, Sachiko Izumi, Kotaro Shibata, Yasuyo Kamimura

CONCEPT

人間の生と死。命の尊さ。自然への畏怖、
1000年先の人々へも伝わる物語。

CATEGORY
Fiction, Documentary, PV, CM

TEL / FAX
+81 (0) 3 5824 1127
+81 (0) 3 5824 1128

E-MAIL
noirmam@sepia.ocn.ne.jp

URL
http://www.kawasenaomi.com

TOOLS
Avid,
Final Cut Pro

Born in Nara, Japan, in 1969. Kawase began attracting attention in film festivals around the world, such as 1995 Yamagata International Documentary Film Festival, for her independent movies "Embracing" (1992) and "Katatsumori" (1994). With her theater debut film "Suzaku" (1996), she was able to become the all-time youngest recipient of Camera D'Or (new director's award) at Cannes in 1997. She later released such films as "Hotaru" (2000), "Kya Ka Ra Ba A" (2001), "Letter From a Yellow Cherry Blossom" (2002), and "Shara" (2003). Kawase holds film retrospectives all over the world, mainly in Europe, and her works continue to receive high praise.

4
Documentary -「きゃからばあ」*Kya Ka Ra Ba A* (2001)
"お父さんが亡くなりました"。携帯に残されたメッセージで、河瀬は1年前の父親の死を知る。「につつまれて」から8年、この世に存在しなくなった父親との決別を想い、生前深く関わった人々、産みの親や養母にインタビューを始めるのだが……。

"Your father has passed away." Through this recorded message on her cell phone, Kawase is informed of her father's death one year after it occurs. This is eight years after "Embracing," and as an act of parting, she begins interviewing people who knew her father while he was alive, the mother that bore Kawase, and her stepmother, but something unexpected comes along.

ProductionCompany: Sent Inc. + Kumie in association with ARTE France
Photography: Naomi Kawase, Masami Inomoto
Sound: Nobuyuki Kikuchi

5
Documentary -「追憶のダンス」*Letter from a Yellow Cherry Blossom* (2002)
写真評論家の西井一夫から「俺の最期を撮ってくれないか？頼んだぞ河瀬」と1本の電話が入る。河瀬はその翌日からホスピス病棟へ通い始める。がん患者の闘病"記録"ではなく、同じ時代をともに生きたもの同士が心を通わせ、今、私たちが生きている"生"の証として、息づき続ける"記憶"の物語。

A phone call comes from the photography critic Kazuo Nishii, saying "Kawase, I would like for you to film the final days of my life." From the next day, she begins visiting him in the hospice. This film isn't just a documentation of one man's fight against cancer. It is a tale of memory, that breathes on as a tribute to the relationship between two comrades who lived in the same age, and to the life that we live today.

Production Company: Sent Inc. + Kumie (Visual Arts College)
Director: Naomi Kawase
Cast: Kazuo Nishii, Chizuko Nishii
Photography: Naomi Kawase

4

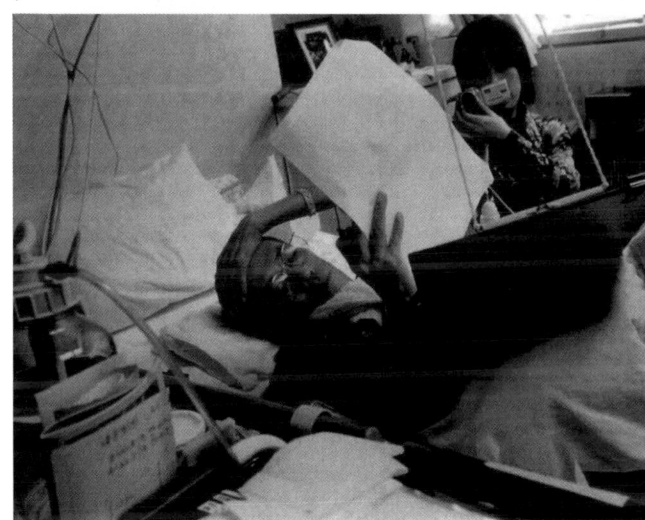
5

The life and death of human beings. An awe towards nature. Stories that can be communicated to even the people living a thousand years in the future.

065 喜田夏記 NATSUKI KIDA

PROFILE

1976年生まれ。東京芸術大学デザイン科大学院修了。在学中からCM、PVなどのさまざまな映像作品を制作。作画から美術制作、撮影、編集までをトータルに行う映像作家。近年では雑誌「VOGUE NIPPON」、「流行通信」などのアートディレクションや、CDジャケットデザインなども手掛ける。2004年にはエジンバラ国際映画祭や、世界最大のデジタル映像フェスティバルonedotzero、RESFESTによる作品招待。2005年には、SICAF Animated Film Festival（韓国）に作品出展ほか。

1

2

CONCEPT

映像のルーツは絵画。素材となるアニメーションの原画や造形物は自ら手作りで制作し、徹底的に美術のクオリティーを重視している。シーンの一つ一つが一枚の絵画としても成立するような完成度を常に追求していきたい。

CATEGORY
Animation, Live Action, Art Direction

TEL / FAX
+81 (0) 3 5785 1780
+81 (0) 3 5785 1784

E-MAIL
post@picsco.net

URL
http://www.picsco.net

TOOLS
Power Mac G5,
Photoshop,
After Effects,
Final Cut Pro

Born in 1976. Graduated from Tokyo National University of Fine Arts and Music Department of Design Graduate School. Kida produced many works including commercials and music videos while she was still in school. She is now a motion graphic artist who does everything from drawing and set design to filming and editing. Recently, she has been doing art direction for magazines such as Vogue and Ryuko Tsushin, and designs for CD covers. In 2004, her work was invited for screening at the world's foremost digital film festivals, Onedotzero and Resfest.

3

4

1
PV - 荘野ジュリ「駅ニテ」Shono Juli, *Ekinite* 」
(Victor Entertainment, 2004)
Director + Art + Animation: 喜田夏記 Natsuki Kida
Animation: 清水修 Osamu Shimizu, 田村香織 Kaori Tamura, 久保コレオ Koreo Kubo, 大野幹 Motoki Oono
Producer: 松居秀之 Hideyuki Matsui
Still-Cam: 渡部幸和 Yukikazu Watabe
Production by P.I.C.S.

2
PV - 荘野ジュリ「マーメイド」Shono Juli, *Mermaid*
(Victor Entertainment, 2004)
Director + Art + Animation: 喜田夏記 Natsuki Kida
Animation: 清水修 Osamu Shimizu, 大野幹 Motoki Oono, 喜田直哉 Naoya Kida
Producer: 松居秀之 Hideyuki Matsui
Still-Cam: 石塚貴雄 Takao Ishizuka
Production by P.I.C.S.

3
PV - 荘野ジュリ「カゲロウ」Shono Juli, *Kagerou*
(Victor Entertainment, 2004)
Director + Art + Animation: 喜田夏記 Natsuki Kida
Animation: 清水修 Osamu Shimizu, 大野幹 Motoki Oono, 池亀沙織 Saori Ikekame, 喜田直哉 Naoya Kida
Producer: 松居秀之 Hideyuki Matsui
DP: 小川幹 Miki Ogawa
Production by P.I.C.S.

4
PV - DEPAPEPE「シュプール -WINTER VERSION '05-」
DEPAPEPE, *Spur -WINTER VERSION'05-* (SME Records, 2005)
Director + Art + Animation: 喜田夏記 Natsuki Kida
Animation: 清水修 Osamu Shimizu, 大野幹 Motoki Oono, 池亀沙織 Saori Ikekame
Camera: 加藤純一 Junichi Kato
Light: 鎌田春樹 Haruki Kamata
Producer: 岩佐和彦 Kazuhiko Iwasa
Production by P.I.C.S.

The foundation of her images lies in painting. She hand-produces the preliminary drawings and sculptures which become the material for the animation, and thoroughly takes heed in aesthetic quality. She aims to constantly pursue a kind of standard of quality in which every scene is aesthetically sufficient enough to be a painting.

066 タナカノリユキ
NORIYUKI TANAKA

PROFILE
1985年、東京芸術大学大学院美術研究科修了。グラフィック、空間造形映像、パフォーマンス、環境デザインなど多様なビジュアル表現を駆使して、活躍するビジュアル・クリエイター。80年代後半より国内外で展覧会、プロジェクトなどのアートワークを手掛ける。サイエンスミュージアムの設計、映画美術、広告、商品開発などさまざまなジャンルで国際的活躍をみせる。ADCなど受賞歴も多数。

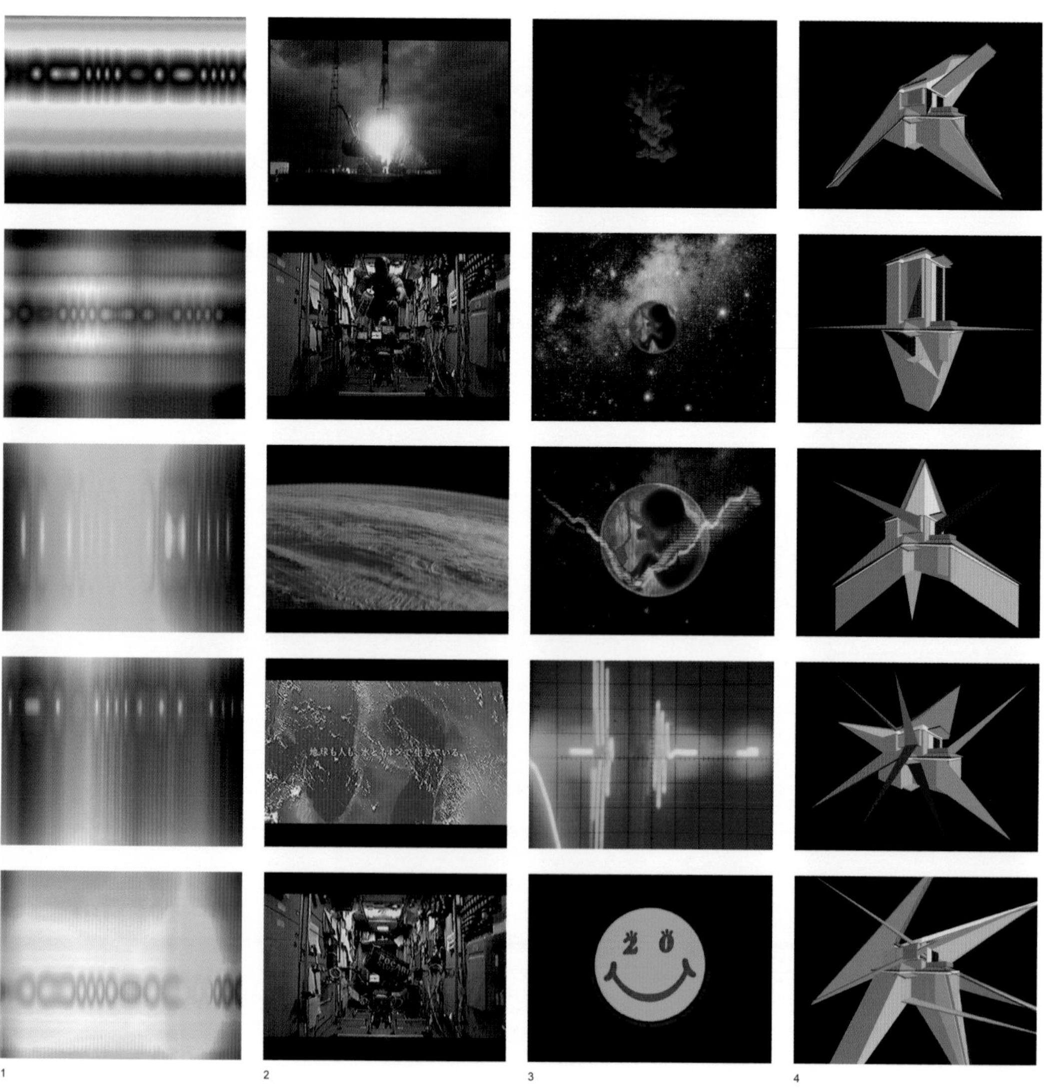

1 2 3 4

CATEGORY
CM, PV, Art etc.

TEL / FAX
+81 (0) 3 5481 4344
+81 (0) 3 5481 4345

E-MAIL
—

URL
—

TOOLS
—

Completed a Master's Course at Tokyo National University of Fine Arts and Music. Tanaka is a visual creator that utilizes diverse mediums including graphics, spatial form design, motion graphics, performances, and environmental design. In the latter half of the 1980's, he began holding exhibitions both domestically and overseas, and also handling many art projects. He is vigorously active around the world, taking on various projects such as the planning of a science museum, artwork for movie sets, production of advertisements, and product development. He has also won numerous awards,

5 6 7 8

1 Private Work - *VISUAL ADDICT* (2004)
2 CF - Pocali Sweat, *IN SPACE* (Otsuka Pharmaceutical Co., Ltd., 2002) AD+Director: Noriyuki Tanaka
3 *Tower Records 20th* (TOWER RECORDS, 1999) AD+Director: Noriyuki Tanaka
4 PV - KEN ISHII, *Islands & Continents 600MHz* (Sony Music Entertainment Inc., 1998) AD+Director: Noriyuki Tanaka
5 CF - UNIQLO, *OUTLAST FLEECE* (UNIQLO, 2004) CD+AD+Director: Noriyuki Tanaka
6 CF - UNIQLO, *.COM* (UNIQLO, 2000) CD+AD+Director: Noriyuki Tanaka
7 CF - NIKE just do it, *Blind Jumper* (NIKE JAPAN, 1997) CD+AD+Director: Noriyuki Tanaka
8 Private Work - *VISUAL ADDICT* (2004)

067 パワーグラフィックス
POWER GRAPHIXX

PROFILE

1996年よりパワーグラフィックスとして活動開始。国内外を問わずグラフィック関連のメディアに多数の作品を寄稿。クライアントワークはロゴマーク、ロゴタイプ、装丁、ポスター、広告、TV番組タイトル、ミュージックビデオなど多岐に渡る。1999年にVibe Station ID Contestにて「SMASH」が準グランプリ受賞。GAS BOOKへオリジナル映像を提供、RESFEST、onedotzeroなどの映像祭にも精力的に参加してきた。また、コンポーザー寺田創一との共同プロジェクト「OMODAKA」では競艇をテーマにした音楽と映像を展開中。

1

2

1
Video Game Opening Movie - KONAMI, *METAL GEAR AC!D2 Opening Movie*
(©1987-2005 KONAMI)
Director: Shinta Nojiri
Producer: Hideo Kojima, Noriaki Okamura
Music: Akihiro Honda
Director + Art Direction + Motion Graphic + CGI: Power Graphixx

2
ART - Power Graphics, *Roundscape* (2005)
Director + Motion Graphic: Power Graphixx
Music: Tesushi Takahashi

CONCEPT

観る者に爽快感を与える映像表現。

Motion graphics that let the viewer feel refreshment.

CATEGORY
Station ID, CI, CM, PV, etc.

TEL / FAX
+81 (0) 3 3414 3065
+81 (0) 3 3414 3065

E-MAIL
support@power-graphixx.com

URL
http://www.power-graphixx.com

TOOLS
Canon XV1,
Illustrator,
Photoshop,
After Effects,
CINEMA 4D

Became active in 1996 as Power Graphixx. They have submitted numerous works to media dealing with graphics around the world. His client work covers a wide variety, including logos, book design, posters, advertisements, TV program titles, and music videos. In 1999, They work “SMASH” won second place in Vibe Station ID Contest. They have provided GAS BOOK with original graphics, and have also been vigorously participating in motion graphic festivals such as RESFEST and Onedotzero.

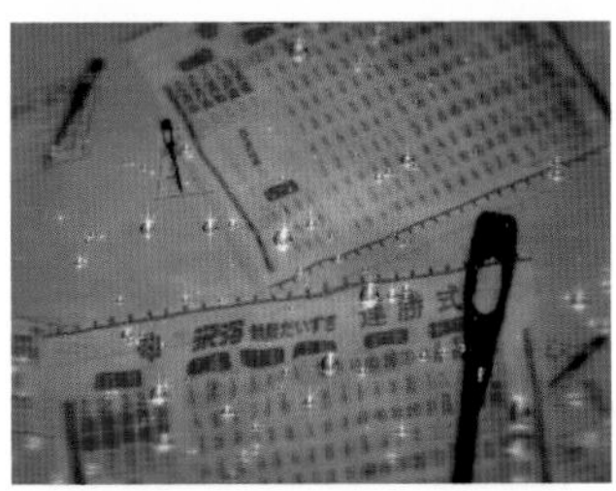

3

4

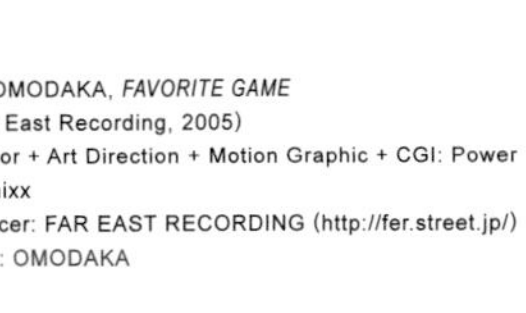

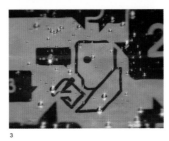

3
PV - OMODAKA, *FAVORITE GAME*
(©Far East Recording, 2005)
Director + Art Direction + Motion Graphic + CGI: Power Graphixx
Producer: FAR EAST RECORDING (http://fer.street.jp/)
Music: OMODAKA

4
ART - Power Graphics, *Hide and Seek Exhibition "HELLO-KITTY"*
(©1976-2005 Sanrio Co., Ltd. & ©AllRightsReserved Ltd., 2005)
Dir & Motion Graphic: Power Graphixx
Sound: except Iwamoto

068 黒川良一
RYOICHI KUROKAWA

PROFILE

1978年生まれ。映像・音響アーティスト。オーディオビジュアル作品を、レコーディング、インスタレーション、上映、ライブパフォーマンスなど、さまざまな形態で発表している。緻密で繊細な音と映像で構成される作品は国内外で高い評価を得ており、多くのフェスティバルや、展覧会へ招待されている。コラボレーションも積極的に行っており、SKETCH SHOWやACOのライブビジュアルなども担当。2005年には、ヨーロッパやアジアの多くのアートフェスティバルで作品が展示・上映され、より国際的な活動へと進展している。

1

2

3

4

5

6

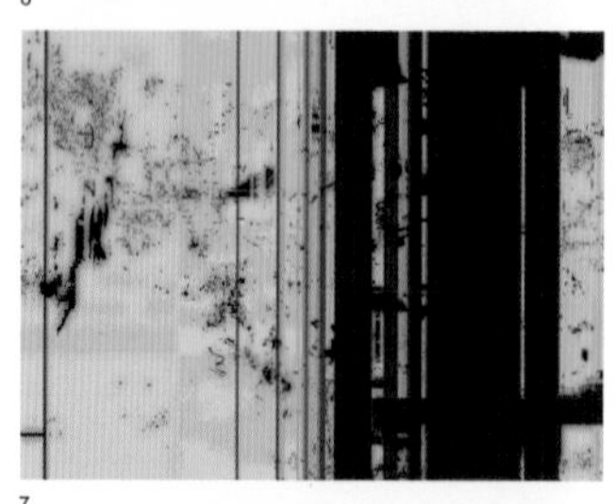

7

8

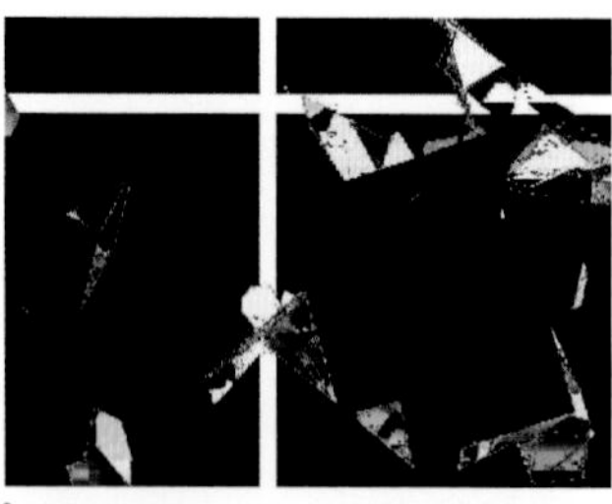

9

10

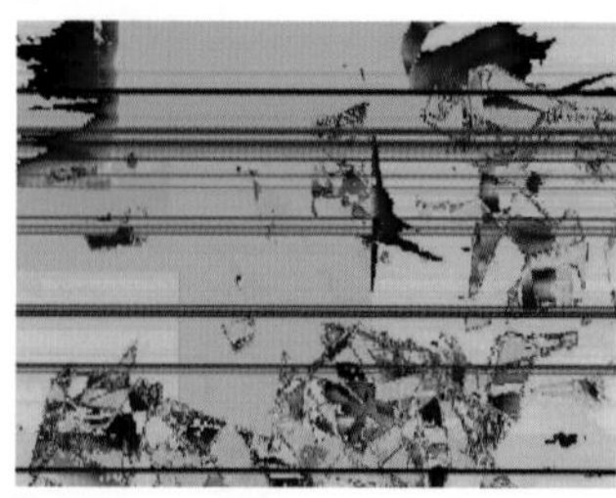

11

12

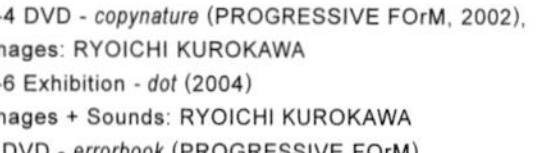

1-4 DVD - *copynature* (PROGRESSIVE FOrM, 2002), Images: RYOICHI KUROKAWA
5-6 Exhibition - *dot* (2004)
Images + Sounds: RYOICHI KUROKAWA
7 DVD - *errorbook* (PROGRESSIVE FOrM)
Images + sounds: RYOICHI KUROKAWA

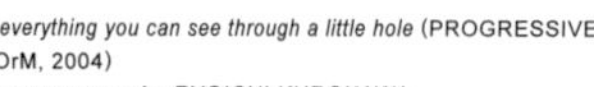

8 *everything you can see through a little hole* (PROGRESSIVE FOrM, 2004)
Images + sounds: RYOICHI KUROKAWA
9 *opside* (PROGRESSIVE FOrM, 2002)
Images + Sounds: RYOICHI KUROKAWA
10-11 *OOL* (PROGRESSIVE FOrM 2002)
Images + Sounds: RYOICHI KUROKAWA

12 *polygonaloop* (Yokohama Arts Foundation, 2005)
Images: RYOICHI KUROKAWA, Sounds: Yoshihiro HANNO
13 DVD - *read #3* (daisyworld discs / cutting edge - avex inc, 2004) Images + Sounds: RYOICHI KUROKAWA
14 DVD - *read #5* (daisyworld discs / cutting edge - avex inc, 2004) Images + Sounds: RYOICHI KUROKAWA

CATEGORY
Video Art

TEL / FAX
—
—

E-MAIL
info@ryoichikurokawa.com

URL
http://www.ryoichikurokawa.com

TOOLS
Power Mac G5,
PowerBook G4,
Final Cut, Shake,
Processing, Isadora,
After Effects, Blender

Born in 1978. A motion graphics / sound artist. Kurokawa presents audio-visual works through various forms, such as recording, installation, screening, and live performance. His works, which are composed of intricate sounds and images, have received much praise both domestically and overseas. Kurokawa has collaborated with such artists as SKETCH SHOW and ACO. Since the beginning of 2005, his creative activities have been entering a more global scale, as his works are shown at many art festivals and exhibitions in Europe and Asia.

13 14 15 16 17 18 19 20 21

15-16 DVD - *readme #2* (daisyworld discs / cutting edge - avex inc, 2004) Images + Sounds: RYOICHI KUROKAWA
17 Performance - *Visual Live Performance with Yoshihiro HANNO [sounds]*, boa, Luzern, 2005
18-19 DVD - *read #0* (daisyworld discs / cutting edge - avex inc, 2004) Images + Sounds: RYOICHI KUROKAWA
20 DVD - *read #1* (daisyworld discs / cutting edge - avex inc, 2004) Images + Sounds: RYOICHI KUROKAWA
21 DVD - *read #2* (daisyworld discs / cutting edge - avex inc, 2004) Images + Sounds by RYOICHI KUROKAWA

069 サッカク SAKKAKU

PROFILE
空間ビジュアルアーティスト集団として、映像プロデューサー、ディレクター、ペインティングアーティスト、DJが集まり2002年5月に結成。多数の円形スクリーンと複合的なプロジェクションを使用した視覚効果的な空間映像インスタレーションで数々のアートイベント、パーティ、ライブなどで精力的に活動中。
メンバー： MASA-XL (PRODUCER), KUNIHIKO OKAZAKI (VISUAL DIRECTION), OHJI OGAWA (VISUAL DIRECTION), a16 (PAINTING ARTIST), KIICHI (ANIMATION), HIKO (DJ), TAKURO (CAMERA)

1 2 3 4

CONCEPT
現実と幻想の境界の探求。

The exploration of the boundary between reality and fantasy

CATEGORY
Space Image Production, VJ

TEL / FAX
+81 (0) 3 5717 9626
+81 (0) 3 5717 9627

E-MAIL
info@sakkaku.net

URL
http://www.sakkaku.net

TOOLS
Roland V-4,
KORG kaptivator,
PowerBook G4,
Final Cut,
After Effects

The members of SAKKAKU, including a motion graphic producer, a director, a painting artist, and a DJ, got together and formed the group in May of 2002. Utilizing circular screens and multiple projections, they show their motion graphic installations vigorously at numerous art events, parties, and concerts.
The members are: MASA-XL (PRODUCER), KUNIHIKO OKAZAKI (VISUAL DIRECTION), OHJI OGAWA (VISUAL DIRECTION), a16 (PAINTING ARTIST), KIICHI (ANIMATION), HIKO (DJ), TAKURO (CAMERA)

5

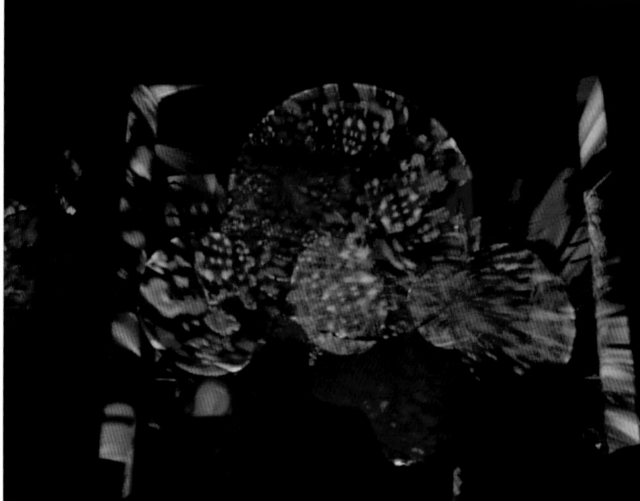

6

7

1 Original Work - *New century of Tokyo Electro Funk*, Graz003 Austria (2003) SAKKAKU & code e aka ebizoo tanuma
2 Space Image Production- *mugenkyo*, Toyama Castle park (2004.8)
3 Original Work - *babylon* (2004)
SAKKAKU & code e aka ebizoo tanuma
4 Original Work - *flowers* (2004)
SAKKAKU & code e aka ebizoo tanuma
5 Original Work - *NATURAL* (2003)
SAKKAKU & Kuniyuki Takahashi
6 Space Image Production - *arcadia*, Roppongi Spiral (2004.7)
7 Space Image Production - *SAKKAKU NIGHT*, toyama BAU (2004.8)

070 ヨシマルシン SHIN YOSHIMARU

PROFILE
1972年、岩手県盛岡市生まれ。保育園時代、愛読していた「テレビマガジン」（講談社）付録のげんとうきで初VJ。八重樫王明とのユニット「モリンコララバイ」〜「バリンコララモイ」を経て、現在はソロ・フリー。VJをはじめ、テレビやインターネットなどの映像、アニメーション、グラフィック、イラストなどを手掛け、広範囲に活動中。

1　2　3

CATEGORY
VJ, Animation

TEL / FAX
+81 (0) 422 40 4808
+81 (0) 422 40 4808

E-MAIL
yosimaru@sage.ocn.ne.jp

URL
http://www.yoshiru.com

TOOLS
Power Mac G4, Note PC,
DV Handycam, LCP Projector,
Canopus Converter, After Effects,
Flash, Illstrator, Photoshop,
Fireworks, Cubase

Born in Morioka-shi, Iwate Prefecture on Jul. 29, 1972. Yoshimaru's first VJ experience was during pre-school, using a magic lantern that came attached with "Televi Magazine," his favorite magazine at the time. After working in a creative unit with Kimiaki Yaegashi, Morinko Lullaby (later became Barinko Lullamoy), he now works solo. Yoshimaru practices a wide range of activities, including motion image, graphics, animation, illustrations, and VJ, on various media such as television and the internet.

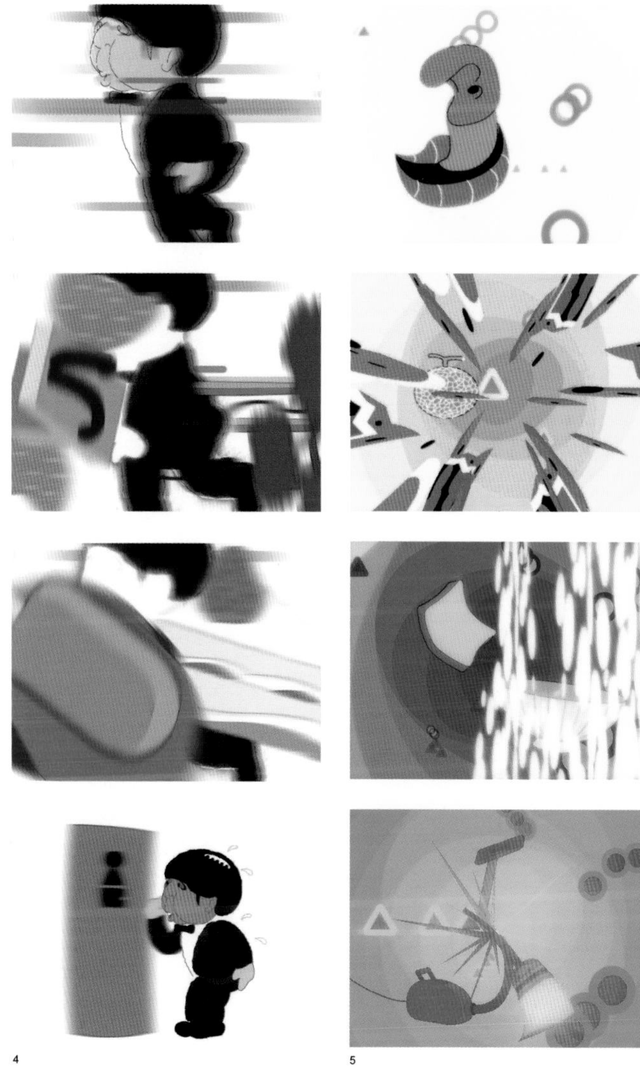

4

5

1
Self Mix -「秘密のフランボワーズ」朝日美穂
Asahi Miho, *Himitsu no Framboise* (2005)

2
DVD - *Default* (2005)
土川藍 Ai Tsuchikawa, 戸田誠司 Seiji Toda
"There She Goes Again" collection

3
Original Animation -「クレープ」*Crape* (2005)

4
DVD -「バナナマンのシャブリなコメディ / あいうえお」
(©CLUBKING CO., LTD. 発売元:東北新社
TOHOKUSHINSHA FILM CORPORATION, 2005)

5
TV -「みごろ！ たべごろ！ ナントカカントカ」
(テレビ朝日系 ザ・ワークス, 2003)
Migoro! Tabegoro! Nantokakantoka (THE WORKS, 2003)

071 シンポ
SIMPO

PROFILE

1978年生まれ。大阪のコアパーティ「FLOWER OF LIFE」の誕生とともにキャリアをスタートして以来、パーティVJというスタンスで日本全国のアンダーグラウンドDIYパーティに参加。2004年にはnutron&EXPEのVJでFUJI ROCK FESTIVALに出演。YOSHITAKE EXPEと共に美術館やギャラリーでインスタレーションライブも行う。ほんわかと冷静が同居したSIMPOの脳から溢れ出すイメージは、パーティの「陶酔」や「きらめき」を表現するスタイルで、FANTASTIC & RADIANCE!!

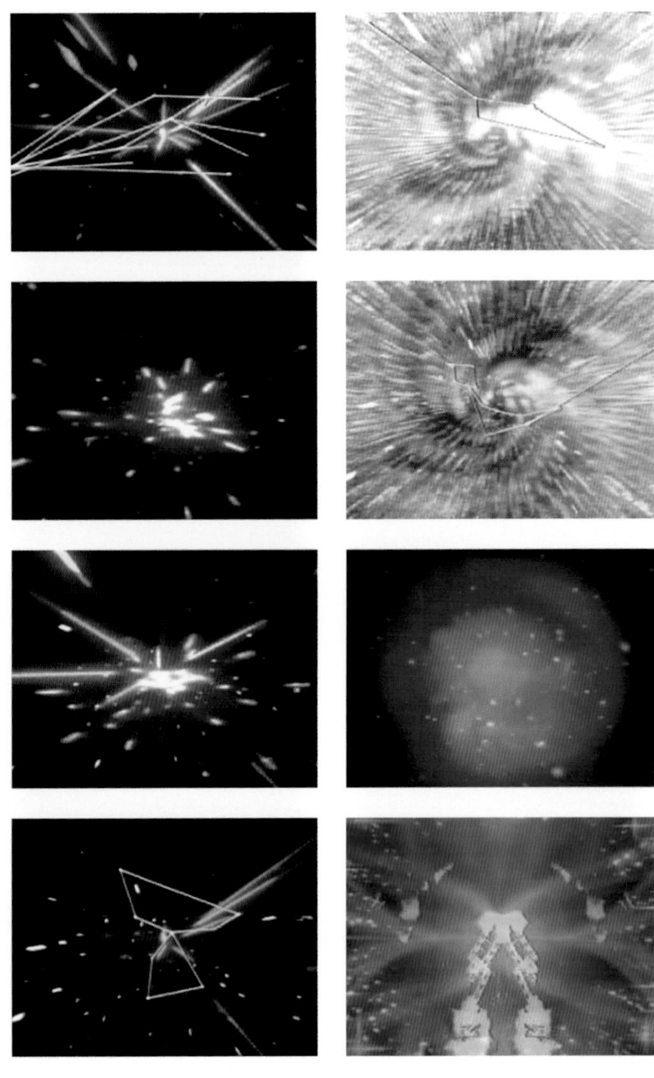

CONCEPT

音、雰囲気、ヴァイブレーションを大切に、そこからつながっていくVISIONをつくる。

To cherish the sound, atmosphere, and vibes, and to create visions that connect to these.

CATEGORY
VJ

TEL / FAX
—
—

E-MAIL
hag27410@yahoo.co.jp

URL
http://www.flower-of-life.org

TOOLS
Sony XV-Z10000,
Sony XV-C900,
iMovie,
Freewares

Born in 1978. After beginning his career with the start of "FLOWER OF LIFE," an underground party in Osaka, Simpo has been participating in D.I.Y.-style parties all around Japan as a "Party V.J.." In 2004, he V.J.ed for nutron & EXPE at Fuji Rock Festival. Together with YOSHITAKE EXPE, he has done live installations at art museums and galleries. The images that spill out of SIMPO's mind, which houses both cool composure and warm easygoing-ness, take a style that aims to express the intoxicating glitter of club parties, and can be described as fantastic and radiating.

PV - nutron, *BIRD7* SIMPO (2004)

072 大月 壮
SOU OOTSUKI

PROFILE
1977年生まれ。東洋美術学校視覚伝達デザイン科デジタルグラフィック専攻卒業。卒業生最高賞受賞。在学中、カナダ・ケベック大学デザイン科留学。卒業後、映像作家の星健太が主宰する映像制作会社、ANALOGICAL に入社。同社退社後、漫画家タナカカツキの元で仕事に関わる。現在フリーランスとしてTV映像、音楽PV、携帯映像、Web配信映像、DVD オーサリングなど幅広い映像制作を行う。

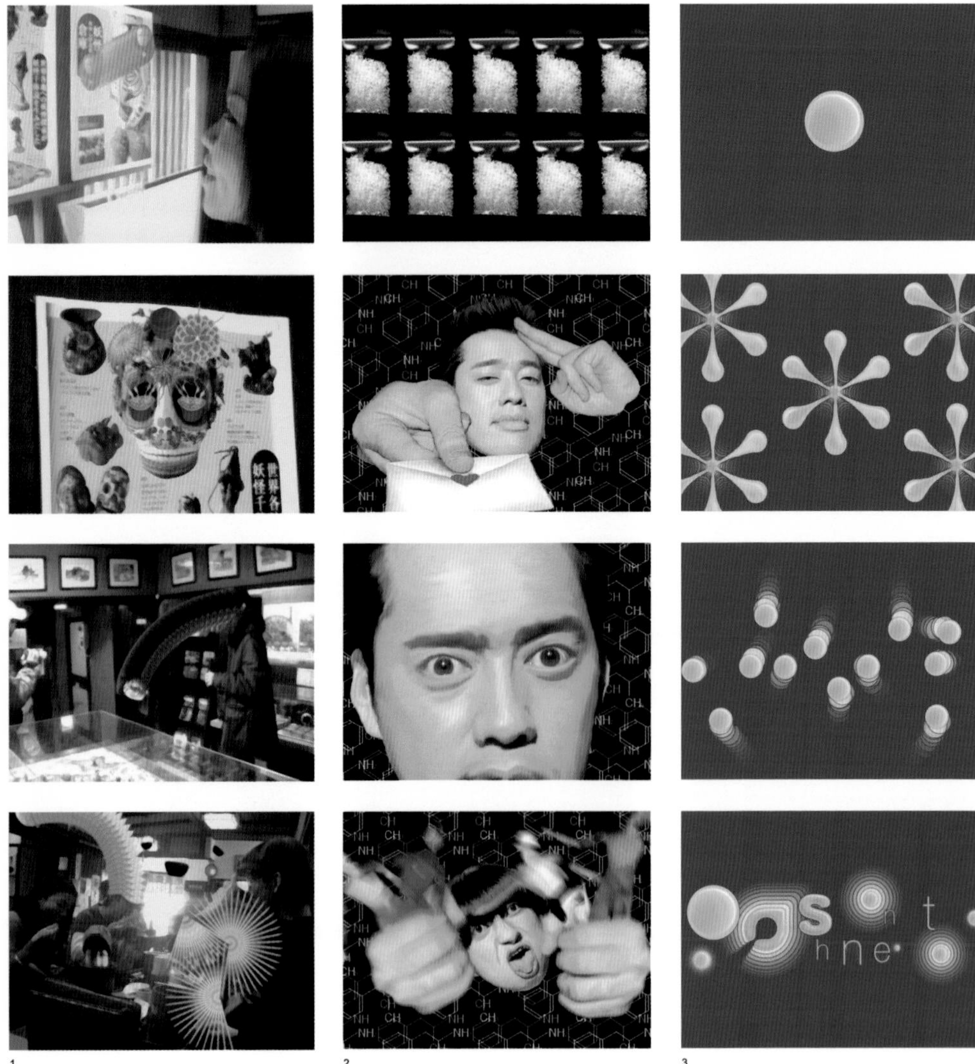

1 2 3

CONCEPT
生命と愛。ぬくもりを感じるような質感のある映像表現。

Life and love. Motion graphics that have a quality of warmth.

CATEGORY
PV, VJ, TV

TEL / FAX
+81 (0) 44 866 4090
+81 (0) 44 866 4090

E-MAIL
oo2ki@unnon-web.com

URL
—

TOOLS
After Effects,
Final Cut Pro,
DVD Studio,
Photoshop,
Illustrator

Born in 1977. Graduated from Toyo Institude of Art and School Department of Visual Communication Design, majoring in Digital Graphics. Upon graduating, he entered ANALOGICAL, a motion graphic production company headed by Kenta Hoshi. After leaving the company, he began working under the manga author Katsuki Tanaka. Currently, he practices a wide variety of motion graphic production as a freelance artist, including television, music videos, motion graphics for mobile phones and internet, and DVD authoring.

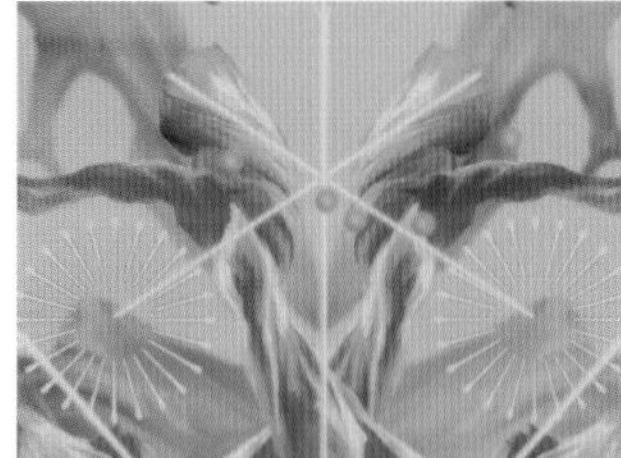

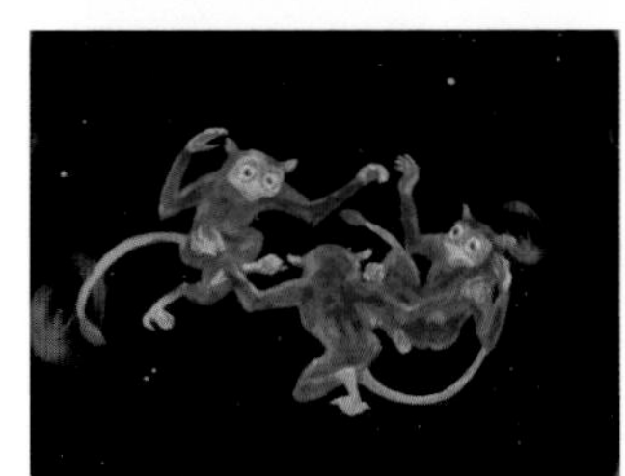

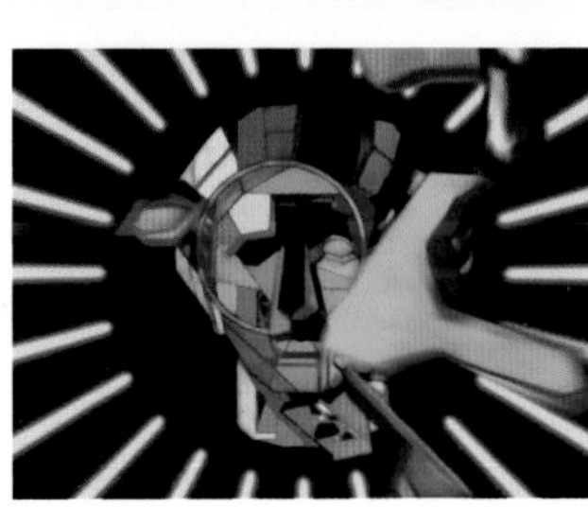

4

5

1
DVD - Fuuri DVD「Fuuriの休日 鬼太郎茶屋 DUB」
Fuuri's Holyday Kitaro Jaya Dub (nos Inc., 2005)

2
DVD -「バナナマンのシャブリなコメディ / もっと燃えろ」
Bananaman's Chablis Comedy / Motto Moero
(©CLUBKING CO., LTD. 発売元：東北新社
TOHOKUSHINSHA FILM CORPORATION, 2005)

3
Station ID - *so-net channel 749 Station 10* (Maltese, 2005)

4
DVD - CLUB KING, *Comedy News Show DVD vol.2*
(©CLUBKING CO., LTD., 2005)
Published by Universal Music K.K.

5
PV - Fuuri, *NANA SONG* (nos Inc., 2005)
Animation: Sou Ootsuki, Teppei Maki

073 菅原そうた SOTA

PROFILE

1979生まれ。漫画家・デザイナー・映画監督。「トニオちゃん」の産みの親。実兄がボーカルを務めるバンド「B-DASH」のトータルアートディレクション、漫画、アニメ、グラフィックを手掛ける。2005年にはニッポン放送ファンタスティックシアターにて初監督の映画「SOTA WORLD」を一週間上映。

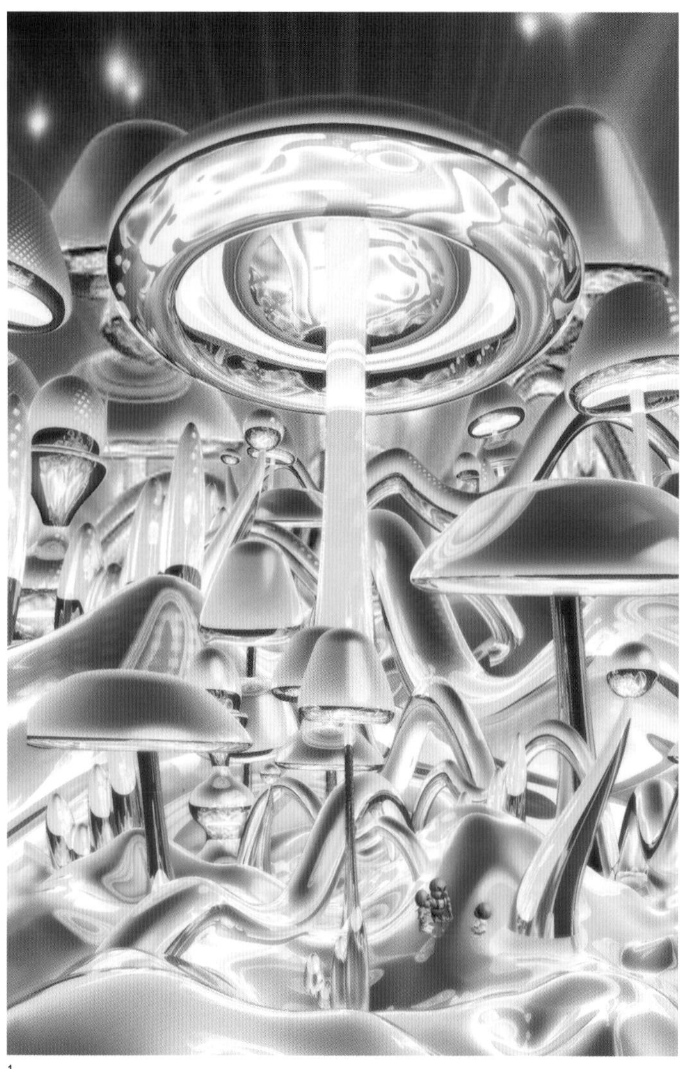

1

1
Movie - *Tonio Movie* (2004)
Music: B-Dash
Director + Modeling + Animation + Editor: Sota

2
Toon -「みんなのトニオちゃん」*Minna no Tonio* (2003)

3
Film - *Sota World* (2005)
Music: B-Dash
Director + Modeling + Animation + Editor: Sota

CATEGORY
PV, VJ, 3D CG Comic, 3D Animation

TEL / FAX
+81 (0) 3 763 6500
+81 (0) 3 763 6500

E-MAIL
sota@suga.gr.jp

URL
http://www.b-dash.com/tonio/index.html

TOOLS
3ds Max,
Illustrator,
Photoshop,
Premiere, ComicStudio,
After Effects, Poser, Shade

Born in 1970. A manga author, designer, and movie director. Sota is the creator of the manga character "Tonio-chan," who was featured in his first manga work. He works on manga, animation, and graphics, taking a stance in which he will take on anything that seems interesting. Sota began handling the CD covers, visuals, and music videos for the band "B Dash," in which his elder brother is the vocalist, and he was soon producing many motion graphic works. In 2005, his first directed movie, "Sota World," was screened at Nippon Broadcasting System's "Fantastic Theater."

2

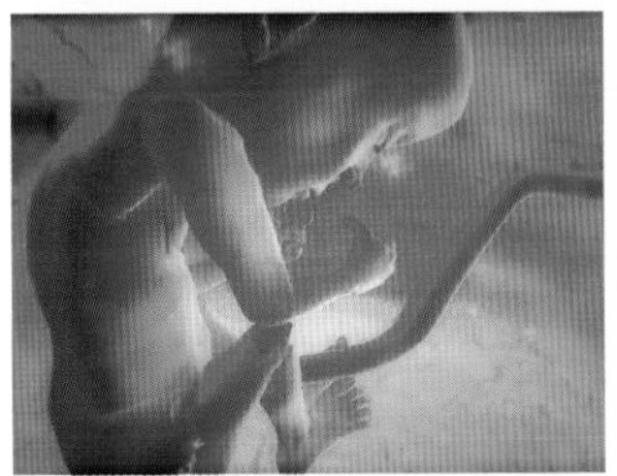

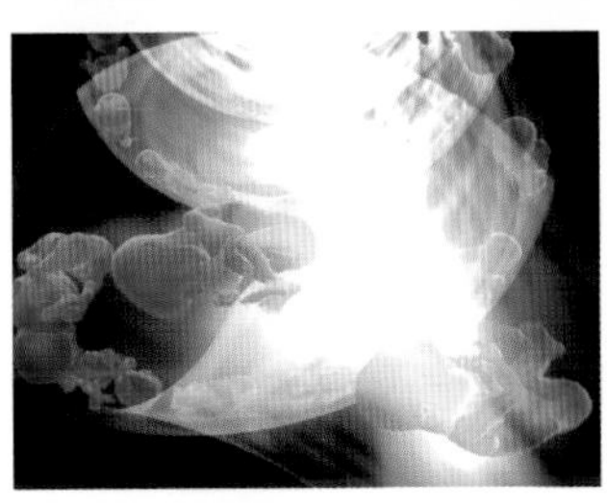

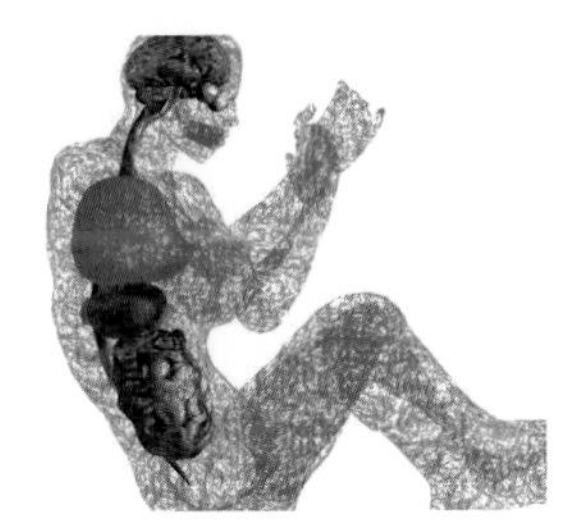

3

074 山本信一
SYNICHI YAMAMOTO

PROFILE

90年代初め、ポストプロダクションでCMエディターをしながら、映像作家として国内外のフェスティバルなどに多く出品。90年代後半から、モーショングラフィックスでイベント映像やスポットCMなどの演出を手掛ける。また、その音楽制作の依頼を通じてレイハラカミ、パードン木村、MASAといった個性的な音楽家とコラボレーションする。2000年以降は、アート作品とコマーシャル作品が良い意味で相関し、コンセプチュアルな企業CIや実験的なタイトルなどを作り続ける。現在は、オムニバスジャパン所属。制作スタイルは独特であり先鋭的。

CONCEPT

頭の中にあるイメージ実現に固執せず流れにまかせ、デスクトップで得られた映像や、音楽家や、関わるスタッフとの行程などにインスパイアされながら制作。時間軸の構成主義、テクノ、ミニマル、音楽の延長線上にある映像。

CATEGORY
Motion Graphic, Video Art

TEL / FAX
+81 (0) 3 6229 0601
+81 (0) 3 6229 0604

E-MAIL
s-yama@omni.co.jp

URL
http://www.wavering.com

TOOLS
Flints 9.2,
Houdini,
Maya,
3ds Max

In the beginning of the 90's, Yamamoto was submitting motion graphic works to many domestic and international film festivals, while working as a post-production editor for TV commercials. From the late 90's, he began directing motion graphics for events and spot commercials. Since 2000, he has been able to construct a successful correlation between art works and commercial works, and has been continually producing conceptual CIs and experimental title sequences. Yamamoto is currently affiliated with Omnibus Japan.

1-2
DVD -「バナナマンのシャブリなコメディ / はげまし数え歌」 bananaman, *Hagemashi Kazoeuta* (©CLUBKING CO., LTD. 発売元 : 東北新社 TOHOKUSHINSHA FILM CORPORATION, 2005)
3DCG: 宗片純二 Jyunji Munekata, モフジ Mofj
Published By: Tohoku Shinsha

3-4
CM - *Yes* (TOWER RECORDS, 2005)
3DCG: 古賀庸郎 Yasuo Koga
Music: SALAD

5-7
Opening Title -「黄金騎士 GARO」*Ougonkishi Garo* (テレビ東京 TV TOKYO, 2005)
3DCG: 古賀庸郎 Yasuo Koga, 宗片純二 Jyunji Munekata

8
CI - *Sony Music* (Sony Music, 2002)

9-11
Opening Title -「月曜映画」*Getsuyou Eiga* (日本テレビ Nippon Television Network Corporation, 2001-2005)
Music: Kinocosmo
Co-production: 大塚恭司 Kyoji Otsuka
Illustration: 丸尾末広 Suehiro Maruo
3DCG: モフジ Mofj

12
CI - *NTT DoCoMo* (NTT DoCoMo, 2005)

13-14
Channel ID - *NTV Brand?* (日本テレビ Nippon Television Network Corporation, 2002)
3DCG: モフジ Mofj

15-16
CI - *Panasonic* (Panasonic, 2002)

17-18
Original - *Pine Wheel* (Go-Pha, 1997)
Music: パードン木村 Pardon Kimura

19-20
Original - *TRIPLE FLAT* (1999)
Music: Rei Harakami

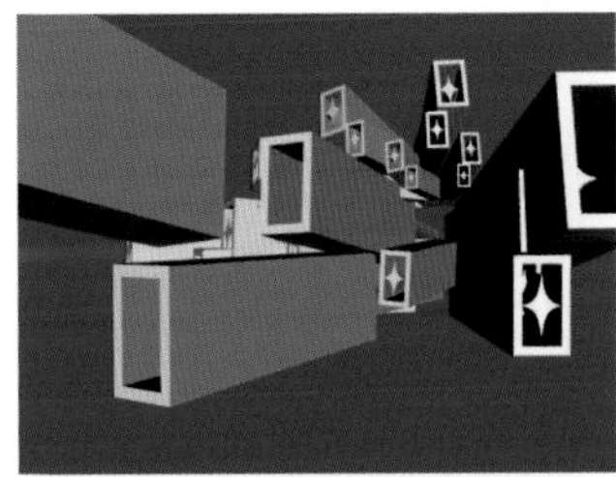
13

14

15

16

17

18

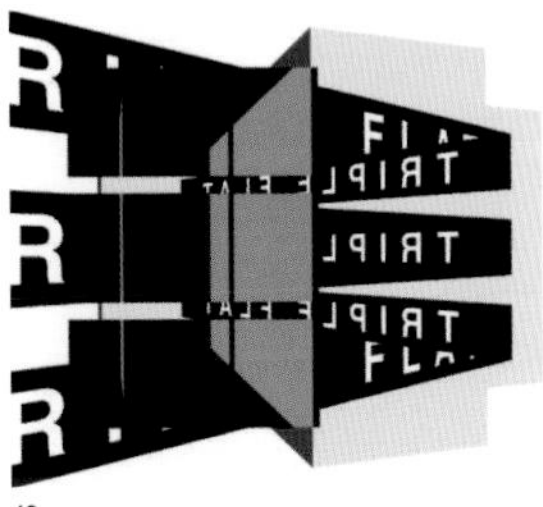
19

20

To not necessarily adhere to the realization of the images within the mind, but to go with the flow, receiving inspiration from motion graphics, music, and interaction with other staff members. To create motion graphics that are derivatives of things such as constructivism of the time axis, techno, minimalism, and music.

075 東芋 TABAIMO

PROFILE

1975年兵庫県生まれ。京都造形芸術大学卒業。「にっぽん」をテーマにしたアニメーションと映像、そして立体を組み合わせたインスタレーションで知られる現代美術家。「キリンコンテンポラリー・アワード1999最優秀作品賞」をはじめ、「第13回五島記念文化賞美術新人賞」(2002)、「日本現代藝術奨励賞」(2005) など数々の賞を受賞。国内のみならず海外でも評価は高く、「サンパウロ・ビエンナーレ」やミネアポリスのウォーカー・アート・センターでの「HOW LATITUDES BECOME FORMS」など、世界各国で展覧会を行う。

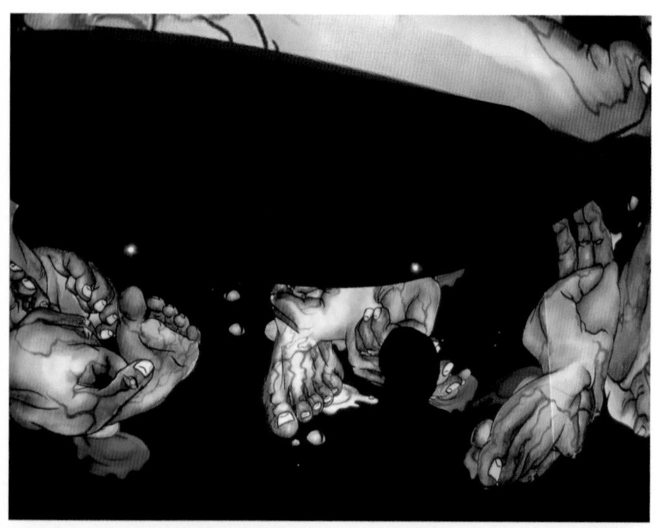

1

2

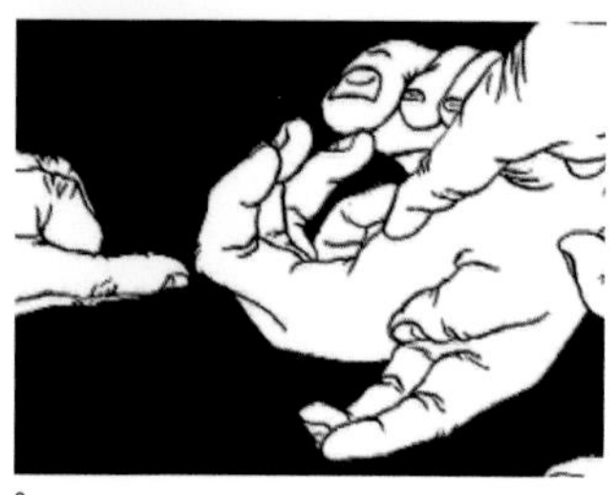

3

4

5

CONCEPT

メディアで受け取った情報を「私」はどのように見ているのか。作品化することでさらに克明に見えてくる「私」をサンプルに、いかに私達が分かったつもりになっているか、いかに何も知らないかを表現する。

CATEGORY
Installation

E-MAIL
tabaimo@js9.so-net.ne.jp

TOOLS
Projector, DVD Player

TEL / FAX
+81 (0)75 723 0370
—

URL
—

Born in 1975 in Hyogo prefecture, Japan. Tabaimo is a contemporary artist who produces works with "Japan" as a main theme, on various media such as animation, motion graphics, and installation. She has won many awards including the Kirin History of Kirin Art Award 1999 Grand Award, the New Artist Award of the 13th Gotoh Memorial Foundation Cultural Awards (2002), and the Nihon Gendai Geijyutsu Shoureisho Award (2005). She receives acclaim overseas as well, and has exhibited at many locations around the globe, such as the Sãn Paulo Biennial.

6

7

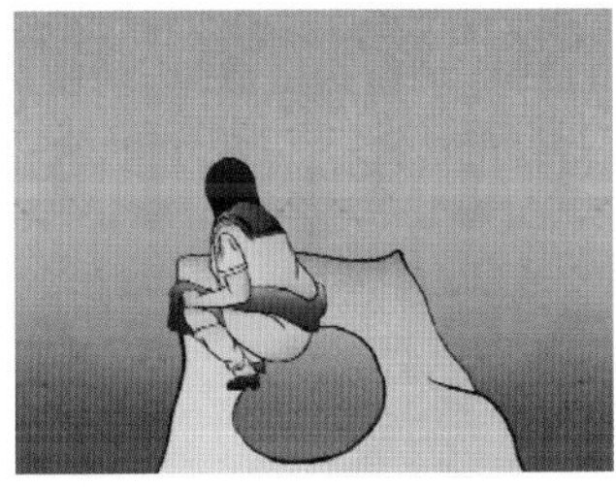
8

1-3
Instalation -「ギニョる」*Guignoller*, KIRIN PLAZA OSAKA (2005)
Photo: Yasushi Kishimoto

4-5
Instalation - *hanabi-ra*, Courtesy of Gallery Koyanagi (2003)

6-8
Instalation -「にっぽんの横断歩道」*Japanese Zebra Crossing*, Kobe Art Village Center, (1999)
Photo: Kiyotoshi Takashima

A question: how do "I" view the information I receive from the media? By using as a sample the "I" that becomes clearer through the process of producing works, Tabaimo aims to express how we believe we know, but essentially do not know.

076 高木正勝
TAKAGI MASAKATSU

PROFILE

1979年生まれ。京都府在住。映像と音楽両方の制作を等価に手掛け、双方の質の高い融合により注目を集めるアーティスト。国内外のレーベルからCD・DVDをリリースすると同時に、アートスペースでのビデオ・インスタレーションや世界各地でのライブなど、分野に限定されない多様な活動を展開している。最近では、デヴィッド・シルヴィアンのワールドツアーへの参加や、UAのミュージックビデオ制作、ダンス作品の映像・音楽を制作するなど、積極的なコラボレーションも行っている。

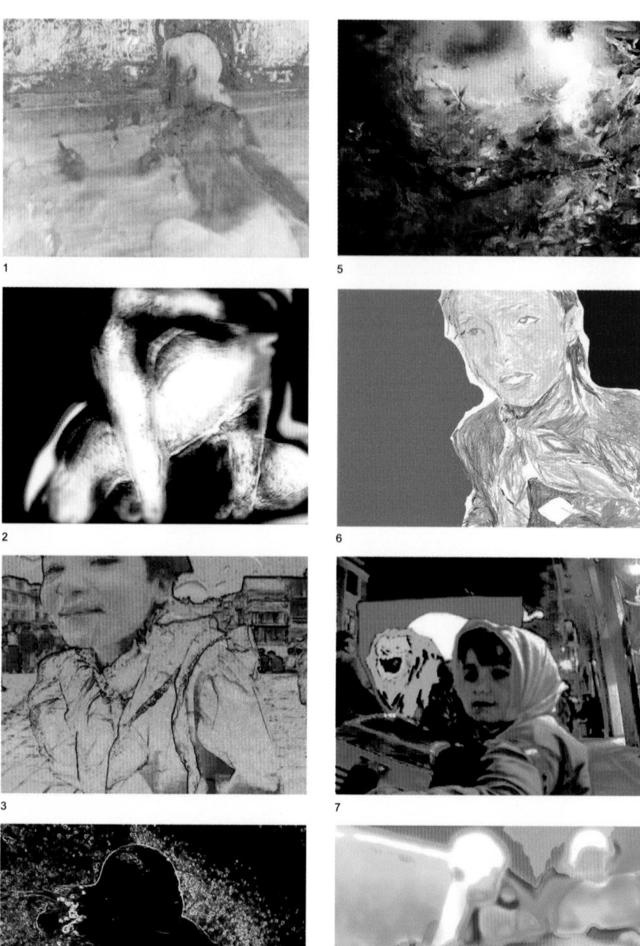

1
Art - *Primo* (©Takagi Masakatsu, 2003)

2
Art - *Pia Flies* (©Takagi Masakatsu, 2004)

3
Art - *Rama* ©Takagi Masakatsu, 2002)

4
Art - *Light Pool* (©Takagi Masakatsu, 2004)

5
Art - *Bloomy Girls* (©Takagi Masakatsu, 2005)

6
Art - *Private Drawing* (©Takagi Masakatsu, 2003)

7
Art - *Sorina Street* (©Takagi Masakatsu, 2002)

8
Art - *Aura* (©Takagi Masakatsu, 2003)

CATEGORY
Art

TEL / FAX
+81 (0) 3 3448 0745 (Epiphany Works)
+81 (0) 3 3448 0745 (Epiphany Works)

E-MAIL
motoutono@mac.com
info@epiphanyworks.net (Epiphany Works)

URL
http://www.takagimasakatsu.com
http://www.epiphanyworks.net (Epiphany Works)

TOOLS
After Effects,
Final Cut

Born in 1979. Resides in Kyoto. Takagi is an artist who produces both visuals and music in equivalence, and attracts much attention for his high quality in fusing the two. Besides releasing CDs and DVDs from labels within Japan and overseas, he also does activities such as video installations in art spaces and live performances all around the world: his wide range of activities do not fit into any one field. Recently, he has been doing much collaborative work, such as participating in David Sylvian's world tour, and producing a music video for UA, and also the motion graphics and music for a dance performance.

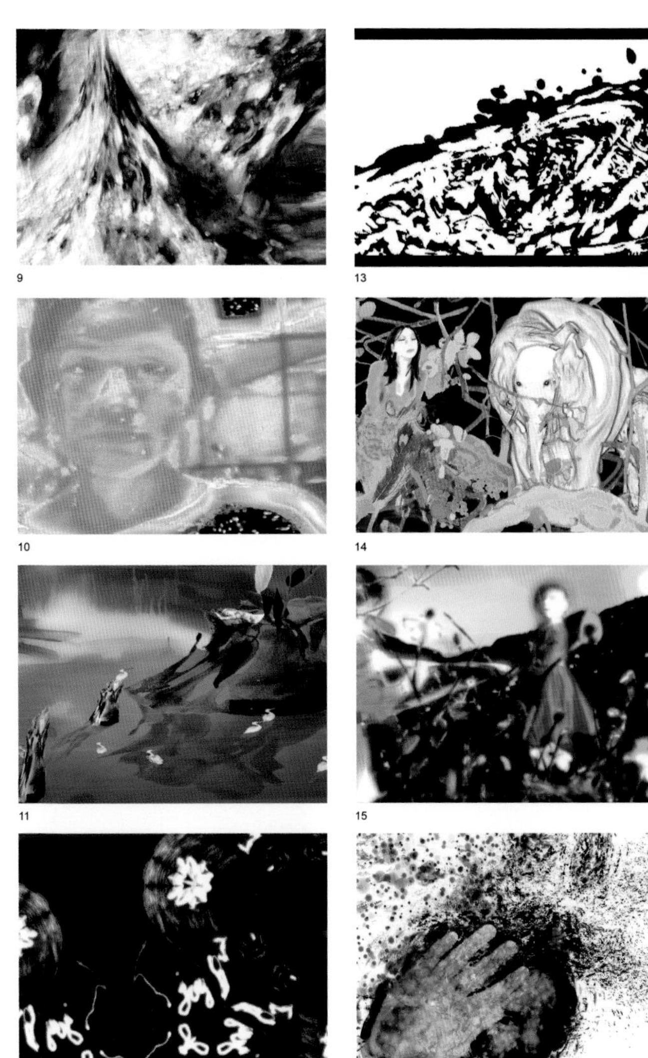

9
Art - *WAVE* (©Takagi Masakatsu, 2004)

10
Art - *CHO CHO THIN GALE*
(©Takagi Masakatsu, 2002)

11
Art - UA, *The Color Of Empty Sky*
(©Takagi Masakatsu + Saeko Takagi, 2005)
Director: Takagi Masakatsu and Saeko Takagi

12
PV - YUKI, *Dramatic*
(©Epic Recrods Japan Inc. / Sony Music, 2005)
Director: Takagi Masakatsu

13
Art - *Maggie's Trip* (©Takagi Masakatsu, 2003)

14
PV - UA, *Lightning* (©SPEEDSTAR RECORDS, 2005)
Director: Takagi Masakatsu and Saeko Takagi

15
Art - *Light Park #3* (©Takagi Masakatsu + Saeko Takagi, 2002)

16
Art - *Girls* (©Takagi Masakatsu, 2003)

077 森田貴宏
TAKAHIRO MORITA / FESN

PROFILE

1975年生まれ。スケートボードとの出会いからそのビデオを撮るようになり、1995年、初のビデオ制作と同時にFESN（far east skate network）を設立。それ以降日本全国のスケートシーンを撮影するため、ビデオカメラと共に日本各地をまわり続けた。現在は地元中野にあるショップ「FATBROS」、デザインチーム「153 laboratory」、クロージングブランド「LIBE BRAND UNIVS」らのすべてでディレクションを務める傍ら、FESNではスケートボード、音楽、ストリートカルチャーを題材にした映像制作を中心に活動。

1　　2

CONCEPT

作品やその対象になる物の「温度」を表現すること。

Expressing the "temperature" of the work and the object.

CATEGORY
Documentary

TEL / FAX
+81 (0) 3 3371 8509
+81 (0) 3 3371 8509

E-MAIL
fesn@par.odn.ne.jp
info@fatbros.net

URL
http://www.fatbros.net (FATBROS)

TOOLS
—

Born in 1975. As Morita began skateboarding, he also began filming skaters. In 1995, he founded FESN as he simultaneously produced his first video work. Afterwards, he roamed all over Japan with his video camera in order to film skating scenes around the country. Currently, he directs "FATBROS," a shop in Nakano, Tokyo, the design team "153 Laboratory," and the clothing brand "LIBE BRAND UNIVS," all while producing films at FESN, with skateboarding, music, and street culture as the material.

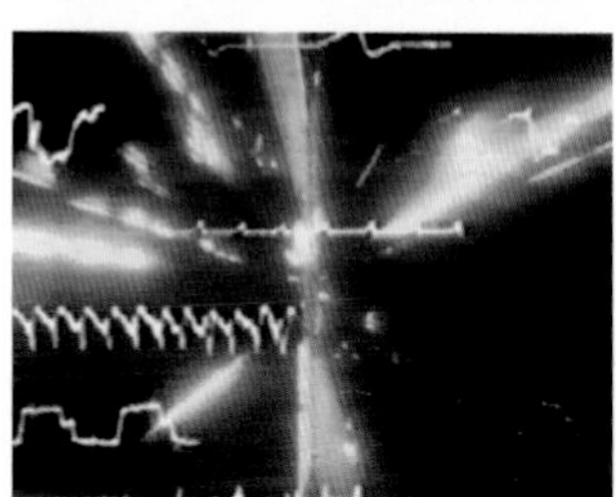

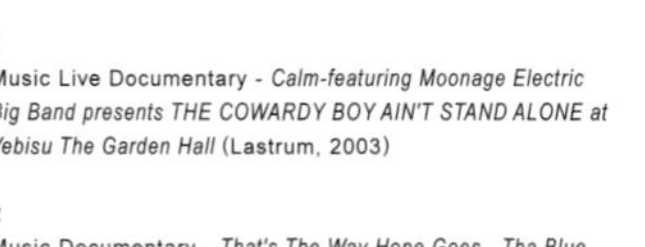

1
Music Live Documentary - *Calm-featuring Moonage Electric Big Band presents THE COWARDY BOY AIN'T STAND ALONE at Yebisu The Garden Hall* (Lastrum, 2003)

2
Music Documentary - *That's The Way Hope Goes - Tha Blue Herb* (THA BLUEHERB RECORDINGS, 2005)

3
Skateboard Video Documentary - *BHIND THE BROAD* (FESN, 2005)

4
Skateboard Video Documentary - *43-26* (FESN, 2000)

3

4

078 山口崇司 TAKASHI YAMAGUCHI

PROFILE
1976年京都生まれ。1998年ナムコ入社。ゲーム開発、CG映像制作に携わる。2001年、SIGGRAPH Electronic Theater入選。退社後、立花ハジメデザインを経て2002年独立。プログラミングを絡めた映像制作、グラフィックデザイン、インタラクションデザインなどと幅広く活動。2005年より活動体「donow」(http://www.do-now.jp)を始動する。

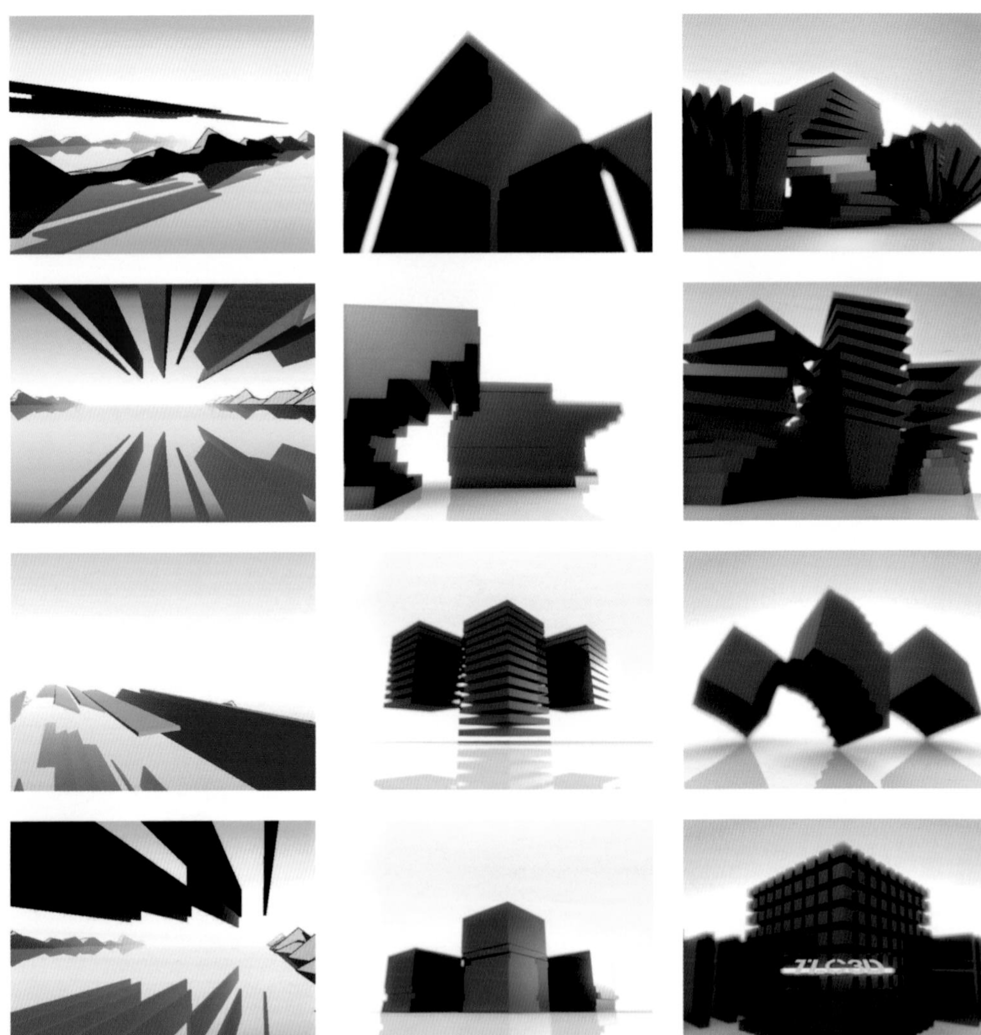

1

2

CATEGORY
PV, Graphic Design, Interaction Design, Interactive Installation

TEL / FAX
+81 (0) 3 3794 4297
+81 (0) 3 3794 4297

E-MAIL
yamag@za3.so-net.ne.jp

URL
http://www006.upp.so-net.ne.jp/ymg/

TOOLS
Maya,
Illustrator,
Photoshop,
Flash,
After Effects,
Director

Born in 1976 in Kyoto. In 1998, Yamaguchi entered Namco, and worked in game development and CG film production. He won an award at SIGGRAPH 2001 Electronic Theater. After leaving Namco in 2002, he participated in Tachibana Hajime Design, and later became independent. He takes on a wide range of activities including motion graphic production, graphic design, and interaction design, often utilizing programming. The activity unit "Donow" has become active in 2005.

3

4

5

1 Original Work - *3dEq* (2004)
Interactive Graphic Equalizer
2 CM - *TLC3D* (BMG JAPAN, 2002)
3 Aprication - *AmbientLED* (2004)
Camera Input Graphics Animation
4-5 Interactive Installation - *NFWR* (NEUT.006 Exhibition ASYL Design, 2005)

079 綿井健陽 TAKEHARU WATAI

PROFILE

1971年大阪府出身。1997年からジャーナリスト活動を始め、1998年から「アジアプレス・インターナショナル」に所属。これまでに、スリランカ民族紛争、スーダン飢饉、東ティモール・アチェ独立紛争、マルク諸島(インドネシア)宗教抗争、米国同時多発テロ事件後のアフガニスタンほかを取材。2003年空爆下のバグダッドから、テレビ朝日系列「ニュースステーション」、TBS系列「筑紫哲也ニュース23」などで映像報告・中継リポートを行う。2005年初監督作品「Little Birds(リトル バーズ) ～イラク 戦火の家族たち～」公開。

CONCEPT

ジャーナリストとして、事実を正確に、より速く、より多くの人に伝える。

To convey facts accurately to as many people as possible, as fast as possible, as a journalist.

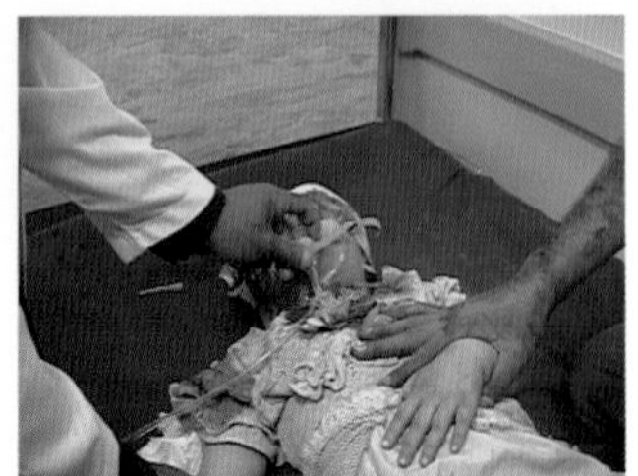

Documentary - *Little Birds,*
(©Projects Little Birds, 2005)
Director: Takeharu Watai
Director of Photography: Takeharu Watai
Producer + Editor: Takaharu Yasuoka
Assistant Editor: Kiyoshi Tsujii
Produced by Yasuoka Films

CATEGORY
Documentary, Journalism

TEL / FAX
—
—

E-MAIL
watai@asiapress.org

URL
http://www1.odn.ne.jp/watai
http://www.littlebirds.net

TOOLS
Sony DCR-VX2000

Takeharu Watai was born in Osaka, Japan, in 1971. He started working as a journalist in 1997, and, since 1998, has worked with Asia Press International, a news agency consisting of a group of independent video journalists. He has worked in many places and on many issues including Sri Lankan civil war, Sudanese famine, East Timor and the Aceh's struggle for independence, the religious strife in Indonesia's Maluku, and in Afghanistan, etc. after the simultaneous multiple terrorist attacks in the U.S.A. In 2003, he sent video reports and messages, and appeared in live broadcasts from air-raided Baghdad for various TV shows.

一切のリアリティを持たず、まるで虚構の出来事のように扱われる戦争。テレビなどを通して入ってくる情報は日々増える一方で、その精細な注釈のついた映像を知れば知るほど、それが個人の身に起こっているという実感は薄れていくばかりだ。平和な国に暮らす人々はマクロな問題に注意を奪われ、個人の悲しみや苦しみから目をそらしている。ジャーナリストとして一線で活躍し、イラク戦争を間近で体験した綿井健陽監督の初監督作品「リトルバード」は、戦争の只中に暮らす人々に焦点を当てた作品である。日常生活に突然割り込む戦闘機、対空砲火、空襲警報の轟音と、それと対照をなすかのような小鳥たちの鳴き声。彼らと同じ目線で、その一部始終を小型カメラが克明に捉える。爆撃で子供を三人なくした父親は残された娘に対して「あの子たちは鳥になって天国を飛んでいる」と語る。綿井監督がイラクで撮りためた123時間の映像を102分にまとめたこの作品は、いまだ続く戦争や現代社会に対して鋭いメッセージを突きつけ、また現存のジャーナリズムのあり方そのものを問い直すものとして、高い評価を得ている。

Before us is a war that is dealt with as if it were fiction, having no feel of reality. The information we receive from the television accumulates each day, and the more we learn about the footage and its detailed captions, the more we lose the sense that these things are happening to the lives of individuals. People living on the peaceful soil become caught up in the macro issues, and take their gazes off of the sadness and pain that individuals are suffering. "Little Bird" is a film that focuses on the people living in the midst of the war. It is the first film directed by Takeharu Watai, who has experienced the War in Iraq first-hand as a journalist. The sounds of fighter jets, ground-to-air firing, and air-raid sirens burst into everyday life, together with the contrasting sounds of the chirps of little birds. The compact camera captures the situation from the beginning to end, from the vantage point of these birds. A father who has lost three children in a bombing tells to his surving daughter, "those children are now birds flying in heaven." 123 hours of footage that Watai filmed in Iraq is organized into the 102 minutes of this film. It has been receiving high acclaim for presenting a strong message to contemporary society and to the war which still goes on, and also for reevaluating the current state of journalism.

080 タケイグッドマン / ウィズ エンターテインメント TAKEI GOODMAN / WIZ ENTERTAINMENT

PROFILE

1968年生まれ。富士山麓で成長。1989年DJスウィンギン シンコ（スチャダラパー）とユニティ「Little Bird」（通称LB Nation）結成。1991年ラップグループ「The Cartoons」結成。スペースシャワー TV（SSTV）参加。「New Wave 90's」（SSTV）でディレクターデビュー。同時に同番組内にてスチャダラパーのコントコーナー「ズームイン・バカ」及びスケートシングのコーナー「Rat Monkey」を開始。その後、スチャダラパーの「後者～The Latter」をはじめ、小沢健二、Tokyo No.1 Soul Set、郷ひろみ、Halcaliなど数多くのアーティストのPVを手掛ける。

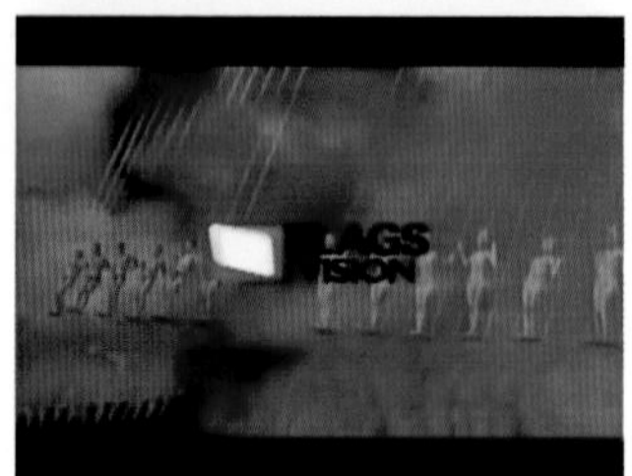

1

2

CONCEPT

新鮮。

Fresh.

CATEGORY
PV, CM, TV Program

TEL / FAX
—
—

E-MAIL
mail@wiz24h.com

URL
http://www.wiz24h.com

TOOLS
Sony HDR-HC1
Mac

Born in 1968, and raised at the foot of Mt. Fuji. In 1989, Takei Goodman formed Little Bird (LB Nation) with DJ Swingin' Shinco of Scha Dara Parr. He participates in the TV channel Space Shower TV (SSTV), and debuted as a director of the program New Wave 90's (SSTV). Within this program, he started Zoom-in Baka, a comic skit section done by Scha Dara Parr, and Rat Monkey, a section featuring Skatething. He has handled music videos for numerous musicians such as Scha Dara Parr, Kenji Ozawa, Tokyo No.1 Soul Set, Hiromi Go, and Halcali.

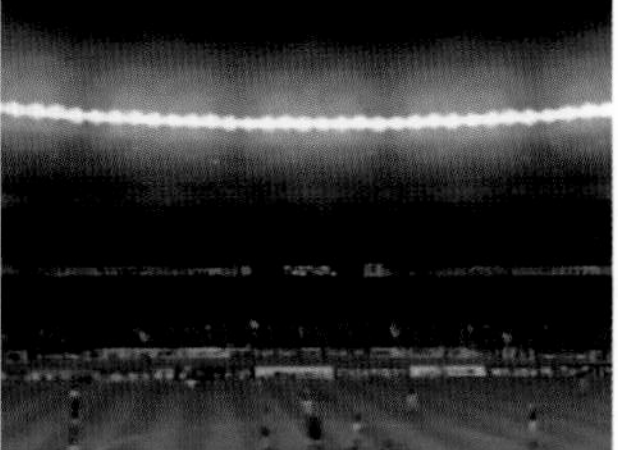

3

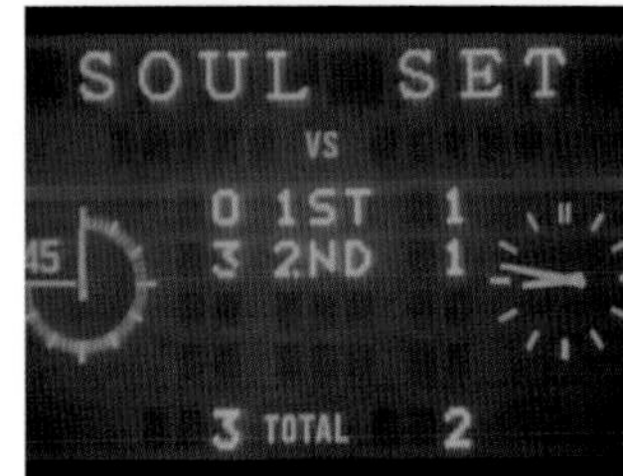

4

1
PV - スチャダラパー「大人になっても」SCHA DARA PARR, *Otona ni nattemo*
(TOSHIBA EMI LIMITED, 1997)

2
CI - *FLAGS VISION* (1998)

3
PV - ハルカリ 「音楽ノススメ」Halcali, *Ongaku no Susume*
(FOR LIFE MUSIC ENTERTEINMENT, 2004)

4
PV - TOKYO No.1 SOUL SET, *SUNDAY*
(VICTOR SPEEDSTAR, 1998)

081 井上 卓 TAKU INOUE

PROFILE

1975年生まれ。東京工芸大学芸術学部卒。1998年MTV Station IDコンテスト受賞をきっかけに、MTV JAPAN入社。現在はCM、PV、MTV On Air Promotion などのディレクターとして、クリエイティブプロダクションP.I.C.S.に所属。2003年 PROMAX&BDA USA プラチナ賞受賞をはじめ、2004年 エジンバラ国際映画祭や世界最大のデジタル映像フェスティバルonedotzeroによる作品招待、「SHOTS」掲載など、海外での作品上映や受賞多数。

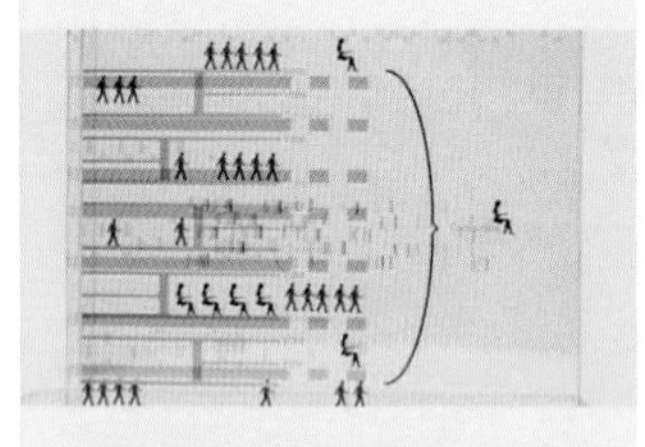

1 2

CATEGORY
Animation, Live action, Illustration

TEL / FAX
+81 (0) 3 5785 1780
+81 (0) 3 5785 1784

E-MAIL
post@picsco.net

URL
http://www.picsco.net

TOOLS
Power Mac G4,
Photoshop,
After Effects

Born in 1975. Graduated from Tokyo Polytechnic University Faculty of Arts. Inoue entered MTV Japan after winning an award for the 1998 MTV Station ID Contest. He is currently affiliated with P.I.C.S.. He was awarded the Platinum Award of Promax&BDA USA 2003, and his work has been invited for screening at many festivals, including the Edinburgh International Film Festival 2004, and Onedotzero, the most prominent digital film festival in the world. He has had many screenings and has won many awards around the globe, and his work has been featured in the magazine "Shots."

3

4

1
Visuarize Movie - RIZE, *SPIT&YELL* (U'S MUSIC・TENSAIBAKA RECORDS, 2005)
Total Direction + Caractor Design: 井上卓 Taku Inoue,
Director: 志賀匠 Takumi Shiga, 市村幸卯子 Yuko Ichimura,
Producer: 松居秀之 Hideyuki Matsui,
Production by P.I.C.S.

2
On Air Promotion - *MTV CONSENSUS* (2004)
Director: 井上卓 Taku Inoue
Producer: 下田伸貴 Nobutaka Shimoda
Camera: 吉田好伸 Yoshinobu Yoshida
Music: 久保田テツ Tetsu Kubota
Production by P.I.C.S.

写真提供: MTV JAPAN

3
NIKE PRESTO (NIKE, 2000)
Director + Animation: 井上卓 Taku Inoue
Producer: 寺井弘典 Hironori Terai
Production by P.I.C.S.

4
PV- Dragon Ash feat.SHUN, SHIGEO *Episode4* (Victor Entertainment, 2004)
Director: 井上卓 Taku Inoue
Producer: 小浜元 Hajime Kohama
CG: 松本空 Sora Matsumoto
Production by P.I.C.S.

082 森 達也
TATSUYA MORI

PROFILE

1956年生まれ。ディレクターとして、テレビ、ドキュメンタリー作品を数多く制作。1998年オウム真理教の荒木浩を主人公とするドキュメンタリー映画「A」を公開、ベルリン・プサン・香港・バンクーバーなど各国映画祭に出品し、海外でも高い評価を受ける。2001年「A2」を完成。最近は米国同時多発テロ問題について雑誌・新聞などでの発言が頻出しており、近著に「ベトナムから来たもう一人のラストエンペラー」(角川書店) がある。

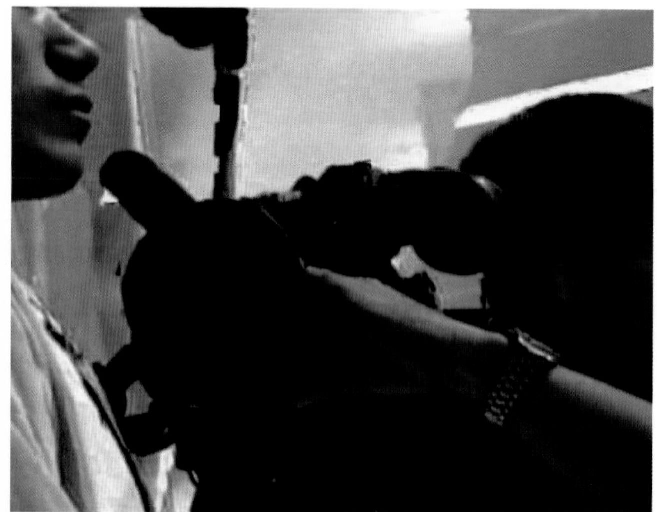

Documentary - 「A」

地下鉄サリン事件以降、加熱する報道合戦の渦中にあったオウム真理教(現アレフ)で、自身の信仰と社会との軋轢の間で苦悶する信者たちに、手持ちカメラひとつで光を当てたドキュメンタリー作品。当初、テレビ放映のドキュメンタリーとして撮影を開始したが、制作会社との見解の違いから会社に所属しての制作を断念。フリーランスの立場で撮影を続行した。その後も、放映先が見つからず、結局は自主制作の映画として上映された。揺れ動くカメラの視線は人間としての彼らと私たちの同質性、そして哀れなほど交差することのない矛盾した世界同士の対立を浮かび上がらせている。

Documentary - *A*

This is a documentary work that sheds light upon the members of Aum Shinrikyo, who, within the midst of a storm of news reportage after the Tokyo subway sarin gas attacks, were anguished by the conflict between their faith and their friction with society. Production began as a documentary to be aired on television, but as differences in opinion with the production company escalated, creating this work as a member of the company became impossible. It was ultimately presented as an independently produced movie. The shaky gaze of the camera exposes the similitude between us and them, and the discord between two contradicting worlds that never intersect.

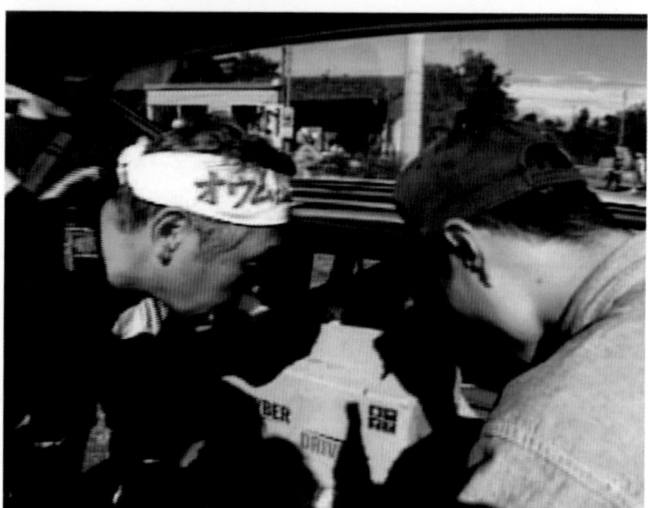

Documentary - 「A2」

オウム真理教の広報副部長、荒木浩を主人公に据えて展開された「A」に対し、その続編「A2」ではオウムの信者たちが暮らす日本各地の拠点を巡り、信者と地域住民たち、そしてそれをとりまく異なった立場にいる人々との関係が描かれる。事件によって生まれた憎悪は、いかなる場所に行こうとしているのか。住民、民族派右翼、メディア関係者など、さまざまな人々がその憎悪をそれぞれの人間模様の中で表現していく。その有り様は、悲しくも可笑しい悲喜劇である。オウム真理教を焦点にして、日本社会の心性を暴き出し、ひいては我々の赤裸々な現実面に至るまで臆することなく迫ったドキュメンタリー作品。

Documentary - *A2*

"A" revolved around Hiroshi Araki, the manager of public affairs of Aum Shinrikyo, but in the sequel "A2," the film crew visits locations all over Japan where Aum mebers reside, and depict the relationships between the locals, the cult members, and the various people between them. Much hostility was born from the tragic incident, but where is it heading? The people in this film manifest this hostility in their human interactions. By focusing on Aum Shinrikyo, this documentary film is able to barge into the bare reality of our own selves.

CATEGORY
Documentary

TEL / FAX
090 1105 4169
+81 (0) 471 49 0561

E-MAIL
tatsuyamo@jcom.home.ne.jp

URL
http://www.jdox.com/mori_t/index.html

TOOLS
—

Born in 1956. Mori has created many television programs and documentary works as a director. In 1998 he released "A," a documentary film centering on Hiroshi Araki, a former member of the Aum Shinrikyo cult, and the work received high international acclaim. In 2001, the sequel "A2" was completed. Recently, he has been frequently making comments about the 9.11 terrorist attacks, on magazines and newspapers. Some of Mori's recent books are "Vietnam kara Kita Last Emperor," "Documentary wa Uso wo Tsuku," and "Akuyaku Wrestler wa Warau" .

Documentary -「ミゼットプロレス伝説～小さな巨人たち～」(1992 年放送)

かつて日本のプロレス黎明期には、興業の花形として一世を風靡した存在でありながら、現在はメディアから黙殺され続けている小人プロレス。現役は2人しか残っていなかったが、かつて逃げ出した選手がまた復帰を願い出た。OB たちも続々集まってきて、実に30年ぶりにテレビマッチが実現する。森達也は実現不可能と言われていたこの企画を通した後にプロデューサーに回り、ディレクターには後に「こどもの時間」で映画デビューする野中真理子を起用した。

Documentary -*Midget Pro Wres Densetsu [The Legend of Midget Pro Wrestling]*

Chiisana Kyojintachi [The Small Giants] (Aired in 1992)
Midget pro wrestling was a star attraction of great popularity during the dawn of Japanese pro wrestling, but it is now given the silence treatment by the media. There were only two active wrestlers left at the time of the filming, but one who went AWOL in the past came back, and a TV match was realized for the first time in thirty years. Mariko Nonaka, who debuted with "The Children's Hour," was later appointed as director.

Documentary -「職業欄はエスパー」
(1998 年 2 月 24 日放送)

ドキュメンタリー映画「A」の編集作業と並行する形で、撮影・編集が進められた作品。秋山眞人、堤祐司、清田益章という、「エスパーであること」を職業に選定した3人の超能力者の日常を撮りながら、彼らを包みこむメンタリティが、「信じること」と「信じないこと」をキーワードに少しずつ露わにされてゆく。企画自体は、1993 年に一度正式に決まりかけたが、清田益章がカメラの前でスプーン曲げを披露することを拒絶してロケ途中で頓挫した作品。

Documentary -*Shokugyoran wa Esper [ESP is My Occupation]* (Aired on February 24, 1998)

This is a film that was produced and edited in parallel with "A." It is about the everyday life of three men who chose to become professional "psychics." Their mentality is gradually made visible, centering around the keywords "to believe" and "to not believe." This project came to a deadlock when Masuaki Kiyota, one of the psychics, refused to bend a spoon with his powers in front of the camera.

Documentary -「1999 年のよだかの星」
(1999 年 10 月 2 日放送)

宮沢賢治の童話「よだかの星」にインスパイアされた森達也が絵本と実写とのコラボレーションという手法で動物実験というジャンルに挑んだ作品。あらゆる化学物質の商品化の際に義務づけられる動物実験は、特に製薬や化粧品など、大手クライアントの公にされない業務に触れざるを得ないため、テレビ業界ではやはり「タブー」に近いジャンルとなっている。しかし動物実験の是非を正面から問うのではなく、愛護団体や実験研究者たちの内面の葛藤を描くことで、「生の営み」の絶対的な矛盾が呈示される。

Documentary -*1999nen no Yodaka no Hoshi [The Nighthawk Star of 1999]* (Aired on Oct. 2, 1999)

Inspired by Kenji Miyazawa's children's story "The Nighthawk Star," Mori attempted to take on the topic of animal experiments, combining actual footage with children's books. Law requires animal experiments to be performed when commoditizing any chemical substance, but it is a topic that is a near-taboo in the television industry. By depicting the conflicting feelings within the hearts of animal rights activists and the researchers conducting the experiments, the essential contradiction involved in "living our lives" is displayed.

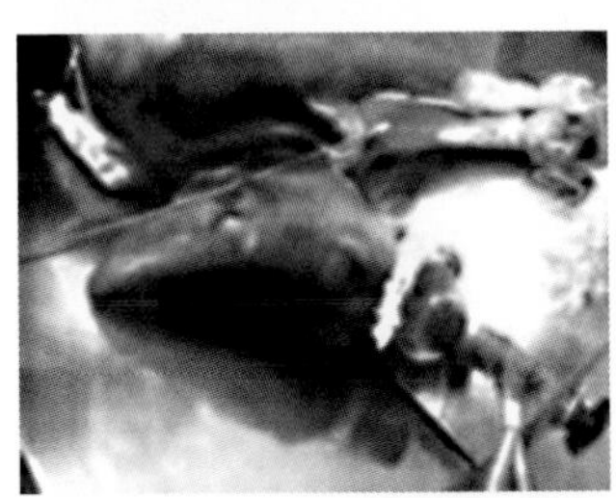

Documentary -「放送禁止歌～歌っているのは誰？規制しているのは誰？～」(1999 年 11 月 6 日放送)

歴代の放送禁止歌を番組内で紹介し、過去のタブーの変遷を検証する趣旨で始まったが、各局ドキュメンタリー番組担当からは「放送禁止歌を放送できるわけがない」と一蹴され続けた。フジテレビ NONFIX で放送が決まり、撮影が進むにつれて、放送禁止歌の実体が実はどこにもないことに気づき、企画の趣旨は「過去の規制の検証」ではなく「現在の規制の主体を炙りだす」ことに徐々に変質してゆく。

Documentary -*Housou Kinshika [Songs Prohibited from Being Aired] Who are Singing Them? Who is Prohibiting Them?* (Aired on Nov. 6, 1999)

It began as a project centering around the introduction of the prohibited songs and the inspection of the history of taboo, but the documentary departments of all the television stations kept rejecting it, saying that they couldn't possibly air the prohibited songs. However, as the filming progressed, it began to turn out that there was no actual substance in the prohibitions, and so the objective of the project gradually transformed from "the inspection of past prohibitions," to "smoking out today's entity behind the prohibitions."

083 ティ・ビィ・グラフィックス TEEVEE GRAPHICS

PROFILE
1995年3月設立。コマーシャル、ミュージックビデオ、映画、ファッション、VJなどの映像の企画演出、制作を行う。オリジナルショートフィルムの制作にも積極的に取り組み、その作品はRESFESTやonedotzeroなど海外の映画祭でも注目を集めている。Jam Films 2の1本として劇場公開された「机上の空論」は、RESFEST 2003にてオーディエンスチョイスアワードを受賞。作品集DVD「VIDEO VICTIM 1・2」が好評発売中。

1 2 3

CONCEPT
Cool & Strange.

CATEGORY
PV, CM, VP

TEL / FAX
+81 (0) 3 3400 6455
+81 (0) 3 5468 7048

E-MAIL
info@teeveeg.com

URL
http://www.teeveeg.com

TOOLS
Windows, Mac
LightWave, 3D Studio MAX,
Illustrator, Photoshop,
After Effects, Speed Razor,
Combustion,
Smoke, Flame, Inferno

Founded in March of 1995. teevee graphics handles the planning-direction and production of motion graphics in the fields of commercials, music videos, movies, fashion, and VJing. They actively produce original short films as well, and these works have attracted much attention at overseas film festivals such as RESFEST (USA) and onedotzero (UK). "Kijyou no Kuuron," screened at theatres as one of the films of Jam Films 2, received the "Audience Choice Award" at RESFEST 2003. The DVD "VIDEO VICTIM 1 & 2," a collection of their work, is currently available for sale.

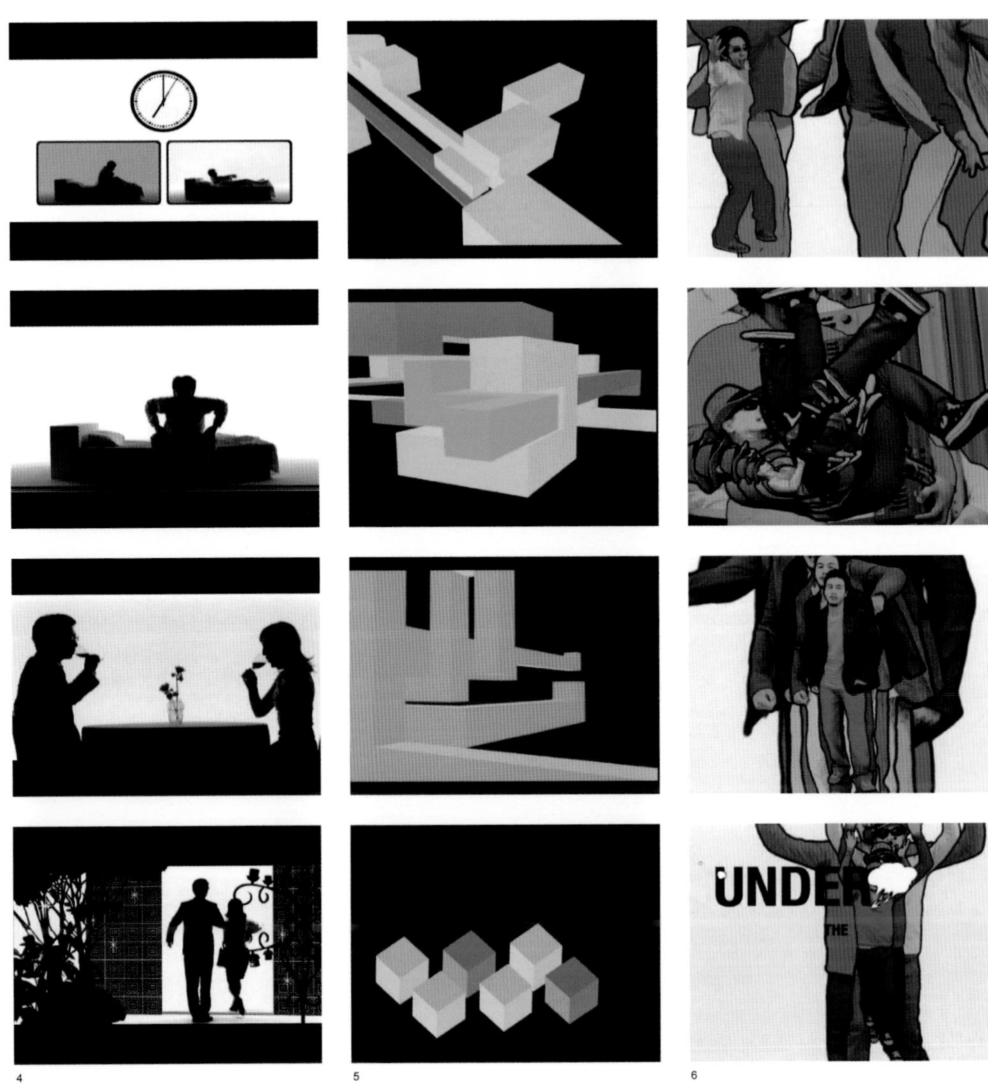

4

5

6

1 Opening Title - 日本テレビ放送網「NNN document」
NNN document (Nippon Television Network Corporation, 2002)
2 Opening Title - 日本テレビ放送網「ナイナイサイズ！」
nainai size (Nippon Television Network Corporation, 2005)
3 CM - au by KDDI INFOBAR「登場篇」
au by KDDI INFOBAR "toujou hen" (KDDI, 2003)

4 PV - Fantastic Plastic Machine, *Tell Me* (avex, 2005)
5 PV - KENISHII, *Strobe Enhanced* (2003)
6 PV - RIP SLYME, *UNDER THE SUN* (Warner Music Japan, 2005)

084 永戸鉄也
TETSUYA NAGATO

PROFILE
1970年東京都生まれ。高校卒業後渡米。帰国後、1996年より作家活動を開始。個展、グループ展などで作品を発表する。音楽、雑誌、書籍、広告などの分野ではアートディレクター・グラフィックデザイナーとして活動。最近ではサザンオールスターズやUAなどのCDジャケット、PVの制作など、映像の分野でも広く活躍をみせる。

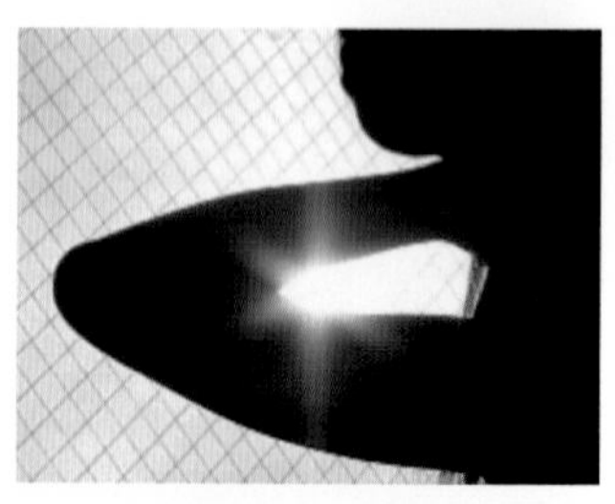

1

2

CONCEPT
ケースバイケース。状況に応じて、最良の方法で対応する。

Case by case. To use the best method according to the situation.

CATEGORY
CG, PV

TEL / FAX
+81 (0) 3 5346 3689
+81 (0) 3 5346 3689

E-MAIL
info@nagato.org

URL
http://www.nagato.org

TOOLS
Photoshop,
Illustrator,
Final Cut Pro

Born in Tokyo in 1970. Nagato went to the United States after graduating from high school. He began his creative activity in 1996, after returning from the United States. He has exhibited his work at a number of personal and group exhibitions. He works as an art director and graphic designer in the fields of music, magazines, book publication, and advertisements. Recently, he has been active in the field of motion graphics, as he has handled the CD covers and music videos of Southern All Stars and UA.

3

1
PV - UA, *BREATHE*
(©Victor Entertainment, Inc. + SPEEDSTAR RECORDS, 2005)
Director: Yasunori Kakegawa, Tetsuya Nagato

2
PV - HOTEI, *IDENTITY* (©TOSHIBA EMI LIMITED, 2005)
Director: Yasunori Kakegawa
AD:Tetsuya Nagato

3
PV - AIR, *ONE WAY* (©TOSHIBA EMI LIMITED, 2004)
Director: Tetsuya Nagato

085 村田朋泰
TOMOYASU MURATA

PROFILE

1974年東京生まれ。東京芸術大学大学院デザイン科専攻伝達造形修了。2002年TOMOYASU MURATA COMPANY.設立。東京芸術大学の卒業制作「睡蓮の人」でPFFアワード2002審査員特別賞、第5回文化庁メディア芸術祭アニメーション部門優秀賞ほか多数受賞。以後、生み出す作品が次々と各国映像フェスティバルで賞賛を浴びる。また、「Mr.Children」のPVを手掛けるなど、各方面で注目を集めている。2006年2月、目黒区美術館にて「俺の路／村田朋泰展」開催。

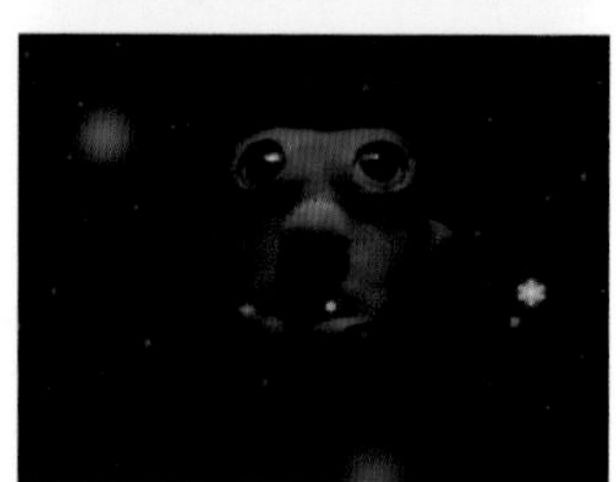

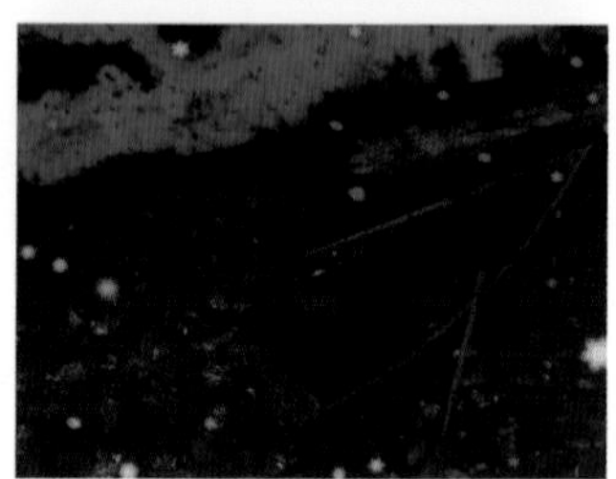

1

2

CONCEPT

自分の体験や記憶に基づいて物語をつくる。一つの技法に限定せず、多面的な表現に絶えず挑戦する。

To create stories based on his own experiences and memories. To constantly pursue a multi-aspectual form of expression, and not limit himself to one particular methodology.

CATEGORY
Animation, PV, CM, Installation

TEL / FAX
+81 (0) 3 3809 3480
+81 (0) 3 3809 3480

E-MAIL
tomoyasu.m@sweet.ocn.ne.jp

URL
http://www.tomoyasu.net/

TOOLS
After Effects,
Final Cut,
Oil Painting,
Hand Painting,
3D

Born in Tokyo in 1974. After graduating from the Graduate School of the Tokyo National University of Fine Arts and Music, Murata founded Tomoyasu Murata Company Corp. in 2002. His graduate project “Suiren no Hito” won many awards including “the 2002 PFF Award's Special Juries” Award, and the 5th Media Arts Festival Agency for Cultural Affairs Excellence Prize. His works thereafter have received much acclaim in film festivals all over the world. He has handled music videos for the band Mr. Children, and is attracting attention from many fields.

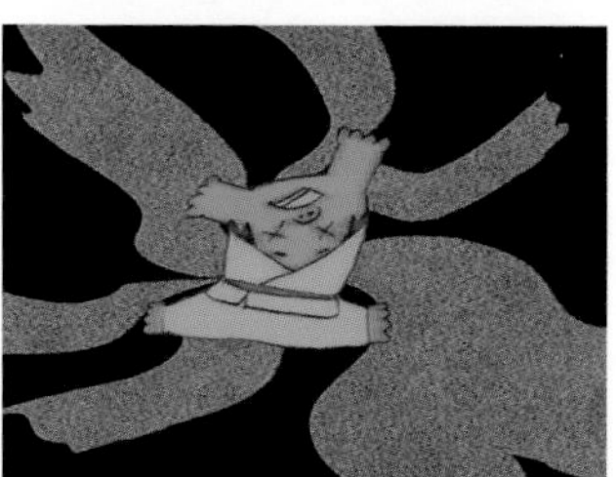

3

4

1
Short Movie - 「睡蓮の人」 *Suiren no Hito,*
(©Tomoyasu Murata Company., 2000)

2
PV - Mr.Children, *HERO*
(©2002 Oorong-Sha Co.,Ltd., 2002)

3
Short Movie - 「さかだちくん、ひたすら走る！」
Sakadachi-*kun Hitasura Hashiru!*
(©Tomoyasu Murata Company., 2005)

4
Short Movie - 「冬の虹」 *Fuyu no Niji*
(©Tomoyasu Murata Company., 2005)

086 長谷川踏太
TOTA HASEGAWA / TOMATO

PROFILE

1972年東京生まれ。英ロイヤル・カレッジ・オブ・アート（RCA）インタラクションデザイン科卒。ソニーデザイナーを経て、2001年よりロンドンを拠点に世界中で活躍するクリエイター集団TOMATOに参加。以降TOMATOとして活動し現在に至る。インターネット広告やCIなどの分野でインタラクティブな作品を多く発表している。

1

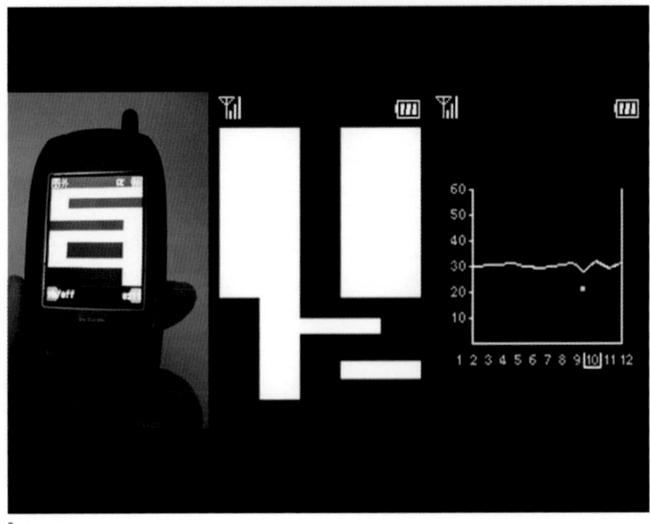

2

1
Products - *Seiko Spectrum SVRD001*
セイコーとのコラボレーションによって製作された、腕時計。電子インク技術を応用した大型曲面ディスプレイにより、斬新な機能とデザインを実現。液晶部分のグラフィックデザインを担当。

2
Application - *wobble clock & water clock For The END* (2002)
PR: 立花ハジメ
D + CO: TOMATO, 立花ハジメ
携帯サイト theEND 用に製作したJAVAアプリ 2点

（中）wobble clock：上下の数字が時間を表しており、5秒置きに上の数字の縦幅が増え、下の数字がつぶされていく。上下の数字の縦幅の比率が分を表らわしている。

（右）water clock：5秒置きに、画面上部から水の粒が落ちてきて、水面を揺らす。水面の高さが分を表している。

3
Workshop - *ICC NEWSCHOOL 9 Reactive / Creative* (NTT ICC, 2004)
PR: NTT ICC
Workshop講師: TOMATO+クワクボリョウタ
デバイスアーティストのクワクボリョウタ氏と共にNTTICCにて行った、ワークショップでの製作物。参加者は、毛糸を立体的な空間につないでいくことによって、コンピューター上でどのように立体が計算されているかを体感する。

4
Tool - *STIJL IDENTITY* (DMOVE Co., Ltd. / XING INC., 2005)
D + AD + CO: TOMATO
音に反応するタイポグラフィーを元に作られた、ロゴとそれを生成するためのツール。流す音やパラメーターの設定によって、ロゴの形、動きが変わってくる。

CATEGORY
—

TEL / FAX
—
—

E-MAIL
tota@tomato.co.uk

URL
http://www.tomato.co.uk

TOOLS
—

Born in 1972 in Tokyo. Graduated from Royal College of Art Department of Interaction Design, in Great Britain. After working as a designer for Sony, Hasegawa began participating in Tomato, a group of creators based in London and active worldwide. He is a still active as a member to this day. He has released numerous interactive works in the fields of internet advertisement and corporate identity.

3

4

1
Products - *Seiko Spectrum SVRD001*
A watch that was produced in collaboration with Seiko Corp.. Innovative functions and design have been realized through the use of a large curved display applying electronic ink technology.

2
Application - *wobble clock & water clock For The END* (2002)
PR: Hajime Tachibana
D + CO:TOMATO, Hajime Tachibana
Two Java applications made for The END, a website for mobile phones.

(middle) Wobble Clock: The numbers on the top and bottom represent the time. Every five seconds, the top number expands vertically, and proportionately crushes the number on the bottom. The vertical ratio of the two numbers represent the minutes.

(right) Water Clock: A drop of water falls from the top of the screen every five seconds, shaking the surface of the water.

3
Workshop - *ICC NEWSCHOOL 9 Reactive / Creative* (NTT ICC, 2004)
PR: NTT ICC
Workshop instructors: Tomato+Ryota Kuwakubo
A work created at a workshop with device artist Ryota Kuwakubo, held at NTT ICC. By connecting wool string in a three dimensional space, the participant experiences how space is calculated within a computer.

4
Tool - *STIJL IDENTITY* (DMOVE Co., Ltd. / XING INC., 2005)
D + AD + CO: TOMATO
A logo constructed from sound-reactive-typography, and the tool that creates these logos. By altering the generated sound and various parameters, the shape and movements of the logo change.

087 塚越有人
TSUKAGOSHI ARIHITO

PROFILE
1974生まれ、横浜出身。音楽を介したコミュニティにて映像、グラフィックを展開する中、精神のあり方を服を通して提案する「イズネス」の設立に参加。現在、「イズネス」のアートディレクターとしての活動を中心に、自分や友人のため、団体や企業のための映像研究、発表を続けている。

1　2

CATEGORY
PV, CM, Documentary

TEL / FAX
+81 (0) 3 3487 9421
+81 (0) 3 3487 9421

E-MAIL
arihito@is-ness.com

URL
http://www.is-ness.com

TOOLS
Photoshop,
Illustrator,
After Effects,
Final Cut Pro,
Flash

Born in 1974, in Yokohama. While Tsukagoshi develops his graphic and motion graphic designs within a music-related community, he has also participated in the founding of "Is-ness," which proposes through clothing how the human spirit should be. While his central activity is working as art director for "Is-ness," he has also been researching and presenting motion graphic works for himself, friends, organizations, and companies.

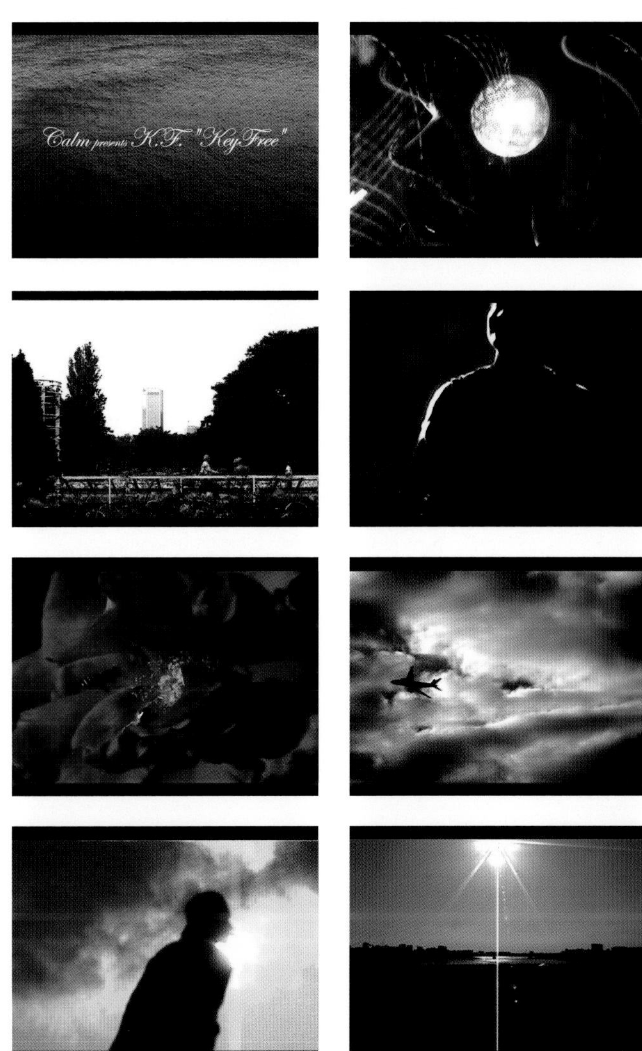

3

1
Private Work - is-ness, *Neu! Type* (2003)
Camera: Nakazawa Koutor

2
Promotion - *Intentionallies & Amadana* (2005)
Director: Kimura Kazufumi
Producer: Takano Yoshikazu

3
PV - *Calm presents K.F. KeyFree* (2004)
Director+Editor+Camera: Tsukagoshi Arihito

088 広岡 毅 TSUYOSHI HIROOKA

PROFILE
1973年東京生まれ。グラフィックデザイナー。1997年よりフリーデザイナーとして活動。2000年5月よりLEVEL1として活動開始。2003年より個人名義で活動開始。2Dグラフィックデザインを中心に、ロゴマーク、Tシャツ、エディトリアル、映像制作、VJなどを手掛ける。

1 2 3

CATEGORY
PV, Promotion

TEL / FAX
+81 (0) 3 3419 3637
+81 (0) 3 3419 3637

E-MAIL
hirooka_tsuyoshi@ybb.ne.jp

URL
http://hiro-ka.jpn.org

TOOLS
Illustrator,
Photoshop,
After Effects

Born in 1973. A graphic designer. Hirooka has been active as a freelance designer since 1997. He began working as "LEVEL1" in May of 2005, and began working with his actual name in 2003. His core activity is 2D graphic design, but also does a variety of activities such as logo design, T shirt design, editorial design, motion graphic design, and VJing.

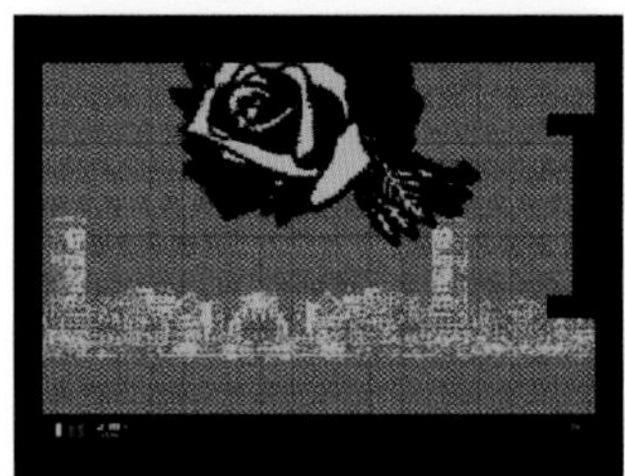

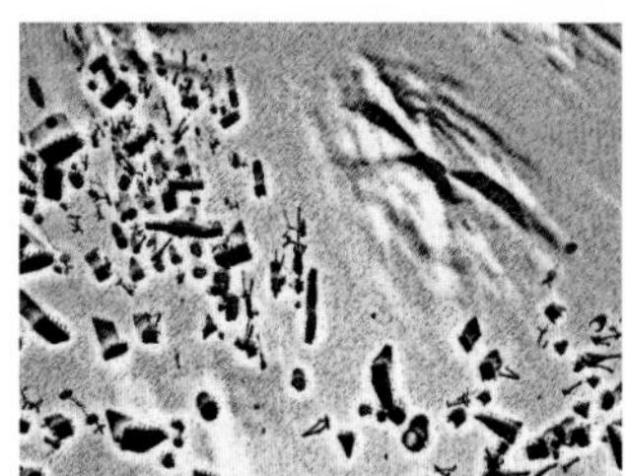

4

5

1
Station ID - MTV JAPAN, *Filler*
(©MTV Japan Inc., 2003)

2
CM - MTV JAPAN, *M size* (©MTV Japan Inc., 2005)
AD: Tsuyoshi Hirooka
CG: Yoshiyuki Komatsu

3
PV - HONDALADY, *ADAD*
(©WARNER ARTISTS INC., 2003)

4
Private Work - Tsuyoshi HIrooka, *His Livolbing Lantern*
(©CLUBKING CO., LTD., 2002)

5
CM - MTV JAPAN, *SUMMER SONIC '05 LIVE Digests Special*
(©MTV Japan Inc., 2005)
AD: Tsuyoshi Hirooka
CG: Yoshiyuki Komatsu
MO: Yuji Kizu

089 宇川直宏 UKAWA NAOHIRO

PROFILE
ヒグマのような雑食性!!
なので、極めて多岐に渡りすぎて書ききれません!!!!!!!!!!!!!!!

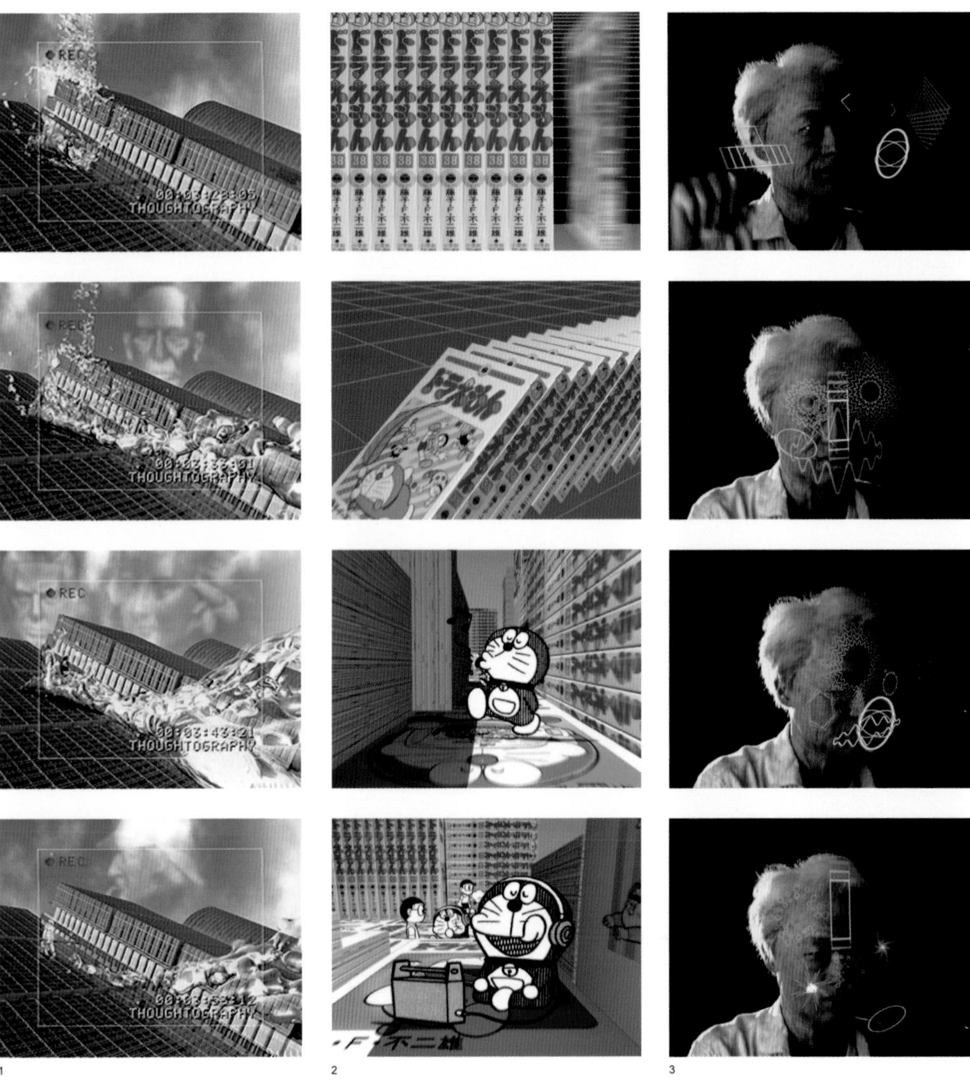

1 2 3

CATEGORY
PV, VJ, Art

TEL / FAX
—
—

E-MAIL
info@momndadproductions.com

URL
http://www.momndadproductions.com/

TOOLS
鍬から斧まで
From a hoe to an axe

I'm omnivorous like a brown bear!! Thus my activity takes up extremely so various that it's not possible to list everything!!!!!! !!!!!!!!

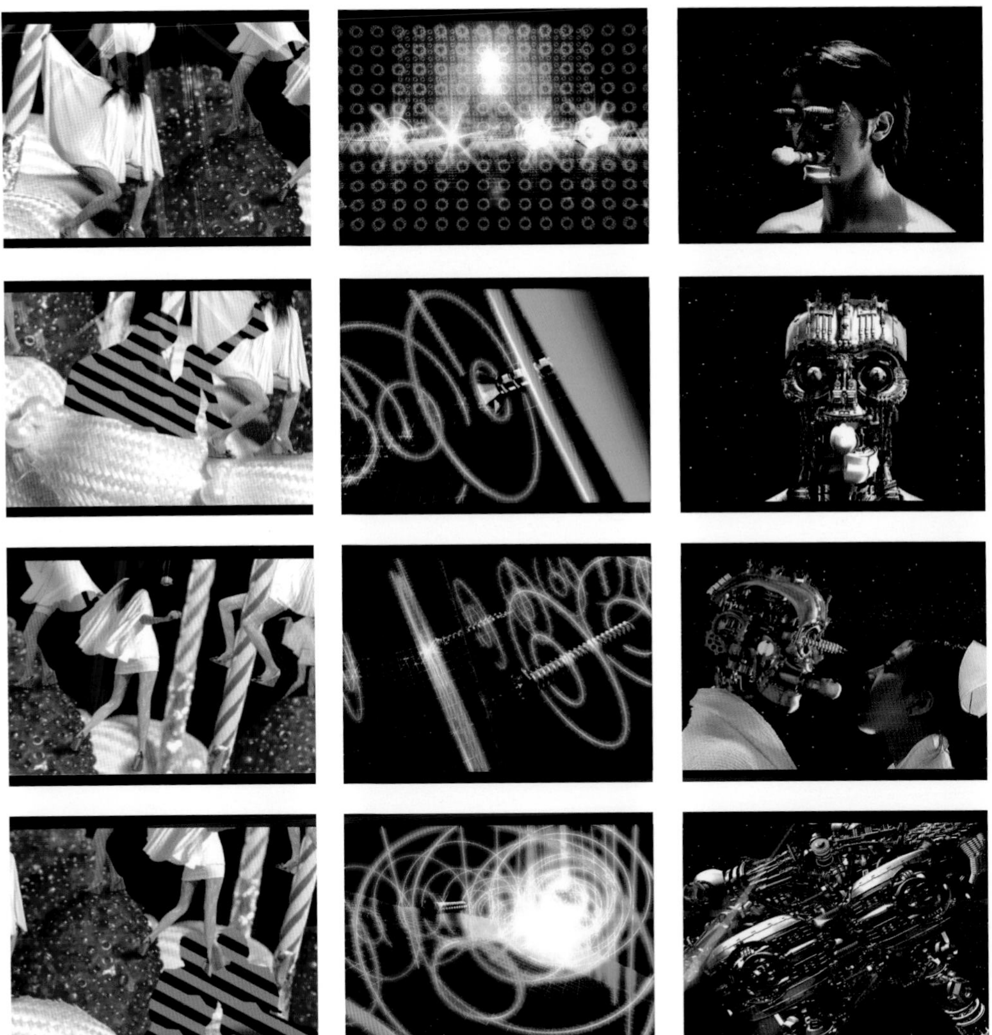

4

5

6

1 PV - SUPERCAR, *BGM* (©Ki/oon Records Inc. / Sony Music Entertainment Inc., 2004)
Director: Ukawa Naohiro
2 PV - THE ORB, *FROM A DISTANCE* (©Fujiko-Pro, Shogakukan, LAD MUSICIAN, V2 Records Japan Inc., 2003)
Director: Ukawa Naohiro
3 PV - CICADA, *KUSSA* (©P-VINE RECORDS, blues interactions, inc., 2005)
Director: Ukawa Naohiro
4 PV - MAKI NOMIYA ♥ m-flo, *BIG BANG ROMANCE* (©avex entertainment inc, 2005)
Director: Ukawa Naohiro
5 PV - Denki Groove × Scha Dara Parr, 「TWILIGHT#1 アブストラクトな林檎たち」 *TWILIGHT#1 Abstruct Na Ringo Tachi* (©Ki/oon Records Inc. / Sony Music Entertainment Inc., 2005) Director: Ukawa Naohiro
6 PV - Denki Groove × Scha Dara Parr, 「TWILIGHT#2 ふぞろいのネジ屋敷」 *TWILIGHT#2 Fuzoroi No Neji Yashiki* (©Ki/oon Records Inc. / Sony Music Entertainment Inc., 2005) Director: Ukawa Naohiro

<u>090</u>

梅川良満
UMEKAWA YOSHIMITSU

PROFILE
1976年生まれ。ハイエンドな表現の中に、イルでドープかつフレッシュな霊界メッセージを込めたマッシヴな作風をドロップする写真家。日本国内外の雑誌、CD、広告等を中心に幅広く活動。アートプロジェクト「IN RAM」を2003年より始動、その第1弾としてホームページ「UMEKAWAYOSHIMITSU.COM」をドロップ。またアートディレクターとしてPVのディレクションも行う。

1

2

CONCEPT
O.M.A.

CATEGORY
Steel, PV, Documentary

TEL / FAX
—
—

E-MAIL
x@umekawayoshimitsu.com

URL
http://www.umekawayoshimitsu.com/

TOOLS
Sony DCR-VX2100,
After Effects,
Final Cut Pro,
Illustrator

The most wanted R.I.P. photographer known for his "massive style" made out of very sophisticated technique and ill'n'dope'n'fresh "MESS:AGE" that he receives from spiritual zone. His works can be seen in various media, from Japanese and foreign magazines, advertising campaigns to CD jackets. In 2003, Mr. Umekawa droped a highly conceptual art project "IN RAM." The first work of the project is the website called "DANCE HOLE," in which visitors can experience the sort of psychic browser crashing while appreciating his conceptual works. HTTP://WWW.UMEKAWAYOSHIMITSU.COM. He has also worked as Art Director, Film Director and has shot

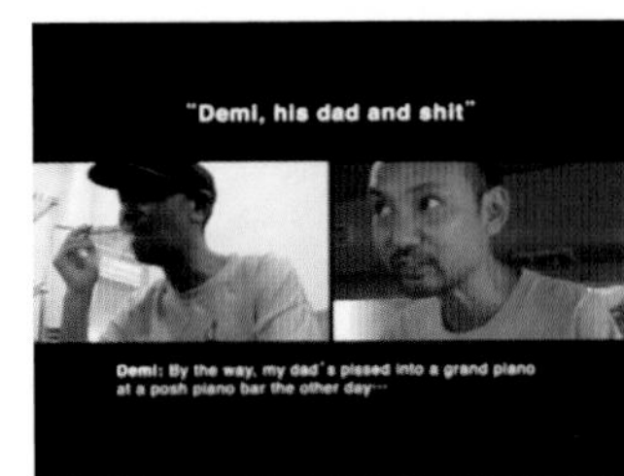

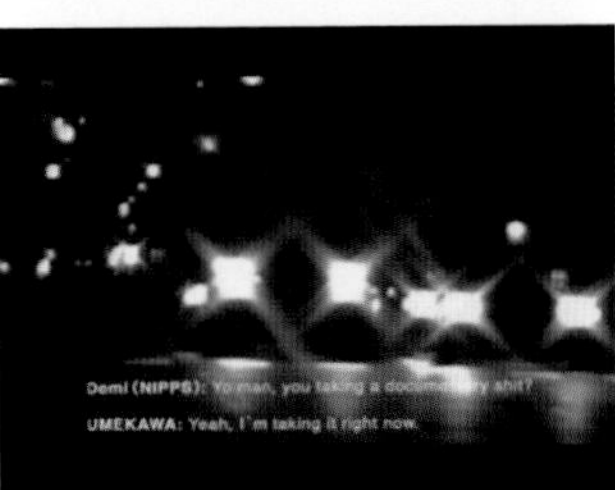

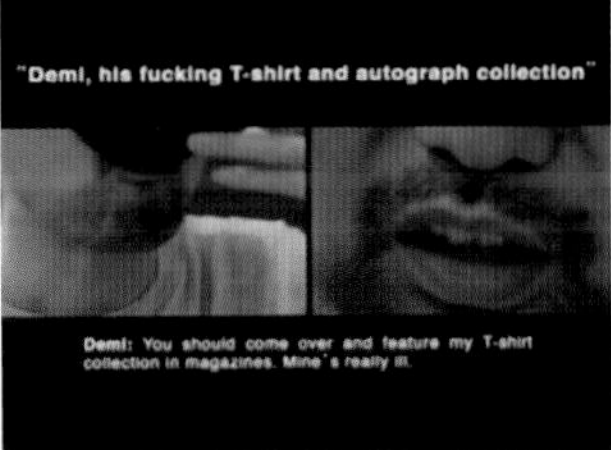

3

1
PV - METALCHICKS, *10000 db* (Musicmine, Inc., 2005)
Director: Kou Chihara & Yoshimitsu Umekawa
AD: Kou Chihara
Camera: Yoshimitsu Umekawa
CG: Muneyoshi Sasao (Hikaru J)
Editor: Yuki Hasegawa (Hikaru J)
Assistant: Jun Kawaguchi
Music: METALCHICKS
Plan: Musicmine
Plastic Model: TAMIYA

2
PV - *BIJIN SUSHI* (HOU CO., LTD, 2005)
Staring: Reko Yuyama a.k.a.Bijin Sushi, Ko San (BAR TERA)
Director + Camera: Umekawa Yoshimitsu
Editor: Hikaru J
Title Design: Hikaru J
Transrator: Kei Sato

3
Documentary - *DEMISAN* (2004)
Staring: Demisan a.k.a. NIPPS (Buddah Brand), 963, KZA (Force of Nature), Keita Ishiguro (JAY PEG)
Director + Camera: Umekawa Yoshimitsu
Camera: Umekawa Yoshimitsu & Hikaru J
Video Scratch: Hikaru J
Transrator: Kei Sato

091 ウオヌマ UONUMA

PROFILE

WOW所属の新潟出身デザイナー阿部伸吾、丸山紗綾香によるユニット。メンバーがそれぞれ個性的な作品を手掛けながら培った技術、アイデアをひとつに落とし込む手法で映像を中心に活動。そのほかにも、グラフィックなど多岐に渡った活動を展開し、濃厚な世界観を表現している。2005年制作のオリジナル作品「4F」でDigi-Con入賞。その他クラブイベントのイメージ映像を制作するなど、ジャンル、場面を問わず見る者に刺激を与える作品を作り続けている。

1 5 2 6 3 7 4 8

CONCEPT

身の回りにある多くの事象・事物のパーツをミックスし、組み合わせ重ねていく。なおかつ要素は整理され、理屈抜きで共感できる、見る者の感覚に直接訴える作品を常に意識しながら表現すること。

CATEGORY
Motion Graphic, Graphic

TEL / FAX
+81 (0) 3 5775 0055
+81 (0) 3 5775 0056

E-MAIL
uonuma@w0w.co.jp

URL
http://www.w0w.co.jp

TOOLS
Photoshop,
Illustrator,
After Effects,
CINEMA 4D,
Quartz Composer

A unit formed by Shingo Abe, a designer from Niigata Prefecture who is a member of WOW, and Sayaka Maruyama. Uonuma takes on a wide menu of activities to express their dense worldview, centering around motion graphics production, but also including things such as graphic design. Their original work from 2005, "4F," was awarded at Digi-Con. They also handle activities such as producing motion graphics for club events, and generally create works that stimulate the audience, no matter the genre or situation.

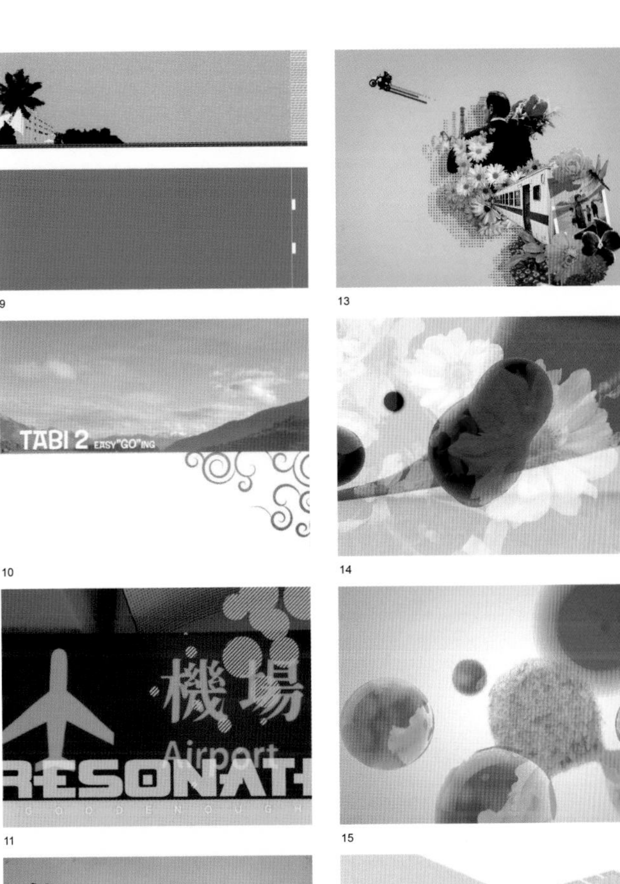

9 13 10 14 11 15 12 16

1-4
Original Work - *4F* (2005)
By Shingo Abe, Sayaka Maruyama

5-6
PV - *asagi* (smt, 2004)
By Shingo Abe

7
Original Work - *box* (2005)
By Sayaka Maruyama

8
Original Work - *M* (2005)
By Sayaka Maruyama

9
Original Work - *moment* (2005)
By Sayaka Maruyama

10-11
Imagefilm - *TABI 2* (BURTON, 2005)
By Shingo Abe, Sayaka Maruyama

12
PV - *TDB* (TDB, 2004)
By Shingo Abe

13
Original Work - *travel* (2005)
By Sayaka Maruyama

14-15
Original Work - *vermilion* (2004)
By Shingo Abe

16
Original Work - *work* (2005)
By Sayaka Maruyama

Mixing, combining, and layering the parts of various objects and phenomena in our everyday lives. Producing works through the concept of creating things that have organized elements, appeal to the viewer's senses, and attract sympathy without the necessity of logic.

092 生西康典
YASUNORI IKUNISHI

PROFILE
掛川康典と共に映像作品、映像を使用したライブパフォーマンスの演出を手掛け、田名網敬一、大竹伸朗、山口小夜子、大友良英、山本精一など、さまざまな領域の作家たちと独自の世界観を展開した作品を生み出している。2004年、2005年には美術館でインスタレーション作品を発表。またライブイベント「映像作家徹底研究」を企画。これまでに松本俊夫、かわなかのぶひろなどが出演した。

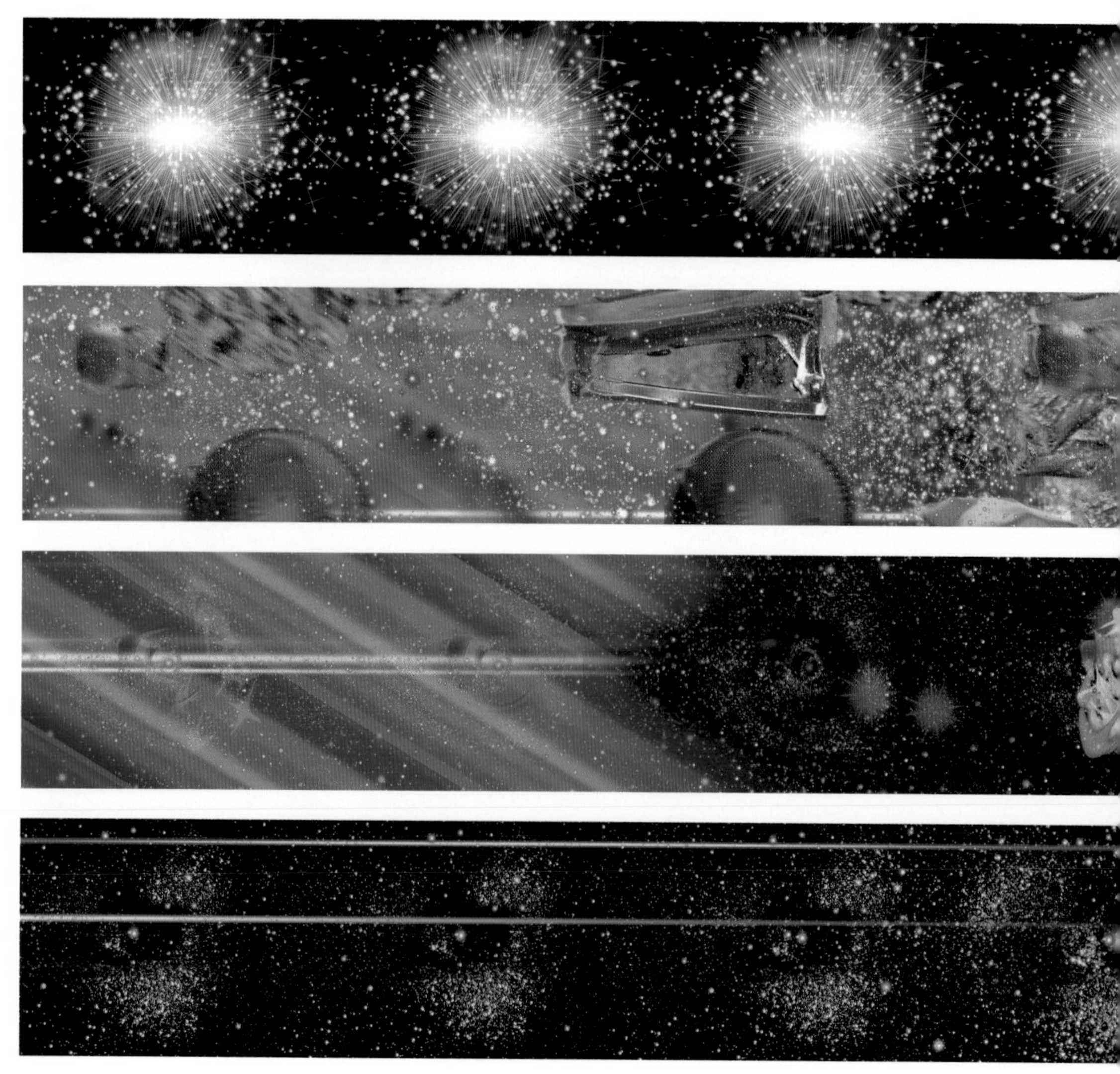

CONCEPT
自分の興味に忠実につくる。

Staying true to his interests.

CATEGORY
Art, VJ, PV

TEL / FAX
—
—

E-MAIL
ikunishi@nyc.odn.ne.jp

URL
—

TOOLS
—

An art director. Together with Yasunori Kakegawa, Ikunishi has handled stage direction for many live performances utilizing motion graphics. He creates works that express an inovvative worldview, collaborating with artists from diverse realms including the likes of Keiichi Tanaami, Shinro Ohtake, Sayoko Yamaguchi, Yoshihide Ohtomo, and Seiichi Yamamoto. He has exhibited installations at art museums in '04 and '05. He also organizes the live event "Eizo Sakka Tettei Kenkyu [Exhaustive Investigations of Motion Graphic Artists]," in which Toshio Matsumoto and Nobuhiro Kawanaka have been featured so far.

Art - GUNDAM GENERATION FUTURES, *Breath upon the Universe* (©SOTSU AGENCY SUNRISE CO., LTD. / SUNRIZE + Ikunishi Yasunori × Kakegawa Yasunori × kuknacke × shu × m.magic Kobayashi × Tetsuya Nagato, 2005)
Artists: Ikunishi Yasunori, Kakegawa Yasunori, Kuknacke, shu, M.Magic Kobayashi, Nagato Tetsuya

093 掛川康典
YASUNORI KAKEGAWA

PROFILE

1972年群馬県生まれ。1996年日本大学芸術学部美術学科絵画コース卒業。同年よりteevee graphicsに参加。TVCM、MUSIC VIDEO、ドキュメンタリー、ファッションショーなどの映像演出からビデオ&サウンドパフォーマンス、さらにVJとしての顔も持つ。ROBERT ASHLEYのオペラ「DUST」、UA全国ツアー「UA SUN 2004」の映像制作などを手掛け、また森美術館で行われた「六本木クロッシング」への出展やデレクジャーマン、田名網敬一のDVDへのオリジナル作品の提供など幅広く活動中。

1

2

1
PV - ASA-CHANG & 巡礼 feat. ハナレグミ「カな」
Asa-chang & Junrei feat. Hnaregumi, *Kana* (ki/oon Records, 2004)
Director: Yasunari Kakegawa

2
PV - HOTEI「弾丸ロック」*Dangan Rock* (TOSHIBA EMI LIMITED, 2004)
Director: Yasunari Kakegawa

3
Documentary - 「デヴィッド・リンチの Hollywood Drive」
David Lynch's Holly Wood Drive (WOWOW, 2004)
Director: Yasunari Kakegawa

4
PV - UA「泥棒」Dorobou
Director: Yasunari Kakegawa, Ysunari Ikunishi
(Victor Entertainment, 2004)

5
PV - キリンジ Kirinji, YOU AND ME
Director: Yasunari Kakegawa (TOSHIBA EMI LIMITED, 2004)

CATEGORY
PV, VJ, Documentary,
Opening Title, TV Program

TEL / FAX
+81 (0) 3 3400 6455 (teevee graphics, inc)
+81 (0) 3 5468 7048

E-MAIL
kake@teeveeg.com

URL
http://www.teeveeg.com

TOOLS
—

Born in 1972, in Gunma Prefecture. Graduated from Nihon University College of Art, Department of Fine Art in 1996, majoring in painting. In the same year, He joined Teevee Graphics. He works in diverse fields including TV commercials, music videos, documentaries, motion graphics for fashion shows, video and sound performances, and VJing. He has produced works for Robert Ashley's opera "Dust," and singer UA's Japan tour "UA Sun 2004." He has also had works exhibited at Mori Art Museum's "Roppongi Crossing," and has provided original works for the DVDs of Derek Jarman and Keiichi Tanaami.

3

4

5

094 栗田やすお
YASUO KURITA

PROFILE
1975年大阪府生まれ。京都精華大学ビジュアルデザイン科に在学中、カットアウトアニメーションを経験し、興味を覚える。卒業制作で同技法を用いた「ロボロボ」(1997)を制作し、国内外の映画祭から高い評価を受ける。スポンジと針金を使い、パペットアニメーションを制作するカリキュラムを京都造形大学で受講。以降独学と自主制作で「緑玉紳士」のパイロット版というべき「RED SLOT MACHINE」(1999)を制作。2005年「緑玉紳士」が完成。

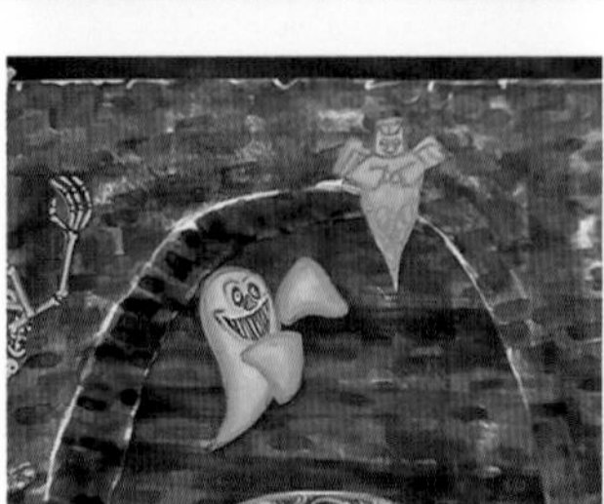

1

2

CONCEPT
見たことのない世界観やデザインであるにもかかわらず、懐かしさが感じられたり、子供のころに絵本を読んでワクワクした気持ちを呼び起こすようなもの。クライアントが求め想像したものよりも、素晴らしいものを作ることを心掛けている。

To create works that induce a feeling of nostalgia even though they depict worldviews and designs that are fresh, and also that feeling of excitement that we had as kids when we read illustrated children's books. To create works that surpass the client's expectations.

1
Pupet Animation - *Robo Robo* (1997)
Director + Written + Editor + Charactor Design: Yasuo Kurita

2
Pupet Animation - *RED SLOT MACHINE* (1999)
Director + Written + Editor + Charactor Design: Yasuo Kurita

3
Pupet Animation - 「緑玉紳士」 *Monsieur Greenpeas* (©Yasuo Kurita + Monsieur Greenpeas Production Committee, 2004)
Director + Written + Editor + Charactor Design: Yasuo Kurita
Production: Grasshoppa!
Produce: Monsieur Greenpeas Production Committee, RENTRAK JAPAN & KLOCK WORX

CATEGORY
Puppet Animation Film, Character Design, Puppet Miniature, Set Making

TEL / FAX
+81 (0) 726 84 1383
+81 (0) 726 84 1383

E-MAIL
ryokutamashinshi@hotmail.com

URL
—

TOOLS
LunchBox Sync,
Premiere

Born in Osaka in 1975. Kurita studied general visual design at Kyoto Seika University. His graduation project "Robo Robo (1997)" received much acclaim both domestically and internationally. On the same year, he was heavily inspired by "Wallace and Grommet / Beware of the Penguins! (1993)" and took a curriculum for producing puppet animation using sponges and wire. Through self-education and independent production, he produced RED SLOT MACHINE (1999) and later MONSIER GREENPEAS (2005).

3

095 児玉裕一 / クイックポップ
YUICHI KODAMA / QUICKPOP

PROFILE
1975年生まれ。映像ディレクション・モーショングラフィックアーティスト。大学在学中より仙台にて映像制作の活動を開始。広告代理店勤務を経てミュージックビデオ、番組、CMなどを手掛けるフリーのディレクターになる。

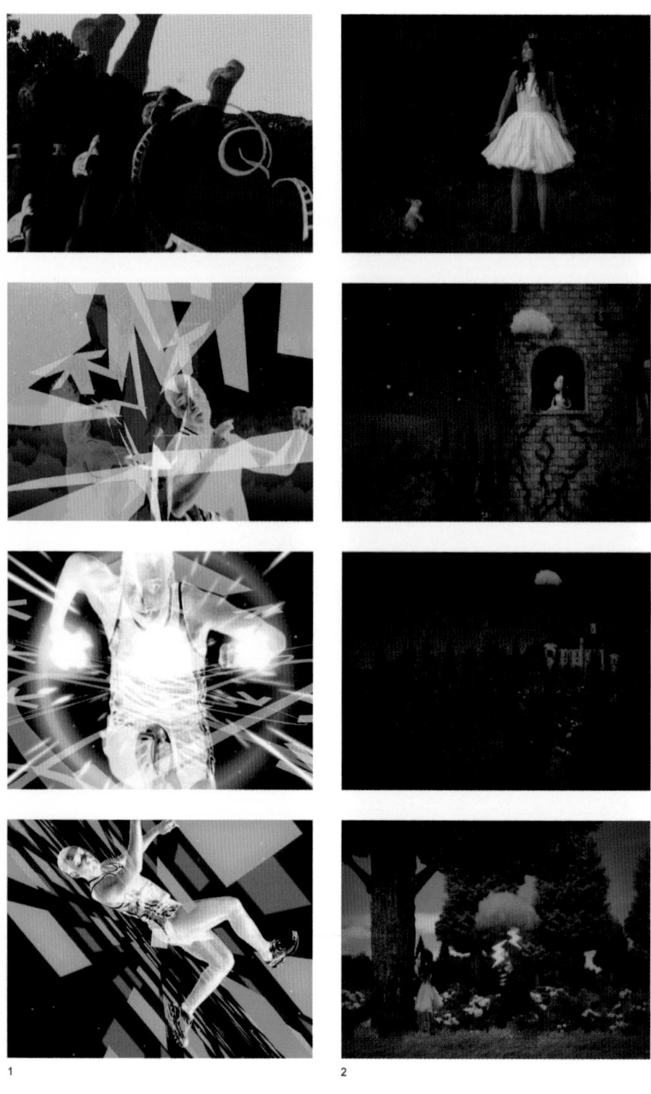

1　2

CONCEPT
何度でも繰り返し見たくなるような映像。

Motion graphics that makes the viewer want to see again and again.

CATEGORY
PV, CM

TEL / FAX
+81 (0) 3 3498 8485
+81 (0) 3 3498 8485

E-MAIL
quickpop@violet.plala.or.jp

URL
http://www.quickpop.tv

TOOLS
Final Cut Pro,
After Effects

Born in 1975. A motion graphic director and artist. Kodama began creating motion graphic works as a University student in Sendai, Japan. After working at an advertisement agency, he became a freelance director of music videos, TV programs, and commercials.

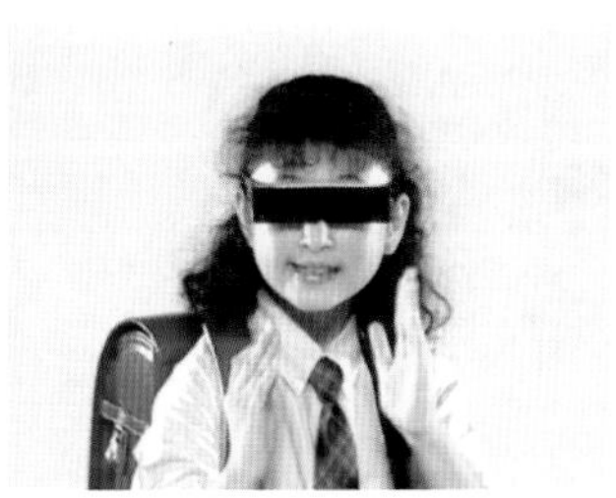

3

1
PV - WRENCH, *TAKE AWAY*
(©Victor Entertainment, Inc., 2004)

2
PV - Yuko Ando, 「さみしがり屋の言葉達」
Samishigariya no Kotobatachi (©cutting edge, 2005)

3
PV - POLYSICS, *I My Me Mine*
(©Ki/oon Records Inc., 2005)

<u>096</u>

河村勇樹
YUKI KAWAMURA

PROFILE
1979年京都生まれ。立地条件の良さ、映画製作を国が支援していることなどに共感し、20歳のころパリに移住する。それ以来、パリを拠点に活動。その作品は、鑑賞者の奥底にある純粋な美の感覚へと語りかける。繊細かつ夢想的な映像は互いに織り合わされ、探求の記憶と消えることのない美の永遠性を共に持つ。彼の映画や短編映像において、鑑賞者は作品にある目的地を発見できる。音楽家の半野喜弘とコラボレーションしたDVD作品集「SLIDE」は、フランスのLowaveからリリースされた。

1

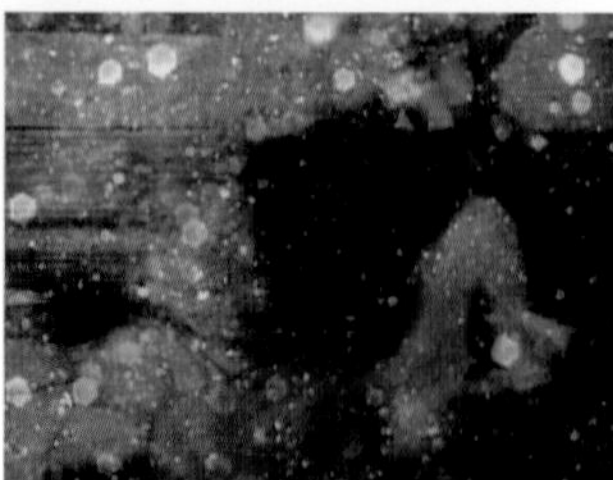

2

1
Video Art - *LETHE*
Music: MASAFUMI KOMATSU
Audio Engineer: François Colin

二人の恋人がレーテ河で泳ぐ（ギリシャ神話に登場する「忘却の河」）。だが、二人は逢えず、そして離れてしまう。少女は悲しい愛を忘れるため、その河に飛び込む。
Two lovers swim in a river called lethe (from Greek mythology: river of forgetfulness). They never meet and thus go apart. A girl dives into the river to forget an unhappy love.

2
Video Art - *JOUR DE REVE*
Music:Yoshihiro HANNO
(CQCD005 entrada de para_iso)

遊ぶ子供たちの連鎖するエネルギーが、噴水の夢のように湧き出る。
Connected energy of playing children emerges like a fountain dream.

3
Video Art - *PLAY AT DUSK*
Music: Yoshihiro HANNO
(SR212 meno)

煙、雲、そしてさまざまなオブジェクトが空に出現する。視点は最も高い位置まで昇り、宇宙の無限性を明かす。
Smoke, clouds and objects appear in the sky. The frame of view travels above to its upmost point demonstrating the infinity of the universe.

4
Video Art - *PORT*
Audio Engineer: François Colin

回転ドアを通して見える空港から発着する人々。時間と空間を移動する現代の生活。
People arriving and departing from the airport seen through a revolving door. Modern life as it moves on in time and space.

5
Video Art - *SCENE H*
Music: Yoshihiro HANNO
(PFCD04 .+)

雪景色の中で走る。イメージは、記憶と同じように，到来しては過ぎ去る。
Running in a snow landscape. Images come and go as memory does.

6
Video Art - *SLIDE*
Music: Yoshihiro HANNO
(CQCD001 Lab suite-edite)

人々が光の空間へと歩み入るにつれ、彼らの輪郭は転回する。全ては全てと繋がっている。空間が他の空間へと入り込むにつれ、物質は変容し、人間は塵と化す。
Outlines of people turn as the people themselves walk into a light space. Everything is connected to each other. Material is transformed as spaces slide into other spaces and people become dust.

7
Video Art - *VE*
Music: Yoshihiro HANNO
(CQCD005 metmOcfetlNiamncEneaile)
Audio Engineer: François Colin
Production: ESEC, David Sauerwein, Maxime Collin, Paula Vélez Bravo, Vivien Yu, Etienne Salonçon

ガラスの破片が虚空のなかを、ほぼ無重力で浮かぶ。とてもはかなく、お互いに衝突すると壊れる。はかなさは、持続しない美しさを表象している。
Pieces of glass float almost weightlessly in a void. Due to high fragility they fall apart when they clash. Fragility stands for beauty which is short lasting.

8
Video Art - *VOISIN*
Music:Yoshihiro HANNO
(CQCD005 Sulpice_Sostenuto)

木の枝が水面に反射する。イメージの動きや色彩は全くの自然であり、加工されていない。隣接するオブジェクトは、観る者の視点を通して、内在する美を露にする。
Branches of trees reflect onto the surface of the water. The movement and colors of the images are completely natural and unprocessed. Neighboring objects reveal their intrinsic beauty through the eyes of the viewer.

text by a-v-e-c.org

CATEGORY
Video Art

TEL / FAX
—
—

E-MAIL
info@yukikawamura.com

URL
http://www.yukikawamura.com

TOOLS
Power Mac G4,
PowerBook G4,
Premiere

Born in 1979, in Kyoto. Kawamura moved to Paris at the age of twenty, because he felt an affinity towards the location and the fact that the government was supporting film production. The base of his activities has been Paris ever since. His works speak straight to the viewers' innermost sense for pure aesthetics. Fragile appearing, lightly dreamy images are interweaving but all have in common the search of memory and eternity of unfading beauty.

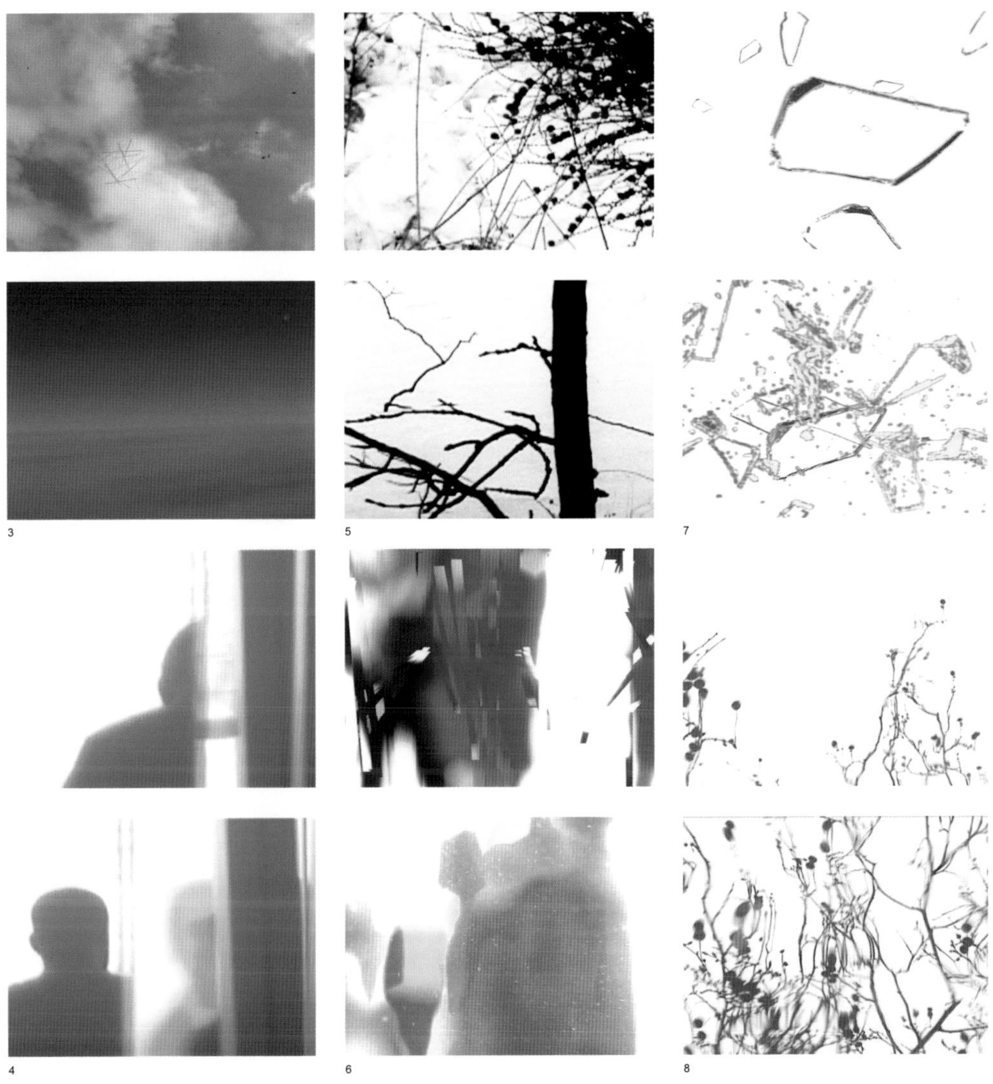

3

5

7

4

6

8

097 宅野祐介 YUSUKE TAKUNO

PROFILE
1974年生まれ。京都芸術短期大学映像専攻科卒業。1998年 MTV JAPAN入社。現在はPV、CM、MTV On Air Promotionなどのディレクターとして、クリエイティブプロダクションP.I.C.S.所属。B'z、矢井田瞳、TRICERATOPSなど数々のミュージックビデオ作品を中心に手掛ける。

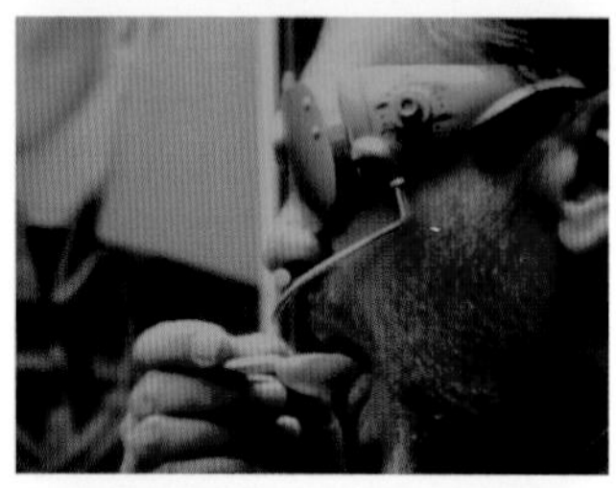

1

2

CONCEPT
基本的に最初のインスピレーションと幼いときから大好きだったモノ、それらを大切にして制作すること。

In the creative process, Takuno cherishes initial inspirations, and the things he was fond of as a child.

CATEGORY
Live Action, Motion Graphics

TEL / FAX
+81 (0) 3 5785 1780
+81 (0) 3 5785 1784

E-MAIL
post@picsco.net

URL
http://www.picsco.net

TOOLS
—

Born in 1974. Takuno graduated from Kyoto Junior College of Art Department of Film. He entered MTV Japan in 1998, and is currently a director of music videos, TV commercials, MTV on-air promotion, and more, as a member of the creative production firm P.I.C.S.. He has handled music videos for many musicians including B'z, Hitomi Yaida, and Triceratops.

3

4

1
Station-ID - MTV Station-ID「ファクトリー篇」
MTV Station-ID, *Factory* (2003)
Director: 宅野祐介 Yusuke Takuno
Producer: 清水忠 Tadashi Shimizu
Camera: 吉田好伸 Yoshinobu Yoshida
Music: 益田泰地 Taichi Masuda
Production by P.I.C.S.

写真提供: MTV JAPAN

2
DVD - L'Arc~en~Ciel, *CHRONICLE2* (Epic Visual, 2001)
Director: 宅野祐介 Yusuke Takuno
Producer: 下田伸貴 Nobutaka Shimoda
DP: 河津太郎 Taro Kawazu
Production by P.I.C.S.

3
PV - 矢井田瞳「マワルソラ」
Hitomi Yaida, *Mawaru Sora* (AOZORA RECORDS, 2005)
Director: 宅野祐介 Yusuke Takuno
Producer: 岩佐和彦 Kazuhiko Iwasa
Camera: 橋本清明 Kiyoaki Hashimoto
Light: 清水健一 Kenichi Shimizu
CG: 志賀匠 Takumi Shiga
Production by P.I.C.S.

4
On Air Promotion - FEELING OF MTV「クラブ篇」
FEELING OF MTV, *Club* (2001)
Director: 宅野祐介 Yusuke Takuno
Producer: 下田伸貴 Nobutaka Shimoda
Camera: 河津太郎 Taro Kawazu
DP: 河津太郎 Taro Kawazu
Gaffer: 中川大輔 Daisuke Nakagawa
Production by P.I.C.S.

写真提供: MTV JAPAN

2001 PROMAX&BDA 銅賞

098 土屋 豊 / W-TV オフィス・ビデオアクト
YUTAKA TSUCHIYA / W-TV OFFICE・VIDEO ACT!

PROFILE

1966年生まれ。明治大学文学部文学科演劇学専攻卒業。大学在学中から記録映画の助監督を務める。卒業後、マルチメディアプロダクションに就職し、CG / ゲームソフトのディレクションを担当。1990年より本格的に独自の映像制作を開始する。1994年より複製自由のフリービデオ「WITHOUT TELEVISION」を発行。同年、「W-TV OFFICE」設立。1998年から自主ビデオの流通プロジェクト「VIDEO ACT !」を主宰し、メディア・アクティビストたちのネットワークを広げるための活動を続けている。

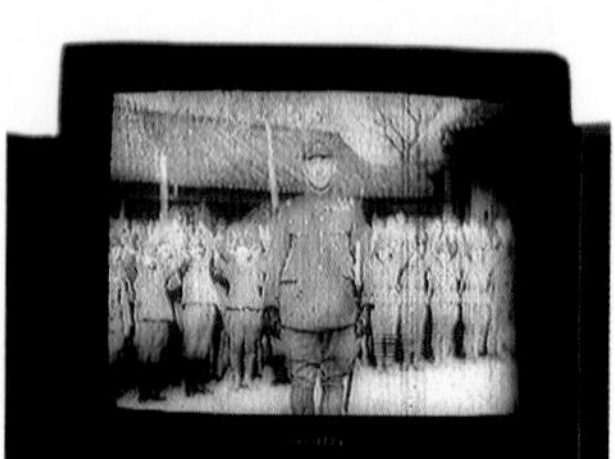

1

2

1
Documentary - 「あなたは天皇の戦争責任についてどう思いますか? <96.8.15 靖国篇 >」
What Do You Think About The War Responsibility Of Emperor Hirohito? (Part Yasukuni, Aug. 15, 1996) (1997)
Director: Yutaka Tsuchiya
Camera: Yutaka Tsuchiya, Wine Akano

1996 年 8 月 15 日、終戦記念日に靖国神社に参拝しに集まった人々に「あなたは天皇の戦争責任についてどう思いますか ?」という質問を投げかけ、その一部始終を記録。土屋のドキュメンタリー初監督作品。山形国際ドキュメンタリー映画祭 97 参加作品。台湾ドキュメンタリーフェスティバルインターナショナルコンペティションノミネート作品。

On August 15, 1996, Tsuchiya asked the question: "What do you think about the war responsibility of Emperor Hirohito?" to people who came to Yasukuni Shrine to worship on the anniversary of the end of the Pacific War. This was the first documentary film that Tsuchiya directed. It was a participating work at Yamagata International Documentary Film Festival '97, and it was nominated at Taiwan International Documentary Film Festival '98's International Competition.

2
Documentary - 「新しい神様」*The New God* (1999)
Director: Yutaka Tsuchiya
Staring: Karin Amamiya, Hideto Ito, Yutaka Tsuchiya

民族派右翼バンドの若い男女と天皇制に反対する監督自身との交流の記録。互いに立場を分かちつつも、撮ることと撮られることを繰り返す中で、彼らの間に不思議な信頼関係が生まれていく。ドキュメンタリー作家としての評価を確かなものにした土屋の代表作。山形国際ドキュメンタリー映画祭'99・国際批評家連盟賞特別賞受賞。ベルリン国際映画祭、香港国際映画祭等、出品多数。

This is a documentation of the exchanges between the young members of a nationalist right-wing band and the director, who is against the imperial system. Through the acts of continuously filming and being filmed, a relationship of trust was somehow built between them even though they have conflicting stances. This is the work that established Tsuchiya's reputation as an author of documentary films. It received the FIPRESCI Special Mention Prize at Yamagata International Documentary Film Festival '99, and has been submitted to Berlin International Film Festival, Hong Kong International Film Festival, and more.

CONCEPT

アイデンティティ、メディア、天皇制。社会的な存在である「私」を出発点とし、その「私」と「世界」の接点をめぐる問いかけが創作の原点。

Identity, media, and the social system based around the imperial family. The origin of his creative process lies in asking questions about the connection between "I" and the between "I" and "the world," with "I" as a social entity being the point of departure.

CATEGORY
Documentary, Fiction

TEL / FAX
+81 (0) 3 5496 7088
+81 (0) 3 5496 7078

E-MAIL
info@videoact.jp / yt_w-tv@st.rim.or.jp

URL
http://www.videoact.jp
http://www.peeptvshow.net
http://www1.cts.ne.jp/~w-tv

TOOLS
Mac,
Windows,
Premiere,
Final Cut,
Director,
Photoshop

Born in 1966. Graduated from Meiji University School of Arts and Letters Department of Literature, majoring in Drama. From the time he was attending university, Tsuchiya worked as an assistant director for documentative movies. A year later, he entered a multimedia production company, and directed CG works and video games. In 1990, he began to seriously produce his own films. In 1994, he released "Without Television," a freely-duplicable free video. In the same year he found "W-TV OFFICE". Since 1998, he has been directing "Video Act!," a distribution project for independent videos, and has been making an effort to widen the network of media activists.

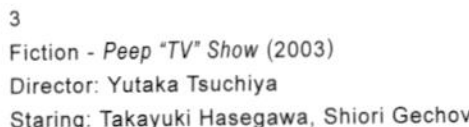

3
Fiction - *Peep "TV" Show* (2003)
Director: Yutaka Tsuchiya
Staring: Takayuki Hasegawa, Shiori Gechov

2001 年 9 月 11 日のニューヨークの映像を「美しい」と感じてしまった盗撮魔の男と、その男に共感するゴスロリの少女を主人公としたフィクション。世界への違和感をもてあます二人の「リアル」を奪還する闘いを描く。物語の核となる台詞以外は設定せず、出演者に即興で演じさせるという実験的な手法で撮影された。

This is a fictional work that revolves around a voyeuristic-footage maniac who felt that the footage of the 9.11 terrorist attacks were "beautiful," and a goth-loli girl who sympathizes with him. The film depicts how these two people, who perceive the world as a strange place, fight to regain what is "real." An experimental method was used for the production of this film, in which the actors improvise all the script lines besides those that form the foundation of the story.

3

099 ゼロ・グラビティ・オプティカルアート ZEROGRAVITY OPTICAL ART

PROFILE
2003年結成。ZEROGRAVITYのヴィジュアル部門として、ZEROGRAVITY OPTICAL ARTを立ち上げる。映像、Webデザイン、インスタレーション、グラフィックデザイン、フォトグラフィ、屋外広告、空間演出など視覚表現全般を手掛ける。

1

2

CONCEPT
重力の束縛から魂を解放させるために結成。人類の進化が目的。

Formed to liberate the soul from the restraints of gravity. The goal is the evolution of humankind.

CATEGORY
PV, Promotion, Art

TEL / FAX
—
—

E-MAIL
tloc3@clock.ocn.ne.jp

URL
—

TOOLS
Illustrator,
Photoshop,
Final Cut Pro,
After Effects,
Flash

Formed in 2003. Optical Art was started up as the visuals section of Zero Gravity. They handle anything visual, including motion graphics, installations, graphic design, photography, outdoor advertisements, and space production.

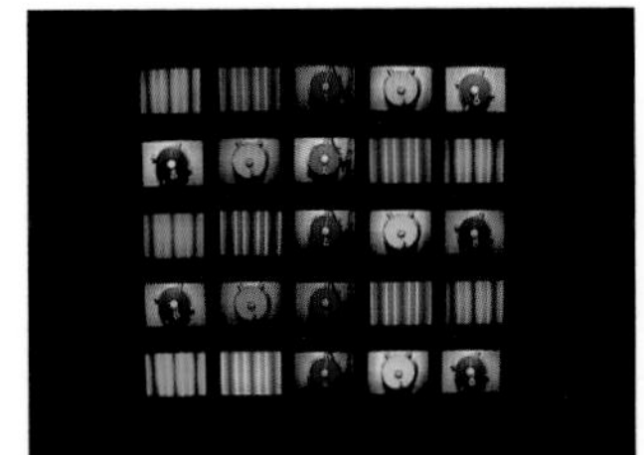

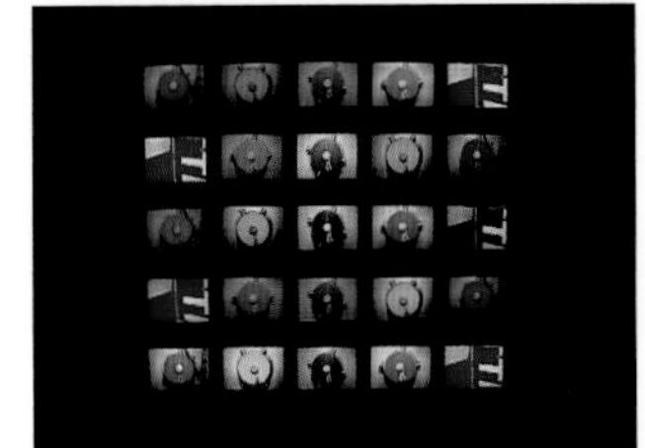

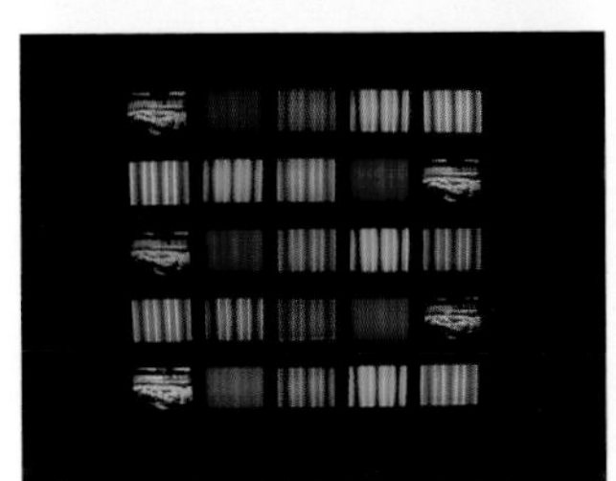

3

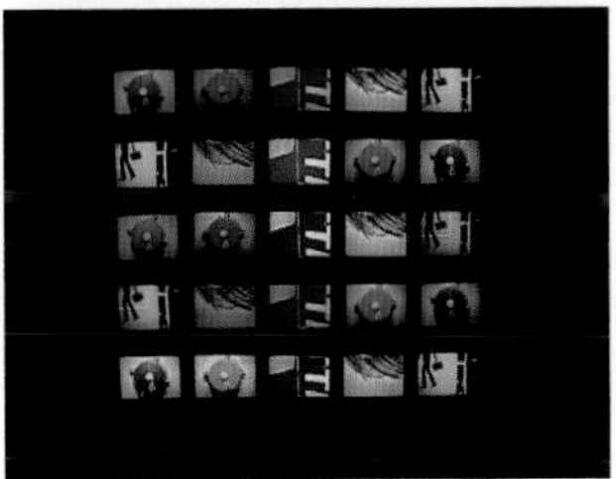

4

1
PV - NAN, *The Election* (2004)
Director + Animation + Photo:
ZEROGRAVITY OPTICAL ART
Planing + AD: NAN
Music: Void Village

2
Web Opening Movie - *2005 Sputnik* (2005)
Director + Animation + AD + photo:
ZEROGRAVITY OPTICAL ART
Music: FRANKY

3
Instalation - *CITY*
(©ZEROGRAVITY OPTICAL ART, 2005)

4
Instalation - *COLOR GRAFFITI*
(©ZEROGRAVITY OPTICAL ART, 2005)

100 ズームグラフィックス ZOOM GRAPHICS

PROFILE
東洋美術学校卒業後、谷田一郎に師事。1999年独立。CM演出、CGイラストからWebデザインなど幅広く活躍中。

1

2

CONCEPT
愛情をもって丁寧に。

Creating with love and carefulness.

CATEGORY
CM, Motion Graphics

TEL / FAX
+81 (0) 3 3443 3804
+81 (0) 3 3443 3806

E-MAIL
zoom-g@k3.dion.ne.jp

URL
—

TOOLS
Illustrator,
Photoshop,
After Effects,
Final Cut Pro,
Motion

After graduating from Toyo Institute of Art and Design, Yusaku began working under Ichiro Tanida. In 1999, he went independent. He handles a wide range of activities including TV commercial production, CG illustrations, and webpage design.

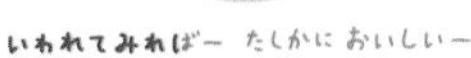

3

4

1
Movie - *Black Bird & Invaders*
MACHINE=EROS PROJECT 出展作品
(©ヤマハ株式会社 YAMAHA CORPOLATION・ヤマハ発動機株式会社 Yamaha Mortor Co., Ltd., 2004)

2
CM - *music.jp*
(©読売広告 YOMIO Advertising & MTI Ltd., 2005)

3
DVD Opening Movie -「バナナマンのシャブリなコメディ / オープニング映像」
Bananaman's Chablis Comedy Opening Movie
(©CLUBKING CO., LTD. 発売元：東北新社 TOHOKUSHINSHA FILM CORPORATION, 2005)

4
CM, VP - グリコ GLICO「熟カレー」*Juku Curry*
電通西日本 , エンジンフィルム (©GLICO LTD., 2005)

映像作家 100人
ワークプロフィール

ADDITIONAL INFO
ABOUT THE CREATORS

P056-057
001 ゼロスタジオ / 松川昌平
000STUDIO / SHOHEI MATSUKAWA

1999-2002 映像制作 -「SIMULATION」伊東豊雄『Blurring Architecture展』
2000 映像制作 - 山本理顕 はこだて未来大学
2001 映像制作 -『布・技と術展』– 京都芸術センター
2002 映像制作 - 池田亮司『 formula [ver.1.0]〜[ver.2.3] 』
2003 映像制作 -『Integrated Identity』池田昌弘展
2003 展示 - sparks cafe*『cyberscape パフォーマンス』
2004 映像制作 - 池田亮司インスタレーション『data.spectra [prototype]』
2004 映像制作 - 池田亮司『C4I』
2004 展示 -『Modern Style in EAST ASIA 2004』– Beijing
2004 展示 -『Modern Style in EAST ASIA 2004』– Kyoto

P058-059
002 テンケイ / アウターリミッツ
10K / OUTERLIMITS Inc.

2000- 日本各地のパーティ・イベントでVJ
2005 映像制作 -「GOTHIC FUTURISM」THE RAM:ΣLL:ZΣΣによる初の公式映像作品集『Service Of Arms』(トライエイト) 収録
2005 ライブ・ドキュメンタリー映像 - NUDE JAZZ「bonus ライブ films」(アルバム『CYNODONTIA』収録Mpeg movie)
2005 映像制作 - ALTZ「BOOGIE ALTZ」BAKI3主演 (時空 / ラストラム)
2005 映像制作 -「ライブ AT DREAM」PORTRAL with 10K (STORY)
2005 映像制作 -「screw」ライブ mixed by DJ DOPANT / smoked & chopped by VJ 10K (STORY)

P060-061
003 AC部
AC-BU

2000 受賞 -「フードファイト」(日本テレビ) ドラマ番宣
2000 受賞 -「ユーロボーイズ」(デジタル・スタジアム / NHK) 年間グランプリ
2003 オリジナル作品 -「ロイヤルドラゴン」RESFEST 2003にノミネート
2003 コーナータイトル -「ベラベラステーション」(Sma STATION-2 / テレビ朝日)
2003 番組タイトル -「チョナン・カン」(フジテレビ)
2003 映像制作 -「哲学するマントヒヒ」(みんなのうた / NHK)
2003 コーナータイトル -「ベラベラステーション」(Sma STATION-3 / テレビ朝日)
2003 コンサート用映像 - SMAP LIVE '03「MIJ TOUR」
2004 PRアニメ制作 - 東京都浴場組合「家庭の風呂より銭湯がいい!そのわけは?」
2004 PV - ビットルズ「ア・イ・ツ」(天才ビットくん / NHK)
2004 CM -「きっかけはフジテレビ / レアルマドリード編」(フジテレビ)
2004 PV - ザマギ「ショッキングブラック」
2004 PV - ザマギ「マジカルDEATH」
2004 ステーションID - スペースシャワー TV「クリスマス編・正月編」
2005 PV - Half Way Music「プリズム」CGパート
2005 番組タイトル、ロゴデザイン -「STUDIO GROWN」(スペースシャワー TV)
2005 PV - sunbrain「emotion」アニメーションパート制作
2005 アニメーション制作 -「天才ビットくん」レギュラーコーナー「BIT-MEN」1話〜12話 (NHK)
2005 PV - グループ魂「本田博太郎」アニメパート制作
2005 PV - KANKAWA×DJ KENSEI「BUTAMANMAN」
2005 PV - ザマギ「It's So Good Now (い・そ・ぐ・な)」
2005 CG制作 -「こどもちゃれんじ教材DVD」(ベネッセコーポレーション) 一部分
2005 オープニング映像 -『東京国際ファンタスティック映画祭2005』

P062-063
004 馬場 淳
ACCI BABA

1996 入選 -『MTV ステーション ID コンテスト』ファイナリスト
2003 映像演出・制作 -『六本木ヒルズカウントダウン』
2004 招待 -『ロサンゼルス映画祭オフィシャルセレクション』
2004 ノミネート -『オランダアニメーション映画祭コンペ部門』
2004 衣装 - ジャッキー・チェン氏衣装、墨絵描画
2005 映像パフォーマンス -『インディーズムービー・フェスティバル』開会式
2005 映像演出・制作 -『東京国際映画祭』オープニングPIGI

P064-065
005 アダプター
ADAPTER

2004 個展 -『CAMPAIGN』– ROCKET、BEAMS-T
2005 個展 -『MORE THAN HUMAN』– パリ
2005 PV - 三上ちさこ「相対形」

P066-067
006 エイジズ・ファイブ・アンド・アップ
AGES5&UP

1997 アプリケーション -「PoPoRon」(DIGITALOGUE)
1998 インタラクティブ -「clickart」(Hot-Wired)
1998 映像制作 -「ズキューン」MOTION GRAPHICS '98 – AXIS / 六本木
1999 インタラクティブ -「a gritty slippery hardy flaby thing」(Hot-Wired)
1999 映像制作 -「ずぼらや」motion graohics osaka – ATC / 大阪
1999 インタラクティブ -「lab」、「©1999 Ages5&up」、「SHELL」(gasbook 6、7)
1999 ステーションID -「Viewsic2000」(エスエムイー・ティーヴィ)
2000 インスタレーション -『ロッテルダム国際映画祭』TECH. POP.JAPAN
2000 映像制作 -「すいみん不足」motion graphics 2000
2001 ステーションID -「Viewsic2001」(エスエムイー・ティーヴィ)
2001 出展 -『テレビゲーム展 / ビットジェネレーターズ』– 水戸芸術館現代美術センター
2001 インタラクティブ -「○」MIND THE BANNER PROJECTNTT data
2001 iアプリ -「cldc」 BUZZ CLUB: NEWS FROM JAPAN – P.S.1 MoMA / ニューヨーク
2002 iアプリ -「h/m/s」、「union」–The END / JAVA PROGRAMMING FOR MOBIL WEB Vol.1 (D&D DEPARTMENT)
2002 映像制作 -「SS_union」OPEN MIND – 森美術館 / 六本木
2003 iアプリ -「union_v」Sony Ericsson SO505i
2003 フライングロゴ - 世界グラフィックデザイン会議『visualogue』– 名古屋国際会議場
2004 インスタレーション -「cell」、「DOTS. Expansion, shringkage」– ヴァージンTOHOシネマズ 六本木ヒルズ×森美術館
2004 Facade アニメーション - 銀座CHANEL

P068-069
007 亜妃子
AKIKO

2004 VJ -『JAZZ GROOVE DJ NIGHT』– モーション・ブルー・ヨコハマ
2004 VJ -『Impression』– モーション・ブルー・ヨコハマ
2005 VJ -『Percussion Session』– アップルストア銀座
2005 VJ -『afrontier』– モーション・ブルー・ヨコハマ

P070-071
008 手塚 敦 / フラヌール
ATSUSHI TEZUKA / FLANEUR

1999 PV - united future organization「ボン・ボヤージュ」
1999 PV - chari chari「Spring to Summer」
1999 PV - Small Circle of Friend「LOVE POTION No.5」
2005 映像制作 - バナナマン「Bananaman DVD Comedy Movie」

P072-073
009 ベータランド
BetaLand

2000 ビデオ -「BetaLand presents UFO ENCOUNTERS feat AOA & Burningman '98 '99」バーニングマン1998、1999とAOAをフューチャリングしたビデオ
2001 PV - OOIOO「OPEN YOUR EYES YOU CAN FLY」
2002 DVD -「EXPANDA（エクスパンダ）」DJ KENSEIとのコラボレーションライブミックスDVD
2004 PV・劇場用、TV用スポット - EGO-WRAPPIN'「マンホールシンドローム」スペースシャワーTVのミュージックビデオアワードでベストグルーヴビデオにノミネート
2004 リミックス映像 - 映画「マインドゲーム」DVDボックスセット特典映像
2005 VJミックス・ライブ映像 -「Service Of Arms」N.Yの伝説的ヒップホップ・アーティスト、THE RAM:ΣLL:ZΣΣのDVD

P074-075
010 キャッチパルス
CATCHPULSE

1998 自主作品 -「star」（8ミリフィルム）
1999 自主作品 -「非凡なる一日のおわりに」
1999 展示 -「CUT」映像（8ミリループフィルム）とフォトスライド
2000 映像制作 -「EMIT←」TATEDOREE
2001 映像と音楽 -「XXXRUXXXX」ソロ野外パフォーマンス
2003 ドラム教則映像 -「HYSTRICDRUM 第2弾」砂十島NANI監督作品
2003 ドラム教則映像 -「HYSTRICDRUM 第4弾」砂十島NANI監督作品
2003 自主作品 -「35」
2003 自主作品 -「1000000000000000PANIC!!!!!!!」ZIGZAGMIX
2004 自主作品 -「HYSTRICDRUM 第5弾」砂十島NANI監督作品ドラム教則映像
2004 ダンス・音楽・映像のコラボレーション -「白夜」
2004 PV - nanycal zuinosin「祭壇前最前列2004時ドラムスメーマン産まれる前」
2005 PV - ZUINOSIN「school oi」（MUZIKHIZOMISSIONERSION）協力：Tatsuki Saito
2005 ドキュメンタリー - ZUINOSIN、オシリペンペンズ「インスタントBOYテクノ御飯おかわりLOVEツアー」
2005 自主作品 -「Park」（製作中）

P076-077
011 キャビア
CAVIAR

2005 PV - YUKI「JOY」（エピックレコード）
2005 CM -「ヴィセシリーズ」（コーセー）
2005 プロモーション映像 -「M5 Project」（USコカ・コーラ）
2005 ショートムービー -「Ten Short Movies」（パナソニック）
2005 CM -「フレシネ」（サントリー）

P078-079
012 松本 力
CHIKARA MATSUMOTO

2005 展示 -『アニエスb. ショー＆パーティー』– 高輪プリンスホテル貴賓館 / 高輪
2005 展示 -『GAW展PART V』– tomorrow / 新宿ゴールデン街
2005 展示 -『showimagino vol.7.1-7.4』– アップルストア心斎橋、アップルストア名古屋栄、アップルストア銀座、アップルストア渋谷
2005 展示 -『How far to utopia ∞月スピリット』– トーキョーワンダーサイト渋谷
2005 展示 -『どこかの星のうえで』– takefloor / 恵比寿
2004 展示 -『TOKYO STYLE in STOCKHOLM』– リードマルホテル / ストックホルム
2004 ワークショップ -『大阪市立大学医学部附属病院小児科病棟プロジェクト2003～アートもクスリ～「ようこそマイルームへ –スイッチ、ザ.カーテン！ オープン、ザ.ウィンドウ！–」』– 大阪市立大学医学部附属病院 / 大阪
2003 展示 -『夜の町長、海へ行く あくつちひろ_松本力 展』– HIGURE 17-15 CAS / 西日暮里
2003 展示 -『NORASCOPE 清水寛子&松本力コラボレーション展』– ラ.ガルリ.デ.ナカムラ / 早稲田
2002 展示 - CANON ART PROJECTS PRESENTS 映像展覧会『URBANLENZ』– TNプローブ / 北青山
2002 展示 -『アニメーション工場と絵巻物マシーン3台』– トーキョーワンダーサイト / 本郷
2002 展示 -『Young Video Artists Initiative』– 六本木ヒルズ インフォメーションセンター THINK ZONE
2002 展示 -『第3回国際共同美術展シティビデオインスタレーション秋葉原TV / akihabara TV_03』– 秋葉原電気街
2001 ワークショップ -『アートー日小学校』– ワタリウム美術館 / 神宮前
2001 オープニング映像 -「美と出会う」アニメーション（NHK教育放送）

P080-081
013 橋本大佑
DAISUKE HASHIMOTO

2002 CM - anan「のびる睫毛編」（マガジンハウス）ディレクション＋アニメーション
2003 CM - コラックスEX「奏でる肌編」（メナード）アニメーション
2004 CM - 爽健美茶 緑茶ブレンド「緑の水墨画編」（日本コカ・コーラ）アニメーション
2005 CM - フランジア「グラスタワー編」（キリン）アニメーション
2005 PV - LUKIA「Ki ra me ki-LUKIA」（セイコーウォッチ）ディレクション

P082-083
014 北山大介 / オレンジ フィルムス
DAISUKE KITAYAMA / ORANGE FILMS

2000 PV - コーネリアス「EUS/VHS」（トラットリア / ポリスター）
2001 PV - TAHITI80「Wallpaper For The Soul」（Atomospheriques / フランス）
2002 PV - カジヒデキ「Footballing Weekenders」（トラットリア / ポリスター）
2002 PV - サロン・ミュージック「Eagle Rock Sinfonia」（トラットリア / ポリスター）
2003 DVD - コーネリアス「Five Point One」（フェリシティ / ポリスター）
2003 PV - カジヒデキ「Fantastic Game」（フェリシティ / ポリスター）
2003 PV - つじあやの「ありきたりなロマンス」（ビクターエンタテインメント）
2003 PV - エレファントカシマシ「生命讃歌」（フェイスミュージックエンタテインメント）
2003 PV - Syrup16g「ex.人間」（コロムビアミュージックエンタテインメント）
2003 PV - L.A.M.N.S.「HEAT OF THE MOMNET」（フェリシティ / ポリスター）
2005 PV - STRAIGHTENER「Against The Wall」（東芝EMI）
2005 PV - SHOPLIFTER「浮雲」（Citys / ポリスター）
2005 PV - HARCO「Night Hike」（コアレコーズ）
2005 PV - 琉球ディスコ「KAJI NU UTA」（プラチック）
2005 PV - ANA「血湧き肉踊る」（コンパクトサウンズ）

P084-085
島田大介 / 四つ葉加工房
015 DAISUKE SHIMADA / YOTSUBA KAKOUBOU

2003 PV - BACK DROP BOMB「PERSPECTIVE」(トイズファクトリー)
2003 PV - Mr.Children「掌」(トイズファクトリー)
2004 PV - BRAHMAN「A WHITE DEEP MORNING」(トイズファクトリー)
2004 PV - トルネード竜巻「ブレイド」(スピードスターレコーズ)
2004 PV - 明星 / Akeboshi「Hey There」(エピックレコード)
2004 PV - 小島麻由美「BLUE MELODY」(ポニーキャニオン)
2005 PV - SHAKALABBITS「Ladybug」(cl.evil design / XTRALARGE RECORDS)
2005 PV - 槇原敬之「traveling」(キャピトルミュージック)
2005 PV - 木村カエラ「BEAT」(ビクターエンタテインメント)
2005 PV - Great Adventure「ANY PLACE ROCKS」(レザボアレコーズ)

P086-087
デラウエア
016 DELAWARE

2005 出展 -「CUSTOMIZE ME」– バルセロナ
2005 出展 -「D-DAY Design Today」
2004 CDアルバムリリース - 5thアルバム
2004 CDアルバムリリース - 6thアルバム
2004 出展 -「This Monkeys Goes To Heaven」– Non Profit Art / サウス・メキシコ
2004 CM -「ケイコとマナブ」(リクルート)
2004 ライブ -「AG Idea International」
2004 ライブ -「Idn Myfavorite Conference」
2004 出展 -「la Triennale di milano / Utopia & betrayal」
2004 作品集 -「1st Solo Book CD-ROM『Designing In The Rain』」
2004 出展 -「44th Cracow Film Festival」– ポーランド
2004 音楽映像作品 - ディーゼル「dreammaker」
2004 出展 -「Tokyo Style」– スウェーデン

P088-089
デバイスガールズ
017 DEVICEGIRLS

1998 映像インスタレーション -『flow#6: Komaba Domitory Project』
1999 展示 - 国際ビデオインスタレーション『秋葉原 TV』
1999 映像出品 - 作品集「GASBOOK 7」
1999 カバー・特集記事掲載 - 雑誌「design plex 8月号」
2000 映像制作・VJ -『東京国際映画祭』チャーリーズ・エンジェルレセプション
2000 オープニング映像制作 - NHKスペシャル「21世紀ネットワーク市民が世界を変える」
2001 展示 -『Buzz Club News From Japan展』– PS1 MoMA Contemporary Art Center / ニューヨーク
2001 映像制作・VJ - 石野卓球ソロLIVE『KARAOKENIGHTSCOOP』
2001 展示 -『Music Concerned Motion Graphics展』
2002 ステーション ID - CS『So-net Channel』
2002 映像制作・VJ - EVENT『MILLENNUM COUNTDOWN 2002』
2003 映像制作 - 鹿児島県民交流センター『生命と環境の学習館』エントランス及び展示用映像制作
2003 インスタレーション -『chanson d'amor』– 横浜赤レンガ倉庫
2004 PV - 琉球ディスコ『ZAN (in waves)』
2005 映像制作・VJ - EVENT『WIRE05』– 横浜アリーナ
2005 映像制作・VJ - KAGAMI LIVE『SPARK ARTS vs SPARK GIRLS』
2005 映像制作・VJ - Porno Graffitti LIVE『SWITCH』– 日本武道館

P090-091
ドラびでお
018 DORAVIDEO

1997 参加 - 想い出波止場『VUOY』
2001 参加 -『アシッドマザーテンプル』UK / USツアー
2005 受賞 -『ARS Electronica』Digital 音楽部門 Honorary Mention賞
2005 CM -「ラフォーレグランバザール」

P092-093
エレクロトニック
019 ELECROTNIK

2001 CM -「toss and turn」
2001 PV - m-flo「prism」(エイベックス)
2002 PV - m-flo「dispatch」(エイベックス)
2002 PV - THE MAD CAPSULE MARKETS「flyhigh」(スピードスターレコーズ)
2002 タイトル映像 -「body and soul」
2003 PV - KENISHII「PRESTO」(ミュージックマイン)
2003 PV - AUDIO ACTIVE「Frozen Head」(ビートインク)
2004 タイトル映像 -「ZOOM」
2004 CM - コカ・コーラ「C2」ビルボード
2004 CM - マルイ「sparkling sale2004 お正月」出演：ASA-CHANG
2005 PV - HIFANA「www.hifana.com」(©W+K東京LAB / ポリスター)
2005 PV - bonobos「THANK YOU FOR THE MUSIC」(ドリーミュージック)
2005 DVD - ZAMURAI TV「GAGLE, KENTARO, TUCKER」(スペースシャワー TV)
2005 PV - m-flo loves LISA「TRIPOD BABY」(エイベックス)
2005 タイトル映像 -「スペースシャワー TV」

P094-095
エンライトメント
020 ENLIGHTENMENT

2000 出展 -『ENLIGHTENMENT』– コレット / パリ
2000 フリーペーパー創刊 -「Display」全10号
2000 個展 -『2-Delight』– パルコギャラリー / 渋谷
2000 作品集 -『2-Delight』(コンポジット・プレス)
2001 出展 -『スーパーフラット展』– LA MOCA、Henry Art Center
2001 出展 -『ACTIVE WIRE展』– 韓国
2001 出展 -『JAM展』– バービカンセンター・アートギャラリー / ロンドン
2001 出展 -『PLANET UNDER A GROOVE展』– ブロンクス美術館 / アメリカ
2002 出展 -『JAM展』– 東京オペラシティアートギャラリー
2002 出展 -『スーパーフラット』展 – Walker Art Center / アメリカ
2003 個展 -『79787562』– 京都造形芸術大学
2003 個展 -『Both Sides』– 名古屋現代美術館
2003 個展 -『Complete Display』– 青山 Gallery 360°
2003 作品集 -「Both Sides」(エンライメント・パブリッシング)
2003 出展 -『PLANET UNDER A GROOVE展』– Kulturreferat / ミュンヘン
2004 出展 - アートフェスティバル『Fiac』に参加 – パリ
2004 出展 - アートフェスティバル『Artissima』– イタリア
2004 出展 -『北京アートフェスティバル』– 北京
2005 グループ展 -『Shanghi cool』– 上海 / 多論美術館
2005 個展 -『LIE OF MIRROR』– HIROMI YOSHII Gallery
2005 作品集 -「LIE OF MIRROR」(エンライメント・パブリッシング)
2005 出展 -『ART FAIR TOKYO』– HIROMI YOSHII Gallery
2005 出展 - アートフェスティバル『Fiac』– パリ
2005 個展 -『LIE OF MIRROR』– Changing-Role Move Over Gallery / イタリア
2005 個展 -『Mind Pleats』– Canon S Gallery / 東京

P096-097 エキソニモ

021 EXONEMO

2004 出展 -『しだ展』– nou LABORATORY / 東京
2004 出展 -『六本木クロッシング』– 森美術館 / 東京
2004 出展・ライブ -『Mediarena: contemporary art from Japan』– Govett-Brewster Art Gallery / New Plymouth / New Zealand
2004 出展 -『ネクスト:メディア・アートの新世代』- ICC / 東京
2004 出展 -『Navigator』– 國立台灣美術館 / 台湾
2004 出展 -『トーキョー・スタイル・イン・ストックホルム 』2004 – Beckmans School of Design / Stockholm
2004 出展 -『リアクティビティ：反応＝再生する可能性』– ICC / 東京
2004 出展 -『ナム・ジュン・パイク アワード2004』– PhoenixHalle / ドイツ
2004 ネット展 -『56kTV - bastard channel』 – http://www.56k-bastard.tv/
2005 出展 -『アート・ミーツ・メディア：知覚の冒険』– ICC / 東京
2005 オーガナイズ -『ドークボット・トーキョー』– SuperDeluxe / 東京
2005 出展 -『愛知万博』– エキスポビジョン / 名古屋
2005 出展 -『Beijing International New Media Arts Exhibition』– China Millennium Museum / 北京
2005 出展 -『O.K. Video 2005』– ジャカルタ / インドネシア
2005 出展 -『Rock the Future』– FACT / リバプール / イギリス
2005 出展 -『MobLab』– IAMAS, ICC, smt, YCAM...etc. / 日本

P098-099 フクーピィ / キュウオブキュウ

022 fc∞py / QofQ

1996-1997 出演・映像制作 –「SONY TECHNO T.V」(MX TV)
1998 映像制作 - BOREDOMS「SUPER SEEEEEE!!!!!!」(ワーナーミュージック・ジャパン)
2000 TV -「Chi Chi 5 MILK」(Music Link)
2000 展示 -『J-WAY 』– リドマルホテル / ストックホルム QofQとしてライブ&インスタレーションを発表
2000 PV - Museum of Plate「F#」塚本サイコ (Museum of Plate)
2001 TV -「George's Magic Van」(Viewsic) 情報コーナー「fc∞pscope」制作
2001 映像制作 -「PUNKALOID」(Viewsic)
2001 展示 -「アートー日小学校 」– ワタリウム美術館 / 東京 QofQとしてインスタレーション「ひみつのおんがくしつ」を2ヶ月に渡り発表し、子供達にワークショップやパーティをプレゼント
2002 PV - 清水靖明「Human Cuckoo Clock」(Sateto)
2003 PV - OOIOO「Kila Kila Kila」(エイプサウンズ)
2004 PV - 16bit「basic」(16bit)
2004 展示 -『Christmas Paradise 2004』– 東南植物楽園 / 沖縄市 エレクトリカル・ミュージカル「MOMO」にて映像制作
2005 PV - 桜なだれ「並木道」(DISCUS)
2005 展示 -『Christmas Paradise 2005』– 東南植物楽園 / 沖縄市 エレクトリカル・ミュージカル「月と一万匹の鯉」にて映像制作

P100-101 ギフト

023 GIFT

2004 オープニング映像 -「IdN My Favourite Conference」
2005 PV -「ALLRIGHTSRESERVED for Press」
2005 PV -「Leno Promotion Movie」(ヤマハ)
2005 PV -「新星堂ミュージックトレジャー」(スペースシャワー TV)

P102-103 ゴーモーション

024 GO MOTION

2001 CM -「Tower Records Bounce.com」(タワーレコード)
2004 コンサート用映像 -「PornoGraffitti 6th Live Circuit『74ers』」
2005 DVD -「バナナマンのシャブリなコメディ / 337拍子、足しちゃった」(クラブキング)
2005 オープニングモーション -「Seeds & Ground WEB」

P104-105 グルーヴィジョンズ

025 GROOVISIONS

1997 PV - Fantastic Plastic Machine「Dear Mr. Salesman」(日本コロムビア)
1997 PV - DREAMS COME TRUE「PEACE!」(東芝EMI)
2000 PV - Spanova「SPEAK LOUD」(ワーナーミュージック・ジャパン)
2000 番組タイトルバック -「トップランナー」(NHK)
2000 モーションロゴ -「Warner Innovation! 30th Anniversary」(ワーナーミュージック・ジャパン)
2001 番組タイトルバック -「キューピー3分クッキング」(味の素)
2002 PR DVD用映像 -「GRV1756 (Nike presto)」(Nike, Neverstop)
2003 PV - ゆず「三番線」(セーニャ・アンド・カンパニー)
2004 PV - 福山雅治「虹～もうひとつの夏～」(ユニバーサルミュージック)
2004 PV - 森山直太朗「今が人生～飛翔編～」(ユニバーサルミュージック)
2004 Art Work -「WATARIDORI GRV2153」Music by cornelius (ガス アズ インターフェイス)
2005 PV - セカイイチ「石コロブ」(トイズファクトリー)
2005 PV - CHEMISTRY「キミがいる」(デフスター・レコーズ)
2005 PV - RIP SLYME「GOOD JOB!」(ワーナーミュージック・ジャパン)
2005 PV - スネオヘアー「悲しみのロックフェスティバス」(エピックレコード)

P106-107 本木秀明

026 HIDEAKI MOTOKI

2003 自主作品 -「ZOUNDS」
2004 PV - Rays「MOONFLOWERS」(HORIZON / liquid recordings)
2005 PV - 琉球ディスコ「CHURAZIMA」(プラチック)

P108-109 稲葉英樹

027 HIDEKI INABA

2004-2005 展覧会 -『NEW LINE』
2004 DVDアートディレクション -「AUDIOVISUALJAPAN」

P110-111 田中秀幸 / フレイムグラフィックス

028 HIDEYUKI TANAKA / FRAME GRAPHICS

2001 CM -「ジャイアント・ブラ」(ラフォーレ原宿)
2001 アニメーション -「OH! スーパーミルクチャン」(©FG, SSNW, SPLX, RTK, ADV)
2005 CM -「スキーキャンペーン」(ジャパン・スノー・プロジェクト)
2005 PV - DJ TASAKA「スピーカー・タイフーン」(キューンレコード)
2001 受賞 - ADC制作者賞
2005 受賞 - ADC賞
2005 受賞 - ACCベストアートディレクション賞

P112-113
光J
029 HIKARU J

2003 PV - レッキンクルー「MACHO BULL」
2003-2004 VJ - 恵比寿みるくレギュラーパーティー『Sustem』
2004 映像作品 - 映画「tori」リミックス
2005 CG・編集 -「デミさん」
2005 映像作品出展 -『Central East TOKYO』
2005 VJ -『Central East TOKYO』
2005 VJ -『Public image』
2005 VJ -『DK SOUND』
2005 VJ -『DISCO TWINS』
2005 CG・編集 - METALCHICKS「10000DB」
2005 PV - DJ KOHNO（fromケツメイシ）& DJ TATSUTA「お客様が神様です」

P114-115
小池 光
030 HIKARU KOIKE

1999 映像制作 -「Dot Slasher」
2004 映像制作 -「うごく【絵】じてん -ピアノ-」(NHK)
2005 フラッシュ制作 - BEYES：Moritz Rogosky (BEYES, 2005)
2005 インスタレーション - DANBOXEL（KDDIデザイニングスタジオ）

P116-117
井口弘史
031 HIROSHI IGUCHI

2002 Art -「HELL」
2002 Art -「Inside」
2001 ステーションID -「GANG STA」（スペースシャワー TV）
2004 DVD オープニング -「SOUND×VISION」

P118-119
木津裕史 / エムティヴィージャパン
032 HIROSHI KIZU / MTV JAPAN

2003 タイトルムービー -「MTV WORLD CHART EXPRESS」（エム・ティー・ヴィー・ジャパン）
2003 チューンイン -「MTV's LIVE SELECTION」（エム・ティー・ヴィー・ジャパン）
2004 オープニングムービー -「MTV COOL CHRISTMAS」（エム・ティー・ヴィー・ジャパン）
2004 オープニングムービー -「THE SUPER DRY LIVE 2005『REDANGER!!』」（エム・ティー・ヴィー・ジャパン）

P120-121
中尾浩之
033 HIROYUKI NAKAO

2003-2005 ショートフィルム -「trash」「ZERO」「ザ・シークレットショウ」
2002 CM - ツーカーホン関西「いいんかいおじさん篇」「いいんかいおかん篇」
2005 CM - 少年サンデー「先生篇」「おやじ篇」（小学館）
2004 オープニング映像 -「ロンブー龍」（日本テレビ）
2006 「trainsurfer」「スチーム係長」3月10日DVD発売予定

P122-123
谷田一郎 / ジョン・アンド・ジェーン・ドォ
034 ICHIRO TANIDA / JOHN AND JANE DOE INC.

1986 BISE入社
1987 ヒロ杉山氏とNeo-Art Group 結成
1996 John and Jane Doe Inc.を設立
1987 受賞 -『日本グラフィック展』審査員賞
1990 受賞 -『日本グラフィック展』協賛企業賞
1992 受賞 - パルコ賞
1996 受賞 - 東京ADC賞
1999 受賞 - N.Y. ADC銀賞
2004 佐藤可士和氏とART DESIGNを結成し、ショートフィルムを制作

P124-125
今井トゥーンズ
035 IMAITOONZ

2004 アニメーション映画 -「DEAD LEAVES」（プロダクションI.G、マンガエンターテインメント）公開
2004 番組パッケージ -「M size」（エム・ティー・ヴィー・ジャパン）
2005 オープニング映像 -「MTV COOL CHRISTMAS」（エム・ティー・ヴィー・ジャパン）
2005 番組パッケージ -「MTV amp」（エム・ティー・ヴィー・ジャパン）
2005 イベントオープニング映像 -「MTV THE SUPER DRY LIVE 2005」（MTVジャパン）
2005 番組パッケージ -「MTV学祭応援団」（エム・ティー・ヴィー・ジャパン）
1996 番組OPタイトルアニメーション -『MTV TOP OF JAPAN』（エム・ティー・ヴィー・ジャパン）
1999 選考 -「SPIDEAD」Digital moving image festival in association with film fore - London
2000 ノミネート -「オランダ・ロッテルダム国際映画祭」エクスプローディングシネマ部門

P126-127
西郡 勲
036 ISAO NISHIGORI

2003 オープニングパーティ映像 - Cartier銀座
2005 オープニング映像 - 科学未来館プラネタリウム
2005 CM - LUKIA「光の軌跡篇」（セイコーウォッチ）
2005 CM - パナソニック モバイルコミュニケーションズ P901i「ズーム篇」
2003 番組パッケージ - エム・ティー・ヴィー・ミュージック・アワーズ

P128-129
出雲重機
037 IZMOJUKI

2001 メカニックデザイン - XBOX用ゲームソフト「鉄騎 –STEEL BATTALION–」（カプコン）
2004 映像制作 - MTV Japanキャンペーン「Music and More」

P130-131
影山二郎 / 右脳事件
038 JIRO KAGEYAMA / unou-jiken inc.

2003 劇場用映像 -「Shochiku Sound Gate」（松竹）
2003 VP 演出・編集 -「シノアドア」（資生堂）
2004 モーションデザイン -「GAS TV SOUND×VISION」（ガスアズ インターフェイス）
2004 映像制作 -『SOUND×VISION 2004』展 – 東京
2005 VP 演出・編集 -「dプログラム」（資生堂）
2005 VP 演出・編集 -「マキアージュ」（資生堂）

P132-133
堀切 潤 / ポータブルコミュニティ
039 JUN HORIKIRI / PORTABLE[K]OMMUNITY

2002 映像展覧会 + パフォーマンス - 『urbanlenz』 portable[k]ommunity – 表参道 TN Probe / 東京
2002 パフォーマンス - 『Tokyo Art Jungle』 – 東京国際フォーラム / 東京
2002 パフォーマンス - 『Port』大阪築港・赤レンガ倉庫 – 大阪
2002 パフォーマンス - 『Farmers Manual Presentation Live』 – THINK ZONE / 六本
2002 パフォーマンス - 『sonar sound tokyo』 – THINK ZONE / 六本木
2002 パフォーマンス - 『電子芸術国際会議 ISEA2002』 Farmers Manual Presentation – 名古屋ダイヤモンドホール / 愛知
2002 パフォーマンス - 『Open Mind』 – 森美術館 / 東京
2003 展示 - 『Sónar 2003』 – Sonar Cinema バルセロナ / スペイン
2004 展示 - 『リアクティヴィティ 反応=再生する可能性』 – NTTインターコミュニケーションセンター / 東京
2004 展示 - 『SOUND×VISION 2004』 – ラフォーレ原宿 / 東京、せんだいメディアテーク / 仙台、YCAM / 山口
2004 展示 - 『Game Commons』 – Yarba Buena Center for the Arts, San Francisco / アメリカ
2004 展示 - 『portable[k]ommunity』 – La Casa Encendida / スペイン
2004 パフォーマンス - 「Anti-Format」スペースシャワー TV 番組内
2005 展示 - 『Ubiquitous Sounds』 – 東京都写真美術館 / 東京
2005 展示 - 『AudioVisual works』 – 金沢21世紀美術館 / 石川
2005 パフォーマンス - 『Ryuichi Sakamoto Japan Tour 2005』 – Zepp / 東京、大阪、名古屋、福岡

P134-135
ジュウリョク
040 JURYOKU

2004 アニメーション - TVCM「PARCO-Christmas」
2005 リアルタイム・モーショングラフィックス - 「Fit-ment」

P136-137
タナカカツキ
041 KATSUKI TANAKA

1999 オンラインTシャツショップ「GbM」(http://kuromatsu.jp/gbm/) スタート
2001 アニメーション - 「モシャとクッシャ」デジタルハイビジョンジャパン
2001 映像制作 - DVD「スーパー一人ごっつ」
2001 TVタイトルデザイン - 「やり逃げコージー」(テレビ東京)
2001 TVタイトルデザイン - 「くりぃむしちゅーのたりらりラ～ン」(日本テレビ)
2001 著書 - 「バカドリル」(扶桑社)
2001 著書 - 「ブッチュくんオール百科」(ソニーマガジンズ)
2001 著書 - 「オッス! トン子ちゃん」(扶桑社)
2002 DVD作品集 - 「SUNDAY」(ナウオンメディア http://www.nowondvd.net/)
2004 展示 - 『六本木クロッシング-日本美術の新しい展望』
2004 展示 - 『KITTY EX.展』 – 森美術館、ラフォーレミュージアム原宿
2004 展示 - 『岡本太郎TributeTシャツ展』 – 森美術館、ラフォーレミュージアム原宿
2004 DVD作品集 - 「赤ちゃん」(DDDDVDレーベル http://www.ddd-dvd.jp/) 発売中

P138-139
若野 桂 / ガール・スタジオ
042 KATSURA MOSHINO / GIRL STUDIO

1995 PV - AUDIO ACTIVE「Happy Shopper」
1997 PV - AUDIO ACTIVE「Paint Your Face Red」
1999 CM - ナイキ・バスケットボールCM「ティム・ダンカン」、「ケヴィン・ガーネット」、「ジェイソン・ウィリアムス」の3バージョン キャラクターデザイン&ディレクション ラップ：ZEEBRA from KING GIDORA、TWIGY from KAMINARI KAZOKU、DEVLAGE from BUDDHA BRAND
2000 CM - 「モード学院」 音楽：DJ KRUSH
2000 PV - DJ YAS from KAMINARI KAZOKU「サブマリン」
2001 ショートムービー - 「SIGN」 音楽：竹村ノブカズ
2002 PV - SOUL SCREAM「緑の森」
2003 BGV - The Orb (ヨーロッパツアー)、The Orb (メタモルフォーゼ苗場)
2003 BGV - DJ KRUSH (アメリカツアー)
2004 PV - nobodyknows+「ココロオドル」

P140-141
カワイオカムラ
043 KAWAI+OKAMURA

1997 個展 - 『オーバー・ザ・レインボウ』 – アートスペース虹 / 京都
1998 グループ展 - 『どないやねん~現代日本の創造力~』 – フランス国立高等美術学校 / パリ
1999 個展 - 『今日の表現11「四角いジャンル」』 – 京都市四条ギャラリー
1999 グループ展 - 『ドーナッツ展』 – オン・サンデーズ / ワタリウム美術館 / 神宮前
2000 短編 - 「バミリオン・プレジャー・ナイト」(テレビ東京) 短編6作品制作
2000 イベント - 『ティップ・コレクション vol.3』 – 扇町ミュージアムスクエア / 大阪
2001 出品 - 『The Images Festival of Independent Film and Video』 – ニスタウンホール / トロント
2001 グループ展 - 『キョウト×アムステルダム―ニュー・ダイレクションズ』 – 京都芸術センター / 京都、smart project / アムステルダム
2001 上映 - 『関西発!!!アニメーション・セレクション』 – アップリンク・ファクトリー / 東京
2002 受賞 - 『調布映画祭 / 第5回ショートフィルムコンペティション』「ヘッドレス-3001」シリーズ 特別賞
2002 グループ展 - 『ビデオ・ラリー展』 – ギャラリーそわか / 京都
2003 グループ展 - 『Premonition-M'』 – 大阪成蹊大学綜合芸術研究センター / 京都
2005 受賞 - 『第1回アンダー 10ミニッツデジタルシネマフェスティバル』「ヘコヒョン7」グランプリ
2005 グループ展 - 『キリンアートプロジェクト2005』 – タマダプロジェクトアートスペース / 東京、KPOキリンプラザ大阪 / 大阪

P142-143
森野和馬
044 KAZUMA MORINO

1992 入選 - 「SLEEPER」キリンコンテンポラリー・アワード 映像アート部門 – 日本
1993 入選 - 「STRIPE BOX」Electronic Theater – SIGGRAPH / アメリカ
1993 入選 - 「STRIPE BOX」WELLINGTON FILM FESTEVAL – イギリス
1994 入選 - 「Control<->Color：Flags」Screening Room Art and Design Program [USA] – SIGGRAPH / USA
1995 入選 - 「Free-Quent Objects」「ACC CM Festival」「Canon BJ Printer」Electronic Theater – SIGGRAPH / USA
1995 受賞 - 「Japan Information-Culture Society」第1回情報文化大賞
1996 入選 - 「Metal Hat」Electronic Theater – SIGGRAPH / アメリカ
1997 入選 - 「Runners」「UNYSIS Japan CM」Electronic Theater – SIGGRAPH / アメリカ
1997 入選 - 「Runners」 – CARTOOMBRIA / イタリア
1998 受賞 - 「Runners」 – Prix Ars Electronica / オーストリア Computer Animation Visual Effect：Distinction
1998 受賞 - 「Runners」 – PRIX PIXEL-INA ART MENTION SPECIALE DU JURY / Imagina / フランス
1998 入選 - 「Runners」 – Anima mundi / ブラジル
1998 入選 - 「Motion Graphics '98 Openning movie」「Charge S: SPACE SHOWER TV JINGLE」 - NICOGRAPH / JAPAN2002

入選 -「Line」Art Gallery – SIGGRAPH / アメリカ
2002 入選 -「Build」– Digital Content Grand Prix アート部門最優秀賞 / 日本
2003 入選 -「Build」Art Gallery – SIGGRAPH / アメリカ

P144-145
北岡一哉 / エディトリアル
045 KAZUYA KITAOKA / EDITREAL

1995 PV - CHAR「MUSTANG」(EDOYA RECORDS)
1996 PV - United Future Organization「Spy's Spice」(ユニバーサル ミュージック)
1996 PV - PEACE FORCE「Mr. FREEDOM cd-extra」(BMG)
1997 PV - 朝日美穂「勉強」「momotie」
1998 PV - silent poets「Suger man (featuring Terry Hall)」(トイズファクトリー)
1998 PV - Small Circle Of Friends「HEADPHONE LOVER」(スカイラーキン)
1999 CM - 任天堂「ドンキーコング」
2002 PV - EGO-WRAPPIN'「サイコアナルシス」(マイナースウィング / ユニバーサル・ポリドール)
2004 コラボID - DMBQ vs HYSTERIC GLAMOUR
2004 PV - SKA FLAMES「太陽」

P146-147
黒坂圭太
046 KEITA KUROSAKA

1984 アニメーション -「変形作品第2番」
1988 アニメーション -「海の唄」
1990 アニメーション -「個人都市」
1991 アニメーション -「春子の冒険」
1991 出品 -『ロッテルダム国際映画祭』
1991 出品 -『ロンドン国際映画祭』
1991 出品 -『メルボルン国際映画祭』– オーストラリア
1992 出品 -『ベルリン国際映画祭』– ドイツ
1992 出品 -『シュツットガルド国際アニメーション映画祭』– ドイツ
1993 出品 -『マドリッド国際映画祭』– スペイン
1993 出品 -『オーバーハウゼン国際短編映画祭』
1993 出品 -『レティナ国際映画祭』– ハンガリー
1994 アニメーション -「ATAMA」
1997 アニメーション -「パパが飛んだ朝」(エム・ティ・ヴィー・ジャパン)
2003 アニメーション -「冬の日」
2005 アニメーション -「壁男」
2005 アニメーション -「餅兵衛」

P148-149
横井 謙
047 KEN YOKOI

2002 オープニング映像・イベント映像 -「デジスタ・アウォード2002」(NHK-BS2)
2003 オープニング映像BGV -「スーパーカー・ライブ」(NHK-BS2)
2003 映像制作 -「M市とC市とG町の戯画 (Modern Chouju Giga)」(NHK BS-hi)
2003 オープニング映像 -「デジタルアートフェスティバル東京2003」(NHKエンタープライズ)
2003 PV - 布袋寅泰「GREAT ESCAPE」DVD、「DOBERMAN DVD」収録
2004 記念式典セレモニー映像・CG制作 -『第55回全国植樹祭』– 宮崎県
2004 オープニング映像 -「送ってみよう! ケータイ俳句」(NHK-BS2)
2005 TV番組内使用BGV -「デジタル・スタジアム」(NHK-BS2)
2005 オープニング映像 -「デジスタ・アウォード2005」(NHK-BS2)

P150-151
辻川幸一郎
048 KOICHIRO TSUJIKAWA

2002 PV - コーネリアス「Drop」(ポリスター)
2002 PV - コーネリアス「TONE TWILIGHT ZONE」(ポリスター)
2003 PV - SKETCH SHOW「EKOT」(デイジーワールド)
2003 PV - SKETCH SHOW「MARS」(デイジーワールド)
2004 ショートフィルム –「eyes」(Getty Images) Music：コーネリアス
2005 CM - 資生堂 HAKU (資生堂)
2005 CM - ヱビスビール「ヱビス・ちょっと贅沢なビール」(サッポロビール)
2005 PV - RIP SLYME「GALAXY」(ワーナーミュージック・ジャパン)
2005 CM - 明治ミルクチョコレート (明治製菓)
2005 CM - HITACHI「つくろう。」(日立製作所)
2005 CM - 資生堂 マジョリカマジョルカ (資生堂)

P152-153
森本晃司 / スタジオ4℃
049 KOJI MORIMOTO / STUDIO4℃

1995 PV - KENISHII「EXTRA」
1995 アニメーション -「MEMORIES (彼女の想いで)」
1997-1998 アニメーション -「永久家族」
1997 アニメーション -「音響生命体ノイズマン」
1999 PV - GLAY「サバイバル2.7-D」
2003 アニメーション -「ANIMATRIX (BEYONDO)」

P154-155
西田幸司
050 KOJI NISHIDA

2005 ウェブ -「EIGHT THE PROJECT」(マクロメディア)
2005 ウェブ -「よろしゅおあがり TASTE OSAKA」(大阪市ゆとりとみどり 振興局/財団法人 大阪観光コンベンション協会)
2005 ウェブ -「YAZAWANOWHERE vol.1」(YAZAWA'S DOOR)
2004 スクリーンセーバー -「artelligent chiristmas」(六本木ヒルズ)
2004 ウェブ -「Flip along Thailand with Kura」(タイ国政府観光庁) 文化庁メディア芸術祭・審査員推薦作品
2004 バナー -「NOODLE TIME」(日清) カンヌ広告際・ショートリスト
2004 ウェブ -「WORLD CITY TOWERS」(住友不動産) ニューヨークフェスティバル・ファイナリスト

P156-157
山村浩二
051 KOJI YAMAMURA

1991 アニメーション -「ふしぎなエレベーター」第4回国際アニメーションフェステイバル広島大会・子ども向けのアニメーション部門第1位
1993 アニメーション -「カロとピヨブプト」シカゴ国際児童映画祭・アニメーション映画最優秀監督賞、ズーリン国際映画祭・プラハ賞、第5回国際アニメーションフェステイバル広島大会・子ども向けのアニメーション部門・第2位
1995 アニメーション -「キップリングJr.」シカゴ国際児童映画祭・特別名誉賞受賞
1996 アニメーション -「バベルの本」'97 ソウルアニメーションエクスポ TVアニメーション部門・第1位、シカゴ国際児童映画祭・第1位
1999 アニメーション -「どっちにする?」シカゴ国際児童映画祭・第1位、ソウル国際家族映画祭・審査員特別賞、オタワ国際アニメーション映画祭・Children's film 最優秀賞
2000 アニメーション -「ジュビリー」オランダ国際アニメーション映画祭・審査員特別賞、第4回 Music Video Awards '99 - BEST MALE VIDEO
2002 アニメーション -「頭山」第75回アカデミー賞短編アニメー

ション部門ノミネート、グランプリ：アヌシー国際アニメーションフェスティバル2003、第16回ザグレブ国際アニメーション映画祭、第10回広島国際アニメーションフェスティバル、レンコントレス国際アニメーション映画祭、第15回ドレスデン国際アニメーション&短編映画祭、メディアウェーブ2003、最優秀短編アニメーション賞：第2回国際アニメーションフェスティバル アニフェス2003トシェボニュ、第8回マンチェスター国際短編映画祭、準グランプリ コンピュータ・アニメーション、ビジュアル・エフェクト部門：アルス・エレクトロニカ・フェスティバル

2005 アニメーション -「年をとった鰐」第3回ビリニュス国際アニメーション映画祭-Tindirindis・グランプリ、シナニマ2005・B部門最優秀賞、第6回ヴィッセンブール・アニメーション映画祭・最優秀脚本賞

P158-159

空気モーションググラフィックス
052 KOO-KI MOTION GRAPHICS

2000 CM -「クッキーアンドクリーム」（ハーゲンダッツ）Director：竹清仁、Animator：高村剛

2000 CM -「モッズ・ヘア」（mod's hair）Director：竹清仁、Animator：木綿達史、Animator：白川東一

2001 CM -「WEGA」（ソニー）CG Director：田中賢一郎

2001 ショットガンCM -「ジップアップ」（リーバイス）Director：竹清仁

2002 CI -「Xbox」Director：竹清仁（マイクロソフト）

2002 アニメーション -「FEVER」（エム・ティー・ヴィー / アディダス）Director：竹清仁、Animator：高村剛

2003 CM -「世界柔道選手権大会」（フジテレビ）Director：江口カン フジテレビ広報局クリエイティブ大賞 N.Y.フェスティバルファイナリスト2004

2003 CI -「JCB」Director：村上ヒロシナンテ（JCB）

2003 イベント映像 -「PROJECTION WORLD」（エプソン）Director：竹清仁、Animator：新田健士

2004 アニメーション -「MOVIE ROAD」（ホンダ）Director：白川東一

2005 CM -「暴君ハバネロ」（東ハト）Director：江口カン

2005 CI -「GAME CUBE」（任天堂）Director：木綿達史

2005 オンエアパッケージ -「SUPER HITS」（スペースシャワーTV）Director：木綿達史

2005 イベント映像 -「FIFA Club World Championship TOYOTA Cup Japan 2005」（FIFA）Director：竹清仁

2005 ステーションID -「DISH」「UFO」「DANCE」（ANIMAX）Director：白川東一

P160-161

小野浩太
053 KOTA ONO

1996 映像制作 - HOI VOO DOO「FAST 映像」 生西康典氏と共同製作

2000 PV - CALM「noon at the moon」（ラストラム）

2000 PV - COMPUTER SOUP「dream mons」（sampless+山辺圭司との共作）

2001 VJ -「static circuit」neon inn（加藤一郎・ADAM・青山政史・斉藤夏美・小野浩太）として参加。

2002 音と映像のパフォーマンス -「Sound Garden at Hara Museum」（原美術館） minamo（杉本佳一・安永哲郎・笹本奈美子・岩下裕一郎）+ neon inn（青山政史・斉藤夏美・ADAM・小野浩太）

2003 VJ -「SOUND and Vision」（アップリンク・ファクトリー）neon inn（菊原清史・青山政史・ADAM・小野浩太）小野以外のメンバーは各自ソロで音と映像のパフォーマンスを行なう。小野はminamo演奏時に映像を担当。

2003 企画展 -「visitors」（アップリンク・ギャラリー）neon innとゲストを招いて美術作品展示とライブパフォーマンス

2004 映像と音のライブ -「7songs」主催：360°rrecords 音楽：niji（360°records）

2004 出品 -「SOUND × VISION 2004」

2004 展示 -「one day exhibision」 音楽：THE PITCHSHIFTERS 荒木健太 - 代々木ギャラリー OFF SITE

2005 VJ -「ku-ki vol8」- Spiral Hall 音楽：kinka（acca）+yogurt（upsets）

2005 VJ -「MusicNight」– 銀座 アップルストア銀座 音楽：三富栄治（guitar electoronics）Decoration：THE PITCHSHIFTERS

P162-163

加藤久仁生
054 KUNIO KATO

2000 アニメーション -「ヘンリエッタの幸福と悲劇」

2000 アニメーション -「ROBOTTING」共同監督：栗原崇

2001 アニメーション -「The Apple Incident」卒業制作

2001 アニメーション - NHK教育「英語であそぼ」おどれタイポ「LALALA」制作 共同監督：栗原崇、NHKエデュケーショナル、音楽：Eric Jacobsen（©NED・NHK）

2001 アニメーション - NHK教育「英語であそぼ」おどれタイポ「MMM...」制作 共同監督：栗原崇、音楽：Eric Jacobsen NHKエデュケーショナル（©NED・NHK）

2003 アニメーション -「『或る旅人の日記』全6話 WEB アニメーション」 音楽：近藤研二、プロデューサー：日下部雅謹・松本絵美、SE：日高貴代美（ONPa）、制作：ROBOT shockwave.comサイト内で公開 / 2005年1月 ジェネオンエンタテイメントよりDVD発売（©ROBOT）

2003 アニメーション -「MY LITTLE LOVER WEB アニメーション『FANTASY』 全5話」作画スタッフ：森川耕平・飯島有、音楽：小林武史、烏龍舎（©Oolong-Sha・ROBOT）

2004 アニメーション -「MUSIC FLOWER」作画スタッフ：森川耕平（©MTV ART BREAK PROJECT）

2004 アニメーション -「或る旅人の日記『赤い実』」音楽：近藤研二、プロデューサー：日下部雅謹・松本絵美、SE：日高貴代美（ONPa）、作画スタッフ：森川耕平・真取輝和・亀島耕、制作：ROBOT「或る旅人の日記」DVD収録（発売元：ジェネオンエンタテイメント、©ROBOT）

2005 アニメーション -「KIRIN 淡麗グリーンラベル webアニメーション」全3話 作画スタッフ：森川耕平・飯島有

2005 アニメーション - NHKみんなのうた「セルの恋」作曲：めけて、唄：中川晃教、プロデューサー：飯野恵子、作画スタッフ：森川耕平・飯島有・博多哲也、制作：NHKエンタープライズ（© NHK・ROBOT）

2005 自主制作アニメーション -「おはよう」

P164-165

ランリュウ
055 LANRYU

2001 映像作家AFGとともにビジュアルアートコミューン「合掌-gassyo-」を立ち上げる

2003 参加DVD -「biomass」 製作: AFG

2004 1st DVDリリース -「lifepack」

2005 参加コンピレーションDVD -「ONE」 制作: BAMBIENT.com

P166-167

ルドビック・グザスデラ
056 LUDOVIC XASDERA

2003 映像展示 -『The Usual Passages』Mike Sheetal for Kyoko Ebata's - ThinkZone –六本木

2003 映像パフォーマンス - Heavy Sick Zero 音楽：Philippe Chatelain

2003 映像展示 -「Takeyabu yaketa」

2003 映像展示 -「Segments」音楽：Roddy Schrock

2003 映像パフォーマンス - ダンス：Jou（dance）- Tokyo wondersite

2003 映像パフォーマンス -「dance city」 共演 Ch. Charles - uplink factory

2003 映像パフォーマンス -「Tokyo Designer Week」 共演：Christophe

Charles
2003　映像音楽イベント -「s-o-u-n-d-s-c-r-e-e-n」- Phaidros cafe
2003　映像パフォーマンス - 音楽：Ch. Charles　ダンス：and Jou - Daikanyama Classics
2003　映像パフォーマンス - 共演：柴崎正道（Shibasaki Masamichi）
2004　映像 -「DANSTROMA #003」- uplink gallery waseda
2004　映像パフォーマンス - 共演：伊藤虹 + 和歌子 - Phaidros cafe
2004　VJ -「Eurasia festival café party」DJ：Sasaki Takashi
2004　パフォーマンス -「poetry reading session」　谷川俊太郎
2004　映像パフォーマンス -「coded：decoded」　音楽：Mjuc　ダンス：Alessio Silvestrin – ICC / 東京
2004　映像ライブ - 共演：pasadena – Loopline
2004　映像パフォーマンス - 共演：Peter Slade
2004　音楽パフォーマンス -「Placard」– 代々木公園
2004　映像パフォーマンス - 共演：Isanoid – idee-r bar / 青山
2004　映像パフォーマンス - Asahi building　共演：Mjuc
2004　ワークショップ - VJ / Aftereffects workshop（Dance & media Japan）共演：michi – Uplink gallery
2005　映像パフォーマンス - Coppe+Legofriendly – Superdeluxe / 六本木
2005　映像パフォーマンス -「Vanishing Points 3.0」– Orbie Hall

P168-169
057 マジック・コバヤシ M.MAGIC.KOBAYASHI

2001　DVD -「Super Star Series」
2004　インスタレーション -「ドランクタワー」
2005　Art - GUNDAM GENERATION FUTURES「Breath upon the Universe / Breath in the Universe」（創通エージェンシー、サンライズ）

P170-171
058 石浦 克 / ティ・ジー・ビー・デザイン MASARU ISHIURA / TGB design.

2003　PV - CUBE JUICE「EXPLOSION」（ビクターエンタテインメント）
2003　映像制作 -「perceived Quallty Design Department」（日産デザイン）
2003　DVD - CUBE JUICE「cube world –music is our message?–」（ナウオンメディア）
2005　映像作品 - COM.A,「Lights, Camera, Hallvcination: COM.A」

P172-173
059 明鏡止水 MEIKYOSHISUI

2000　Art - 響現
2002　Art - 千總友禅アートプロジェクト
2002　ファッションブランドとのコラボレーション -「輪廻転生コレクション」（FINAL HOME）
2003　DVD - FINAL DROP「elements」
2004　CDカバー - GoRo「dub shanti」
2004　ウェブ - ナイキ（US）「NIKE FREE『DESIGN BY NATURE』」
2004　広告 - 和歌山県「紀伊山地の霊場・参詣道」世界遺産登録記念ビジュアル
2004　DVD参加 -「AUDIOVISUALJAPAN」
2004　展示 - Transplant Gallery – NY
2005　LIVE VISUAL - DJ KRUSH & 森田柊山
2005　グラフィックコラボレーション - 田名網敬一
2005　水の結晶写真江本氏との地球瞑想
2005　LIVE VISUAL - juzu a.k.a moochy「MOMENTOS」
2005　展示 - 93 FEET EAST　– LONDON
2005　Art -「靈氣」現代霊気ヒーリング協会代表・土居裕による監修
2005　広告 - 日本再生プロジェクト「うまれかわる日本・惟神」

P174-175
060 michi / 石多 未知行 michi a.k.a. MICHIYUKI ISHITA

2003　演出・映像 -『ku-ki vol.6』– CAY（Spiral B1）/ 青山
2003　VJ・空間演出 -『蟲の響 final』– 梅ケ谷の森キャンプ場 / 青梅
2004　VJ -『Metamorphose』– 苗場スキー場
2004　映像・空間演出 - mjuc presents『crossing of high density』– ASAHI ART AQUARE / 浅草
2004　映像・空間演出 -『art ライブ [sound+dance+visual] vol.4、vol.5』– BankART1929 YOKOHAMA・馬車道 / 横浜
2004　映像・空間演出 -『あがた森魚ライブ』– Art Place / 新宿
2005　映像・空間演出 -『Electric Love Station』– Bar TUNE モーション・ブルー・ヨコハマ / 横浜赤レンガ倉庫
2005　映像・空間演出 -『CYPRESS』– ageha / 新木場
2005　映像・空間演出 -『Neutral inf.』– Butterfly / 福岡
2005　映像・空間演出 - オペラ『忘れられた少年』欧州巡演 – ポルトガル
2005　映像・空間演出 -『Apple Store ライブ』– アップルストア渋谷
2005　企画・映像・演出 - michi produce『conscious-意識-』公演 – スパイラルホール / 青山
2005　映像・空間演出 - オペラ『魔笛』宗像公演 – 福岡

P176-177
061 ミズヒロ・サビーニ MIZUHIRO SAVINI

2000　PV - audio active「スクリュードライマー」（ビートインク）
2001　PV - 奥田民生「and i love car」（SME）
2001　PV - ACO「ハートを燃やして」（キューンレコード）
2003　CM - ロッテ「紗々」（LOTTE）
2004　PV - 日暮愛葉「ユメミタイ」（キューンレコード）
2004　CM - KIRIN「フランジア」（キリン）
2004　CM - USEN「光ファイバー」（ユーセン）
2005　CM -「アオキGOGOGO!」（アオキインターナショナル）

P178-179
062 野田 凪 NAGI NODA

2002　CM -「ラフォーレ Butterfly Ribbon」（ラフォーレ原宿）
2003　PV - YUKI「センチメンタルジャーニー」（ソニーミュージック）
2003　CM -「A Small Love Story About Alex & Juliet」（フランフラン）
2003　CM -「LAFORET Wedding」（ラフォーレ原宿）
2004　映像作品 -「For Being Appraised As An『ex-fat Girl』」

P180-181
063 生意気 NAMAIKI

2000　ステージデザイン・ビデオディレクション -「L'Arc~en~Ciel『Real Tour 2000』」
2001　グループ展 -『JAM：London – Tokyo』The Barbican – ロンドン
2001　ステージデザイン - Strange Kinoko Dance Company「Frill (Mini)」
2001　グループ展 -『TOKYO ART JUNGLE』– 東京国際フォーラム
2001　個展 -『Ultradeluxe Osakaaa!!』– KPOキリンプラザ大阪
2003　グループ展 -『JPG』– バルセロナ
2003　展示 -『2x2』– 原美術館・中庭に展示（2006年3月まで）
2004　グループ展 -『Graphic Wave 2004 工藤青石×GRAPH×生意気』- ギンザ・グラフィック・ギャラリー / 東京
2004　グループ展 -『FUSION：Architecture+Design in Japan』– イスラエル博物館
2004　出展 - アートフェスティバル『Tokyo Style in Stockholm』– ストックホルム
2005　グループ展 -「きのうよりワクワクしてきた。」– 国立民族学博物館 / 大阪
2005　タイトル映像 -「MTV Video Music Awards Japan '05」（エム・ティ・ヴィー・ジャパン）

P182-183
河瀬直美 / 遷都
064 NAOMI KAWASE / SENT

1992 ドキュメンタリー -「につつまれて」
1993 フィクション -「白い月」
1994 ドキュメンタリー -「かたつもり」
1996 ドキュメンタリー -「現しよ」往復書簡 河瀬直美×是枝裕和
1996 フィクション -「萌の朱雀」(WOWOW + バンダイビジュアル)
1997 ドキュメンタリー -「杣人物語(そまうどものがたり)」
1999 ドキュメンタリー -「万華鏡」
2000 フィクション -「火垂(ほたる)」(火垂製作委員会)
2000 CM - 住友生命「介護保障」ACC賞受賞
2001 ドキュメンタリー -「きゃからばあ」
2001 PV - JUDY AND MARY「PEACE」(エピックレコード) best shooting 賞受賞
2002 ドキュメンタリー -「追臆のダンス」
2003 フィクション -「沙羅双樹」(沙羅双樹製作委員会)
2004 フィクション -「影 - shadow」(T-artist + ムービングピクチャーズジャパン)
2005 ドキュメンタリー -「主人公は君だ!」インターネットムービー(総務省提供)

P184-185
喜田夏記
065 NATSUKI KIDA

1999-2000 TVスポット -「日テレ営業中」「日テレ式」(日本テレビ)
2001 PV - 宇多田ヒカル「Traveling」アニメーション一部
2002 ステーションID - MTV「Cage篇」
2004 PV + CDジャケット制作 - 荘野ジュリ「駅ニテ」「マーメイド」「カゲロウ」
2004 CM - Ora2「エッセンスビューティー篇」(サンスター) Art + アニメーション
2005 CM - 資生堂 TISS ディープオイルN「ポロポロン篇」(資生堂) ディレクター + アニメーション

P186-187
タナカノリユキ
066 NORIYUKI TANAKA

1997 CM -「Blind Jumper」(ナイキ)
1998 PV - ケンイシイ「Islands&Continents 600MHz」
1999 映像制作 -「Tower Records 20th」(タワーレコード)
2000 CM -「.com」(ユニクロ)
2002 CM -「ポカリスエット IN SPACE」(大塚製薬)
2004 映像作品 -「VISUAL ADDICT」
2004 CM -「OUTLAST FLEECE」(ユニクロ)

P188-189
パワーグラフィックス
067 POWER GRAPHIXX

2002 DVD -「PGDVD」(ガス アズ インターフェイス)
2003 選考 - 潟高「FORTUNATE 1 MARK」onedotzeroワールドツアー
2004 受賞 -「Roundscape」文化庁メディア芸術祭アート部門審査員推薦作品
2004 ステーションID -「日本テレビステーションID」(日本テレビ)
2005 TVスポット映像制作 -「イサム・ノグチ展」
2005 シンボル映像制作 -「ROBOCUP 2005 ヒューマノイドリーグ」(ルイ・ヴィトン)
2005 映像制作 -「Samurai Jack」(カートゥーンネットワーク)

P190-191
黒川良一
068 RYOICHI KUROKAWA

2003 CD・DVDリリース -「COPYNATURE」CD、DVD (PROGRESSIVE FOrM)
2003 映像ライヴ - Sketch Show「SONAR」– バルセロナ
2004 DVDディレクション -「M/Wild Sketch Show」(デイジーワールド、cutting edge / エイベックス)
2004 映像ライブ -「ACO (Sony) irony tour」– 東京他
2004 映像ライブ - Taeji Sawai, ACO「Tokyo Style」– ストックホルム
2004 CD・DVDリリース -「READ」(デイジーワールド、cutting edge)
2004 映像ライブ - Human Audio Sponge「sonarsound」– 東京
2004 音楽・映像ライブ -「SOUND × VISION」– 東京
2005 展示 -「CHALET.05 – club transmediale」– ベルリン
2005 展示 -「B!AS International Sound Art Exhibition」– 台北市立美術館
2005 上映 -「SONAR」– バルセロナ
2005 上映 -「OPTRONICA」– ロンドン
2005 上映 -「backup_festival. new media in film」– ワイマール
2005 上映 -「CIMATICS Festival」– ブリュッセル
2005 上映 -「IMPAKT Festival」– ユトレヒト

P192-193
サッカク
069 SAKKAKU

2002 空間映像演出 -『The big chill』– イギリス
2003 MEDIA MIX ライブ -『The cutting edge of japanese underground 1』– グラーツ市 / オーストリア
2003 MEDIA MIX ライブ・VJ -『JAPAN NIGHT』– ザグレブ市 / クロアチア
2003 MEDIA MIX ライブ・VJ -『The cutting edge of japanese underground 2』– グラーツ市 / オーストリア
2004 空間映像演出 -『The big chill Meeting JAPAN』– omamori 代官山・gallery BAU / 富田市
2004 展示 - 時空+4 – gallery BAU / 富山市
2004 空間映像演出 & VJ -『FUJI ROCK FESTIVAL '04』– 苗場
2004 空間映像演出 -『BIG BBQ』– 琵琶湖
2004 空間映像演出 -『夢幻境』– 富山城趾公園
2004 空間映像演出 -『鎌倉花火大会PARTY』– VENUS CAFE / 鎌倉
2004 空間映像演出 - INORAN『ANOTHER ROOM』– LIQUID ROOM / 恵比寿
2004 空間映像演出 -『MO'WAVE』– Zing / 大阪
2004 空間映像演出 -『COMMUNICATEMUTE』– 久多キャンプ場 / 京都
2004 空間映像演出 -『groundrhythm』– Air / 代官山 charichari a.k.a. kaoru inoue氏のレギュラーパーティ
2005 空間映像演出 -『nagisa music festival』– お台場オープンコート
2005 空間映像演出 -『FUJI ROCK FESTIVAL』ボードウォークの映像アートワーク – 苗場
2005 空間映像演出 -『MOTHER S.O.S』– 白馬栂池高原
2005 空間映像演出 -『roocs 音の盆』– みるく / 恵比寿
2005 MEDIA MIX ライブ -『nagisa music festival』– お台場オープンコート

P194-195
ヨシマルシン
070 SHIN YOSHIMARU

2003 アニメーション -「みごろ! たべごろ! ナントカカントカ」(テレビ朝日系)
2003 映像制作 -「FUZZ」(スペースシャワー TV)
2003 映像制作 -「BBL WORLD」(スペースシャワー TV)
2003 アニメーション -「みごろ! たべごろ! デンセンマン」(テレビ朝日)
2004 ロゴムービー制作 -「ミニッツTV」
2004 映像制作 - スペースシャワー TV「BBL WORLD」
2004 アニメーション -「HOW TO お葬式」(MXTV)

2004　宣伝番組アニメーション -「愛情イッポン！」（日本テレビ）
2005　DVD -「GALACTiKA 07」miroqueライヴVJ収録
2005　DVD -「Panasocic：CQ」カニムービー
2005　PV - 朝日美穂「秘密のフランボワーズ」
2005　PV -「Default」（戸田誠司DVD『There She Goes Again』収録）
2005　着モーション -「プラチナメロディー」
2005　DVD -「バナナマンのシャブリなコメディ」（クラブキング）

P196-197
シンポ
071 SIMPO

2002-　VJ -『FLOWER OF LIFE』
2003　VJ -『FUJI ROCK FESTIVAL 2004』YOSHITAKE EXPE/nutronのVJとして参加
2004　PV - nutron「BIRD7」

P198-199
大月 壮
072 SOU OOTSUKI

2004　ジングル - so-net channel 749「No Title」（マルチーズ）
2004　映像作品 -「panasonic CQ『卓球いじめ』」（ナウオンメディア）
2004　映像作品 - プラチナムービー「香港カラオケおばさん」（フィッシュグローブ）
2005　DVD -「COMEDY NEWS SHOW DVD vol.2」（クラブキング）
2005　DVD -「バナナマンのシャブリなコメディ」（クラブキング）
2005　映像制作 - REDFOX企業VP（WEBTOWER）

P200-201
菅原そうた
073 SOTA

2004　映像作品 -「Tonio Movie」
2005　映画 -「Sota World」

P202-203
山本信一
074 SYNICHI YAMAMOTO

1997　オリジナル作品 -「Pine Wheel」
1997　オリジナル作品 -「Chromatic Cliff」
1998　オリジナル作品 -「Mirror Line」
1999　オリジナル作品 -「TRIPLE FALT」
1999　DVDオープニング制作 - 布袋寅泰「Tonight I'm In Yours」
2000　オープニング&CM -「MTV TOWER TOP 40」
2000　CM -「TOKIO Best Album」
2001　オープニング - NTV「月曜映画」
2001　PV - パードン木村「Fisherman's Blues」
2001　映像制作 - テクモ社ゲームソフト「DEAD OR ALIVE」エンディング
2002　モーショングラフィック - FIFA World Cup 2002 スタジアム用公式「GOAL」
2002　タイトル制作 - NHK「ソルトレークオリンピック」
2002　オープニング制作 - B'z ライブ
2004　モーションロゴ制作 -「ソニー銀行」
2005　映像制作 - 愛知万博トヨタ館
2005　DVD -「バナナマンのシャブリなコメディ」（クラブキング）

P204-205
束芋
075 TABAIMO

1999　インスタレーション -「にっぽんの横断歩道」神戸アートビレッジセンター
1999　受賞 -『キリンコンテンポラリー・アワード1999』最優秀作品賞
2000　受賞 - 平成12年度咲くやこの花賞（美術部門）
2001　出品 -『横浜トリエンナーレ2001』– 横浜
2002　出品 -『第25回サンパウロ・ビエンナーレ』– サンパウロ
2002　受賞 - 第13回五島記念文化賞美術新人賞
2003　インスタレーション -「hanabi-ra」– Courtesy of Gallery Koyanagi
2003　出品 -『ODORO ODORO』– 東京オペラシティ
2005　出品 -『Fairy Tales Forever』– デンマーク
2005　インスタレーション -「ギニョる」– KPOキリンプラザ大阪
2005　受賞 - 第23回京都府文化賞奨励賞
2005　受賞 - 日本現代藝術奨励賞

P206-207
高木正勝
076 TAKAGI MASAKATSU

2001　Art -「pia」（carpark records）
2002　Art -「eating」（karaoke kalk）
2002　Art -「opus pia」（carpark records）
2002　Art -「JOURNAL FOR PEOPLE」（デイジーワールド、エイベックス）
2003　Art -「rehome」（W+K東京LAB、フェリシティ）
2003　Art -「eating2」（karaoke kalk）
2003　Art -「セイル」（デイジーワールド、エイベックス）
2003　Art -「world is so beautiful」（デイジーワールド、エイベックス）
2004　Art -「COIEDA」（W+K東京LAB、フェリシティ）

P208-209
森田貴宏
077 TAKAHIRO MORITA / FESN

2000　スケートボードビデオドキュメント -「43-26」（FESN）
2001　ビデオ作品 -「THE BOOTLEGGERS-reconstructive43-26」（FESN）
2001　オリジナルサントラアルバム -「43-26」サウンドスケープ（FESN）
2001　レーベルロゴデザイン -「LIFE LINE RECORDS」サウンドスケープ（FESN）
2003　ミュージックライブドキュメント -「Calm-featuring Moonage Electric Big Band presents THE COWARDY BOY AIN'T STAND ALONE at Yebisu The Garden Hall」ラストラムコーポレーション（FESN）
2005　ミュージックドキュメント -「That's The Way Hope Goes - Tha Blue Herb」サウンドスケープ（FESN）
2005　スケートボードビデオドキュメント -「BHIND THE BROAD」（FESN）

P210-211
山口崇司
078 TAKASHI YAMAGUCHI

1998-　ナムコにてゲーム、映像開発
2002　携帯Webサイト - The END（2003年度 TDCインタラクティブデザイン賞）
2005　展示 - Delawareとのコラボレーション（ポンピドゥーセンター）携帯電話作品

P212-213
綿井健陽
079 TAKEHARU WATAI

2003-2004　「ニュースステーション」（テレビ朝日系列）、「筑紫哲也のNEWS23」（TBS系列）などでイラク戦争の映像報告、中継リポートを行う
2003　受賞 -「ボーン・上田記念国際記者賞」特別賞

2003　受賞 - 第41回「ギャラクシー賞」（報道活動部門）優秀賞
2005　ドキュメンタリー映画 - 「Little Birds（リトル バーズ）~イラク 戦火の家族たち~」
2005　著書 - 「リトルバーズ 戦火のバグダッドから」（晶文社）
2005　受賞 - ロカルノ国際映画祭 人権部門 最優秀賞受賞
2005　受賞 - JCJ大賞（日本ジャーナリスト会議大賞）受賞
2005　受賞 - 韓国EBS国際ドキュメンタリー映画祭スピリットアワード受賞

P214-215

タケイグッドマン / ウィズ エンターテインメント
080 TAKEI GOODMAN / WIZ ENTERTAINMENT

1991　PV - TheCartoons「Cartoons is Coming」
1993　番組 - 「100000000%ビースティボーイズ」（スペースシャワーTV）
1994　ジャケット写真 - 小沢健二「LIFE」
1994　CDジャケットアートディレクション - Tokyo No.1Soul Set「ロマンティック伝説」
1995　映画 - 「What's Happening of the GOODMAN」BOX東中野にて劇場公開
1996　CM - 「森永ダース」（1996）ディレクター &コピー「12コだからダースです」
1997　参加&アートディレクション - かせきさいだぁ「ウィンド・ブレイカー」
1999　Video - SDP VIDEO-PACK「Funkey-4-View」
2000　PV - 郷ひろみ「ハレルヤ・バーニング・ラヴ」
2003　番組 - 「中原昌也TV#001：SpikeJonze」（スペースシャワーTV）
2004　PV - Halcali「音樂ノススメ」
2005　番組 - 「視聴覚交感TV」BSフジ

P216-217

井上 卓
081 TAKU INOUE

2002　PV - BOOM BOOM SATELLITES「Crimson Labyrinth」
2003-2005　CM - 任天堂DSシリーズ
2003　CM - PENTAX Optio S「METAL SPACE」篇
2004　ショットガンCM - BEAMS
2005　番組パッケージ - NHK TOP RUNNER

P218-219

森 達也
082 TATSUYA MORI

1992　プロデュース - 「ミゼットプロレス伝説～小さな巨人たち～」ディレクター：野中真理子
1995　ドキュメンタリー - 「ステージ・ドア」 制作：フジテレビ + ジャパンウェイブ
1997　ドキュメンタリー - 「教壇が消えた日」 制作：フジテレビ + グッドカンパニー
1998　ドキュメンタリー - 「職業欄はエスパー」 制作：フジテレビ + グッドカンパニー
1998　ドキュメンタリー - 「A」
1999　ドキュメンタリー - 「1999年のよだかの星」 制作：フジテレビ + グッドカンパニー
1999　ドキュメンタリー - 「放送禁止歌」～歌っているのは誰? 規制しているのは誰? ～ 制作：フジテレビ+グッドカンパニー
2001　ドキュメンタリー - 「A2」
2001　執筆 - 「スプーン一超能力者の日常と憂鬱」（飛鳥新社）
2003　執筆 - 「世界はもっと豊だし、人はもっと優しい」（晶文社）
2004　執筆 - 「戦争の世紀を超えてその場所で語られるべき戦争の記憶がある」共著：姜尚中（講談社）
2004　執筆 - 「世界が完全に思考停止する前に」（角川書店）
2004　執筆 - 「池袋シネマ青春譜」（柏書房）
2004　執筆 - 「下山事件」（新潮社）
2004　執筆 - 「いのちの食べかた」YA新書 よりみちパン!セ（理論社）
2005　執筆 - 「ドキュメンタリーは嘘をつく」（草思社）

P220-221

ティ・ビィ・グラフィックス
082 TEEVEE GRAPHICS

2000　展示 - 「映像 VICTIM」 - 原宿ROCKET
2000　PV - ACO「ハートを燃やして」、audio active「スクリュードライマー」ほか
2001　オリジナルDVD - 「映像 VICTIM」
2001　ブロードキャストデザイン - 「ぐるぐるナインティナイン」（日本テレビ）ほか
2001　PV - K.「ECHO」、砂原良徳「LOVEBEAT」、松崎ナオ「太陽」、K.「最後のサイダー」、キリンジ「Drifter」他
2002　展示 - 「Cut Out」 – THINK ZONE ／六本木
2002　ロゴアニメーション – NTT DoCoMo、POLAほか
2002　PV - YUKI「The end of shite」、ACIDMAN「今、透明か」「赤橙」「アレグロ」、DRY & HEAVY「NEW CREATION」、キリンジ「鋼鉄の馬」、ホフディラン「SEASON」ほか
2003　CM - 資生堂「プラウディア/胸騒ぎ篇」、京セラ「ファインカム / 二人侍篇」ほか
2003　ブロードキャストデザイン - ANIMAX Graphic Package 2003、「真夜中の王国03」NHK BS-2 ほか
2003　PV - Ken Ishii「Strobe enhanced」、HYDE「HELLO」、SOFFet「君がいるなら☆」、ACIDMAN「リピート」、堂島孝平「銀色クリアデイズ」、キリンジ「カメレオンガール」ほか
2004　劇場公開 - 「机上の空論」Jam Film 2
2004　音楽と映像 - 鬼束ちひろ「いい日旅立ち・西へ」「私とワルツを」、ニルギリス「KING」、奥村愛子「冬の光」ほか
2005　オリジナルDVD - 「映像 VICTIM 2」
2005　コマーシャル - 三菱電機「MUSIC PORTER」、ボルヴィック「気持ちすっきり篇」、ソニー「スゴ録」ほか
2005　ブロードキャストデザイン - 「ナイナイサイズ」日本テレビ ほか
2005　PV - BENNIE K「Dreamland」、「叙情詩」L'Arc~en~Ciel、RIP SLYME「UNDER THE SUN」、Fantastic Plastic Machine「Tell Me」ほか

P222-223

永戸鉄也
084 TETSUYA NAGATO

2004　PV - AIR「ONE WAY」（東芝EMI）
2005　PV - HOTEI「IDENTITY」（東芝EMI）
2005　CM - 「NUDY」アートディレクション（カネボウ）
2005　PV - UA「BREATHE」（ビクターエンタテインメント＆スピードスターレコーズ）

P224-225

村田朋泰
085 TOMOYASU MURATA

2000　ショートフィルム - 「睡蓮の人」
2002　ショートフィルム - 「朱の路」
2002　受賞 - 「睡蓮の人」第5回文化庁メディア芸術祭アニメーション部門 優秀賞
2002　受賞 - 「朱の路」東京芸術大学大学院美術学部デザイン科修了制作 大学買い上げ賞 首席
2002　受賞 - 「睡蓮の人」 PFFアワード2002 審査員特別賞
2002　受賞 - 「朱の路」第9回広島国際アニメーションフェスティバル 優秀賞
2002　PV - Mr.Children「HERO」
2002　出展 - 「カフェ・イン・水戸」 - 水戸芸術館
2003　個展 - 「美術を楽しむために2003村田朋泰」 - 富岡市立美術博物館
2004　出展 - 「国際交流基金企画『未来への回路-日本の新世代アーティスト』」
2004　出展 - 「カフェ・イン・水戸2004」 – 水戸芸術館

2004 ショートフィルム -「PINK」(Mr.Children Tour シフクノオト 2004)
2004 PV - Bank Band「糸」
2005 ショートフィルム -「冬の虹」
2006 個展 -「俺の路/村田朋泰展/東京モンタージュ」– 目黒区美術館(開催予定)

P226-227
086 長谷川踏太 TOTA HASEGAWA / TOMATO

2002 iアプリ -「wobble clock & water clock For The END」PR：立花ハジメ D + CO：tomato
2003 「Walk on the Hill」PR：DELAWARE D：DELAWARE+Tomato CO：tomato
2003 連載 - モノサシに目印 (Web Designing / 毎日コミュニケーションズ) PR：今里了次 D + AD + 文章：Tomato
2004 展示 -「KITTY'S eye view for KITTY EX」(サンリオ) PR：デジタルハリウッド AD + D + CO：Tomato
2004 ワークショップ -「ICC NEWSCHOOL 9 リアクティヴ/クリエイティヴ」(NTT ICC) PR:NTT ICC ワークショップ講師：Tomato+クワクボリョウタ
2005 アプリケーション -「STIJL IDENTITY」(株式会社 ディムーブ / 株式会社 エクシング) D + AD + CO: tomato
2005 「YOU ME WHO?」(KDDI DESIGNING STUDIO) PR: ガスアズ インターフェイス D + AD + CO: tomato
2004 着ムービー -「bowwaus」(ディムーブ／エクシング) D + AD + CO：tomato、音楽：Anthony Caple
2005 携帯用時計 -「遊スタイル」PR：field system D + AD：tomato
2005 プロダクト -「Seiko Spectrum SVRD001」(セイコーウオッチ)

P228-229
087 塚越有人 TSUKAGOSHI ARIHITO

2003 自主作品 - is-ness「NEU TYPE」
2004 PV -「Calm presents K.F. KeyFree」
2005 プロモーション映像 -「Intentionalies & Amadana」

P230-231
088 広岡 毅 TSUYOSHI HIROOKA

2000 映像作品 -「His Livolbing Lantern」(クラブキング)
2003 PV - HONDALADY「アドアド」(ワーナーミュージック・ジャパン)
2003 映像制作 -「Filler」(エム・ティー・ヴィー・ジャパン)
2004 映像制作 - VJ BG「ファミ通Choice」(エンターブレイン)
2004 映像制作 -「smork exibition」(スモーク)
2005 映像制作 -「j:com ホット! チャンネル オープニング」(フラッグ)
2005 映像制作 -「M size」(エム・ティー・ヴィー・ジャパン)
2005 映像パッケージ -「SUMMER SONIC'05 ダイジェストスペシャル」(エム・ティー・ヴィー・ジャパン)

P232-233
089 宇川直宏 UKAWA NAOHIRO

2000 DVD - ボアダムス「SUPER SEEEEEE!!!!!!」
2001 DVD -「Scanning of Modulations」(アップリンク・ファクトリー)
2003 PV - THE ORB「FROM A DISTANCE」(藤子プロ・小学館・ラッドミュージシャン・V2レコード)
2004 PV - SUPERCAR「BGM」(ソニーミュージック)
2004 DVD - スーパーカー「SUPERCAR/HIGH BOOSTERU.N.V.J. WORKS」(ソニーミュージック)

2005 PV - 電気グルーヴ×スチャダラパー「Twilight」(ソニーミュージック)
2005 PV - 野宮マキ ♥ m-flo「BIG BANG ROMANCE」(エイベックス)
2005 PV - CICADA「KUSSA」(Pヴァイン・レコード)

P234-235
090 梅川良満 UMEKAWA YOSHIMITSU

2004 撮影 -「THE RAM:ΣLL:ZΣΣ」(スペースシャワー TV)
2005 撮影 - METAL CHICKS「10,000db」(ミュージックマイン)

P236-237
090 ウオヌマ UONUMA

2005 アニメーション -「GAGA USEN C.I」
2005 CGアニメーション -「LOFT 2005Christmas Collection」
2005 アニメーション -「TABI 2 imagefilm」

P238-239
092 生西康典 YASUNORI IKUNISHI

2002 DVD - Black Flag「イメージガーデン」(アップリンク)
2002 映像作品 -「Super Star Series」(ガス アズ インターフェイス)
2003 DVD -「Mouse Escape」(ガス アズ インターフェイス)
2004 映像インスタレーション -「H.I.S. Landscape」六本木クロッシング展 – 森美術館
2005 映像インスタレーション -「Breathe upon the Universe / Breathe in the Universe」(『GUNDAM 来るべき未来のために展』) – サントリーミュージアム天保山、上野の森美術館

P240-241
093 掛川康典 YASUNORI KAKEGAWA

2002 PV - UA「泥棒」
2002 DVD - Super Star Series (ガス アズ インターフェイス)
2003 PV - HOTEI「弾丸ロック」
2004 PV - キリンジ「You & Me」
2003 DVD - MOUSE ESCAPE (ガス アズ インターフェイス)

P242-243
094 栗田やすお YASUO KURITA

1997 映像 -「ロボロボ」
1999 映像 -「RED SLOT MACHINE」
2005 映像 -「緑玉紳士」
2005 CM -「J-WAVE」30秒のCMスポット

P244-245
095 児玉裕一 / クイックポップ YUICHI KODAMA / QUICKPOP

2002 PV - WRECH「FACT」
2002 PV - スネオヘアー「アイボリー」
2002 PV - スネオヘアー「訳も知らないで」
2003 PV - スネオヘアー「ピント」
2003 PV - スネオヘアー「冬の翼」
2004 PV - スネオヘアー「Over the River」

2004　PV - スネオヘアー「ウグイス」
2004　PV - スネオヘアー「セイコウトウテイ」
2004　PV - YUKI「ハローグッバイ」
2004　PV - WRECH「When New Winds Blow」
2004　PV - WRECH「TAKE AWAY」
2004　PV - YOU THE ROCK★「GRAND MASTER FRESH Pt.2」
2005　PV - スネオヘアー「コミュニケーション」
2005　PV - スネオヘアー「ワルツ」
2005　PV - POLYSICS「I My Me Mine」
2005　PV - CHEMISTRY「WINGS OF WORDS」
2005　PV - くるり「Birthday」

P246-247

河村勇樹
096 YUKI KAWAMURA

2003　パフォーマンス - for Yoshihiro HANNO- audio forma#2 -complex – 東京
2003　上映 - Microcinema – ヒューストン
2003　上映 - Sketch gallery – ロンドン
2003　上映 - 森アートミュージアム – 東京
2003　Film -「SCENE H」
2003　Film -「PLAY AT DUSK」
2004　上映 -『Biennnale of Biwako』– 滋賀
2004　上映 -『Palais de Tokyo』– パリ
2004　上映 -『Museum of contemporary art』– リオン / フランス
2004　インスタレーション -「SHIKI」with O.Lamm Vooruit art center – Gent / ベルギー
2004　Film -「LETHE」
2004　Film -「SLIDE」
2005　上映 -『Forum des images』– パリ
2005　上映 -『Le Festival sous la Plage』– パリ
2005　上映 -『Tokyo compe』– 東京
2005　上映 -『Gallery Magda Dansysz』– パリ
2005　上映 -『Rencontres International Paris-Berlin』– パリ
2005　上映 -『Biennale of video and new media』– サンティエゴ / チリ
2005　上映 -『Tirana International Film Festival』– アルバニア
2005　上映 -『Centre Culture Française』– セルビア
2005　上映 -『Tank TV』– ロンドン
2005　上映 -『Dotmov Festival』– 札幌
2005　個展 -『Le Cube』– パリ
2005　Film -「JOUR DE REVE」
2005　Film -「IMAGIN」(Zorba Production) – パリ
2005　Film -「DOLLS」(Zorba Production) – パリ
2005　Film -「SEKAINOHATE」(Zorba Production) – パリ
2005　DVD -「SLIDE」(Lowave / a-v-e-c) – パリ

P248-249

宅野祐介
097 YUSUKE TAKUNO

2000-2001　PV - ゴスペラーズ「永遠に」「ひとり」ほか
2002　CM - MTV+LEGO「ジョセイ篇」「ダンセイ篇」「シャシン篇」
2002　PV - ケツメイシ「トモダチ」
2003　PV - TRICERATOPS「TATTOO」「Rock Music」「赤いゴーカート」
2004　CM - NTT コミュニケーションズ OCN「先行OCNミュージックストア篇」

P250-251

土屋 豊 / W-TV オフィス・ビデオアクト
098 YUTAKA TSUCHIYA / W-TV OFFICE・VIDEO ACT!

1993　ドキュメンタリー -「Identity?」
1994　フリービデオ「WITHOUT TELEVISION」を自主流通により発行
1997　ドキュメンタリー -「あなたは天皇の戦争責任についてどう思いますか? <96.8.15靖国篇>」
1998　自主ビデオの流通プロジェクト「VIDEO ACT !」を主宰
1999　ドキュメンタリー -「新しい神様」山形国際ドキュメンタリー映画祭99<アジア千波万波>国際批評家連盟賞特別賞受賞
2003　フィクション -「PEEP "TV" SHOW」第33回ロッテルダム国際映画祭 タイガーアワード 国際批評家連盟賞受賞、第24回ハワイ国際映画祭・NETPAC特別賞受賞、Montreal International Festival of New Cinema <New Discovery Award, Feature Film Mention>受賞

P252-253

ゼロ・グラビティ・オプティカルアート
099 ZEROGRAVITY OPTICAL ART

2003　PV - NAN「The Election」
2005　映像インスタレーション - FreedamVillage – 大桟橋
2005　映像インスタレーション - Back to school on Halloween IID
2005　映像インスタレーション - design U.K. – イギリス大使館
2005　ウェブオープニング映像制作 - sputnik web move

P254-255

ズームグラフィックス
100 ZOOM GRAPHICS

2004　映像制作 -「Black Bird & Invaders」(ヤマハ)
2005　CM - music.jp (読売広告 & MTI Ltd.)
2005　DVDオープニング映像 -「バナナマンのシャブリなコメディ」(クラブキング)
2005　CM -「熟カレー」(グリコ)

映像作家100人
Japanese Motion Graphic Creators

2006年2月10日 初版第1刷発行
2006年3月31日 初版第2刷発行

制作　4D

編集　古屋蔵人
庄野祐輔
藤田夏海
服部全宏

表紙デザイン　広岡 毅

扉イラスト　井口弘史

翻訳　内山隆太郎

編集協力　大月 壮　shoe　竹田晃洋　岩崎 梓　山口浩司
鈴木恵美子　竹内加奈子

発行人　長谷川新多郎

発売　株式会社ビー・エヌ・エヌ新社
〒163-1111
東京都新宿区西新宿6-22-1
新宿スクエアタワー
FAX 03-3345-1127

印刷　株式会社シナノ

Thanks to　デイヴィッド・ディヒーリ
UNNON　門井隆盛　大橋二郎

Printed In Japan
ISBN4-86100-362-8